T0249867

Integration of AI-Based Manufacturing and Industrial Engineering Systems with the Internet of Things

Integration of AI-Based Manufacturing and Industrial Engineering Systems with the Internet of Things describes how AI techniques, such as deep learning, cognitive computing, and Machine Learning, can be used to analyze massive volumes of data produced by IoT devices in manufacturing environments.

The potential benefits and challenges associated with the integration of AI and IoT in industrial environments are explored throughout the book as the authors delve into various aspects of the integration process. The role of IoT-enabled sensors, actuators, and smart devices in capturing real-time data from manufacturing processes, supply chains, and equipment is discussed along with how data can be processed and analyzed using AI algorithms to derive actionable insights, optimize production, improve quality control, and enhance overall operational efficiency.

A valuable resource for researchers, practitioners, and professionals involved in the fields of AI, IoT, manufacturing systems, and industrial engineering, and combines theoretical foundations, practical applications, and case studies.

Intelligent Manufacturing and Industrial Engineering

Series Editor: Ahmed A. Elngar, Beni-Suef Uni.
Mohamed Elhoseny, Mansoura University, Egypt

Machine Learning Adoption in Blockchain-Based Intelligent Manufacturing
Edited by Om Prakash Jena, Sabyasachi Pramanik, Ahmed A. Elngar

Integration of AI-Based Manufacturing and Industrial Engineering Systems with the Internet of Things
Edited by Pankaj Bhambri, Sita Rani, Valentina E. Balas, Ahmed A. Elngar

For more information about this series, please visit: https://www.routledge.com/Mathematical-Engineering-Manufacturing-and-Management-Sciences/book-series/CRCIMIE

Integration of AI-Based Manufacturing and Industrial Engineering Systems with the Internet of Things

Edited by
Pankaj Bhambri
Sita Rani
Valentina E. Balas
Ahmed A. Elngar

CRC Press is an imprint of the
Taylor & Francis Group, an **informa** business

Designed cover image: © Shutterstock

First edition published 2024
by CRC Press
2385 NW Executive Center Drive, Suite 320, Boca Raton FL 33431

and by CRC Press
4 Park Square, Milton Park, Abingdon, Oxon, OX14 4RN

CRC Press is an imprint of Taylor & Francis Group, LLC

ISBN: 978-1-032-46601-9 (hbk)
ISBN: 978-1-032-46831-0 (pbk)
ISBN: 978-1-003-38350-5 (ebk)

DOI: 10.1201/9781003383505

Typeset in Times LT Std
by SPi Technologies India Pvt Ltd (Straive)

Contents

About the Editors

Dr. Pankaj Bhambri is affiliated with the Department of Information Technology at Guru Nanak Dev Engineering College in Ludhiana. Additionally, he fulfills the role of the Institute's Coordinator for the Skill Enhancement Cell and acts as the Convener for his Departmental Board of Studies. He possesses nearly two decades of teaching experience. Dr. Bhambri acquired a Master of Technology degree in Computer Science and Engineering and a Bachelor of Engineering degree in Information Technology with Honours from I.K.G. Punjab Technical University in Jalandhar, India, and Dr. B.R. Ambedkar University in Agra, India, respectively. Dr. Bhambri obtained a Doctorate in Computer Science and Engineering from I.K.G. Punjab Technical University, located in Jalandhar, India. Over an extended period, he fulfilled many responsibilities including those of an Assistant Registrar (Academics), Member (Academic Council/BoS/DAB/RAC), Hostel Warden, APIO, and NSS Coordinator within his institution. His research work has been published in esteemed worldwide and national journals, as well as conference proceedings. Dr. Bhambri has made significant contributions to the academic field through his role as both an editor and author of various textbooks. Additionally, he has demonstrated his innovative thinking by filing several patents. Dr. Bhambri has received numerous prestigious awards from esteemed organizations in recognition of his exceptional achievements in both social and academic/research domains. These accolades include the ISTE Best Teacher Award in 2022, the I2OR National Award in 2020, the Green ThinkerZ Top 100 International Distinguished Educators award in 2020, the I2OR Outstanding Educator Award in 2019, the SAA Distinguished Alumni Award in 2012, the CIPS Rashtriya Rattan Award in 2008, the LCHC Best Teacher Award in 2007, and several other commendations from various government and non-profit entities. He has provided guidance and oversight for numerous research projects and dissertations at the undergraduate, postgraduate, and Ph.D. levels. He successfully organized a diverse range of educational programmes, securing financial backing from esteemed institutions such as the All India Council for Technical Education (AICTE), the Technical Education Quality Improvement Programme (TEQIP), among others. Dr. Bhambri's areas of interest encompass machine learning, bioinformatics, wireless sensor networks, and network security. Dr. Bhambri possesses a wide array of professional responsibilities, encompassing the duties of an educator, editor, author, reviewer, expert speaker, motivator, and technical committee member for esteemed national and worldwide organizations.

Dr. Sita Rani works in the Department of Computer Science and Engineering at Guru Nanak Dev Engineering College, Ludhiana. Earlier, she served as Deputy Dean (Research) at the Gulzar Group of Institutions, Khanna (Punjab). She completed her B. Tech. and M. Tech. degrees in Computer Science and Engineering from Guru Nanak Dev Engineering College, Ludhiana. She earned her Ph. D. in Computer Science and Engineering from I.K. Gujral Punjab Technical University, Kapurthala, Punjab in 2018.She completed her Post Graduate Certificate Program in Data Science and Machine Learning from the Indian Institute of Technology, Roorkee in 2023. She is also a Post Doctoral Research Fellow at South Ural State University, Russia since May 2022. She has more than two decades of teaching experience. She is an active member of ISTE, IEEE and IAEngg and is the recipient of the ISTE Section Best Teacher Award– 2020, and the International Young Scientist Award–2021. She has contributed to the various research activities while publishing articles in renowned journals and conference proceedings. She has also published seven international patents. Dr. Rani has delivered many expert talks in AICTE-sponsored Faculty Development Programs and organized many international conferences over the course of her 20 years of teaching experience. She is a member of editorial boards and also a reviewer for many international journals of repute. Her areas of research interest include parallel and distributed computing, data science, Machine Learning, Blockchain, the Internet of Things (IoT), and healthcare.

Prof. Valentina E. Balas is currently Full Professor in the Department of Automatics and Applied Software at the Faculty of Engineering, "Aurel Vlaicu" University of Arad, Romania. She holds a PhD in Applied Electronics and Telecommunications from the Polytechnic University of Timisoara. Dr. Balas is the author of more than 300 research papers in refereed journals and international conferences. Her research interests include intelligent systems, fuzzy control, soft computing, smart sensors, information fusion, modeling and simulation. She is the editor-in chief for the *International Journal of Advanced Intelligence Paradigms* (*IJAIP*) and the *International Journal of Computational Systems Engineering* (*IJCSysE*), an editorial board member of several national and international journals and an evaluating expert for national, international projects and PhD theses. Dr. Balas is the director of the Intelligent Systems Research Centre in Aurel Vlaicu University of Arad and the director of the Department of International Relations, Programs and Projects in the same university. She served as general chair of the International Workshop on Soft Computing and Applications (SOFA),which was held in Romania and Hungary on eight occasions between 2005 and 2018. Dr. Balas has participated in many international conferences in a variety of different roles, including organizer, honorary chair, session chair and has also been a member of Steering, Advisory or International Program Committees. She is a member of the EUSFLAT and the SIAM and a Senior Member of the IEEE, and a member of the TC – Fuzzy Systems (IEEE CIS), the TC – Emergent Technologies (IEEE CIS), and the TC – Soft Computing (IEEE SMCS). Dr. Balas was also past vice-president (Awards) of IFSA International Fuzzy Systems Association Council (2013–2015) and is a Joint Secretary of the Governing Council of Forum for Interdisciplinary Mathematics (FIM), a multidisciplinary academic body in India. She is also director of the Department of International Relations, Programs and Projects and head of the Intelligent Systems Research Centre in Aurel Vlaicu University of Arad, Romania.

Dr. Ahmed A. Elngar is an Associate Professor and Head of the Computer Science Department at the Faculty of Computers and Artificial Intelligence, Beni-Suef University, Egypt. Dr. Elngar is also an Associate Professor of Computer Science at the College of Computer Information Technology, and the American University in the Emirates, United Arab Emirates. Dr. Elngar is also Adjunct Professor at the School of Technology, Woxsen University, India. He is the Founder and Head of the Scientific Innovation Research Group (SIRG) and a Director of the Technological and Informatics Studies Center (TISC), Faculty of Computers and Artificial Intelligence, Beni-Suef University. Dr. Elngar has more than 106 scientific research papers published in prestigious international journals and over 25 books covering such diverse topics as data mining, intelligent systems, social networks, and the smart environment. Dr. Elngar is a collaborative researcher and a member of the Egyptian Mathematical Society (EMS) and the International Rough Set Society (IRSS). His other research areas include the Internet of Things (IoT), network security, intrusion detection, Machine Learning, data mining, and Artificial Intelligence, Big Data, authentication, cryptology, healthcare systems, and automation systems. He is an editor and reviewer of many international journals around the world. He has won several awards, including the "Young Researcher in Computer Science Engineering", from Global Outreach Education Summit and Awards 2019, on 31 January 2019 in Delhi, India. He has also been awarded the "Best Young Researcher Award (Male) (Below 40 years)", Global Education and Corporate Leadership Awards (GECL–2018).

Contributors

Saaema Akhtar
National Institute of Technology,
Warangal, Telangana, India

Hutashan Vishal Bhagat
Sant Longowal Institute of Engineering
    and Technology,
Sangrur, Punjab, India

Pankaj Bhambri
Guru Nanak Dev Engineering College,
Ludhiana, Punjab, India

Vidyadevi G. Biradar
NITTE Meenakshi Institute of
    Technology,
Bangalore, Karnataka, India

Yogesh Chhabra
CT University,
Ludhiana, Punjab, India

Dharmavaram Asha Devi
Sreenidhi Institute of Science and
    Technology,
Hyderabad, Telangana, India

M. Dharmananda
NITTE Meenakshi Institute of Technology,
Bangalore, Karnataka, India

M. R. Dileep
NITTE Meenakshi Institute of
    Technology,
Bangalore, Karnataka, India

Aayushi Gautam
Chandigarh Group of Colleges,
SAS Nagar, Punjab, India

Polishetty Gayatri
Sreenidhi Institute of Science and
    Technology,
Hyderabad, Telangana, India

P. Geetha
Sri Venkateswara College of
    Engineering,
Sriperumbudur, Tamil Nadu, India

Madhwaraj Kango Gopal
Mangalore Institute of Technology and
    Engineering,
Moodbidri, Karnataka, India

M. Gopala Krishna
SRM Institute of Science and
    Technology,
Ramapuram Campus, Chennai, Tamil
    Nadu, India

B. S. Harisha
NITTE Meenakshi Institute of
    Technology,
Bangalore, Karnataka, India

D. Sai Surya Harsha
SRM Institute of Science and
    Technology,
Ramapuram Campus, Chennai, Tamil
    Nadu, India

Kusumlata Jain
Manipal University,
Jaipur, Rajasthan, India

T. Kalaichelvi
Pondicherry University,
Pondicherry, Puducherry, India

R. K. Kapila Vani
Sri Venkateswara College of
Engineering,
Sriperumbudur, Tamil Nadu, India

S. Keerthana Sri
Sri Venkateswara College of
Engineering,
Sriperumbudur, Tamil Nadu, India

Charu Krishna
Motilal Nehru National Institute of
Technology Allahabad,
Prayagraj, Uttar Pradesh, India

Divya Kumar
Motilal Nehru National Institute of
Technology Allahabad,
Prayagraj, Uttar Pradesh, India

Naveen Kumar
National Institute of Technology,
Kurukshetra, Haryana, India

Santosh Kumar
Chandigarh Group of Colleges,
SAS Nagar, Punjab, India

Dharmender Singh Kushwaha
Motilal Nehru National Institute of
Technology Allahabad,
Prayagraj, Uttar Pradesh, India

H. Lakshmi
NITTE Meenakshi Institute of
Technology,
Bangalore, Karnataka, India

S. Lakshmi Gayathri
Sri Venkateswara College of
Engineering,
Sriperumbudur, Tamil Nadu, India

Zahid Amin Malik
Kumaun University,
Nainital, Uttarakhand, India

Archana Naik
NITTE Meenakshi Institute of
Technology,
Bangalore, Karnataka, India

A. V. Navaneeth
NITTE Meenakshi Institute of
Technology,
Bangalore, Karnataka, India

Gampa Nikhitha
Sreenidhi Institute of Science and
Technology,
Hyderabad, Telangana, India

Anshuman Priyadarshini
NITTE Meenakshi Institute of
Technology,
Bangalore, Karnataka, India

Rachna Rana
Ludhiana Group of Colleges,
Ludhiana, Punjab, India

Manju Rani
Gurugram University,
Gurugram, Haryana, India

Sita Rani
Guru Nanak Dev Engineering College,
Ludhiana, Punjab, India

S. Ravi
Pondicherry University,
Pondicherry, Puducherry, India

G. Pavan Sundar Reddy
SRM Institute of Science and
Technology,
Ramapuram Campus, Chennai, Tamil
Nadu, India

Hemant Kumar Saini
Chandigarh University,
SAS Nagar, Punjab, India

R. Sathya
SRM Institute of Science and
   Technology,
Ramapuram Campus, Chennai, Tamil
   Nadu, India

Gurjeet Singh
Guru Kashi University,
Bathinda, Punjab, India

Jagdeep Singh
Guru Nanak Dev Engineering College,
Ludhiana, Punjab, India

Manminder Singh
Sant Longowal Institute of Engineering
   and Technology,
Sangrur, Punjab, India

Prem Singh
Guru Nanak Dev Engineering College,
Ludhiana, Punjab, India

Swaran Singh
Chandigarh Group of Colleges,
SAS Nagar, Punjab, India

P. Ushashree
Geethanjali College of Engineering and
   Technology,
Hyderabad, Telangana, India

Anurag Verma
NITTE Meenakshi Institute of
   Technology,
Bangalore, Karnataka, India

Pusa Vineela
Sreenidhi Institute of Science and
   Technology,
Hyderabad, Telangana, India

Preface

Welcome to *Integration of AI-Based Manufacturing and Industrial Engineering Systems with the Internet of Things*. In today's rapidly evolving technological landscape, the convergence of artificial intelligence (AI), manufacturing, industrial engineering, and the Internet of Things (IoT) has brought about a paradigm shift in the way we design, produce, and optimize industrial systems. This book serves as a comprehensive guide that explores the integration of these transformative technologies and their applications in the realm of manufacturing and industrial engineering.

The Fourth Industrial Revolution, often referred to as Industry 4.0, has propelled us into an era where intelligent systems, interconnected devices, and data-driven decision-making are revolutionizing the industrial sector. The marriage of AI-based approaches, such as machine learning, deep learning, and data analytics, with the vast network of IoT devices has opened up a world of possibilities for optimizing production processes, enhancing quality control, improving resource management, and enabling predictive maintenance, among many other applications.

This book aims to provide a holistic understanding of the integration of AI-based manufacturing and industrial engineering systems with the IoT. It delves into the underlying principles, methodologies, and technologies that drive this integration and explores real-world case studies, practical implementations, and emerging trends. Whether you are a researcher, practitioner, student, or an industry professional seeking to stay at the forefront of this rapidly evolving field, this book offers valuable insights and knowledge. Each chapter is authored by experts in their respective domains, ensuring that the content is both comprehensive and up-to-date. Additionally, practical examples, illustrations, and references are provided to facilitate a deeper understanding of the topics covered.

We hope that this book serves as a valuable resource for researchers, educators, students, and professionals interested in exploring the integration of AI-based manufacturing and industrial engineering systems with the Internet of Things. We believe that the knowledge and insights shared within these pages will inspire further advancements and innovations in this exciting field.

We would like to express our gratitude to all the contributors who have dedicated their time and expertise to make this book possible. We also extend our appreciation to the readers for their interest in this subject matter. Together, let us embark on this journey into the integration of AI, manufacturing, industrial engineering, and the Internet of Things.

1 Challenges, Opportunities, and the Future of Industrial Engineering with IoT and AI

Pankaj Bhambri and Sita Rani

Guru Nanak Dev Engineering College, Ludhiana, India

1.1 INTRODUCTION

Industrial engineering is a field that has long been concerned with designing, optimizing, and managing complex systems and processes. However, with the emergence of the Internet of Things (IoT) and Artificial Intelligence (AI), the challenges and opportunities faced by industrial engineers have evolved (Kothandaraman et al, 2022). IoT is a collection of physical objects that are interconnected with the internet, allowing them to exchange information (Kaur et al., 2015). Conversely, AI pertains to machines endowed with the capacity to carry out tasks typically necessitating human intelligence, including learning, decision-making, and problem-solving (Tao et al., 2019).

The integration of IoT and AI into industrial engineering has the potential to revolutionize the field, but it also presents significant challenges. The sheer amount of data generated by IoT devices can overwhelm traditional data management systems, while the vulnerability of IoT devices to cyber-attacks presents a significant security risk. On the other hand, the benefits of IoT and AI are many, including real-time monitoring, predictive maintenance, and predictive quality control (McAfee and Brynjolfsson, 2017).

This chapter will explore the challenges, opportunities, and future of industrial engineering with IoT and AI. We will begin by discussing the challenges that industrial engineers face in the age of IoT and AI, including data management and cybersecurity. We will then examine the opportunities that these technologies offer, including real-time monitoring, predictive maintenance, and predictive quality control. Finally, we will discuss the future of industrial engineering with IoT and AI, including the changes in the nature of work and the skills required for success in this evolving field (Paika and Bhambri, 2013).

1.1.1 Industrial Engineering Role, Processes, and Developments in Brief

Industrial engineering involves the optimization of intricate systems and processes. It involves the application of engineering principles, mathematics, and statistics to improve efficiency, productivity, and quality in a variety of industries (Qureshi and Khan 2019).

The role of an industrial engineer is to analyze existing processes, identify problems and inefficiencies, and develop solutions to optimize the process. They work closely with other professionals, including engineers, managers, and technicians, to identify opportunities for improvement and implement changes (Wang and Liu, 2019). The processes involved in industrial engineering can vary depending on the industry, but some common processes include:

- Process design and improvement: Industrial engineers analyze existing processes and develop new processes that are more efficient, cost-effective, and productive.
- Quality control: Industrial engineers design quality control systems that ensure that products and services meet customer requirements and industry standards.
- Supply chain management: Industrial engineers manage the flow of goods and services from suppliers to customers, optimizing logistics, inventory management, and transportation.
- Human factors: Industrial engineers consider the human factors involved in industrial processes, such as ergonomics, safety, and worker productivity.
- Project management: Industrial engineers are often involved in managing projects, including planning, budgeting, and scheduling.

There have been several significant developments in industrial engineering in recent years. Among the noteworthy advancements, the IoT and AI have emerged as prominent ones. In industrial environments, the prevalence of IoT devices has grown substantially, enabling the collection of real-time data (Rani et al. 2023b). This data serves the purpose of optimizing processes, enhancing quality control, and minimizing wastage. AI algorithms can analyze this data to predict equipment failures, identify quality issues, and optimize supply chain management (Rauschecker and Devaraj, 2019).

Another development in industrial engineering is the increasing use of automation and robotics. Industrial robots are becoming more affordable and capable, allowing them to perform tasks that were previously done by humans. This has the potential to increase efficiency, reduce labor costs, and improve worker safety.

Finally, there is a growing emphasis on sustainability and environmental impact in industrial engineering. Industrial engineers are increasingly concerned with reducing waste, minimizing energy consumption, and developing more environmentally friendly processes. In various industries, ranging from manufacturing to healthcare, industrial engineering assumes a vital role. Its focus on efficiency, productivity, and quality makes it a key driver of economic growth and development. With the continued development of IoT, AI, automation, and sustainability initiatives, industrial engineering is poised to become even more important in the years to come.

1.2 INDUSTRIAL ENGINEERING APPLICATIONS

Industrial engineering is a field that has a wide range of applications across many industries. Its focus on optimizing processes and systems can improve efficiency, productivity, quality, and safety. Here are some of the key applications of industrial engineering:

- **Manufacturing**: The application of industrial engineering in manufacturing is commonly utilized to enhance production processes, minimize waste, and enhance quality control. This can involve the design of manufacturing systems, the optimization of supply chain management, and the development of quality control systems.
- **Healthcare**: In healthcare, industrial engineering can be applied to improve patient flow, reduce wait times, and optimize resource utilization. This can involve the design of hospital layouts, the development of scheduling systems, and the analysis of patient data to identify areas for improvement (Liu and Wang 2018).
- **Transportation**: Industrial engineering is used in transportation to optimize logistics, reduce fuel consumption, and improve safety. This can involve the optimization of transportation networks, the design of routing systems, and the development of safety systems.
- **Service industries**: Industrial engineering can be applied in service industries such as banking, hospitality, and retail to improve customer service, reduce wait times, and optimize resource utilization. This can involve the design of service systems, the development of scheduling systems, and the optimization of supply chain management.
- **Energy**: In the energy industry, industrial engineering is used to optimize energy production processes, reduce waste, and improve safety. This can involve the optimization of energy production systems, the development of safety systems, and the analysis of data to identify areas for improvement (Sundmaeker et al., 2010).
- **Construction**: Industrial engineering is applied in construction to optimize construction processes, reduce waste, and improve safety. This can involve the design of construction processes, the optimization of resource utilization, and the development of safety systems.
- **Agriculture**: In agriculture, industrial engineering can be used to optimize farming processes, reduce waste, and improve resource utilization. This can involve the design of farming systems, the optimization of supply chain management, and the development of safety systems.

Overall, industrial engineering has a wide range of applications across many industries. Its focus on optimizing processes and systems can improve efficiency, productivity, quality, and safety, making it an essential field for driving economic growth and development.

1.3   ARTIFICIAL INTELLIGENCE

AI can be used to optimize production processes, detect quality issues before they become serious, and predict supply chain disruptions. AI has significant implications for society as a whole.

One of the challenges of AI is the development of explainable AI, which refers to the ability to understand how AI algorithms make decisions. This is important for ensuring that AI is transparent and accountable, and for identifying and mitigating any biases or errors in the algorithms. Explainable AI demands the development of techniques and algorithms that can provide explanations for AI decisions, such as decision trees, rule-based systems, and feature importance analysis (Manyika et al., 2011).

Ethical AI involves developing algorithms and techniques that are designed to minimize bias, ensure privacy and security, and prevent harm to individuals and society. AI is also rapidly transforming the nature of work and employment.

It is important to develop techniques for identifying and mitigating bias in AI algorithms, such as ensuring diverse representation in the data used for training, and regularly auditing AI systems for bias. Another challenge of AI is the development of secure AI, which refers to the ability to protect AI systems from cyber-attacks and other security threats. AI systems are vulnerable to various types of attacks, such as adversarial attacks, where malicious actors intentionally manipulate the input data to deceive the AI algorithm, and data poisoning attacks, where malicious actors intentionally inject biased or malicious data into the training data to manipulate the AI algorithm. It is important to develop techniques for securing AI systems and ensuring that they are resilient to cyber-attacks. Despite these challenges, the future of AI is promising, with significant potential for further advancements and applications.

Integration of AI with other emerging technologies, such as the IoT, blockchain, and 5G could lead to new applications and benefits, such as more efficient and automated supply chains, more personalized healthcare, and smarter cities. AI is a rapidly evolving field with significant applications and implications for society. It is important to develop appropriate policies and regulations to ensure that AI is used responsibly and ethically, and to continue to invest in research and development to advance the field and realize its full potential.

However, the deployment of AI also raises concerns around energy consumption and the environmental impact of AI hardware, as well as the potential for unintended consequences and unforeseen environmental impacts. AI is a transformative technology with significant implications for society, the economy, and the environment (Zeng et al., 2019).

Machine Learning (ML) is a highly significant application of AI that entails the creation of algorithms which are capable of learning from data without the need for explicit programming (Bhambri, 2020). The field of machine learning can be broadly classified into three main categories, namely reinforcement learning, supervised learning and unsupervised learning. Supervised learning involves the training of a model on labeled data, wherein the right result is already established. Conversely, unsupervised learning pertains to the process of instructing a model with un-annotated data, wherein the accurate output is unknown. Reinforcement learning is a machine learning technique that entails instructing an instance to make decisions by utilizing a reward and punishment system.

The field of AI encompasses various applications, among which Natural Language Processing (NLP) holds a prominent position. NLP involves the development of algorithms that are capable of comprehending and processing human language. NLP encompasses a wide array of practical implementations, such as language translation, speech recognition, sentiment analysis, and chatbot development (Sumathi et al., 2021). AI has noteworthy implications in diverse sectors, such as finance, healthcare, transportation, & manufacturing. AI has the potential to enhance patient outcomes, decrease expenses, and boost efficiency in the healthcare sector (Bali et al. 2023). AI has the potential to be utilized in the analysis of medical images, resulting in more precise diagnoses. Additionally, AI can be employed in the monitoring of patient health, enabling the detection of potential health concerns before they escalate into critical conditions (Kumar et al., 2022). AI has the potential to enhance fraud detection, risk management, and customer service within the finance industry. AI has the potential to be utilized in the analysis of financial data to identify fraudulent transactions. Additionally, it can offer tailored financial guidance to customers according to their unique requirements and objectives. AI has the potential to enhance efficiency, safety, and sustainability in the field of transportation. AI has the potential to enhance transportation networks by optimizing them, mitigating traffic congestion, and enhancing fuel efficiency (Rani et al., 2022). AI has the potential to enhance quality control, productivity, and supply chain management in the manufacturing industry (Kataria et al. 2022). AI has the potential to enhance production processes, identify quality concerns in advance, and anticipate potential disruptions in the supply chain. AI carries substantial ramifications for the broader society (Rana et al., 2020). The phenomenon under consideration possesses the capacity to generate noteworthy economic and societal advantages, yet it simultaneously engenders ethical and societal apprehensions, including but not limited to issues of privacy, bias, and displacement of employment. Given the increasing sophistication and ubiquity of AI, it is imperative to contemplate these apprehensions and formulate suitable protocols and guidelines to guarantee the responsible and ethical utilization of AI (Sangwan et al., 2021).

A significant hurdle in the field of AI pertains to the advancement of explainable AI. This concept pertains to the capacity to comprehend the decision-making process of AI algorithms. Ensuring the transparency and accountability of AI is crucial, as it enables identification and mitigation of any biases or lapses present in the algorithms. The concept of Explainable AI pertains to the creation of algorithms and methodologies that are capable of furnishing justifications for the decisions made by AI. This may include the utilization of rule-based systems, decision trees, and feature importance analysis.

The development of ethical AI poses a significant challenge in the field of Artificial Intelligence. This pertains to the utilization of AI in a manner that aligns with ethical principles, including but not limited to fairness, transparency, accountability, and the upholding of human rights (Babu et al., 2021). The concept of ethical Artificial Intelligence pertains to the creation of algorithms and methodologies that aim to reduce partiality, guarantee confidentiality and protection, and forestall any detrimental effects on both individuals and the community. The impact of Artificial Intelligence on the field of work and employment is undergoing rapid transformation (Li et al., 2015). AI possesses the capacity to generate novel employment prospects, however, it also harbors the potential to mechanize numerous jobs, thereby resulting in displacement of employment and unemployment. As AI continues to progress and become more integrated into various industries, it is crucial to contemplate the potential consequences for the labor force and establish suitable policies and initiatives to guarantee that employees are adequately equipped to adapt to the evolving work landscape (Bhambri and Gupta, 2012).

The likelihood for discrimination prejudice in AI algorithms is considered to be one of the biggest effects of AI on society. The level of impartiality exhibited by AI algorithms is contingent upon the impartiality of the data utilized in their training. In the event that the data is partial, the algorithm will additionally be partial (Bakshi et al., 2021). The phenomenon under consideration has the potential to engender discriminatory practices in various domains, including but not limited to employment, financial transactions, and the criminal justice system, thereby reinforcing pre-existing disparities in society. The development of techniques for recognizing and minimizing discrimination in AI algorithms is crucial. This can be achieved by ensuring different representations in the information used in training and conducting regular audits of AI systems to detect any bias (Kothandaraman et al., 2022). An additional obstacle in the field of Artificial Intelligence pertains to the advancement of secure AI, denoting the capacity to safeguard AI systems against cyber-assaults and other forms of security hazards (Hossain et al., 2017). AI systems are susceptible to different forms of attacks, including adversarial attacks and data poisoning attacks. Adversarial attacks involve the deliberate manipulation of input data by malicious actors to mislead the AI algorithm, while data poisoning attacks involve the intentional injection of biased or fraudulent information into the training info to alter the AI algorithm (Kothandaraman et al., 2022). The development of techniques aimed at securing AI systems while improving their resilience to cyber-attacks is of paramount importance. Notwithstanding these obstacles, the outlook for Artificial Intelligence is encouraging, as there exists substantial potential for additional progress and utilization. The advancement of Artificial General Intelligence (AGI) is a subject of significant interest, as it pertains to the creation of Artificial Intelligence that can perform any cognitive task that a human is capable of. The development of AGI would constitute a noteworthy advancement in the field of AI and has the potential to generate numerous novel applications and advantages for the community Gupta et al., 2011).

An additional field of inquiry pertains to the amalgamation of AI with other nascent technologies, including the IoT, blockchain, and 5G. The integration of various technologies has the potential to result in novel applications and advantages, including streamlined and automatic supply chains, customized healthcare services, and intelligent urban environments. The field of Artificial Intelligence is characterized by a swift pace of development and holds substantial potential for societal applications and ramifications. AI possesses the capacity to generate substantial advantages; however, it simultaneously elicits ethical and societal apprehensions that necessitate resolution. The formulation of suitable policies and regulations is crucial in ensuring the responsible and ethical utilization of AI. Additionally, sustained investment in development & research is necessary to further the progress of the field and fully actualize its capabilities. Moreover, it is anticipated that AI will have a substantial influence on the labor market and the characteristics of employment (Anand and Bhambri, 2018). AI possesses the capability to generate novel employment prospects; however, it also harbors the potential to mechanize numerous extant jobs, particularly ones that entail monotonous duties. The aforementioned scenario has the potential to result in the displacement of jobs, necessitating the acquisition of novel skills and expertise by workers in order to maintain their competitiveness in the labor market (Gubbi et al., 2013). It is imperative for policymakers as well as business entities to acknowledge and tackle the potential ramifications of the advent of Artificial Intelligence and formulate effective measures to facilitate the welfare of employees and ensure a fair and equitable transition to an economy driven by AI (Ritu and Bhambri, 2022). Furthermore, it is anticipated that Artificial Intelligence will have noteworthy ramifications for the healthcare industry. AI possesses the capability to enhance healthcare results through the facilitation of precise diagnoses, customized treatment plans, and streamlined healthcare administration (Rachna et al., 2022). AI algorithms have the potential to be trained using medical images as well as patient data, which can lead to precise disease diagnosis and identification of optimal treatment options. AI has the potential to facilitate the creation of customized treatment plans that take into account an individual's distinct genetic profile and medical background. The implementation of AI in the healthcare sector has given rise to apprehensions regarding ethical considerations, privacy, and security. One of the major concerns is the possibility of AI exacerbating the existing healthcare disparities (Bhambri and Gupta, 2014).

AI possesses the capability to considerably influence the environment and environmental sustainability (Kaur and Bhambri, 2020). AI has the potential to enhance the efficiency and sustainability of manufacturing processes, optimize consumption of energy in buildings and travel, and monitor and mitigate the effects of climate change (Huang et al., 2017). AI has the potential to enhance the efficiency of systems that generate electricity from renewable sources, for example windmills & solar panels, through optimization of their placement and operation (Kaur et al., 2019). The implementation of AI technology gives rise to apprehensions regarding its consumption of energy and the ecological implications of AI hardware. Additionally, there exists a possibility of inadvertent outcomes and unanticipated environmental effects. AI is a technology that has the potential to bring about significant transformations with far-reaching implications for various aspects of the economy, society, and the environment. AI possesses the capacity to generate substantial advantages; however, it also elicits noteworthy societal, ethical, and environmental apprehensions that necessitate attention. Continuous communication and cooperation among policymakers, corporations, and individuals are crucial to guarantee the ethical, responsible, and sustainable development and implementation of AI. This approach should priorities the advancement of the common good and the enhancement of the overall welfare of all members of society.

1.4 INTERNET OF THINGS

The IoT refers to a system of interconnected devices that are capable of communicating with one another and sharing data via the internet, without the need for human intervention. The IoT is swiftly revolutionizing diverse sectors such as manufacturing, healthcare, transportation, and agriculture, by facilitating instantaneous data analysis and informed decision-making. This section aims to present a thorough exposition of the IoT, encompassing its conceptualization, structural framework, practical implementations, and associated obstacles.

1.4.1 IoT Definition and Architecture

The term IoT refers to the interconnection of tangible entities such as structures, automobiles, and devices, which are equipped with software, network connectivity, and sensors. The interconnectivity of these devices facilitates the acquisition and transmission of data. The IoT is structured into three distinct layers, namely the network layer, the perception layer, and the application layer. The stratum of perception encompasses a range of technological apparatus, including RFID tags, sensors, and analogous devices, which are responsible for gathering data from the surrounding milieu. The network layer provides connectivity among the devices, and the application layer comprises software applications that analyze the data and provide insights.

1.4.2 IoT Applications

IoT is revolutionizing multiple sectors, such as manufacturing, healthcare, transportation, and agriculture. The healthcare sector leverages IoT devices to monitor the patients' well-being and vital signs, thereby facilitating remote medical treatment and diagnosis by physicians. IoT devices find various applications in different industries. In manufacturing, these devices are utilized for monitoring equipment performance, identifying faults, and optimizing maintenance schedules. In transportation, they are employed for tracking the location of vehicles, monitoring fuel efficiency, and enhancing safety. In agriculture, IoT devices are utilized for monitoring environmental factors such as soil moisture, temperature, etc., to optimize crop yield (Rani et al., 2022).

1.5 OTHER TECHNOLOGIES IN INDUSTRIAL PROCESSES

The use of technology has transformed industrial processes by increasing efficiency, reducing costs, and improving product quality. From automation to Artificial Intelligence, there are many technologies that businesses can leverage to streamline their operations and stay ahead of the competition. This section explores some of the most significant technologies used in industrial processes and their impact on the industry (Bhambri and Gupta, 2014).

- Automation: The term "automation" pertains to the utilization of computers, machines, and robots in executing tasks that were previously accomplished by human beings. Automation has been widely adopted in industrial processes to reduce labor costs and improve productivity. For example, in manufacturing, robots are used to assemble products, paint, and weld. This allows companies to produce goods more quickly, efficiently, and with fewer errors. The benefits of automation in industrial processes are many. Firstly, automation reduces the likelihood of human error, which can lead to product defects and quality issues. Secondly, automation improves production speed and output, as machines can work 24/7 without breaks or fatigue. Thirdly, automation can reduce the need for manual labor, which can save companies money on wages and benefits (Singh et al., 2020).

- Artificial Intelligence: AI has revolutionized industrial processes. AI pertains to the replication of human intellect in machines which are designed to emulate human thinking and learning processes (Bandyopadhyay and Sen, 2011). AI is used in many industrial processes, such as predictive maintenance, quality control, and logistics. One of the primary benefits of AI in industrial processes is its ability to improve predictive maintenance. With AI, machines can analyze data from sensors and other sources to predict when equipment is likely to fail. This allows companies to schedule maintenance in advance, reducing downtime and repair costs. AI is also used in quality control, where it can identify defects and anomalies in products more quickly and accurately than humans (Vijayalakshmi et al., 2021).

- Internet of Things: IoT pertains to a system of interconnected devices that are capable of sharing data amongst themselves. In industrial processes, IoT is used to monitor equipment, track inventory, and optimize energy consumption. IoT devices can be connected to sensors and other devices, allowing companies to collect data and analyze it to improve efficiency and reduce waste. One of the primary benefits of IoT in industrial processes is its ability to provide real-time data. With IoT, companies can monitor equipment and processes in real time, allowing them to make adjustments on the fly to improve efficiency and reduce waste. IoT can also be used to track inventory, ensuring that companies have the right amount of supplies on hand at all times (Bhambri et al., 2023).

- Augmented Reality: Augmented Reality (AR) is a technological innovation that overlays computer-generated visual content onto the physical environment. In industrial processes, AR is used to provide workers with information and instructions while they are performing tasks. AR can be used to overlay instructions onto machines, allowing workers to see exactly what they need to do in real-time. One of the primary benefits of AR in industrial processes is its ability to improve worker productivity and safety. With AR, workers can receive instructions and information without having to consult manuals or other materials. This can reduce the likelihood of errors and accidents, improving worker safety and reducing downtime (Bhambri et al., 2022).

- Cloud Computing: Cloud computing pertains to the utilization of off-site servers for the purpose of storing, organizing, and manipulating data. In industrial processes, cloud computing is used to store and analyze data from sensors and other devices. Cloud computing can provide companies with real-time insights into their operations, allowing them to make better decisions and improve efficiency (Atzori et al., 2010). One of the primary benefits of cloud computing in industrial processes is its ability to provide real-time data analysis. With cloud computing, companies can analyze data from sensors and other devices in real-time, allowing them to make decisions quickly and effectively. Cloud computing can also reduce the need for on-premise hardware, reducing costs and improving scalability (Bhambri et al., 2021).

- Blockchain: The blockchain technology offers a decentralized and secure method for the storage and dissemination of information. In industrial processes, blockchain can be used to create a tamper-proof record of transactions, improving transparency and reducing the likelihood of fraud.
- 3D Printing: Additive manufacturing, commonly referred to as 3D printing, is a cutting-edge technology that enables the creation of three-dimensional objects by depositing successive layers of material on top of one another. The utilization of 3D printing technology in industrial processes has the potential to produce prototypes and finalized products, thereby decreasing production costs and lead times (Bose et al., 2021).
- Virtual Reality: The technology of Virtual Reality (VR) generates a computer-generated environment that enables users to engage in interactive experiences. In industrial processes, VR can be used to train workers on new processes and equipment, allowing them to gain experience in a safe and controlled environment (Singh et al., 2021).

Technology has transformed industrial processes in many ways. Various technological advancements, such as automation, AI, IoT, AR, and cloud computing, have the potential to enhance operational efficiency, minimize expenses, and elevate product standards for enterprises. By adopting these technologies, companies can stay ahead of the competition and remain relevant in an increasingly competitive marketplace. However, it is important to note that the adoption of technology in industrial processes is not without challenges. For example, there may be resistance to change from workers who fear job loss due to automation. Additionally, there may be concerns around cyber-security and data privacy when using cloud computing and internet of things technologies (Kuzhaloli et al., 2020). To overcome these challenges, it is important for businesses to involve their workers in the adoption of technology and provide training and support to help them adapt to new processes. Additionally, businesses should prioritize cyber-security and data privacy when implementing new technologies, ensuring that proper measures are in place to protect sensitive information (Rani et al., 2023a). On the whole, the advantages of incorporating technology into industrial operations surpass the obstacles. The adoption of novel technologies by enterprises can enhance operational effectiveness, curtail expenses, and elevate the caliber of their merchandise, thereby enabling them to attain prosperity in a constantly changing commercial sphere (Jabeen et al., 2021).

Overall, the use of technology in industrial processes will continue to evolve and transform the industry. As new technologies emerge, businesses will need to stay up to date and be willing to adapt to remain competitive. By utilizing cutting-edge technologies, enterprises can enhance operational effectiveness, curtail expenses, and elevate product standards, thereby positioning themselves for triumph in an intensifying competitive landscape (Al-Fuqaha et al., 2015).

1.6 APPLICATIONS OF AI AND IoT IN IE

AI and IoT are two technologies that have gained a lot of attention in recent years, and for good reason. These technologies are revolutionizing industrial engineering and enabling businesses to improve their processes, reduce costs, and increase efficiency. In this section, we will explore the applications of AI and IoT in industrial engineering and discuss their potential impact.

1.6.1 APPLICATIONS OF AI IN INDUSTRIAL ENGINEERING

Following are the applications of Artificial Intelligence in industrial engineering:

- Predictive Maintenance: Artificial Intelligence has the capability to forecast equipment malfunction in advance, thereby allowing enterprises to execute maintenance procedures prior to the occurrence of a potential breakdown. This approach has the potential to decrease the amount of time that equipment is out of service and result in cost savings associated with maintenance and repairs.
- Quality Control: Artificial Intelligence has the capability to monitor manufacturing processes and identify any defects in real time. This can both improve product quality and reduce waste.
- Production Planning: AI has the potential to enhance production scheduling and minimize wastage. Through the examination of data such as consumer demand and stock levels, Artificial Intelligence has the ability to generate production strategies that are characterized by enhanced efficiency and cost-effectiveness.
- Supply Chain Management: The implementation of AI has the potential to enhance supply chain management through its ability to forecast demand, minimize inventory, and detect potential disruptions. This can improve efficiency and reduce costs (Chui et al., 2016).
- Autonomous Vehicles: AI can be used to enable autonomous vehicles, such as drones and self-driving trucks, to navigate industrial environments. This can improve safety and efficiency in logistics operations.

1.6.2 APPLICATIONS OF IoT IN INDUSTRIAL ENGINEERING

Following are the applications of Artificial Intelligence in industrial engineering:

- Remote Monitoring: The utilization of IoT sensors enables remote monitoring of equipment and processes, thereby facilitating the identification of potential issues prior to their escalation into significant problems, thereby benefiting businesses. The implementation of this measure has the potential to decrease operational downtime and result in cost savings for maintenance expenses.

- Predictive Maintenance: The utilization of IoT sensors has the potential to facilitate the monitoring of equipment and identification of indications of deterioration, thereby allowing enterprises to conduct maintenance activities proactively and prevent unexpected equipment failures. The implementation of this measure has the potential to decrease periods of inactivity and result in cost savings associated with maintenance (Bhambri & Gupta, 2013).

- Asset Tracking: The utilization of IoT sensors enables the monitoring of the current location and condition of equipment as well as inventory in a timely manner. The implementation of this approach has the potential to enhance the management of supply chain operations and mitigate the occurrence of theft and loss.

- Energy Management: The implementation of IoT sensors in manufacturing facilities and distribution centres can facilitate the monitoring of energy consumption, thereby allowing businesses to pinpoint areas that require optimization and ultimately curtail expenses.

- Condition Monitoring: The utilization of IoT sensors has the potential to facilitate the monitoring of equipment status and the early detection of potential issues, thereby mitigating the likelihood of significant problems. This can improve equipment reliability and reduce maintenance costs (Davenport and Ronanki, 2018).

1.6.3 Potential Impact of AI and IoT on Industrial Engineering

The potential ramifications of the integration of AI and IoT in the field of industrial engineering are considerable (Chen et al., 2019). Through the utilization of these technologies, enterprises can enhance operational effectiveness, curtail expenses, and augment output. For example, predictive maintenance can reduce downtime and save money on repairs, while quality control can improve product quality and reduce waste (Sharma and Bhambri, 2020). Autonomous vehicles can improve safety and efficiency in logistics operations, while remote monitoring and asset tracking can improve supply chain management. Additionally, the use of AI and IoT can enable businesses to make more informed decisions by providing real-time data and analytics. This can lead to better resource allocation, improved production planning, and more efficient supply chain management.

The applications of AI and IoT in industrial engineering are vast and diverse (Rani & Kaur, 2012). The implementation of these technologies harbors the possibility of transforming the industry through the enhancement of operational efficiency, the reduction of expenses, and the augmentation of output. Businesses that embrace these technologies will be better positioned for success in an increasingly competitive marketplace. Nevertheless, it is crucial to acknowledge that the implementation of AI and IoT in the field of manufacturing is not devoid of obstacles. Cyber security poses a significant challenge. The susceptibility of IoT devices to cyber-attacks necessitates that enterprises implement security protocols to safeguard their networks and devices. Likewise, the efficacy of AI systems is contingent upon the quality of the data on which they are trained. Therefore, it is incumbent upon businesses to guarantee the precision and impartiality of their data (Devadutta et al., 2020). Another challenge is the fear of job loss. AI and IoT hold the potential to automate several tasks that were previously carried out by humans, which has raised concerns regarding job displacement. Effective communication of technological advantages and the provision of support and instruction to employees who may be affected by automation are crucial for businesses. Notwithstanding these obstacles, the prospective advantages of AI and IoT in the field of industrial engineering are noteworthy. As businesses continue to adopt these technologies, we can expect to see increased efficiency, reduced costs, and improved productivity in the industry (Bhambri et al., 2022).

To give a real-world example of the impact of AI and IoT in industrial engineering, let us consider the case of a manufacturer that produces automotive parts. By using IoT sensors to monitor its production lines, the manufacturer can detect defects in real time and make adjustments to its processes to improve quality. This can lead to a reduction in scrap and rework, as well as an improvement in customer satisfaction. Additionally, the manufacturer can use AI to optimize its production schedules, reducing lead times and improving efficiency. This can lead to a reduction in inventory and a decrease in production costs. By embracing these technologies, the manufacturer can stay ahead of the competition and remain relevant in an ever-evolving marketplace. The applications of AI and IoT in industrial engineering are numerous and diverse. The implementation of these technologies holds the promise of transforming the industry through enhancements in operational efficiency, cost reduction, and productivity amplification. Businesses that adopt these technologies will be better positioned for success in an increasingly competitive marketplace. It is imperative to acknowledge and tackle obstacles such as computer security and employment displacement in order to effectively actualize the advantages presented by these technologies.

With the ongoing advancements in AI and IoT, it is anticipated that industrial engineering will witness further sophisticated applications. For example, AI algorithms can be used to optimize complex manufacturing processes, such as chemical reactions, to reduce costs and improve efficiency. The utilization of IoT sensors for the purpose of monitoring environmental parameters, such as humidity and temperature, is a viable approach to guarantee the appropriate storage and transportation of goods under ideal circumstances. Furthermore, the use of AI and IoT can enable businesses to achieve sustainability goals by reducing waste and energy consumption. Another area where AI and IoT can make a significant impact is in the field of predictive maintenance. Through the utilization of sensors for equipment monitoring and the application of AI algorithms for data analysis, enterprises can anticipate equipment failure and undertake maintenance procedures in advance of any potential breakdown. The implementation of this approach has the potential to decrease the amount of time that a system is non-operational and result in cost savings with regards to maintenance. For example, in the oil and gas industry, predictive maintenance can help prevent equipment failures that could result in oil spills or other environmental disasters. The use of AI and IoT in industrial engineering also has implications for the workforce. As automation becomes more prevalent, there will be a need for workers with new skills, such as data analytics and programming. This scenario provides a prospect for enterprises to allocate resources towards employee training and development, in order to ensure that their workforce possesses the necessary competencies required for the contemporary digital era. The ongoing advancements in AI and IoT are anticipated to yield more sophisticated industrial engineering applications. Enterprises that adopt these technologies are likely to be better situated for success in a dynamic marketplace.

1.7 CHALLENGES AND FUTURE RESEARCH DIRECTIONS

1.7.1 CHALLENGES

The amalgamation of IoT and AI within the domain of industrial engineering poses a number of challenges that require resolution. Data management poses a significant challenge. IoT generates a massive amount of data, which must be collected, processed, analyzed, and stored. Industrial engineers must develop new data management strategies and tools that can handle this large amount of data efficiently.

Cyber security poses an additional challenge. The susceptibility of IoT devices to cyber-attacks poses a significant threat, as it may result in the compromise of confidential information or the interference with industrial operations. Industrial engineers must develop secure systems and protocols that can protect against cyber threats.

1.7.2 OPPORTUNITIES

Despite the challenges, IoT and AI also offer significant opportunities for industrial engineering. The IoT offers a significant advantage by facilitating the instantaneous monitoring and management of industrial operations. This allows industrial engineers to identify and address problems as they arise, which can lead to increased efficiency and productivity.

AI offers a range of benefits, including predictive maintenance, predictive quality control, and predictive supply chain management. Through the analysis of data obtained from IoT devices, Artificial Intelligence has the capability to anticipate the occurrence of equipment failure, defects, and low inventory levels. This allows industrial engineers to take proactive measures to prevent problems from occurring, which can save time and money.

1.7.3 FUTURE OF INDUSTRIAL ENGINEERING WITH IoT AND AI

The future of industrial engineering is closely tied to the development and implementation of IoT and AI. In the coming years, industrial engineers are likely to use these technologies to develop more efficient and effective processes, improve supply chain management, reduce waste and environmental impact, and improve worker safety.

IoT and AI are also likely to change the nature of work for industrial engineers. As machines become more intelligent and autonomous, industrial engineers may spend more time designing and optimizing processes, and less time on manual tasks. This will require new skills and knowledge, as well as a shift in the way industrial engineers approach their work.

1.8 CONCLUSIONS

In conclusion, IoT and AI present both challenges and opportunities for industrial engineering. Industrial engineers must develop new data management strategies and cyber-security protocols to address the challenges posed by these technologies. At the same time, IoT and AI offer significant benefits, including real-time monitoring, predictive maintenance, and predictive quality control. The integration and implementation of these technologies are expected to shape the future of the industrial engineering field as they continue to advance.

REFERENCES

Al-Fuqaha, A., Guizani, M., Mohammadi, M., Aledhari, M., & Ayyash, M. (2015). Internet of things: A survey on enabling technologies, protocols, and applications. *IEEE Communication Surveys and Tutorials*, 17(4), 2347–2376.

Anand, A., & Bhambri, P. (2018). Character recognition system using radial features. *International Journal on Future Revolution in Computer Science & Communication Engineering*, 4(4), 599–602.

Atzori, L., Iera, A., & Morabito, G. (2010). The internet of things: A survey. *Computer Networks*, 54(15), 2787–2805.

Babu, G. C. N., Gupta, S., Bhambri, P., Leo, L. M., Rao, B. H., & Kumar, S. (2021). A semantic health observation system development based on the IoT sensors. *Turkish Journal of Physiotherapy and Rehabilitation*, 32(3), 1721–1729.

Bakshi, P., Bhambri, P., & Thapar, V. (2021). A review paper on wireless sensor network techniques in internet of things (IoT). *Wesleyan Journal of Research*, 14(7), 147–160.

Bali, V., Bali, S., Gaur, D., Rani, S., & Kumar, R. (2023). Commercial-off-the shelf vendor selection: A multi-criteria decision-making approach using intuitionistic fuzzy sets and TOPSIS. *Operational Research in Engineering Sciences: Theory and Applications*, 12(4), 100–113.

Bandyopadhyay, D., & Sen, J. (2011). Internet of things: Applications and challenges in technology and standardization. *Wireless Personal Communications*, 58(1), 49–69.

Bhambri, P. (2020). Green compliance. In S. Agarwal (Ed.), *Introduction to Green Computing* (pp. 95–125). AGAR Saliha Publication. ISBN: 978-81-948141-5-3.

Bhambri, P., & Gupta, O. P. (2012). A novel method for the design of phylogenetic tree. *International Journal of IT, Engineering and Applied Sciences Research*, 1(1), 24–28.

Bhambri, P., & Gupta, O. P. (2013). Design of distributed prefetching protocol in push-to-peer video-on-demand system. *International Journal of Research in Advent Technology*, 1(3), 95–103.

Bhambri, P., & Gupta, O. P. (2014). Dynamic frequency allocation scheme of mobile networks using priority assignment technique. *International Journal of Engineering and Technology Innovation*, 1(1), 9–12.

Bhambri, P., Singh, M., Dhanoa, I. S., & Kumar, M. (2022). Deployment of ROBOT for HVAC duct and disaster management. *Oriental Journal of Computer Science and Technology*, 15, 1–8.

Bhambri, P., Singh, M., Jain, A., Dhanoa, I. S., Sinha, V. K., & Lal, S. (2021). Classification of gene expression data with the aid of optimized feature selection. *Turkish Journal of Physiotherapy and Rehabilitation*, 32, 3.

Bhambri, P., Singh, S., Sangwan, S., Devi, J., & Jain, S. (2023). Plants recognition using leaf image pattern analysis. *Journal of Survey in Fisheries Sciences*, 10(2S), 3863–3871.

Bose, M. M., Yadav, D., Bhambri, P., & Shankar, R. (2021). Electronic customer relationship management: Benefits and pre-implementation considerations. *Journal of Maharaja Sayajirao University of Baroda*, 55(01(VI)), 1343–1350.

Chen, C., Li, X., & Li, X. (2019). A survey of industrial internet of things: A focus on architecture, applications, technologies, and security. *Journal of Industrial Information Integration*, 15, 100–120.

Chui, M., Manyika, J., & Bughin, J. (2016). The rise of the machines: Prospects and challenges for the internet of things. *McKinsey Global Institute*, 7, 1–11.

Davenport, T. H., & Ronanki, R. (2018). Artificial intelligence for the real world: Don't start with moon shots. *Harvard Business Review*, 96(1), 108–116.

Devadutta, K., Bhambri, P., Gountia, D., Mehta, V., Mangla, M., Patan, R., Kumar, A., Agarwal, P.K., Sharma, A., Singh, M., & Gadicha, A.B. (2020). Method for Cyber Security in Email Communication among Networked Computing Devices [Patent application number 202031002649]. India.

Gubbi, J., Buyya, R., Marusic, S., & Palaniswami, M. (2013). Internet of things (IoT): A vision, architectural elements, and future directions. *Future Generation Computer Systems*, 29(7), 1645–1660.

Gupta, O., Rani, S., & Pant, D. C. (2011). Impact of parallel computing on bioinformatics algorithms. In *Proceedings 5th IEEE International Conference on Advanced Computing and Communication Technologies* (pp. 206–209).

Hossain, M. S., Muhammad, G., & Muhammad, R. (2017). Industrial internet of things (IIoT): Challenges, opportunities, and directions. *Future Generation Computer Systems*, 82, 354–365.

Huang, J., Xu, W., & Li, L. (2017). Industrial big data analytics: Understanding, modeling and predicting maintenance problems. *Engineering Applications of Artificial Intelligence*, 60, 197–210.

Jabeen, A., Pallathadka, H., Pallathadka, L. K., & Bhambri, P. (2021). E-CRM successful factors for business enterprises case studies. *Journal of Maharaja Sayajirao University of Baroda*, 55(01(VI)), 1332–1342.

Kataria, A., Agrawal, D., Rani, S., Karar, V., & Chauhan, M. (2022). Prediction of blood screening parameters for preliminary analysis using neural networks. In *Predictive Modeling in Biomedical Data Mining and Analysis* (pp. 157–169). Academic Press.

Kaur, G., Kaur, R., & Rani, S. (2015). Cloud computing-a new trend in it era. *International Journal of Science, Technology and Management*, 4(6), 1–6.

Kaur, J., & Bhambri, P. (2020). *Hybrid classification model for the reverse code generation in software engineering*. I.K. Gujral Punjab Technical University.

Kaur, J., Bhambri, P., & Sharma, K. (2019). Wheat production analysis based on Naïve Bayes classifier. *International Journal of Analytical and Experimental Model Analysis*, 11(9), 705–709.

Kothandaraman, D., Manickam, M., Balasundaram, A., Pradeep, D., Arulmurugan, A., Sivaraman, A. K., … & Balakrishna, R. (2022). Decentralized link failure prevention routing (DLFPR) algorithm for efficient internet of things. *Intelligent Automation & Soft Computing*, 34(1), 655–666.

Kumar, P., Banerjee, K., Singhal, N., Kumar, A., Rani, S., Kumar, R., & Lavinia, C. A. (2022). Verifiable, secure mobile agent migration in healthcare systems using a polynomial-based threshold secret sharing scheme with a blowfish algorithm. *Sensors*, 22(22), 8620.

Kuzhaloli, S., Devaneyan, P., Sitaraman, N., Periyathanbi, P., Gurusamy, M., & Bhambri, P. (2020). IoT based Smart Kitchen Application for Gas Leakage Monitoring [Patent application number 202041049866A]. India.

Li, S., Xu, L. D., & Zhao, S. (2015). The internet of things: A survey of topics and trends. *Information Systems Frontiers*, 17(2), 261–274.

Liu, Y., & Wang, Z. (2018). Big data analytics with applications. *Journal of Computer Science and Technology*, 33(1), 223–224.

Manyika, J., Chui, M., Brown, B., Bughin, J., Dobbs, R., Roxburgh, C., & Byers, A. H. (2011). Big data: The next frontier for innovation, competition, and productivity. *McKinsey Global Institute*, 1, 1–149.

McAfee, A., & Brynjolfsson, E. (2017). *Machine, Platform, Crowd: Harnessing Our Digital Future*. WW Norton & Company.

Paika, E. V., & Bhambri, E. P. (2013). Edge detection-fuzzy inference system. *International Journal of Management & Information Technology*, 4(1), 148–155.

Qureshi, K. N., & Khan, M. A. (2019). Internet of things (IoT) for industrial applications: Challenges and solutions. *Wireless Networks*, 25(3), 1117–1136.

Rachna, R., Bhambri, P., & Chhabra, Y. (2022). Deployment of distributed clustering approach in WSNs and IoTs. In Pankaj Bhambri, Sita Rani, Gaurav Gupta, & Alex Khang (Eds.), *Cloud and Fog Computing Platforms for Internet of Things* (pp. 85–98). Chapman and Hall/CRC. https://www.routledge.com/Cloud-and-Fog-Computing-Platforms-for-Internet-of-Things/Bhambri-Rani-Gupta-Khang/p/book/9781032101507

Rana, R., Chabbra, Y., & Bhambri, P. (2020). Comparison of clustering approaches for enhancing sustainability performance in WSNs: A Study. In *Proceedings of the International Congress on Sustainable Development through Engineering Innovations* (pp. 62–71). ISBN 978-93-89947-14-4.

Rani, S., Bhambri, P., & Gupta, O. P. (2022). Green smart farming techniques and sustainable agriculture: Research roadmap towards organic farming for imperishable agricultural products. In Vikram Bali, Rajni Mohana, Ahmed A. Elngar, Sunil Kumar Chawla, & Gurpreet Singh (Eds.), *Handbook of Sustainable Development through Green Engineering and Technology* (pp. 49–67). CRC Press. https://www.routledge.com/Handbook-of-Sustainable-Development-Through-Green-Engineering-and-Technology/Bali-Mohana-Elngar-Chawla-Singh/p/book/9780367650926

Rani, S., Bhambri, P., Kataria, A., & Khang, A. (2023a). Smart city ecosystem: Concept, sustainability, design principles, and technologies. In Alex Khang, Sita Rani & Arun Kumar Sivaraman (Eds.), *AI-Centric Smart City Ecosystems* (pp. 1–20). CRC Press. https://www.taylorfrancis.com/books/edit/10.1201/9781003252542/ai-centric-smart-city-ecosystems-alex-khang-sita-rani-arun-kumar-sivaraman

Rani, S., Kataria, A., Kumar, S., & Tiwari, P. (2023b). Federated learning for secure IoMT-applications in smart healthcare systems: A comprehensive review. *Knowledge-Based Systems*, 110658, 1–15.

Rani, S., & Kaur, S. (2012). Cluster analysis method for multiple sequence alignment. *International Journal of Computer Applications*, 43(14), 19–25.

Rauschecker, U., & Devaraj, S. (2019). Artificial intelligence and the future of work. *MIS Quarterly Executive*, 18(3), 49–60.

Ritu, & Bhambri, P. (2022). A CAD System for Software Effort Estimation. *Paper presented at the International Conference on Technological Advancements in Computational Sciences* (pp. 140–146). IEEE. DOI: 10.1109/ICTACS56270.2022.9988123.

Sangwan, Y. S., Lal, S., Bhambri, P., Kumar, A., & Dhanoa, I. S. (2021). Advancements in social data security and encryption: A review. *NVEO-Natural Volatiles & Essential Oils Journal NVEO*, 8(4), 15353–15362.

Sharma, R., & Bhambri, P. (2020). *Energy aware bio inspired routing technique for mobile Adhoc networks*. I.K. Gujral Punjab Technical University.

Singh, G., Singh, M., & Bhambri, P. (2020). Artificial intelligence based flying car. In *Proceedings of the International Congress on Sustainable Development through Engineering Innovations* (pp. 216–227). ISBN 978-93-89947-14-4.

Singh, M., Bhambri, P., Lal, S., Singh, Y., Kaur, M., & Singh, J. (2021). Design of the effective technique to improve memory and time constraints for sequence alignment. *International Journal of Applied Engineering Research (Netherlands)*, 6(02), 127–142.

Sumathi, N., Thirumagal, J., Jagannathan, S., Bhambri, P., & Ahamed, I. N. (2021). A comprehensive review on bionanotechnology for the 21st century. *Journal of the Maharaja Sayajirao University of Baroda*, 55(1), 114–131.

Sundmaeker, H., Guillemin, P., Friess, P., & Woelfflé, S. (2010). Vision and challenges for realising the internet of things. *European Commission Information Society and Media*, 10(2), 1–1.

Tao, F., Zhang, M., & Venkatesh, V. C. (2019). Industrial internet of things and digital innovation: A convergence review. *International Journal of Production Research*, 57(7), 2117–2135.

Vijayalakshmi, P., Shankar, R., Karthik, S., & Bhambri, P. (2021). Impact of work from home policies on workplace productivity and employee sentiments during the Covid-19 pandemic. *Journal of Maharaja Sayajirao University of Baroda*, 55(01(VI)), 1314–1331.

Wang, X., & Liu, J. (2019). An overview of industrial internet of things. *Engineering*, 5(1), 28–40.

Zeng, X., Chen, H., Liao, J., & Wu, Z. (2019). Artificial intelligence-based smart manufacturing: A review. *Engineering*, 5(4), 676–687.

2 Evolution and the Future of Industrial Engineering with the IoT and AI

Rachna Rana
Vansh Infotech, Ludhiana, India

Pankaj Bhambri
Guru Nanak Dev Engineering College, Ludhiana, India

Yogesh Chhabra
CT University, Ferozepur, India

2.1 THE INTRODUCTION OF INDUSTRIAL ENGINEERING WITH IoT AND AI

The use of Artificial Intelligence (AI) innovations will considerably improve the manufacturing industry's capabilities since they operate across a range of business functions and levels, from staffing to product design, to the increasing of efficiency, and improvements in both product quality and worker welfare. In the case of industrial engineering, developments in AI are essential because they enable robots to handle more cognitive tasks and make conscious choices based on environmental input in real time (Bhambri et al., 2023).

The use of IoT and AI involves controlling various factors, including content genres, production techniques, financial constraints, and time restraints. Machine Learning (ML) can be used to manage and assess the concepts and other crucial duties, giving more insight into the most recent designs. In order to forecast equipment failure in industrial engineering, AI is employed in factories to provide the anticipatory monitoring of critical industrial machinery (Bakshi and Bhambri, 2021).

The use of cutting-edge communication and manufacturing systems in industries is referred to as Industry 4.0. This is the phrase currently employed in the industry when discussing the digital revolution. This is a general term that encompasses AI, cyberspace, the IoT, storage, ML, and more. These can all be integrated into industrial production processes (Bhambri et al., 2020).

The use of such systems can permit the rapid analysis of information during the course of the manufacturing process. Through this assessment, new processes are created that can continuously adapt to output changes. In the course of this industrial revolution, various operations are not only more efficiently connected, but also simplified. Industry 4.0 is the foundation for industrial industry digitization, which will transform AI and ML applications and affect how we communicate (Hofmann et al., 2019; Cioffi et al., 2020).

Computerized accounting systems are referred to as "Artificial Intelligence" (AI) when they mimic human brain processes (Kaur and Bhambri, 2016). Intelligent systems, computer vision, the processing of natural language speaker identification and machine vision are all among examples of specific AI applications. The following might all be regarded as types of AI: Machines That React, Small Memory, Concept of Mind, Self-aware, Narrow Artificial Intelligence (ANI), and AGI stands for Artificial General Intelligence, or super intelligence (ASI) (Bhambri et al., 2019).

Using computers to perform tasks that usually require human intelligence is known as AI. This s capable of processing large amounts of data in ways that humans are not capable of. The ultimate goal of AI is to replace human skills such as discernment, pattern recognition, and decision-making (Adhikari and Munusamy, 2021). Figure 2.1 shows how industrial engineering can be innovated through the use of IOT and AI.

Everything and Things A comprehension of the notions of "entities" and "totality" is important when engaging in discourse pertaining to the IoT and the IoE. The term "thing" in the context of the IoT encompasses any object that is capable of establishing a connection. The broad definition allows for a wide range of entities to be classified as "things" within the IoT framework, making it a versatile and inclusive notion. Contrarily, we define it in an opposing manner. An object of a physical nature may possess additional attributes that enable it to meet the criteria for being classified as a "thing." (Jain et al., 2021a).

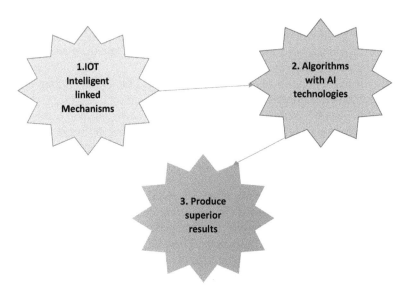

FIGURE 2.1 Innovation of industrial engineering with IOT and AI.

The "thing" (alive or not) should be able to:

1. Generate or gather data;
2. Process data;
3. Dispatch or get data;
4. Identify it.

When considering the Internet of Things, it's crucial to remember that "Situations" are actual things, or events that exists in the actual world. The Internet as we currently understand it is made up of more than just hardware (Sumathi et al., 2021). A website is a virtual entity that does not qualify as a physical object. The same is true for services that are used frequently, such as social networking sites and online shops. Such "intellectual operations" combined "aspects" think up the "every-thing." The connections inside "things" from the physical world and "intelligent services" from the digital world make up the Internet of Everything (Rachna et al., 2022; Bousdekis et al., 2020).

A wide idea known as the Internet of Things (IoT) incorporates a variety of sensors, actuators, data storage devices, and data-processing tools. Therefore, every IoT-enabled device may detect its environment, send, store, and analyse the obtained data, and then take the required action. The next step in responding appropriately depends entirely on the one before it (Kothandaraman et al., 2022).

The actual degree of intelligence of an IoT service is influenced by the amount of computing or operation it is capable of performing (Rachna et al., 2021). The potential of a non-intelligent IoT system will be limited, and it will not possess the capacity to evolve as the requirements evolve. A non-smart IoT system's potential will be constricted, and it won't be talented to alter as the report changes. However, a more intelligent IoT system will have artificial intelligence capabilities and may actually move in the direction of computerization and elasticity (Gupta et al., 2021).

A few instances of current IoT services that use AI at their core are described in this context.

2.1.1 ASSISTANTS WITH VOICE

These speech services operate in the cloud and serve as users' personal assistants on a tabletop. They do a number of tasks via third-party programs and other connected devices (Rachna et al., 2020). Using voice commands from the user, they can answer to inquiries, call cabs, make restaurant bookings, make songs, activate on/off lighting controls, and conduct a number of other functions (Cioffi et al., 2020). Here are a few well-known voice assistants as examples:

- The chatbot Amazon is a feature of Amazon products such as Amazon's Alexa and Amazonian Connect. A particular group of skills, called the Alexa Skills Kit (ASK), can be upgraded and changed to enhance or enhance some talents.
- With the help of additional features, Voice Recognition, which is integrated into Voice Control, can recognize up to six distinct users and get the necessary data to connect with them.

- Apple Airpods uses Alexa from Apple Company to accomplish a similar task.
- These voice assistants can perform a broad range of tasks thanks to the use of many AI subfields. The advancement of technology has led to significant progress in various aspects of voice search, including automated processes, term recognition, text-to-speech conversion, natural language processing, comprehension, experiential rationalization, strategic planning, problem solving, and interactional AI. These developments have virtual assistants to effectively assist individuals in accomplishing tasks in real time(Anand and Bhambri, 2018).
- Robots: The latest advances in this branch of robotics have facilitated the formation of automatons that are more akin to human beings and are intelligent enough to interact with people at the same time as understanding, responding, and displaying some human emotions. Robots are IoTs in themselves because of the various cameras, controllers, and brains they possess (Sangwan et al., 2021).
- One anthropomorphic partner that can converse with people is referred to as Peppers, a mortal robotic from SoftBank Robotics. By observing a person's body language, voice tempo, furrowed brow, and other cues, it can infer their emotional state (Kaur and Bhambri, 2020). It can recognise and appropriately respond with movements, words, and visuals on its screen to the four human emotions of happiness, sadness, anger, and surprise. It has the ability to move and communicate with nearby people and machines. Interleave is widely utilized in various commercial contexts as a means to effectively interact with clients (Potluri et al., 2019).
- Sophia, a Hanson Robotics social robot has a remarkably human-like appearance and is able to convey sentiments through more than 50 different facial expressions. Throughout a discussion, it is competent to preserve gaze by means of the humans at the same time as speaking. She was the first automaton to receive full citizenship in the entire planet. She has even given a concert performance along with many interviews (Panda et al., 2019).
- The Robotic Kitchen by Moley Robotics is a state-of-the-art, completely operational robot that is included within a kitchen. It has robotic arms, a cooktop, an oven, and a finger screen device for social interaction. It also has a recipe database and can make expert-level food (Kaur and Bhambri, 2019).
- The substantial utilization computational linguistics, object recognition, induced, object classification, recognition and tracking, blacklist techniques to analysis input information & answers, face detection, voice commands, monologue techniques, impossible challenge acknowledgment, haptics, etc. has made it possible for these robots to operate effectively (Ritu and Bhambri, 2023).
- Smart Things: In an IoT, there are smart things and devices that support human work as well as voice recognition and robots. Smart things that are automated use technologies such as object classification, face detection, voice search, language and attitude identifiers, multifaceted neural networks learning techniques, processor visualization, etc. (Bhambri et al., 2021).

- The Elegant Microwave by June is capable of providing delicious cuisine. In order to automatically check on the meals while they are being cooked in an oven; it comes with a telephoto lens and a cooking monitor. In addition, it can switch grilling methods as required. This cooker can be managed by Alexa; through its understanding of information about the user, it can advise and put together a scheduled bake schedule (Kuzhaloli et al., 2020).
- Using their smartphone or voice assistant, users of the Honeywell HD WiFi doorbell SkyBell can answer the door. The video doorbell camera delivers a live feed and an alarm to the homeowner's phone to let them know who is at the door. The owner can contact the person using SkyBell even from a distance. This has helped to prevent robbers and trespassers (Singh et al., 2020).
- Mobile devices and the Amazon or Google Home can be used to remotely operate Deako's Smart Lights. They have Internet access, and they occasionally receive software upgrades.
- The Vehicle Machine learning from involuntary muscles refers to a cabin-based Identification Generator that can be utilized in fully autonomous and automated financial systems. Using microphones and cameras, it evaluates the passengers' facial and voice expressions to determine their emotional and mental state.

2.2 SURVEY ON INDUSTRIAL ENGINEERING WITH IoT AND AI

To optimize industrial supply chains, organizations can foresee market movements with the use of AI systems. This gives management a huge advantage in terms of responding to competitive challenges. AI algorithms look for position trends, macroeconomic and socioeconomic characteristics, ecological patterns, status policy, consumer behaviour, and more to estimate market wants (Rana, 2018; Rana et al., 2019).

Manufacturers would be able to minimize production downtime and maximize the overall operational efficiency of their manufacturing lines thanks to this development (Kaur et al., 2019). By generating a predictive study of the equipment's attributes and ultimately optimizing production processes, intelligence and computer training also improve quality control and standardization. With the use of AI, businesses can now make quick decisions based on data, streamline their manufacturing procedures, cut operational expenses, and improve customer service (Dal Mas et al., 2021; Gupta et al., 2021).

Industry will be transformed by a Machine Learning IIoT, which will also save money and enhance service quality (Gupta et al., 2011). Organizations may retain storage by keeping a close watch on inventory levels, estimate arrival dates, and produce the maximum amount of goods by projecting bottlenecks. In order to compute an examination of production processes and analyse phenomena such as microscopic breakage within industrial facilities, the implementation of a computerized visual system could be employed. Machine Learning may flag enterprises to manufacturing problems that could contribute to unsatisfactory quality control. The primary obstacles can be evaded in the initial phases of Industry 4.0's broad technological level (Javaid and Haleem, 2019; Sanchez et al., 2020).

Property breakdown estimates are developed using the artificial neural network and extensive evolutionary computation for replacement prognosis (Ribeiro et al., 2021). To avoid problems with consumer satisfaction, automated systems must inform industrial workers of evolving output problems. This can check for minute differences in the performance of the device, differences in the materials, etc. (Riley et al., 2021).

The minimal and highest limits are commonly defined by the graphic artist to guarantee that what an optimum technique gives results on the inside of the desired range (Babu et al., 2021). The options that have been described can be further evaluated using ML to determine which building style conforms with criteria. AI algorithms are used in quality assurance to alert factories to possible manufacturing problems that could degrade that finished product's level of quality (Koh et al., 2019; Bousdekis et al., 2020).

2.3 CHALLENGES OF INDUSTRIAL ENGINEERING WITH IoT AND AI

The Industrial Internet of Everything is bringing significant advantages to businesses. They are witnessing advances in a variety of areas, including intelligence, discretion, production, investment management, and others. However, there are some big disadvantages to all of those gains, just as with most things. Then again, one wants to make a mechanism more complicated (Bhambri et al., 2022).

The structures that govern nuclear power plants, water meters, safety precautions, and production plants that have the capacity to generate tens of billions of dollars in less than one hour offer just a few examples of the responsive or important structures that these computers frequently track and connect with (Karaca and Cetin, 2021).

The employment of motorized manufacturing facilities driven by water and electricity at the end of the 19th century marked the beginning of the initial agricultural revolution (Dhanalakshmi et al., 2022). When the application of electricity and the division of labour made mass manufacture viable at the start of the 20th century, the second industrial transformation got under way. Later, in the 1970s we saw the start of the machine age, which is still going strong today. And through embedded device of information and technology, this is differentiated by both a better automated level of production and other task processes.

In the fourth technological revolution, new manufacturing methods are being invented by means of humanoid systems (such as those outlined above), thinking devices, and interacting objects. The phrase "Technology 4.0" refers to the logistic place's rising technology, which enables connections between computers, commodities, and individuals utilizing real-time file transfer.

These connections would enable artificially IoT technologies, commodities, and services to change in line with shifting climatic conditions (Kaur et al., 2020). The definition of Industry 4.0's five core components is as follows: (1) digitizing, streamlining, and customization of manufacture; (2) robotics and adaptability; (3) interpersonal contact; (4) significance activities as well as outlets; but instead (5) faster information interchange but also networking. The following problems:

- Personnel as well as working conditions
- Inadequate capital capabilities

- Issues with homogeneity
- Safety worries as well as difficulties with information privacy
- Inferiority danger
- The incorporation of technology
- Communication challenges between business structures
- Insufficient management abilities as well as exercises
- Administrative opposition

The following are among the challenges faced:

- **High Investment Returns**: One of the industrial IoT's most glaring issues is the high costs of adoption. Yes, one of the main promises of IoT is that costs might be brought down through better capital management, access to corporate intelligence, and productivity gains. However, businesses find it difficult to justify the cost when a) they are unsure of the precise ROI to expect and b) they have no significant experience implementing connected systems. According to 29% of the businesses who participated in Microsoft's 2019 IoT Signals research, a lack of resources is one of the biggest obstacles to the adoption of IoT (Figure 2.2).
- **Secure File Management & Storage**: Large quantities of information are produced by the Internet of Things. A vast quantity of information must to be promptly evaluated in order to reveal immediate trends. Regarding the degree of protection required by IIoT platforms, organizations must devise a plan for accelerating tracking, administration, and preservation to enabling speedy reactions to external attackers (Rani and Gupta, 2016).

  Because of this, companies must get ready with both a protracted alternative (the virtualized or corporate centre is located) for processing and also secure choices for summary archiving. To generate increased efficiency as well as prevent unavailability, legitimate analytics also were required. For illustrate, a business might use sensors to assess the operation of crucial gear. In this case, the system ought to be able to detect the deterioration as it happens, enabling users to address issues before production is halted, costing the business money and missed effort.

  It's also critical to bear in mind that integrating every one of these electronic features, algorithms, and monitors could result in the introduction of brand-new data types that a business isn't yet capable of processing. A factory might employ a business intelligence software that employs a Relational Database Management System (RDBMS) to streamline the supply chain, agricultural products, shelf space, sales prices, and pending contracts. The issue is that non-relational databases are used to manage heterogeneous data that IoT devices may produce. Additionally, in order for businesses to benefit fully from a connected system, ERP data, customer information, and IoT insights must be combined into a single, connected picture. Even if an organization is able to integrate all of the necessary sensors, software, and equipment, its ROI can only be realized if the company has the appropriate resources and knowledge in place. This is another significant IIoT difficulty (Dal Mas et al., 2021).

- **Connection problems**: The problem is that the parameter that sensor nodes may output is managed by semi-servers. Secondly, a comprehensive, interconnected portrait made up of information systems data, client data, and IoT observations is required for corporations to reap benefits out of a centralized model (Dhanoa and Bhambri, 2020). Although a corporate is capable of incorporating all of the hardware, algorithms, and sensors, its return will not be fulfilled until the business has the requisite resources and abilities in place. This is yet another important IIoT challenge. For contrast, cellphone communication could be a good option if business device necessitates a significant amount of throughput; however, if you intend to monitoring facilities for a lengthy moment, a moderate pro-tracted alternative might have been our right approach (Arya et al., 2022). A range of dangers in addition to the discomfort of a momentary wireless blackout are brought about by interruptions in the Industrial Internet of Things Whenever it relates to being able to detect threats like dangerous gases, a device failure would essentially be the crucial distinction between life and death. Mistakes of the electric city can cut off the electricity to an entire town. (Gordon and Moore, 2022).
- **Ability Gap**: Owners of industrial IOT projects are aware that the skills gap and how to close it are two of the most difficult problems with industrial IoT (Bhambri and Gupta, 2017). Currently, the industrial landscape is changing quickly, and businesses have expressed concern over a shortage of technical staffing (Kaur and Bhambri, 2015). Numerous sectors of the business are being impacted by the lack of qualified personnel. According to some 29% of businesses in Microsoft's 2019 IoT Signals research, a lack of resources is one of the biggest obstacles to IoT adoption. In addition to the urgent need to modernize and change business operations, finding competent employees to create, deploy, and operate contemporary industrial networks presents a substantial hurdle for many businesses.
- **Analysis of Data**: Adding tools for data gathering, processing, and visual-ization to manufacturing facilities is a typical approach for integrating IoT solutions in industrial settings. These comprise sensors, Network of Things (IoT) interfaces, user interfaces for machines, plus virtualized analysis tools that transform raw device data into useful insights (Bhambri and Gupta, 2016). Making sense of the massive amount of data created every minute by the rapidly growing number of devices, integrated devices, and devices, as well as the developing both vertical and horizontal networking of value chains, depends in large part on data analysis (Rani et al., 2022a).

Many businesses are not efficiently or sufficiently utilizing this crucial data. IoT solutions have not just taken over our homes in recent years; in-dustry is now making increased use of them. IoT implementation is evolv-ing from consumer-focused applications to mission-critical ones in the in-dustrial sector and playing a crucial part in the so-called Industry 4.0, the subsequent stage of factory automation (Tondon and Bhambri, 2017). The industrial Internet of Things (IIOT) enables factories to fully digitize their manufacturing processes by fusing the digital and physical worlds together.

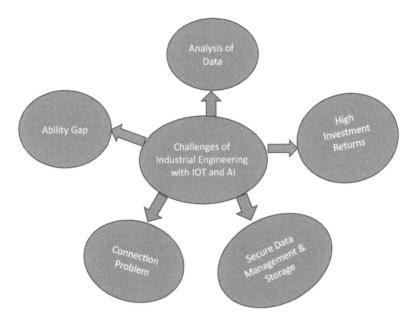

FIGURE 2.2   Challenges of industrial engineering with IOT and AI.

Predictive maintenance, intelligent measuring technologies, asset management, and fleet management are some of the most typical IIOT scenarios (Bhambri and Gupta, 2018).

During the present COVID-19 global financial crisis, an increasing number of industrial organizations are embracing the IIOT to monitoring their systems and prevent unplanned downtime. 85% of firms are working on IoT projects, according to a Microsoft survey, and a recent prediction by Million Insights predicts that, by 2025, global investment in the revolution (Industry 4.0) will reach a startling $992 billion. Despite the fact that IIOT is transforming manufacturing in the future, it does present some important challenges as organizations accelerate their digital transformation. Above are the top 5 issues that organizations must solve throughout the IIOT deployment phase.

2.4   OPPORTUNITIES OF INDUSTRIAL ENGINEERING WITH IoT AND AI

AI enhances IoT through intelligent decision-making, and IoT enables AI capabilities through data exchange. In the end, when combined these two approaches will usher in a brand-new century of interactions and solutions that transform businesses across numerous industries and provide wholly new opportunities (Bhambri and Gupta, 2012). In order to understand how to increase such efficiencies in terms of production output, it is being utilized to examine sensor and Internet of Things (IoT) technologies that are peering into the industrial manufacturing process (Haleem et al., 2021).

The intelligent manufacturing system is quickly integrating into a global production system and offers substantial market opportunities, according to numerous research findings and assessments from different organizations. Intelligent manufacturing is more likely to be used in small and medium-sized firms (Rani et al. 2022b).

According to a McKinsey & Company report that Manyika presented, there is a potential for 60% automation in the production, transportation, and warehouse sectors (Sharma and Bhambri, 2020). 73% of the hospitality and food services are also likely to be automated. Since they offer the biggest potential for automation, these industries are currently the focus of study for applying the most recent technology to improve productivity and performance (Hansen and Bøgh, 2021).

In accordance with the 2017 WBR Report, participants in the study were prepared and eager to revamp with the smart factories mechanism relatively soon. Of these, 38% had intentions to install new technology, 45% had upgrading their current equipment with both the astute supply chain, and 17% had strategies to integrate the two processes. In order to illustrate the impact and usefulness of smart manufacturing/industry application technologies in a production line, we looked into the differences seen between existing production systems as well as the forthcoming production facility (Hofmann et al., 2019). The complexity of the system, machine interactions and relationships, the roles that each subsystem plays, and also the operating practices and interdependencies of those systems, all have an impact on how industrial automation systems are designed (Devadutta et al., 2020). Data and information may now be shared throughout interconnected systems thanks to automation technology, and machine communication has advanced rapidly. This makes handling exceptions and managing adaptable resources and processes easier (Javaid and Haleem, 2019).

The application of sophisticated and automated technologies has enabled the development of this next-generation production plant, also called intelligent industrial activity or smart factories, that use both command line information and information obtained through virtualization to speed up the production of personal and unique data (Vijayalakshmi et al., 2021). To meet the current market demand, a reliable and automated system is needed. This technology has also shortened lead times for product delivery, enhanced design variation, and decreased production costs (Karaca and Cetin, 2021).

The need to educate employees to accommodate changing conditions is one of the biggest obstacles to the introduction of Manufacturing 4.0. In future, alternative techniques of functioning will be necessary, and these methods could both benefit and harm individuals. Problems in corporate settings may result from the altered treatment of workers (Bhambri and Gupta, 2013). Multiple reports have revealed that a lack of funding is one key impediment to the development, and it was discovered that low levels of standards, a lack of knowledge of connection, and worries regarding information protection could potentially prevent the acceptance of Manufacturing 4.0. It was noticed that standardization issues could affect both intra-organizational interactions and the systems and methods used by firms (Sinha et al., 2020).

There are many opportunities for industrial engineering with regard to IOT and AI. IoT and cutting-edge analytics technology can be used by manufacturers for a wide range of opportunities (Figure 2.3).

According to a McKinsey Global Institute analysis, IoT applications in factory settings might generate up to $3.7 trillion in value annually by 2025. Present-day

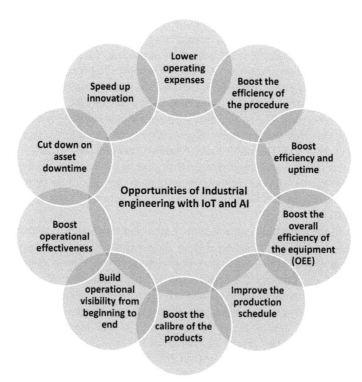

FIGURE 2.3   Opportunities of industrial engineering with IOT and AI.

manufacturers are looking for innovative solutions to better serve the demands of the market, enhance products, streamline processes, boost profits, and lower costs and risk (Jain et al., 2021b). Companies that want to save costs, create new efficiencies, and discover new business prospects with IIoT must implement automation, digitalization, and IIoT. The path to success has become more difficult as a result of the market's shifting dynamics and constantly changing environment (Koh et al., 2019).

With success strongly correlated to the entire availability and reliability of capital assets, product quality, worker performance efficiency, safety, and satisfaction, as well as customer satisfaction, organizations try to achieve aggressive production deadlines and consumer expectations. Operations can succeed or fail based on equipment and worker performance (Rana et al., 2021a; Rana et al., 2021b). Equipment failures that occur unexpectedly might result in missed deadlines and millions of dollars in lost opportunities. Equipment performance declines and staff incompetence or mistakes can reduce profits and cause needless expenses (Oswal et al., 2021).

The Industrial Internet of Things (IIoT) market landscape is described in this white paper, along with the main problems that analytics can solve (Bhambri and Gupta, 2014). It presents streaming analytics for IIoT, lists customer issues that lend themselves to streaming analytics, and offers examples from the industry to help these ideas come to life. It is meant to serve as a guide on how analytics might assist realize the potential of IIoT (Pereira et al., 2020).

A strong ecosystem can offer IIoT solutions that cooperate to address manufacturers' problems. Siemens and SAS have teamed up to provide IIoT and analytics capabilities in Siemens MindSphere because they appreciate the complexity of these situations. The most extensive range of chances for optimizing corporate value can be found by utilizing streaming analytics on the edge and in the *cloud* (Peres et al., 2020).

Our modern world has been greatly moulded and altered by the upbeat outlook of successful entrepreneurs. The extraordinary vision, steadfast beliefs, and unthinkable risks taken by previous entrepreneurs have directly contributed to the world as it is today (Rani et al., 2021). Thomas Edison, Andrew Carnegie, Henry Ford, Bill Gates, Steve Jobs, Jeff Bezos, Larry Page, Sergey Brin, and so forth are among a few of the notable figures mentioned. All of them were initially thought to be dreamers, and their theories were seen as ridiculous, implausible, or, at the very least, impracticable (Bali et al., 2023).

And yet, all the incredible conveniences, eases, and reliefs of this particular millennium are unquestionably attributable to their extraordinary accomplishments, which lends implausible credence to remarkable entrepreneurial traits such as vision, risk-taking, and the capacity for opportunity spotting (Kumar et al., 2022). Sara Blakely, a multibillionaire businesswoman and the creator of Spanx, famously said: "Embrace what you don't know, especially at first, since what you don't know might end up being your greatest asset. It guarantees that you will unquestionably act differently from everyone else" (Paika and Bhambri, 2013).

A few years ago, the Industrial Internet of Things (IIoT) seemed just as far-fetched and remote as the internet, search engines, the World Wide Web and smartphones had previously seemed (Singh et al., 2021a). Isn't the time when we were all satisfied with our Nokia 3310s still recent in our memory, and doesn't it seem like only yesterday? But what is now popular? If we compare today's technological operating level to that of just two decades ago, when the Nokia 3310 first appeared, is it not far more advanced? The IIoT is a clear, diverse, and potentially promising area of entrepreneurial influence and investigation (Radanliev et al., 2021a).

2.5 FUTURE OF INDUSTRIAL ENGINEERING WITH IoT AND AI

The industry's future lies in the fusion of artificial intelligence with the Internet of Things; this is something that tech giants such as Google, Amazon, Tesla, and Uber are actively researching and developing (Kshirsagar et al., 2022). Table 2.1 details common features of industrial engineering with IOT and AI.

The IoT and AI applications are about to experience yet another major uptick in the manufacturing sector, with a projected IoT market size of $2.4 trillion annually by 2027, according to Business Insider. AI will offer useful data that helps business executives create unique and reliable business models. When it comes to seeing patterns and occurrences that a normal person cannot notice clearly, this technique will prove to be quite helpful (Jabeen et al., 2021). AI will generate the data needed to support fact-based, data-driven business decisions. It will in many ways give a more thorough assessment and assist in removing personal prejudices from the calculation (Rani et al., 2022c). In order to uncover growth, extension, and even emerging market prospects, ML and AI technologies can acquire data from a variety of sources.

TABLE 2.1
Features of Industrial Engineering with IoT and AI

Serial No.	Points of Features	Description
1	Effectiveness - and outcome – leaning	• Manufacturing and Industrial internet of things are both geared at streamlining production procedures and preserving the profit and viability of industry.
2	Knowledge -determined	• Without the current creation of high, mobile, combined Internet connectivity, Automation and Industrial internet of things could not be practicable.
3	Citizens -determined	• Automation and Industrial internet of things use of technology only will improve and incorporate new operations. It cannot establish new procedures or take control on its own. The success of this innovation depends on people who can understand, use, and integrate the material and activities it supplies.

As a result, new services and goods will be created (Radanliev et al., 2021b; Sharma et al., 2020a; Sharma et al., 2020b). AI systems may streamline industrial processes, issue early alerts, help with QA and quality control, and forecast equipment failure in machinery in addition to apparent applications like automation and robotics. The secret is acquiring the right data, and, by doing so, manufacturers can create cutting-edge AI applications and set themselves apart from their rivals (Singh et al., 2021b). In the case of their IIoT applications, several firms use a variety of AI algorithms to make choices in real time (Chauhan and Rani, 2021). It's critical to comprehend that data reigns supreme in applications based on Artificial Intelligence. The most crucial step in using AI to optimize an organization and derive insights is gathering, cleaning, and preparing unique data (Soni et al., 2022).

AI engineers frequently spend up to 75% of their time digesting the first data before they can start training their Machine Learning models. Keep in mind that you'll need a data set or set of data sets that reflect the actual conditions and situations you will be working with when the application is live in order to train a Machine Learning model using IIoT devices. The process of constructing a data set involves several steps (Bose et al., 2021). It begins with data that has frequently been gathered over a number of years, and engineers must decide on an overall structure for the data. Any defects, contradictions, or gaps in the data will need to be eliminated before they can transform it into the format the algorithm needs in order to interact with it in a beneficial way (Sanchez et al., 2020; Wang et al., 2019).

2.6 CONCLUSION

The term Artificial Intelligence of Things ("AIoT") refers to the combination of intelligent machines and the internet of devices, moving intelligence from the boundary to the cloud in industrial settings and converting information into useful data for great decisions while preparation is undertaken for activity to be carried out where it is most necessary. The fundamentals of IIoT are the capability to regularly collect massive volumes of data and enable these interconnected datasets mobile and accessible throughout the organization for strategic decision-making. The commercialization of artificial intelligence and machine learning in the industrial domain is achieved via the Internet of Things, which integrates machine learning, IT, applications at scale, and OT domain expertise.

With the use of AI, Industry 4.0 fully automates the management of the various manufacturing process phases. Any step of the production process will be improved in real time in accordance with the product specifications. The entire development process can be integrated, and multiple divisions can share the workload of data processing. AI can be used to integrate data feedback and gathering systems into manufacturing processes. With the help of this technology, manufacturing technology and assembly lines may collaborate more effectively.

To predict repairs and predict asset failure, sophisticated AI systems are deployed. AI and Industry 4.0 integration leads to a number of industrial breakthroughs. AI is better able to control the associated output processes. This technology can produce insightful viewpoints that foster manufacturing creativity. With the use of data-collecting tools like sensors and cameras, every mechanical physical of the production server may be seen in its entirety. Using a cloud link, the data produced by intelligent components is captured, preserved, and processed. This will eventually gather cloud data and ensure that Industry 4.0 runs smoothly.

REFERENCES

Adhikari, M., & Munusamy, A. (2021). ICovidCare: Intelligent health monitoring framework for COVID-19 using ensemble random forest in edge networks. *Internet of Things*, 14, 100385. https://doi.org/10.1016/j.iot.2021.100385

Anand, A., & Bhambri, P. (2018). Character recognition system using radial features. *International Journal on Future Revolution in Computer Science & Communication Engineering*, 4(4), 599–602.

Arya, V., Rani, S., & Choudhary, N. (2022). Enhanced bio-inspired trust and reputation model for wireless sensor networks. In *Proceedings of Second Doctoral Symposium on Computational Intelligence: DoSCI 2021* (pp. 569–579). Springer Singapore.

Babu, G. C. N., Gupta, S., Bhambri, P., Leo, L. M., Rao, B. H., & Kumar, S. (2021). A semantic health observation system development based on the IoT sensors. *Turkish Journal of Physiotherapy and Rehabilitation*, 32(3), 1721–1729.

Bakshi, P., & Bhambri, P. (2021, March). A Review Paper on Wireless Sensor Network Techniques in Internet of Things (IOT). *Wesleyan Journal of Research*, 14(07), 147–160, ISSN: 0975-1386.

Bali, V., Bali, S., Gaur, D., Rani, S., & Kumar, R. (2023). Commercial-off-the shelf vendor selection: A multi-criteria decision-making approach using intuitionistic fuzzy sets and TOPSIS. *Operational Research in Engineering Sciences: Theory and Applications*, 12(4), 100–113.

Bhambri, P., Aggarwal, M., Singh, H., Singh, A. P., & Rani, S. (2022). Uprising of EVs: Charging the future with demystified analytics and sustainable development. In *Decision Analytics for Sustainable Development in Smart Society 5.0: Issues, Challenges and Opportunities* (pp. 37–53). Singapore: Springer Nature Singapore.

Bhambri, P., Dhanoa, I. S., Sinha, V. K., & Kaur, J. (2020). Paddy crop production analysis based on SVM and KNN classifier. *International Journal of Recent Technology and Engineering*, 8(5), 2791–2793.

Bhambri, P., & Gupta, O. P. (2012). A novel method for the design of phylogenetic tree. *Int J IT Eng Appl Sci Res*, 1(1), 24–28.

Bhambri, P., & Gupta, O. P. (2013). Design of distributed prefetching protocol in push-to-peer video-on-demand system. *Int J Res Advent Technol*, 1(3), 95–103.

Bhambri, P., & Gupta, O. P. (2014). Dynamic frequency allocation scheme of mobile networks using priority assignment technique. *Int J Eng Technol Innov*, 1(1), 9–12.

Bhambri, P., & Gupta, O. P. (2016). Phylogenetic tree construction with optimum multiple sequence alignment. *Biological Forum-An International Journal*, 8(2), 330–339.

Bhambri, P., & Gupta, O. P. (2017). Applying distributed processing for different distance based methods during phylogenetic tree construction. *Asian Journal of Computer Science and Information Technology*, 7(3), 57–67.

Bhambri, P., & Gupta, O. P. (2018). *Implementing Machine Learning Algorithms for Distance based Phylogenetic Trees*. I.K. Gujral Punjab Technical University, Jalandhar.

Bhambri, P., Singh, M., Jain, A., Dhanoa, I. S., Sinha, V. K., & Lal, S. (2021). Classification of gene expression data with the aid of optimized feature selection. *Turkish Journal of Physiotherapy and Rehabilitation*, 32, 3.

Bhambri, P., Singh, S., Sangwan, S., Devi, J., & Jain, S. (2023). Plants recognition using leaf image pattern analysis. *Journal of Survey in Fisheries Sciences*, 10(2S), 3863–3871.

Bhambri, P., Sinha, V. K., & Jaiswal, M. (2019). Change in iris dimensions as a potential human consciousness level indicator. *International Journal of Innovative Technology and Exploring Engineering*, 8(9S), 517–525.

Bose, M. M., Yadav, D., Bhambri, P., & Shankar, R. (2021). Electronic customer relationship management: Benefits and pre-implementation considerations. *Journal of Maharaja Sayajirao University of Baroda*, 55(01(VI)), 1343–1350.

Bousdekis, A., Apostolou, D., & Mentzas, G. (2020). A human cyber physical system framework for operator 4.0 – Artificial intelligence symbiosis. *Manufacturing Letters*, 25, 10–15. https://doi.org/10.1016/j.mfglet.2020.06.001

Chauhan, M., & Rani, S. (2021). COVID-19: A revolution in the field of education in India. *Learning How to Learn Using Multimedia*, 1, 23–42.

Cioffi, R., Travaglioni, M., Piscitelli, G., Petrillo, A., & De Felice, F. (2020). Artificial intelligence and machine learning applications in smart production: Progress, trends, and directions. *Sustainability*, 12(2), 492. https://doi.org/10.3390/su12020492

Dal Mas, F., Bagnoli, C., Massaro, M., & Biazzo, S. (2021). Smart technologies and new business models: Insights from artificial intelligence and blockchain. *SIDREA Series in Accounting and Business Administration*, 271–285. https://doi.org/10.1007/978-3-030-80737-5_21

Devadutta, K., Bhambri, P., Gountia, D., Mehta, V., Mangla, M., Patan, R., Kumar, A., Agarwal, P. K., Sharma, A., Singh, M., & Gadicha, A.B. (2020). Method for Cyber Security in Email Communication among Networked Computing Devices [Patent application number 202031002649]. India.

Dhanalakshmi, R., Anand, J., Sivaraman, A. K., & Rani, S. (2022). IoT-based water quality monitoring system using cloud for agriculture use. In *Cloud and fog computing platforms for internet of things* (pp. 183–196). Chapman and Hall/CRC.

Dhanoa, I.S., & Bhambri, P. (2020). Traffic-aware energy efficient VM migrations. *Journal of Critical Reviews*, 7(19), 177–183.

Gordon, N., & Moore, K. W. (2022). The effects of artificial intelligence (AI) enabled personality assessments during team formation on team cohesion. *Information Systems and Neuroscience*, 311–318. https://doi.org/10.1007/978-3-031-13064-9_31

Gupta, B. B., Tewari, A., Cvitić, I., Peraković, D., & Chang, X. (2021). Artificial intelligence empowered emails classifier for Internet of things based systems in industry 4.0. *Wireless Networks*, 28(1), 493–503. https://doi.org/10.1007/s11276-021-02619-w

Gupta, O., Rani, S., & Pant, D. C. (2011). Impact of parallel computing on bioinformatics algorithms. In *Proceedings 5th IEEE International Conference on Advanced Computing and Communication Technologies* (pp. 206–209).

Haleem, A., Javaid, M., Singh, R. P., & Suman, R. (2021). Applications of artificial intelligence (AI) for cardiology during COVID-19 pandemic. *Sustainable Operations and Computers*, 2, 71–78. https://doi.org/10.1016/j.susoc.2021.04.003

Hansen, E. B., & Bøgh, S. (2021). Artificial intelligence and Internet of things in small and medium-sized enterprises: A survey. *Journal of Manufacturing Systems*, 58, 362–372. https://doi.org/10.1016/j.jmsy.2020.08.009

Hofmann, E., Sternberg, H., Chen, H., Pflaum, A., & Prockl, G. (2019). Supply chain management and industry 4.0: Conducting research in the digital age. *International Journal of Physical Distribution & Logistics Management*, 49(10), 945–955. https://doi.org/10.1108/ijpdlm-11-2019-399

Jabeen, A., Pallathadka, H., Pallathadka, L. K., & Bhambri, P. (2021). E-CRM successful factors for business enterprises case studies. *Journal of Maharaja Sayajirao University of Baroda*, 55(01(VI)), 1332–1342.

Jain, A., Singh, M., & Bhambri, P. (2021a). Performance evaluation of IPv4-IPv6 tunneling procedure using IoT. *Journal of Physics: Conference Series*, 1950(1), 012010. https://doi.org/10.1088/1742-6596/1950/1/012010

Jain, A., Singh, M., & Bhambri, P. (2021b, August). Performance Evaluation of IPv4-IPv6 Tunneling Procedure Using IoT. In *Journal of Physics: Conference Series* (Vol. 1950, No. 1, p. 012010). IOP Publishing.

Javaid, M., & Haleem, A. (2019). Industry 4.0 applications in medical field: A brief review. *Current Medicine Research and Practice*, 9(3), 102–109. https://doi.org/10.1016/j.cmrp.2019.04.001

Karaca, K. N., & Cetin, A. (2021). Botnet attack detection using convolutional neural networks in the IoT environment. *2021 International Conference on Innovations in Intelligent Systems and Applications (INISTA)*. https://doi.org/10.1109/inista52262.2021.9548445

Kaur, H., & Bhambri, P. (2016). A prediction technique in data mining for the diabetes mellitus. *Apeejay Journal of Management Sciences and Technology*, 4(1), 1–12.

Kaur, J., & Bhambri, P. (2019). Various DNA sequencing techniques and related applications. *International Journal of Analytical and Experimental Model Analysis*, 11(9), 3104–3111.

Kaur, J., & Bhambri, P. (2020). *Hybrid Classification Model for the Reverse Code Generation in Software Engineering*. Jalandhar: I.K. Gujral Punjab Technical University.

Kaur, J., Bhambri, P., & Sharma, K. (2019). Wheat production analysis based on NaÃve Bayes classifier. *International Journal of Analytical and Experimental Model Analysis*, 11(9), 705–709.

Kaur, K., Dhanoa, I. S., & Bhambri, P. (2020, December). Optimized PSO-EFA Algorithm for Energy Efficient Virtual Machine Migrations. In *2020 5th IEEE International Conference on Recent Advances and Innovations in Engineering (ICRAIE)* (pp. 1–5). IEEE.

Kaur, R., & Bhambri, P. (2015). Information retrieval system for hospital management. *International Journal of Multidisciplinary Consortium*, 2(4), 16–21.

Koh, L., Orzes, G., & Jia, F. (2019). The fourth industrial revolution (Industry 4.0): Technologies disruption on operations and supply chain management. *International Journal of Operations & Production Management*, 39(6/7/8), 817–828. https://doi.org/10.1108/ijopm-08-2019-788

Kothandaraman, D., Manickam, M., Balasundaram, A., Pradeep, D., Arulmurugan, A., Sivaraman, A. K., … & Balakrishna, R. (2022). Decentralized link failure prevention routing (DLFPR) algorithm for efficient internet of things. *Intelligent Automation & Soft Computing*, 34(1), 1–23.

Kshirsagar, P. R., Jagannadham, D. B. V., Ananth, M. B., Mohan, A., Kumar, G., & Bhambri, P. (2022, May). Machine learning algorithm for leaf disease detection. In *AIP Conference Proceedings* (Vol. 2393, No. 1, p. 020087). AIP Publishing LLC.

Kumar, P., Banerjee, K., Singhal, N., Kumar, A., Rani, S., Kumar, R., & Lavinia, C. A. (2022). Verifiable, secure mobile agent migration in healthcare systems using a poly-nomial-based threshold secret sharing scheme with a blowfish algorithm. *Sensors*, 22(22), 8620.

Kuzhaloli, S., Devaneyan, P., Sitaraman, N., Periyathanbi, P., Gurusamy, M., & Bhambri, P. (2020). IoT based Smart Kitchen Application for Gas Leakage Monitoring [Patent appli-cation number 202041049866A]. India.

Oswal, N., Ateeq, K., & Mathew, S. (2021). Trends in recruitment information and com-munication system using artificial intelligence in industry 4.0. *Proceedings of the 3rd International Conference on Finance, Economics, Management and IT Business*. https://doi.org/10.5220/0010503201110118

Paika, E. V., & Bhambri, E. P. (2013). Edge detection-fuzzy inference system. *International journal of management & Information Technology*, 4(1), 148–155.

Panda, S. K., Reddy, G. S. M., Goyal, S. B., Thirunavukkarasu, K., Bhambri, P., Rao, M. V., Singh, A. S., Fakih, A. H., Shukla, P. K., Shukla, P. K., Gadicha, A. B., & Shelke, C. J. (2019). Method for Management of Scholarship of Large Number of Students based on Blockchain (Patent No. IN201911034937A).

Pereira, A. G., Lima, T. M., & Charrua-Santos, F. (2020). Industry 4.0 and society 5.0: Opportunities and threats. *International Journal of Recent Technology and Engineering (IJRTE)*, 8(5), 3305–3308. https://doi.org/10.35940/ijrte.d8764.018520

Peres, R. S., Jia, X., Lee, J., Sun, K., Colombo, A. W., & Barata, J. (2020). Industrial artificial intelligence in industry 4.0 – Systematic review, challenges and outlook. *IEEE Access*, 8, 220121–220139. https://doi.org/10.1109/access.2020.3042874

Potluri, S., Tiwari, P. K., Bhambri, P., Obulesu, O., Naidu, P. A., Lakshmi, L., Kallam, S., Gupta, S., & Gupta, B. (2019). Method of Load Distribution Balancing for Fog Cloud Computing in IoT Environment [Patent number IN201941044511].

Rachna, R., Bhambri, P., & Chhabra, Y. (2022). Deployment of distributed clustering approach in WSNs and IoTs. *Cloud and Fog Computing Platforms for Internet of Things*, 85–98. https://doi.org/10.1201/9781003213888-7

Rachna, R., Chhabra, Y., & Bhambri, P. (2020). Comparison of Clustering Approaches for Enhancing Sustainability Performance in WSNSL a Study. *TEQIP-III Sponsored International Conference on Sustainable Development Through Engineering Innovations* (pp. 62–71), ISBN: 978-93-89947-14-4.

Rachna, R., Chhabra, Y., & Bhambri, P. (2021). Various approaches and algorithms for moni-toring energy efficiency of wireless sensor networks. *Lecture Notes in Civil Engineering*, 761–770. https://doi.org/10.1007/978-981-15-9554-7_68

Radanliev, P., De Roure, D., Nicolescu, R., Huth, M., & Santos, O. (2021a). Artificial intel-ligence and the Internet of things in industry 4.0. *CCF Transactions on Pervasive Computing and Interaction*, 3(3), 329–338. https://doi.org/10.1007/s42486-021-00057-3

Radanliev, P., De Roure, D., Nicolescu, R., Huth, M., & Santos, O. (2021b). Digital twins: Artificial intelligence and the IoT cyber-physical systems in industry 4.0. *International Journal of Intelligent Robotics and Applications*, 6(1), 171–185. https://doi.org/10.1007/s41315-021-00180-5

Rana, R. (2018, March). A review on evolution of wireless sensor network. *International Journal of Advanced Research Trends in Engineering and Technology (IJARTET)*, 5. Available at www.ijartet.com

Rana, R., Chhabra, Y., & Bhambri, P. (2019). A Review on Development and Challenges in Wireless Sensor Network. *International Multidisciplinary Academic Research Conference (IMARC, 2019)*, (pp. 184–188), ISBN: 978-81-942282-0-2.

Rana, R., Chhabra, Y., & Bhambri, P. (2021a). Comparison and evaluation of various QoS parameters in WSNs with the implementation of enhanced low energy adaptive efficient distributed clustering approach, *Webology*, 18(1), (ISSN: 1735-188X).

Rana, R., Chhabra, Y., & Bhambri, P. (2021b). Design and development of distributed cluster-ing approach in wireless sensor network. *Webology*, 18(1), (ISSN: 1735-188X).

Rani, S., Arya, V., & Kataria, A. (2022c). Dynamic pricing-based E-commerce model for the produce of organic farming in India: A research roadmap with main advertence to vegetables. In *Proceedings of Data Analytics and Management: ICDAM 2021, Volume 2* (pp. 327–336). Springer Singapore.

Rani, S., Bhambri, P., & Gupta, O. P. (2022b). Green smart farming techniques and sustainable agriculture: Research roadmap towards organic farming for imperishable agricultural products. In *Handbook of Sustainable Development through Green Engineering and Technology* (pp. 49–67). CRC Press.

Rani, S., & Gupta, O. P. (2016). Empirical analysis and performance evaluation of various GPU implementations of protein BLAST. *International Journal of Computer Applications*, *151*(7), 22–27.

Rani, S., Kataria, A., & Chauhan, M. (2022a). Cyber security techniques, architectures, and design. In *Holistic approach to quantum cryptography in cyber security* (pp. 41–66). CRC Press.

Rani, S., Mishra, K. R., Usman, M., Kataria, A., Kumar, P., Bhambri, P., & Mishra, K. A. (2021). Amalgamation of advanced technologies for sustainable development of smart city environment: A review. *IEEE Access*, 9, 150060–150087.

Ribeiro, J., Lima, R., Eckhardt, T., & Paiva, S. (2021). Robotic process automation and artificial intelligence in industry 4.0 – A literature review. *Procedia Computer Science*, 181, 51–58. https://doi.org/10.1016/j.procs.2021.01.104

Riley, C, J Vrbka & Z Rowland (2021). Internet of things-enabled sustainability, big data-driven decision-making processes, and digitized mass production in industry 4.0-based manufacturing systems. *Journal of Self-Governance and Management Economics*, 6(1), 42. https://doi.org/10.22381/jsme9120214

Ritu, P., & Bhambri, P. (2023, February 17). Software effort estimation with machine learning – A systematic literature review. In *Agile Software Development: Trends, Challenges and Applications* (pp. 291–308). John Wiley & Sons, Inc.

Sanchez, M., Exposito, E., & Aguilar, J. (2020). Autonomic computing in manufacturing process coordination in industry 4.0 context. *Journal of Industrial Information Integration*, 19, 100159. https://doi.org/10.1016/j.jii.2020.100159

Sangwan, Y. S., Lal, S., Bhambri, P., Kumar, A., & Dhanoa, I. S. (2021). Advancements in social data security and encryption: A review. *NVEO-Natural Volatiles & Essential Oils Journal|NVEO*, 8(4), 15353–15362.

Sharma, R., & Bhambri, P. (2020). *Energy Aware Bio Inspired Routing Technique for Mobile Adhoc Networks*. Jalandhar: I.K. Gujral Punjab Technical University.

Sharma, R., Bhambri, P., & Sohal, K. A. (2020a, February). Mobile adhoc networks. *JAC: A Journal of Composition Theory*, XIII(2), 982–985, ISSN: 0731-6755.

Sharma, R., Bhambri, P., & Sohal, K. A. (2020b, March). Energy bio-inspired for MANET. *International Journal of Recent Technology and Engineering (IJRTE)*, 8(6), 5581–5585. https://doi.org/10.35940/ijrte.F8522.038620

Singh, A. P., Aggarwal, M., Singh, H., & Bhambri, P. (2021b). Sketching of EV network: A complete roadmap. *Lecture Notes in Civil Engineering*, 431–442. https://doi.org/10.1007/978-981-15-9554-7_37

Singh, G., Singh, M., & Bhambri, P. (2020). Artificial Intelligence Based Flying Car. In *Proceedings of the International Congress on Sustainable Development through Engineering Innovations* (pp. 216–227), ISBN 978-93-89947-14-4.

Singh, M., Bhambri, P., Singh, I., Jain, A., & Kaur, E. K. (2021a). Data mining classifier for predicting diabetics. *Annals of the Romanian Society for Cell Biology*, 25(4), 6702–6712.

Sinha, V. K., Jeet 2D, R., Bhambri, P., & Mahajan, M. (2020). Empowering intrusion detection in iris recognition system: A review. *Journal of Natural Remedies*, 21(2), 131–153.

Soni, K., Kumar, N., Nair, A. S., Chourey, P., Singh, N. J., & Agarwal, R. (2022). Artificial intelligence. *Handbook of Metrology and Applications*, 1–23. https://doi.org/10.1007/978-981-19-1550-5_54-2

Sumathi, N., Thirumagal, J., Jagannathan, S., Bhambri, P., & Ahamed, I. N. (2021). A comprehensive review on bionanotechnology for the 21st century. *Journal of the Maharaja Sayajirao University of Baroda*, 55(1), 114–131.

Tondon, N., & Bhambri, P. (2017). Technique for drug discovery in medical image processing. *International Journal of Advance Research in Science & Engineering*, 6(8), 1712–1718.

Vijayalakshmi, P., Shankar, R., Karthik, S., & Bhambri, P. (2021). Impact of work from home policies on workplace productivity and employee sentiments during the covid-19 pandemic. *Journal of Maharaja Sayajirao University of Baroda*, 55(01(VI)), 1314–1331.

Wang, Z., Shou, M., Wang, S., Dai, R., & Wang, K. (2019). An empirical study on the key factors of intelligent upgrade of small and medium-sized enterprises in China. *Sustainability*, 11(3), 619. https://doi.org/10.3390/su11030619

3 Applications of Artificial Intelligence and Internet of Things IoT in Marketing

H. Lakshmi, M. Dharmananda, and B. S. Harisha

Nitte Meenakshi Institute of Technology, Bangalore, India

3.1 INTRODUCTION

3.1.1 ARTIFICIAL INTELLIGENCE

A technology that attempts to imitate human intelligence is referred to as Artificial Intelligence (AI), which has the potential to recognize voice, picture recognition, machine learning, and semantic search. The industry-wide adoption of AI has helped companies better position their offerings, gather consumer data, and develop new futuristic products (Jain et al., 2021). Marketers are keen to deploy this technology to modify the marketing mix and improve customer satisfaction and to gain a competitive edge in the industry AI can be classified into three types, namely AI applications, the Machine Learning approach, and applied propensity models (Singh et al., 2021a). AI applications are other varieties of AI that perform tasks that often requires human intervention, such as responding to consumer inquiries or creating new content (Adobe Sensei Team, 2019). Propensity models can be produced using Machine Learning approaches, which use algorithms to "learn" from past data sets. When these propensity models are used to forecast specific occurrences, such as ranking leads according to how likely they are to convert, this is known as applied propensity models (Kaur et al., 2020).

From a marketing perspective, each application of AI plays a unique role in the consumer track record, but they can all be significantly useful for marketers (Adobe, 2019). Some techniques have more appeal for customers, while others can help with conversion or re-engaging previous clients (Kaur and Bhambri, 2019). These techniques are grouped into the Reach, Act, Convert, Engage (RACE) framework. (Reach, Act, Convert, Engage)

3.1.2 RACE FRAMEWORK

1. **Reach - Use various marketing strategies to engage customers**

   Search engine optimization, content marketing appeal to website users and they initiate purchase process. At this point, AI and applied propen-

DOI: 10.1201/9781003383505-3

sity models can be utilized to increase the number of visitors, providing them with value content and making their user experience more enjoyable (Agrawal, 2020).

i. **AI-generated content**
    Certain operations require AI content writing tools that may choose components from a data set and organize them into a content which resonate with human writing. For example, Wordsmith is a self-service platform that offers real-time content updates, comprehensive narrative customization, and a robust API for flexible publishing (Dooley, 2020).

    AI writers are highly helpful for reporting on recurring, data-centric occurrences, namely sports events, market statistics, quarterly reports etc. AI-generated content could be beneficial for content marketing plan for vital and dynamic industries, such as financial services. A free beta edition of its AI writing tool is introduced by software like Wordsmith's creator, automated insights, allowing users to test the technology and determine what might benefit their business (Rachna et al., 2022).

ii. **Programmatic Media Buying**
     For media buying, programmatic advertising use automated technologies and algorithmic techniques (Maruti Tech, 2019). The process for buying and selling adverts in the advertising market is referred to as programmatic media buying. Programmatic advertising uses automation and differs more from traditional media buying process. User behavior is analyzed thoroughly to ensure the correct promotional strategies are adopted for target users at the appropriate time (Sangwan et al., 2021).

iii. **Voice-based search**
      According to Statista 2023, by 2027, the market size for Alexa is expected to reach a total value of $34.4 billion, with a record compound annual growth rate (CAGR) of 22.2%. Voice assistant shipments will total 8 billion units by 2023. Research also suggests that 28% of online users use voice-based searches on their smartphones globally. The rise in smartphone usage and the presence of IoT devices have led to an increase in the popularity of voice searches rather than typing.

iv. **Smart Content Curation**
     AI-enabled content creation provides better user engagement by displaying relevant content based on user choice, preference, and browsing history (Sinha et al., 2020). This method can also be used to more broadly personalize website messaging and is most frequently seen in ecommerce sites offering recommendation to the users such as "customers also bought this". This strategy works well for a subscription-based business model because the better content recommendations get the more users to utilize the service and provide more data for the machine learning algorithm to work with (Bhambri and Chhabra, 2022). For example, Amazon's recommendation system helps users to make better-informed choices. Many businesses, such as Amazon, Netflix, and Spotify, have benefited greatly from the deductions and linkages made by AI's data pairing system with the help of its AI-based clus-

tering system. The Over-the-Top (OTT) service provider Sky has also incorporated AI into its system, allowing material to be delivered to customers according to their current preferences.

3.2 ACT – USE TECHNIQUES THAT APPEALS TO USERS AND PROVIDE THEM PRODUCT AWARENESS

i. Propensity modelling
    The "propensity model" describes a variety of statistical models created to forecast outcomes that can either occur or not. It is a statistical method for estimating the probability that an event will occur (Rani et al., 2021). The Machine Learning algorithm is given historical data from previous years, and it makes use of this data to create a propensity model that can generate accurate predictions about the market. The stages of this procedure are shown in Figure 3.1. Propensity modelling is a potent tool, which can be used to enhance marketing efforts, more precisely target customers, improve business decisions, and even forecast client attrition (Bughin et al., 2019).

ii. **Predictive analytics**
    Propensity modelling can be used in a variety of situations, such as determining which users are most likely to convert, at what price they will probably convert for, or if they're likely to buy the same product. Because it employs analytics data to forecast client behaviour, this application is known as predictive analytics (IBM, 2019). The propensity model works best when the data is error-free; otherwise, it may be unable to generate reliable forecasts (Sweeny, 2020).

iii. **Targeting Advertisements**
    A huge volume of historical data can be analysed by the use of Machine Learning algorithms to determine which advertising works best for which audiences and at what points in the purchase cycle. By using this information, they can provide them with the best content at the ideal time (Enterprise Content Team, 2019). More effective ad placement and advertisement content can be produced by marketers by utilizing machine learning to continuously optimize thousands of variables (Vecteezy.com).

iv. **Lead scores**
    Propensity models created by Machine Learning can be customized on specific criteria such as whether it is worth investing time and effort on a lead. It is crucial in business-to-business (B2B) companies with consultative sales procedures where the sales team must dedicate a substantial amount of time on each sale (Zambito, 2014). The sales team can save time and focus their work where it will be most beneficial by reaching out to the most pertinent leads. The knowledge of a lead's propensity to purchase can also be used to focus special offers and discounts in the right places (Rani et al., 2023).

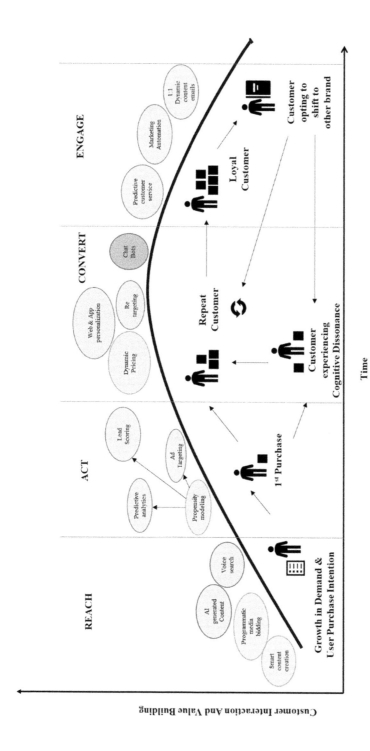

FIGURE 3.1 Fifteen marketing applications of AI across the RACE marketing model. (Source: Fifteen marketing applications of AI across the RACE marketing model Source: Chaffey, D. (2019b). 15 marketing applications of Artificial Intelligence across the RACE marketing model, Dr Dave Chaffey -personal site, Digital Insights, 14 October)

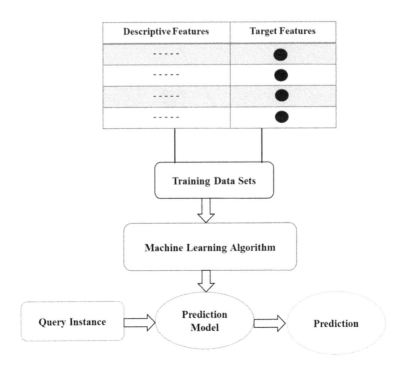

FIGURE 3.2 Steps of propensity modelling. (Source: https://www.smartinsights.com/
managing-digital-marketing/marketing-innovation/15-applications-artificial-intelligence-
marketing/.)

3.3 CONVERT – ENCOURAGE POTENTIAL CUSTOMERS TO CONSUMERS

i. **Dynamic pricing**

Dynamic pricing comprises solutions that are adaptable and expansible for
re-pricing, which involves continuously altering the price of products based
on important variables such as demand and supply, industry and market
trends, competition, customer expectations, site user behaviour etc. (Puri
et al., 2022). It examines how much a product is worth in respect of other
products on the market (Chaffey, 2019a). With this pricing method, companies may respond to shifting market conditions without disclosing any personal information or breaching the privacy of customers (Clifford, 2018).
To give an example: For all of its express trains, Indian Railways has shifted
to dynamic pricing based on demand and season. As a result, the revenue
has increased by an estimated 20%.

Algorithmically, self-improving Machine Learning equations are
used to calculate dynamic prices (Singh et al., 2021b). These algorithms
consider a wide range of pricing optimization factors, including profit
analysis, the forecast of price and market trends, price automation, market analysis, competitor price analysis, personalized pricing for loyal
customers, and the flexibility to adjust and adapt to new scenarios (Deakin
et al., 2019).

ii. **Chatbots**

A chatbot is a software program that is used to simulate conversation with humans. Chatbot systems often require constant tuning and testing in order to accurately mimic how a human would act as a conversation partner. A chatbot answers user questions through instant chats which resolve customer queries. Many types of chatbots are used by companies, including menu-based chatbots-, language-based chatbots, keyword chatbots, voicebots, and Machine Learning chatbots. Presently, the Machine Learning chatbot and the voicebot are widely adopted as it uses technology that adds value to the company and the customer (Levine, 2018).

3.4   MACHINE LEARNING CHATBOTS

These chatbots respond according to a user's previous history, with the aid of Machine Learning and Artificial Intelligence techniques. The user queries and questioning style is analysed and these chatbots use it to improvise themselves. Say, for example, generally in food ordering app, the user preference, frequency of food purchase, is stored based on the previous purchase. Over a period of time, when the user interacts with these chatbots, they recollect their data, such as location, food preference, payment method and assist only in payment confirmation. The user can place an order with a single click or swipe. This simplifies the valuable user experience (Bali et al., 2023).

3.5   VOICEBOTS

Companies have increasingly adapted to voice-based bots because of its seamless assistance. Owing to the convenience the voice-bots, such as Amazon's Alexa or Apple's Siri, conversation is more personal, quick and hassle-free; this is the prime reason for its growing popularity in recent years. A recent study by Statista (2023) states that users find voice search more than typing, as they feel it is more personal (Vicioso, 2019).

iii. **Web & App Personalization**

The propensity model is used for website personalization. It is a process of creating a unique browsing experience for a user every time they visit a website. Companies providing a personalized web experience is possible with the help of cookies, which are unique and exclusive, and cater to the user's specific requirements. Thus, it offers customized tailormade information that appeals to the user rather than general and mass information.

Customized mobile apps can also be developed using a propensity model. This helps to cater to a niche segment of the target audience. A tailormade, unique user experience is offered such as language, information on the app, recently viewed items, payment preferences, offers and promotion schemes are made in mobile apps (Derek, 2018).

iv. **Re-targeting**

Machine Learning helps to identify content that makes users revisit the website. Advertisements are optimized accordingly using predictive analysis and websites alter the content that is most viewed by the users. This also works based on user interest and the choice of preferences.

3.6 ENGAGE – USE TECHNIQUES TO MAKE USERS REVISIT WEBSITE OR APP

i. **Predictive customer service**

Getting repeat sales for existing users is far simpler than gaining new customers. Thus, maintaining the current clientele is essential to the success of a business (Ritu and Bhambri, 2023). This is especially true for businesses that rely on subscriptions, when a high degree of turnovers can be quite expensive. The predictive analysis technique helps to identify those factors that make a customer likely to discontinue the service. Marketers can get in touch with these clients with promotions, reminders, or help to stop them from leaving.

ii. **Automated Marketing**

The majority of marketing automation techniques contain a set of rules that, when activated, initiate customer interactions. Through the analysis of billions of consumer data points, Machine Learning can determine the best times to contact customers, the best subject lines, and much more. Your marketing automation activities can then be made more effective by using these insights (Suthar, 2020).

iii. **1:1 dynamic emails**

Any email content that alters based on the information, preferences, and behaviours of the subscribers is referred to as dynamic content in email marketing. A marketing email is sent to the entire database; however, some content modules are dynamic and change depending on a determined attribute (Dhanalakshmi et al., 2020).

3.7 IoT AND MARKETING APPLICATION

The implementation of IoT has transformed business operations in the present era. It facilitates the collection of a sizable volume of data from a variety of sources (Ritu and Bhambri, 2022). The use of the IoT is changing how businesses operate in the modern world. This makes it possible to gather a sizable amount of data from multiple sources. IoT is the prime factor for the development of increasingly intelligent devices, which creates new potential across all situations and industries, not just in the B2B landscape (Kaur et al., 2019).

The Industrial Internet of Things (IIoT) emerged as a result of the longest-running IoT applications in the industrial sector. The emergence of Industry 4.0 has boosted the IIoT sector and it is experiencing the fastest growth and popularity due to developments in automation and robotics. This has been made possible by the innovation in production systems brought on by the adoption of IoT. The concept of the Phygital (blending the Physical with the digital) evolved which opened avenues to introduce new products and new services that are useful to the market (Chhabra and Bhambri, 2021). Production facilitated by smart connected devices enables the ability to understand customer specifications and, as a result, the ability to suggest brand-new practical services to support these products.

Businesses may get real-time sales information, understand where and how their items are bought, and get prompt customer feedback. As a result, real-time strategic planning that is constantly being adjusted is produced. The IoT is the foundation for

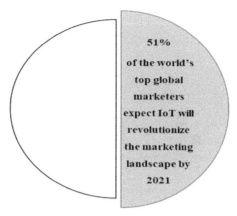

FIGURE 3.3 Global Marketers expectation about IoT and consumer adoption. (Source: Economic Insights, Gartner; Salesforce, Verizon Enterprise, Marketo.)

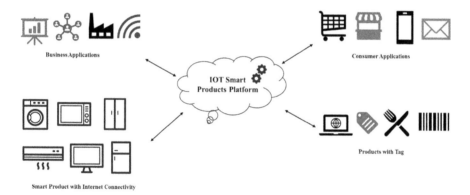

FIGURE 3.4 Applications of IoT in consumer and business applications. (Source: The Internet of Things in a marketing consumer and application context as seen on the website of Chiefmartec – the leading marketing technology blog of Scott Brinker http://chiefmartec. com/2015/06/marketing-internet-things-closer-think/.)

the development of connected devices, or items that network their capacity to detect contextual information. In reality, connected products enable process modifications in response to actual customer needs by integrating with production systems during the product generation phase.

With the use of the internet and AI, any network can transform connected products into smart products. It is feasible to build a network of connected, intelligent items that will provide people with new value services. In order to personalize offerings, marketers can, for instance, use this new communication channel to connect with people who own and use products. Additionally, customer service and management can be better contextualized and adapted to each customer's needs.

Future consumers will reportedly be less inclined to type their requests on a gadget and more convinced that their wants must be acknowledged and satisfied. IoT makes it possible for better and more precise advertising: it can help to provide

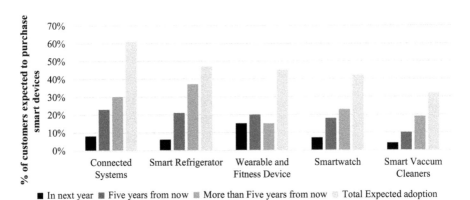

FIGURE 3.5 Projected new adoption of smart devices and connected technology. (Source: Economic Insights, Gartner; Salesforce, Verizon Enterprise, Marketo.)

relevant and helpful messages that are in line with the consumer's profile, behaviours, and previous purchases. It has been estimated that the worldwide market for IoT solutions in 2013 was $1.9 trillion and in 2020 it was $7.1 trillion; similarly, the estimated number of IoT-connected devices in 2015 was 2.9 billion and in 2020 it was 13 billion (Economic Insights, Gartner; Salesforce, Verizon Enterprise, Marketo).

3.7.1 IoT in Digital Marketing

1. **Product development**
   IoT enables digital marketers to better understand what consumers genuinely want from their brands, which thereby helps to raise the quality of their goods. The IoT not only improves product quality, but also helps in demand forecasting and new product planning. Businesses will be able to make better decisions more quickly and efficiently if they have access to data from IoT devices.
2. **User buying behavior analysis**
   IoT provides a comprehensive picture of user buying habits from the start until the end of the decision-making process. It also helps to study consumer demands, buying habits, how trends affect those habits, and geographic location so that marketers may tailor their products appropriately. IoT can deliver more precise data on consumer preferences.
3. **Tracking of data**
   IoT devices facilitates data tracking, which helps companies to predict the user need for a particular product or service. Real-time customer information helps marketers increase sales. It is also used to determine the best time for sales.
4. **Customer analysis**
   Smart devices allows marketers to understand their customers better. Large amounts of data are provided by smart devices, and provide insights about

customers on their daily habits Information gathered from smart devices is also more detailed and significant. It enables digital marketers to advertise products reflecting the data that has been gathered.

5. **Big Data**

   With the help of smart gadgets, marketers collect innumerable customer data which will be applied to successful marketing efforts. IoT devices have more sensor-based data about consumers than is typical with traditional research. Big Data gives marketers more precise insights that will lower risk and enhance opportunities.

6. **Automated Marketing**

   Typically, gathering client data requires a lot of work and time from marketers. However, IoT helps by saving the time required by marketers for data collection and analysis.

7. **More connection with end users**

   Any smart gadget can be utilized as a channel in the IoT to connect with consumers. Therefore, any intelligent product will enable marketers to communicate with their clients, increasing the level of customer engagement (Bhambri et al., 2020).

8. **Micro-Personalization**

   Personalization is a powerful tool for connecting with and involving the audience. Real-time communication with customers is made possible by IoT. The effectiveness of the marketing effort is increased as a result of better audience targeting (Anand and Bhambri, 2018). IoT enables you to collect a range of customer-related data that will enable you to decide what kind of campaign would best engage them. Marketers can deliver the best message at the ideal time to complete the buying journey based on the data which they have gathered. Furthermore, marketers can exploit it to create better-targeted adverts.

9. **Customer satisfaction**

   Everyone expects the fastest customer service in the modern digital age, and every marketer must prioritize this aspect. Real-time data allows marketers to respond to clients more quickly.

| Analyze Customer buying behavior across platforms | Gather previous data to understand user interaction with devices and products | Gain deeper insights about a consumer's buying pattern | Provide real time point of sale data and target ads | Quickly resolve issues and keep customers happy and satisfied |

FIGURE 3.6   How will IoT be used by marketers? (Source: Economic Insights, Gartner; Salesforce, Verizon Enterprise, Marketo.)

3.8 CONCLUSION

In the future, the role of both the Internet of Things (IoT) and Artificial Intelligence (AI) will be crucial. The increasing need for technologies in businesses and governments is fuelled by a variety of sources. Technologists, engineers, and scientists have already begun to implement it at various levels. In the digital marketing industry, IoT developments will empower marketers to design and execute successful marketing strategies. They establish a connection between consumers and marketers that enables them to fulfil one another's demands.

REFERENCES

Adobe Sensei Team. Adobe. AI: Your behind-the-scenes marketing companion. https://www.adobe.com/insights/sensei-ai-for-marketers.html (Accessed 7 June 2019).

Adobe. Artificial intelligence unlocks the true power of analytics. https://www.adobe.com/au/insights/ai-unlocks-the-true-power-of-analytics.html (Accessed 4 June 2019).

Agrawal, A. (2020). How the IoT helps transform the field in different impactful ways – From machine efficiency to worker safety, *CustomerThink*, February 21. Retrieved from http://customerthink.com/how-the-iothelps-transform-the-field-in-different-impactful-ways-from-machine-efficiency-to-worker-safety/?

Anand, A. and Bhambri, P. (2018). Character recognition system using radial features. *International Journal on Future Revolution in Computer Science & Communication Engineering*, 4(4), 599–602.

Bali, V., Bali, S., Gaur, D., Rani, S. and Kumar, R. (2023). Commercial-off-the shelf vendor selection: A multi-criteria decision-making approach using intuitionistic fuzzy sets and TOPSIS. *Operational Research in Engineering Sciences: Theory and Applications*, 12(4), 100–113.

Bhambri, P. and Chhabra, Y. (2022). Deployment of distributed clustering approach in WSNs and IoTs. In Pankaj Bhambri, Sita Rani, Gaurav Gupta, Alex Khang (Eds.), *Cloud and Fog Computing Platforms for Internet of Things* (pp. 85–98). Chapman and Hall/CRC.

Bhambri, P., Dhanoa, I. S., Sinha, V. K. and Kaur, J. (2020). Paddy crop production analysis based on SVM and KNN classifier. *International Journal of Recent Technology and Engineering*, 8(5), 2791–2793.

Bughin, J., Catlin, T. and LaBerge, L. (2019). *A Winning Operating Model for Digital Strategy, Digital McKinsey*, McKinsey & Company, January. Retrieved from https://www.mckinsey.com/capabilities/mckinsey-digital/our-insights/a-winning-operating-model-for-digital-strategy

Chaffey, D. (2019a). 15 applications of artificial intelligence in marketing, *Smart Insights*, 31 January. Retrieved from https://www.smartinsights.com/managing-digital-marketing/marketing-innovation/15-applications-artificialintelligence-marketing/

Chaffey, D. (2019b). 15 marketing applications of artificial intelligence across the RACE marketing model, Dr Dave Chaffey – Personal site, *Digital Insights*, 14 October. Retrieved from https://www.davechaffey.com/digital-marketingglossary/artificial-intelligence-for-marketing/

Chhabra, Y. and Bhambri, P. (2021). Various approaches and algorithms for monitoring energy efficiency of wireless sensor networks. In *Sustainable Development Through Engineering Innovations: Select Proceedings of SDEI 2020* (pp. 761–770). Springer Singapore.

Clifford, Catherin. (2018). Google CEO: A.I. is more important than fire or electricity, *CNBC.com*. February 1, 2018. Retrieved from https://www.cnbc.com/2018/02/01/google-ceo-sundar-pichai-ai-is-more-important-than-fire-electricity.html (Accessed 6 June 2019).

Deakin, J., LaBerge, L. and O'Beirne, B. (2019). *Five Moves to Make During a Digital Transformation*, McKinsey &Company, April. Retrieved from https://www.mckinsey.com/capabilities/mckinsey-digital/our-insights/five-moves-to-make-during-a-digital-transformation

Dhanalakshmi, R., Vijayaraghavan, N., Sivaraman, A. K. and Rani, S. (2020). Epidemic awareness spreading in smart cities using the artificial neural network. In Alex Khang, Sita Rani, Arun Kumar Sivaraman (Eds.), *AI-Centric Smart City Ecosystems* (pp. 187–207). CRC Press. https://www.taylorfrancis.com/books/edit/10.1201/9781003252542/ai-centric-smart-city-ecosystems-alex-khang-sita-rani-arun-kumar-sivaraman?refId=4f506ea6-341a-422c-b932-e03649e8f883&context=ubx

Derek, Thompson. (2018). The Atlantic. Where did all the advertising jobs go? February 7, 2018. Retrieved from https://www.theatlantic.com/business/archive/2018/02/advertising-jobs-programmatic-tech/552629/ (Accessed 1 June 2019).

Dooley, J. (2020). UX is the top brand differentiator among marketers in 2020, *ClickZ*, February 25. Retrieved from https://www.clickz.com/ux-is-the-top-brand-differentiator-among-marketers-in-2020/

Enterprise Content Team. The magic of AI in a content-driven world. Using AI to create content faster. Retrieved from https://www.adobe.com/insights/the-magic-of-AI-in-a-content-driven-world.html (Accessed 5 June 2019).

https://appinventiv.com/blog/ai-and-iot-will-transform-your-business/

https://martechvibe.com/martech/top-10-applications-of-ai-in-marketing/

https://www.automationworld.com/process/iiot/article/21723170/iot-applied-to-marketing

https://www.clariontech.com/blog/ai-and-iot-blended-what-it-is-and-why-it-matters

https://www.i-scoop.eu/internet-of-things-iot/internet-things-marketing/

https://www.linkedin.com/pulse/15-applications-artificial-intelligence-marketing-robert-allen/

https://www.mckinsey.com/capabilities/mckinsey-digital/our-insights/the-internet-of-things-the-value-of-digitizing-the-physical-world

https://www.mckinsey.com/capabilities/mckinsey-digital/our-insights/the-internet-of-things-the-value-of-digitizing-the-physical-world

https://www.smartinsights.com/managing-digital-marketing/marketing-innovation/15-applications-artificial-intelligence-marketing/

https://www.techtarget.com/iotagenda/definition/Artificial-Intelligence-of-Things-AIoT#:~:text=AI%2Dintegrated%20IoT%20devices%20can,Data%20analytics%20done%20by%20AI

https://www.tutorialspoint.com/internet_of_things/internet_of_things_media_marketing_and_advertising.htm

IBM. How to get started with cognitive computing. https://www.ibm.com/watson/advantage-reports/getting-started-cognitivetechnology.html (Accessed 6 June 2019).

Jain, A., Singh, M. and Bhambri, P. (2021, August). Performance evaluation of IPv4-IPv6 tunneling procedure using IoT. *Journal of Physics: Conference Series*, 1950(1), 012010.

Kaur, J. and Bhambri, P. (2019). Various DNA sequencing techniques and related applications. *International Journal of Analytical and Experimental Model Analysis*, 11(9), 3104–3111.

Kaur, J., Bhambri, P. and Sharma, K. (2019). Wheat production analysis based on Naïve Bayes classifier. *International Journal of Analytical and Experimental Model Analysis*, 11(9), 705–709.

Kaur, K., Dhanoa, I. S. and Bhambri, P. (2020, December). Optimized PSO-EFA algorithm for energy efficient virtual machine migrations. In *2020 5th IEEE International Conference on Recent Advances and Innovations in Engineering (ICRAIE)* (pp. 1–5). IEEE.

Levine, Barry. (2018). Marketingland.com. Adobe adds new features to its data management platform, December 3, 2018. Retrieved from https://marketingland.com/adobe-adds-new-features-to-its-data-management-platform-252944 (Accessed 2 June 2019).

Maruti Tech. 14 powerful chatbot platforms. Retrieved from https://www.marutitech.com/14-powerful-chatbot-platforms/ (Accessed 8 June 2019).

Puri, V., Kataria, A., Solanki, V. K. and Rani, S. (2022, December). AI-based botnet attack classification and detection in IoT devices. In *2022 IEEE International Conference on Machine Learning and Applied Network Technologies (ICMLANT)* (pp. 1–5). IEEE.

Rani, S., Kataria, A., Sharma, V., Ghosh, S., Karar, V., Lee, K. and Choi, C. (2021). Threats and corrective measures for IoT security with observance of cybercrime: A survey. *Wireless Communications and Mobile Computing, 2021,* 1–30.

Rani, S., Pareek, P. K., Kaur, J., Chauhan, M. and Bhambri, P. (2023, February). Quantum machine learning in healthcare: Developments and challenges. In *2023 IEEE International Conference on Integrated Circuits and Communication Systems (ICICACS)* (pp. 1–7). IEEE.

Rachna, R., Bhambri, P. and Chhabra, Y. (2022). Deployment of distributed clustering approach in WSNs and IoTs. In Pankaj Bhambri, Sita Rani, Gaurav Gupta, Alex Khang (Eds.), *Cloud and Fog Computing Platforms for Internet of Things* (pp. 85–98). Chapman and Hall/CRC.

Ritu, P., and Bhambri, P. (2022). A CAD system for software effort estimation. *Paper presented at the International Conference on Technological Advancements in Computational Sciences* (pp. 140–146). IEEE. DOI: 10.1109/ICTACS56270.2022.9988123.

Ritu, P. and Bhambri, P. (2023, February 17). Software effort estimation with machine learning – A systematic literature review. In Susheela Hooda, Vandana Mohindru Sood, Yashwant Singh, Sandeep Dalal, Manu Sood (Eds.), *Agile software development: Trends, challenges and applications* (pp. 291–308). John Wiley & Sons, Inc.

Sangwan, Y. S., Lal, S., Bhambri, P., Kumar, A. and Dhanoa, I. S. (2021). Advancements in social data security and encryption: A review. *NVEO-Natural Volatiles & Essential Oils Journal|NVEO,* 8(4). 15353–15362.

Singh, A. P., Aggarwal, M., Singh, H., and Bhambri, P. (2021a). Sketching of EV network: a Complete Roadmap. In *Sustainable Development Through Engineering Innovations: Select Proceedings of SDEI 2020* (pp. 431–442). Springer Singapore. https://www.statista.com/?kw=statista&crmtag=adwords&gclid=Cj0KCQjwxuCnBhDLARIsAB-cq1qE3kNDwfV7dZ8Hl3AgcZ2ntiUcvbehp3VwIl8b6FgRoLX8UUHHMwEaAiH_EALw_wcB (accessed on dated 04.04.2023)

Sinha, V. K., Jeet 2D, R., Bhambri, P. and Mahajan, M. (2020). Empowering intrusion detection in iris recognition system: A review. *Journal of Natural Remedies,* 21(2), 131–153.

Singh, M., Bhambri, P., Singh, I., Jain, A. and Kaur, E. K. (2021b). Data mining classifier for predicting diabetics. *Annals of the Romanian Society for Cell Biology,* 25(4), 6702–6712.

Suthar, S. (2020). 6 proven ways to revamp your digital customer experience, *CustomerThink,* February 21. Retrieved from http://customerthink.com/6-proven-ways-to-revamp-your-digital-customer-experience/?

Sweeny, T. (2020). Best practices for support web site design, *CustomerThink,* February 20. Retrieved from http://customerthink.com/best-practices-for-support-web-site-design/?

Vecteezy.com Licence Attribution: Home Appliances Vectors by Vecteezy. https://www.vecteezy.com/free-vector/home-appliances

Vicioso, Sara. (2019). Seer interactive. Programmatic advertising 101: How it works, August 27, 2015. https://www.seerinteractive.com/blog/programmatic-advertising-101-works/ (Accessed 6 June 2019).

Zambito, T. (2014). The future of modern marketing is human-centered, *Business 2 Community,* May 17. Retrieved from https://www.business2community.com/marketing/future-modern-marketing-human-centered-

4 An Introduction to Multi-Objective Decision Programming with Fuzzy Parameters

Zahid Amin Malik
Kumaun University, Nainital, India

4.1 DEFINITIONS

Decision-maker(s): The person(s), stakeholder(s), or organization(s) to whom the strategic decision issue under investigation relates are referred to as the decision-maker(s).

Decision variable(s): A decision variable(s) represents those variable(s) that can be controlled by the decision-maker. For example, consider a bakery production firm that must select how many different varieties of baked items to produce in the coming month, and in what quantities. All of the factors explain the situation thoroughly and lead to the decision to be made.

Criterion: A criterion is indeed a single measure which can be used to assess the performance of a decision problem's solution the system to a decision problem. Criteria can be of numerous types and come from a variety of areas of application. However, many of the most frequently raised concerns, at the best level, are related to:

- Profit
- Cost
- Time
- Distance
- Production planning
- Personal preferences of the decision-maker
- Commercial or organizational strategy
- System performance

A multi-criteria decision aid (MCDA) problem exists when a decision problem comprises one or more criteria. This is referred to as a multi-criteria decision-making (MCDM) problem.

Criteria space: The criterion space is the space generated by a set of criteria.

Objective: The objective will be used as a criterion in the current study, with information on whether to maximize or minimize, and the decision-maker(s) will choose one criterion scale (e.g., minimize unwanted goal deviations). A problem with several objectives is called a multi-objective optimization problem. However, we observe that such objectives would be competing, implying that they can't achieve their optimal values at the same time, and, if they do, that the problem would be resolved as a single-objective problem. The space defined by the values of a set of objectives is known as objective space.

Achievement function: The achievement function is the one in which we must reduce the unwanted deviations from our desired outcomes in the model.

Goal: A goal is a desired target level set by the decision-maker(s) to accomplish under specific conditions.

There are three possible types of goals:

- **A lower, unilateral goal**: This goal establishes a lower limit, below which one does not want to fall (but exceeding the limit is acceptable). As an example, aim to manufacture at least 20 products.
- **A higher, unilateral goal**: This goal establishes an upper limit, which one does not wish to exceed (but it is acceptable to go below the limit). As an example, maintain costs within the 1 lakh Rs (Indian) budget.
- **A two-sided goal**: This goal sets specific targets that we do not want to miss on either side. As an example, aim to engage exactly 20 employees.

Deviational variable: A deviational variable is a variable that calculates the overall difference between the desired goal and the value attained in a given solution.

Positive deviational variable: If the attained value exceeds the desired target level, then the difference is determined by the value of the positive deviational variable.

Negative deviational variable: If the attained value is less than the desired target level then the difference is determined by the value of the negative deviational variable.

Constraint: The constraint is a limitation imposed on the decision variables that should be satisfied to attain a practical solution. A generic decision variables function involving equality or inequality can be used as a constraint.

Sign restriction: A sign constraint restricts a single decision or deviation variable from falling inside a specific value range. The most common sign constraint is that the variable is quasi and continuous.

Feasible region: The feasible region is generated by a set of solutions in goal programming which fulfils all those constraints and sign limitations in decision space, and this type of solution is required to be implementable in practice.

Ideal point: In the objective space the ideal point represents that point where each goal in a multi-objective optimization problem is optimized individually within the feasible area and achieves its optimal value. When the goals are incompatible, this ideal point will just be beyond the feasible area in the objective space, and it will be referred to as an infeasible point.

Fuzzy theory: Zadeh (1965) proposed a fuzzy set theory to deal directly with the vagueness, uncertainty, and ambiguity of human behaviour and judgements. Fuzzy set theory is a method of data refinement that uses mathematical formulae or operations to overcome particular uncertainties connected with human reasoning and thinking.

Fuzzy sets: Fuzzy sets are an extension of Boolean or crisp sets. A fuzzy set $\widetilde{F}$ is specified on just about any discourse universal set, say Z, and is determined by a certain membership function related to every element z of Z, represented by $\mu_{\widetilde{F}}(z)$. The fuzzy set $\widetilde{F}$ is expressed as a collection of ordered pairs of basic elements y and their associated membership functions $\mu_{\widetilde{F}}(z)$, i.e.

$$\widetilde{F} = \left\{ \left(z, \mu_{\widetilde{F}}(z) \right) \mid z \in Z, \mu_{\widetilde{F}}(z) \in [0,1] \right\}$$

Convex fuzzy set: A fuzzy set is defined to be convex if any point placed between two other points does have a greater membership degree than these points' minimum membership degree.
i.e.

$$\mu_{\widetilde{F}}\left(\lambda z_1 - (1 - \lambda) z_2 \right) \geq \min\left(\mu_{\widetilde{F}}(z_1), \mu_{\widetilde{F}}(z_2) \right) \; \forall z_2, z_2 \in Z, \lambda \in [0,1]$$

When at least one of its components obtains the highest attainable membership grade, the fuzzy set is referred to as a normalized fuzzy set.

Fuzzy numbers: A fuzzy number is defined as a convex and normalized fuzzy set with a membership function specified in R and piecewise continuous.

Optimizing: The term "optimize" in decision-making refers to choosing the final decision that delivers the best value of some measure among all possible decisions on the specified real-life problems. The ultimate goal of such judgments is to guide production planning in order to generate a profit, i.e., to obtain desired advantages or to minimize the amount of effort and needed resources used in the production process.

Classical optimization techniques are the work of Newton, Cauchy and Lagrange in solving optimization problems arising in physics and geometry by applying differential calculus approaches and calculus of variations. These may be expanded to handle scenarios where the variables must be non-negative and the constraints are inequalities, but these generalizations are largely theoretical and do not define computing techniques.

Satisficing: Satisficing is derived a combination of the words 'satisfy' and 'suffice'. It refers to a type of behaviour in which decision-makers seek to achieve a set of predefined goals. If they fulfil those goals, it is sufficient for them in that decision scenario, and they are therefore fulfilled.

Mathematical modelling: Mathematical modelling is the process of turning real-life events under certain circumstances into mathematical formulations using various mathematical structures such as graphs, equations, diagrams, and so forth.

Mathematical programming problems: Mathematical programming problems are used to express a wide number of real-world optimization problems that are no longer solvable using classical optimization methodologies. There has been significant progress in the theory and strategies for tackling different types of mathematical programming problems.

Production: Production is one of the most important roles in organizations/industries since it deals with converting input assets (resources) into desired outputs (products). In other words, production comprises the transformation of one material shape into another using chemical or mechanical procedures in order to create or improve the product's efficacy for users. Production is a type of process in which valuable commodities and services are- manufactured to make a profit.

Production planning: Production planning is the backbone of every organization or industry. Production planning's primary function is to direct manufacturing systems towards achieving desired goals with efficiency and effectiveness. Its major aim is to provide a strategy for what we need to achieve inside the production system, how we need to get there, and the materials we'll need to make it happen.

Production system: The tactics and procedures utilized to manufacture desired items for the market are referred to as production systems. Production systems make use of the resources available in the manufacturing sector to create products.

4.2 INTRODUCTION

Mathematical programming is a powerful tool for dealing with real-world issues, notably in the industrial sector (Kaur et al., 2020). To survive in today's competitive environment, the manufacturing sector has always encountered adversity in selecting the best decision support system. Mathematical programming methodologies are among the most common methods for dealing with production planning issues in the manufacturing sector. In a real-world setting, the ultimate goal of most of this decision-making is to either maximize the optimal outcome or minimize the utilized effort. Previously, profit maximization or cost reduction were the only objectives or goals of the production system or small-scale industrial organization. Linear programming is a technique that just applies to one goal, such as minimizing costs or increasing profits. In practice, the manager of industrial management must meet various objectives, including such product quality, employment stability, labour and working conditions, profit maximization, and so on, even though the primary goal is profiting maximization because industries were indeed established to make a profit. When the parameters are not in crips, goal programming is a standard way for dealing with many objectives in decision-making situations.

As a result, the proposed research work investigates the fuzzy goal programming approach in the manufacturing sectors to assist production management and decision analysis using fuzzy parameters. The primary advantage of goal programming would be that environmental, strategic planning and organizational objectives are examined and included in the model at various goal levels. Goal programming attempts to achieve a counterbalance between mathematical optimization and the decision-maker's (DM's) determination to obtain specific goals. The primary goal of goal programming is to accomplish multiple objectives simultaneously. Goal programming is the process of condensing all desired objectives into a single goal and arriving at a satisfactory solution.

The goal programming approach has been widely used in operations research (OR). Goal programming, according to Charnes, Cooper, and Ferguson, was the first attempt to initiate the concept of goal programming (1961). Ijiri (1965), Lee (1972), Ignizio (1976), Flavell (1976), and others have expanded on this strategy. This goal programming technique is a mathematical way of resolving multi-objective problems in a variety of industries in order to ensure effective, opportune, and proper decisions. Goals, along with the customary constraints of the given problem, are considered constraints in goal programming, with the goal of minimizing goal deviation as just an objective and assigning weights to allocate priorities to the several goals. The goal programming model is then utilized to solve such a problem; thus, sensitivity analysis is also feasible (Singh et al., 2021). Goal programming could be an approach for enhancing the effectiveness of management decisions. Goal programming can assist with such widely available decision issues involving multiple objective functions.

4.3   MATHEMATICAL FORMULATION

Goal programming is the popular approach while dealing with production problems to obtain maximum benefits. The general goal programming problem can be represented (Charnes & Cooper, 1977; Ignizio, 1976; Malik et al., 2019b):

Minimize:

$$Z = \sum_{l=1}^{m} \left(h_l^- + h_l^+ \right)$$

Subject to:

Goal constraints:

$$\sum_{t=1}^{n} E_{lt} y_t + h_l^- - h_l^+ = p_l \text{ for } l = 1, 2, 3, \ldots, m$$

Hard constraints:

$$\sum_{t=1}^{n} E_{lt} y_t \begin{pmatrix} \geq \\ = \\ \leq \end{pmatrix} p_l \text{ for } l = m+1, \ldots, m+g$$

$$y_t, h_{\bar{l}}^-, h_l^+ \geq 0,$$

$(l = 1, 2, 3, 4, \ldots, m)$ and $(t = 1, 2, 3, 4, \ldots, n)$,

Where

Z is the objective function (summation of unwanted deviations);
h_l^+ represents the positive deviational variable and is the amount abovethe desired l^{th} goal;
h_l^- indicates the negative deviational variable and is the amount below the desired l^{th} goal;
p_l represents the goals for $l = 1, 2, 3, 4, \ldots, m$;
y_t designates the decision variables;
E_{lt} denotes the decision variable coefficients.

It should be noted that one or even both variables must be zero; that is,

$$h_l^+ * h_l^- = 0$$

Both of these variables also meet the non-negativity requirement; that is,

$$h_l^+ * h_l^- \geq 0$$

4.3.1 WEIGHTED GOAL PROGRAMMING (WGP) OR ARCHIMEDEAN GOAL PROGRAMMING

The objective function (Z) in the weighted goal programming approach is actually the weighted sum of the deviations for the related problem's desired targets, with weights assigned based on the decision-maker's choice. In terms of representation, the weighted goal programming strategy takes the following form(Charnes & Cooper, 1977; Ignizio, 1976; Romero, 2004):

Minimize:

$$Z = \sum_{l=1}^{m} \left(f_l^+ h_l^+ + f_l^- h_l^- \right)$$

Subject to:

Goal constraints:

$$\sum_{t=1}^{n} E_{lt} y_t + h_l^- - h_l^+ = p_l \text{ for } l = 1,2,3,\ldots,m$$

Hard constraints:

$$\sum_{t=1}^{n} E_{lt} y_t \begin{pmatrix} \geq \\ = \\ \leq \end{pmatrix} p_l \text{ for } l = m+1,\ldots,m+g$$

$$y_t, h_l^-, h_l^+, f_l^+, f_l^- \geq 0$$

$$\left(l = 1, 2, 3, 4, \ldots, m\right), \left(t = 1, 2, 3, 4, \ldots, n\right)$$

where h_l^+ denotes the positive deviation; h_l^- denotes the negative deviation; f_l^+ and f_l^- are real numbers denoting the relative weights allotted inside a priority level to the unwanted deviational variables and both reflect the decision-maker's choice on the relative position to each target; p_l denotes the desired targets or goals for l = 1, 2, 3, 4, ..., m; y_t denotes the decision variables; E_{lt} are the decision variable coefficients.

These weights define the norms' determining criteria, and are arbitrary. Jyoti and Mannan (2016) and Orumie and Ebong (2014) have used the goal programming formulations mentioned above.

4.3.2 LEXICOGRAPHIC GOAL PROGRAMMING (LGP) OR NON-ARCHIMEDEAN GOAL PROGRAMMING OR PRE-EMPTIVE GOAL PROGRAMMING

The lexicographic goal programming variant was used in the great majority of the initial goal programming formulations (for example, Lee, 1972). The presence of multiple priority levels helps to distinguish lexicographic goal programming from those other goal programming strategies (Kaur and Bhambri, 2019). Each prioritized level contains several unwanted deviations that must be minimized within constraints. The decision-maker in this approach needs to prioritize the problem's desired goals (Ritu and Bhambri, 2023). The model is then optimized by focusing as precisely as possible on the most important objective before moving onto the next higher goal, and so on until the minimal goal is reached., i.e., the objective functions are arranged in such a way that achieving the very first goal is frequently more vital than achieving the second goal, which is significantly more important than achieving the third goal, and so on. As a result, a lower-priority goal never disregards the best value of a higher-priority goal. The lexicographic goal programming was mentioned by Iserman (1982), Sherali (1982), and Ignizio (1985) in their research.

The following is the proposed lexicographic goal programming model:

Minimize:

$$Z = \sum_{l=1}^{m} r_l \left(h_l^- + h_l^+\right)$$

Subject to:

Goal constraints:

$$\sum_{t=1}^{n} E_{lt} y_t + h_l^- - h_l^+ = p_l \text{ for } l = 1, 2, 3, \ldots, m$$

Hard constraints:

$$\sum_{t=1}^{n} E_{lt} y_t \begin{pmatrix} \geq \\ = \\ \leq \end{pmatrix} p_l \text{ for } l = m+1,\ldots,m+g$$

$$y_t, h_l^-, h_l^+ \geq 0,$$

$$\text{And } \left(l = 1,2,3,4,\ldots,m\right), \left(t = 1,2,3,4,\ldots,n\right)$$

where r_l denotes the pre-emptive factor or priority level assigned to each relative desired goal in rank order ($r_1 > r_2 > r_3 > \ldots > r_m$); h_l^+ denotes the positive deviation; h_k^- denotes the negative deviation; p_k denotes the desired targets or goals for $l = 1, 2, 3, 4, \ldots, m$; the decision variables are represented by y_t; The decision variable coefficients denoted by E_{lt}.

Furthermore, Charnes and Cooper (1977)proposed the goal programming model by combining pre-emptive priorities and weightings, as defined (Ijiri, 1965);

Minimize:

$$Z = \sum_{l=1}^{m} \sum_{j=1}^{n_k} r_l \left(f_{lj}^+ h_l^+ + f_{lj}^- h_l^- \right)$$

Subject to:

Goal constraints:

$$\sum_{t=1}^{n} E_{lt} y_t + h_l^- - h_l^+ = p_l \text{ for } l = 1,2,3,\ldots,m$$

Hard constraints:

$$\sum_{l=1}^{n} E_{lt} y_t \begin{pmatrix} \geq \\ = \\ \leq \end{pmatrix} p_l \text{ for } l = m+1,\ldots,m+g$$

$$n_l, y_t, h_l^-, h_l^+, f_{lj}^+, f_{lj}^- \geq 0$$

$$(l = 1, 2, 3, 4, \ldots, m), (t = 1, 2, 3, 4, \ldots, n)$$

Here f_{lj}^+ and f_{lj}^- can be real numbers denoting the relative weights allotted inside the lth category; ($j = 1, 2, 3, 4, \ldots, n_l$) to which is ascribed the non-Archimedean transcendental value of r_l; h_l^+ denotes the positive deviation; h_l^- denotes the negative deviation; the desired target or goals are denoted by p_l for $l = 1, 2, 3, 4, \ldots, m$; y_t are the decision variables; E_{lt} are the decision variable coefficients.

4.3.3 FUZZY GOAL PROGRAMMING (FGP)

As with real-world issues, there is significant uncertainty, i.e., if the decision-maker becomes unable to identify a goal at a given target level, the fuzzy sense emerges. As a result, some sort of fuzzy programming modelling is needed. The notion of fuzzy decision-making was presented by Bellman and Zadeh (1970). Zimmermann addressed fuzzy set optimization in 1976. Zimmermann (1978) investigated the interconnection of such membership functions correlating to consider the optimal solution could be an alternative in the decision space that maximizes the least achievable aspiration phases in decision-making, as noted by such pertaining membership functions.

The fuzzy goal programming approach may be represented as follows:

Find

$$Y(y_1, y_2, y_3 \ldots y_n)$$

To satisfy:

$$M_l(Y) \cong \begin{pmatrix} \tilde{\geq} \\ \cong \\ \tilde{\leq} \end{pmatrix} P_l \tag{4.1}$$

Subject to:

$$EY \begin{pmatrix} \tilde{\geq} \\ \cong \\ \tilde{\leq} \end{pmatrix} a, \tag{4.2}$$

$$Y \geq 0,$$

Here $M_l(Y)$ is the lth goal of fuzzy; P_l is the objective level related to $M_l(Y)$; $\tilde{\geq}$, $\cong$ and $\tilde{\leq}$ denotes the fuzziness of the objective level (i.e., approximately greater than or equal to, approximately equal to and approximately less than or equal to); $EY\left(\tilde{\geq},\cong,\tilde{\leq}\right)a$ reflects a set of constraints in the vector notation.

The membership function attributed to the objectives in a fuzzy decision-making condition is actually achieved by trying to define allowed variations of up and down, and the kind of membership function is influenced by the nature of the goal. If the goal is not implemented fully, the decision-maker is comfortable up to a certain tolerable limit, according to the aspirational level of the fuzzy goal in (4.1). According to Zimmermann, a linear membership function, μ_l, can indeed be asserted (Zimmermann, 1976, 1978).

The limitation of the type $\tilde{\geq}$, μ_l will be algebraically framed as follows:

$$\mu_l = \begin{cases} 1 & \text{if } M_l\left(Y\right) \geq P_l \\ \dfrac{M_l\left(Y\right)-L_l}{P_l-L_l} & \text{if } L_l \leq M_l\left(Y\right) \leq P_l \\ 0 & \text{if } M_l\left(Y\right) \leq L_l \end{cases} \tag{4.3}$$

Here L_l denotes the least tolerance limit for the fuzzy goal $M_l(Y)$.

For the type $\tilde{\leq}$ limitation, μ_l would be algebraically framed like this:

$$\mu_l = \begin{cases} 1 & \text{if } M_l\left(Y\right) \leq P_l \\ \dfrac{U_l-M_l\left(Y\right)}{U_l-P_l} & \text{if } P_l \leq M_l\left(Y\right) \leq U_l \\ 0 & \text{if } H_l\left(Y\right) \geq U_l \end{cases} \tag{4.4}$$

Here U_l represents the higher tolerance limit for the fuzzy goal $M_l(Y)$.

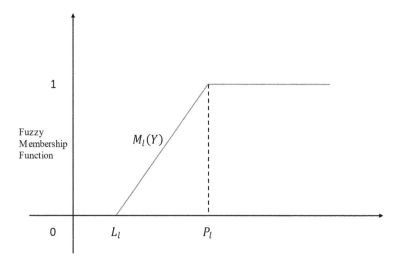

FIGURE 4.1 Membership function form of Equation (4.3).

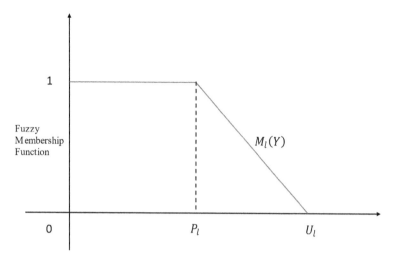

FIGURE 4.2 Membership function form of Equation (4.4).

The restriction of type $\cong$, μ_l will be algebraically framed as follows:

$$\mu_l = \begin{cases} 1 & \text{if } M_l(Y) = P_l \\ \dfrac{U_l - M_l(Y)}{U_l - P_l} & \text{if } P_l \le M_l(Y) \le U_l \\ \dfrac{M_l(X) - L_l}{P_l - L_l} & \text{if } L_l \le M_l(Y) \le P \\ 0 & \text{if } H_l(Y) \ge U_l \\ & \text{if } H_l(Y) \le L_l \end{cases} \quad (4.5)$$

The additive model would be expressed by the combination of the membership functions with the fuzzy goal programming problem (4.1):

Maximize:

$$Z(\mu) = \sum_{l=1}^{m} \mu_l$$

Subject to:

$$\mu_l = \frac{M_l(Y) - L_l}{P_l - L_l}$$

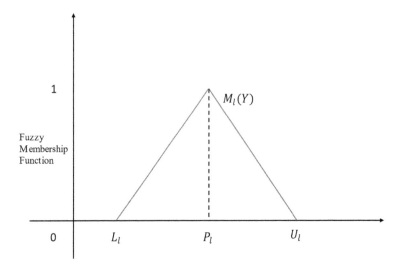

FIGURE 4.3 Membership function form of Equation (4.5).

$$\mu_l = \frac{U_l - M_l(Y)}{U_l - P_l}$$

$$EY \begin{pmatrix} \geq \\ = \\ \leq \end{pmatrix} a$$

$$\mu_l \leq 1$$

$$Y, \mu_l \geq 0,$$

$$l = 1, 2, 3, 4 \ldots m,$$

where $Z(\mu)$ is a fuzzy decision function or fuzzy achievement function; $EY(\geq, \leq, =)$ a in vector notation reflects a set of restrictions.

4.3.4 WEIGHTED FUZZY GOAL PROGRAMMING

Maximize:

$$Z(\mu) = \sum_{l=1}^{m} f_l \mu_l$$

Subject to:

$$\mu_l = \frac{M_l(Y) - L_l}{P_l - L_l}$$

$$\mu_l = \frac{U_l - M_l(Y)}{U_l - P_l}$$

$$EY \begin{pmatrix} \geq \\ = \\ \leq \end{pmatrix} a$$

$$\mu_l \leq 1$$

$$Y, \mu_l \geq 0,$$

$$l = 1, 2, 3, 4 \ldots m,$$

where $Z(\mu)$ is a fuzzy decision function or fuzzy achievement function; f_l denotes the relative weight to the lth fuzzy goal; $M_l(Y)$ denotes the lth goal of fuzzy.

To transmit the relative order of the desired goals, the weighted fuzzy goal programming process is widely employed in goal programming and multi-objective optimization methods. This method imitates the relative value of the aspects by allocating differential based on the coefficients of each term in the fuzzy achievement function (Kaur et al., 2019).

4.3.5 PRE-EMPTIVE FUZZY GOAL PROGRAMMING

Goals in some actual situations will not have the same demonstrable units, but they may still be proportionate. Additionally, extra goals shouldn't be evaluated when a subset of them is reached. Weighting fuzzy goal programming is not a good technique in these circumstances. The pre-emptive priority method could be expressed as $r_l \geq r_{l+1}$, which signifies that the desired goals in the lth priority level has greater priority than the goals in the $(l+1)^{th}$ priority level, i.e., no matter how large N (a number), r_l cannot be equal to Nr_{l+1} (Ignizio, 1976; Sherali & Soyster, 1983). Using this strategy, the problem may be divided into l sub-problems, wherein l is the number of priority levels. The primary priority levels of the fuzzy goals are the only ones that have been witnessed in the preliminary sub-problem. The membership data initially gathered at higher priority levels have been adjusted to add extra limits for other priority levels (Chhabra and Bhambri, 2021).

The broad pre-emptive sub-problem can be written as:

Maximize:

$$Z(\mu) = \sum_{l=1}^{m} (\mu_l) r_s$$

Subject to:

$$\mu_l = \frac{M_l(Y) - L_l}{P_l - L_l}$$

$$\mu_l = \frac{U_l - M_l(Y)}{U_l - P_l}$$

$$EY \begin{pmatrix} \geq \\ = \\ \leq \end{pmatrix} a$$

$$\mu_l \leq 1$$

$$(\mu) r_s = (\mu^*) r_s$$

$$Y, \mu_l \geq 0,$$

$$l = 1,2,3...m, \ s = 1,2,3...,j-1$$

where $(\mu_l) r_s$ denotes the membership functions of the goals in the lth priority level; $(\mu^*) r_s$ representsas attained membership value in the sth ($s \leq j-1$) priority level; $Z(\mu)$ is a fuzzy decision function or fuzzy achievement function.

Many decision-makers in the manufacturing sector have used fuzzy goal programming, a kind of goal programming, to highlight various benefits. For an inventory control model utilized for a sizable chemical factory, Golany et al. (1991) created a goal programming technique to give an effective compromise solution and decision-making completion with many fuzzy goal values. Due to the fact that, with this approach, goals and limits can be deterministic or fuzzy and the accomplishment of several goals simultaneously is possible, the fuzzy goal programming model is anticipated to perform better than the goal programming model (Chalam, 1994). Mohamed

(1997) established a connection between goal programming and fuzzy programming, which enables membership objectives of best degree attainment to be met by lowering under-deviation variables. Numerous fuzzy goal programming approaches mentioned in the literature were examined (Chanas & Kuchta, 2002). Furthermore, a unique method for resolving problems with fuzzy-based multi-objective fractional goal programming was developed (Pal et al., 2003; Toksarı, 2008). Pal and Moitra (2003)investigated at a case study and created a fuzzy goal programming model for a long-term land allocation plan in the agricultural sector. Ghiani et al. (2003) used fuzzy set theory to develop a mixed-integer linear methodology for assigning production batches to subcontractors in an Italian textile sector, which substituted the management's previous hand-made solutions. Kumar et al. (2004) addressed the problem of multiple target vendor selections using a fuzzy mixed integer goal optimization technique. Biswas and Pal (2005) proposed fuzzy goal programming to successfully simulate and address land-use planning challenges in agricultural sectors for the optimal production of many seasonal crops within a planning year. Iskander (2006) offered an exponential membership function and a chance-constrained method to transform his stochastic fuzzy goal programme structure into its deterministic-crisp counterpart.

Petrovic and Aköz (2008) used a fuzzy goal programming method to overcome batch-processing computer loading and organization challenges. The channel allocation problem with priority in the steel sector was addressed by Tsai et al. (2008) using a fuzzy mixed-integer multiple-goal programming technique. Yimmee and Phruksaphanrat (2011) employed the fuzzy goal programming technique for aggregate production and logistics planning to maximize profit and minimize variations in the labour level. The fuzzy goal programming technique was created by Biswas and Modak (2012) to discover the optimal answer by minimising the deviational variables. Fazlollahtabar et al., (2013)proposed that the virtual intelligent agent could be used to optimize the service industry market by utilising a fuzzy goal programming technique. Mekidiche et al. (2013) developed a weighted additive fuzzy goal programming method to address the issue of aggregate production planning. For fuzzy multi-objective linear fractional programming (MOLFP) issues with a tolerance limit inside of an ambiguous environment, are investigated by a goal programming approach (Dangwal et al., 2013). In order to effectively handle the problem, they also applied the linear goal programming (LGP) technique, introducing the methodology of variable change within a predetermined tolerance of the membership and non-membership goals, in addition to the model's fuzzy goal.

Fuzzy goal programming was used by Dáz-Madroero et al. (2014) to solve the issue of required materials planning for a first-tier supplier in an automobile supply chain by referring to the optimization of numerous competing objectives: reduction of normal, overtime, and subcontracted manufacturing total costs of final products plus inventory costs of finished goods, components and raw materials; reduction of idle time; reduction of backorder amounts. Hajikarimi et al. (2015) presented the fuzzy goal programming approach to boost productivity by forming productivity components such as data, process, output, business cycles, rivals, and government policies. This strategy employs a systematic approach to advancing elements in three productivity areas: materials, capital, and human resources, resulting in a well-rounded image of real-world production and sales systems. In fuzzy goal programming, Iskander (2015) proposed an exponential membership function that operated within the two main processes of the fuzzy goal programme. When used to a fuzzy textile production planning issue where the membership functions of the fuzzy objectives are regarded as exponential with either an increasing or decreasing rate of change, it compared the lexicographical procedure to the pre-emptive goal hierarchy. In order to foresee and address environmental issues related to the construction industry, Naithani et al. (2016) sought to show the efficiency of fuzzy goal programming (FGP) in the field of mathematical programming. Patel et al. (2016) looked into how farmers in the Patan region in North Gujarat, India, may plan their agriculture using fuzzy optimization approaches.

In order to solve multi-objective transportation problems, Rivaz et al. (2020) established a fuzzy goal programming method, and they include numerical examples to highlight the usefulness and advantages of the suggested model. A unique and integrated intuitionistic fuzzy multi-objective linear programming solution addressing portfolio selection issues was developed by Yu et al. (2021). They improved the common intuitionistic fuzzy (IF) inequalities and IF theory by creating non-membership functions using pessimistic, optimistic, and mixed techniques.

4.4 MATHEMATICAL VALIDATION

To determine the mathematical validation and applicability of the proposed approach, the production planning problem is illustrated. A set of bakery products are addressed as a descriptive case. The problem taken for this study is proposed by Malik et al. (2019a) (Tables 4.1 to 4.4).

The factory would like to achieve the following goals subject to the given constraints:

Goal 1: Maximizing Profit (560Rs).
Goal 2: Utilization of Labour Time (430 minutes).
Goal 3: Machine Time (430 minutes).

The weight is assigned to the goals based on the decision-maker's preference. The general framework for weighted goal programming is as follows:

TABLE 4.1
The Cost, Price, and Profit Margins for All Products

Product	Price (Rs)	Costs (Rs)	Profit (Rs)
Muffins	1.00	0.20	0.80
Cake	2.90	1.40	1.50
Cream puff	1.50	0.42	1.08
Egg tart	1.50	0.14	1.28
Cheese tart	1.15	0.20	0.95

TABLE 4.2
The Major Components for Each Product (in Grams) for One Item

Ingredients	Muffin	Cake	Cream Puff	Egg Tart	Cheese Tart
Margarine	5.025	8.520	4.801	4.573	5.000
Flour	8.000	9.100	5.012	9.262	8.523
Egg	8.000	9.000	8.300	6.322	2.021
Sugar	7.472	10.122	2.607	3.010	2.322
Evaporated milk	0.000	0.000	4.231	6.012	0.000
Cream cheese	0.000	0.000	0.000	0.000	4.215

TABLE 4.3
The Raw Material Available for Each Day

Raw Material	Total Offered for Each Day(Grams)
Margarine	2800
Sugar	2600
Flour	4000
Cream cheese	450
Eggs	3400
Evaporated milk	1100

TABLE 4.4
The Time Required for Each Product (Minutes)

	Muffin	Cake	Cream Puff	Egg Tart	Cheese Tart
Labour	1.45	0.30	1.00	0.60	0.80
Machine	1.30	0.80	1.00	0.55	0.50

Minimize

$$S = 2h_1^- + 4h_2^+ + 6h_3^-$$

Subject to:

Goal constraints:

$$0.80y_1 + 1.50y_2 + 1.08y_3 + 1.28y_4 + 0.95y_5 - h_1^+ + h_1^- = 560$$

$$1.45y_1 + 0.30y_2 + 1.00y_3 + 0.60y_4 + 0.80y_5 - h_2^+ + h_2^- = 430$$

$$1.30y_1 + 0.80y_2 + 1.00y_3 + 0.55y_4 + 0.50y_5 - h_3^+ + h_3^- = 430$$

Hard constraints:

$$5.025y_1 + 8.520y_2 + 4.801y_3 + 4.573y_4 + 5.000y_5 \leq 2800$$

$$8.000y_1 + 9.100y_2 + 5.012y_3 + 9.262y_4 + 8.523y_5 \leq 4000$$

$$8.000y_1 + 9.000y_2 + 8.300y_3 + 6.322y_4 + 2.021y_5 \leq 3400$$

$$7.472y_1 + 10.122y_2 + 2.607y_3 + 3.010y_4 + 2.322y_5 \leq 2600$$

$$0.000y_1 + 0.000y_2 + 0.000y_3 + 0.000y_4 + 4.215y_5 \leq 450$$

$$0.000y_1 + 0.000y_2 + 4.231y_3 + 6.012y_4 + 0.000y_5 \leq 1100$$

$$y_1, y_2, y_3, y_4, y_5 \geq 0$$

And $h_1^-, h_1^-, h_2^+, h_2^-, h_3^+, h_3^- \geq 0$,
y_1, y_2, y_3, y_4, y_5 are five products to be produced in a factory.
h_k^+ are positive deviational variables; h_k^- are negative deviational variables for $k = 1, 2$ & 3.

4.4.1 RESULTS

$$h_1^- = 8.9415, h_2^+ = 0, h_3^- = 0$$

Goal (1) = 551.0584, Goal (2) = 430, Goal (3) = 430, S= 17.88.
Assume the decision-maker disregards the above solution because the profit target level is not fully met and the objective value is 17.88. Therefore, the study investigates the applicability of the fuzzy goal programming technique. Considering the concept of fuzzy goal programming the tolerance limit is given to the goals.
Let the tolerance limit of the above goals be 550, 440, and 425.
Now the above problem is formulated in fuzzy goal programming (with equal weights) as;

Maximize:

$$Z(\mu) = \sum_{l=1}^{3} \mu_l$$

Subject to:

Goal Constraints:

$$\mu_1 = \left(0.80y_1 + 1.50y_2 + 1.08y_3 + 1.28y_4 + 0.95y_5 - 550\right) / \left(560 - 550\right)$$

$$\mu_2 = \left(440 - 1.45y_1 + 0.30y_2 + 1.00y_3 + 0.60y_4 + 0.80y_5\right) / \left(440 - 430\right)$$

$$\mu_3 = \left(1.30y_1 + 0.80y_2 + 1.00y_3 + 0.55y_4 + 0.50y_5 - 425\right) / \left(430 - 425\right)$$

Hard constraints:

$$8.000y_1 + 9.100y_2 + 5.012y_3 + 9.262y_4 + 8.523y_5 \le 4000$$

$$5.025y_1 + 8.520y_2 + 4.801y_3 + 4.573y_4 + 5.000y_5 \le 2800$$

$$7.472y_1 + 10.122y_2 + 2.607y_3 + 3.010y_4 + 2.322y_5 \le 2600$$

$$8.000y_1 + 9.000y_2 + 8.300y_3 + 6.322y_4 + 2.021y_5 \le 3400$$

$$0.000y_1 + 0.000y_2 + 0.000y_3 + 0.000y_4 + 4.215y_5 \le 450$$

$$0.000y_1 + 0.000y_2 + 4.231y_3 + 6.012y_4 + 0.000y_5 \le 1100$$

$$\mu_l \le 1,$$

$$\left(l = 1, 2, 3\right)$$

4.4.2 RESULTS

$\mu_1 = 1$, $\mu_2 = 1$, $\mu_3 = 0.5280$
$y_1 = 149.04$, $y_2 = 84.39$, $y_3 = 94.27$, $y_4 = 88.96$, $y_5 = 51.02$, Objective value = 2.52
Goal 1 = 560, Goal 2 = 429.8, Goal 3 = 427.64

It has been found, by the applicability of fuzzy goal programming, that the decision-maker would achieve all the desired objectives and better results than the usual goal programming models. In the fuzzy goal programming approach, the decision-maker faces negligible deviation and hence the decision-maker will utilize the proposed approach to enhance efficient and effective production processes to earn maximum benefits from their efforts. The mathematical method used in this study to describe the indeterminate lifetime determines the best schedules for maximizing production and minimizing cost as a sign of high efficiency in the manufacture of baked products.

4.5 CONCLUSION

This chapter studies and investigates the applicability of fuzzy goal programming for production planning problems. It has been found that the proposed mathematical programming formulation would deliver better results than other mathematical models. The fuzzy goal programming outlined in this chapter is expected to play an important part in the decision-making process of any production sector. The suggested model offers a useful method for developing management plans to choose different manufacturing processes in a decision support system. Making the best use of certain resources is frequently a goal of decision-makers, along with increasing profit and reducing labour and production expenses. Thus, an effort was made to enhance operational planning strategies in the agricultural and industrial sectors via constructing fuzzy goal programming approaches by simultaneously incorporating every one of these objectives into the suggested model. The model can be used to address many of the problems and issues associated related to the production sectors in their decision support system and related production planning problems.

REFERENCES

Bellman, R. E., & Zadeh, L. A. (1970). Decision-making in a fuzzy environment. *Management Science*, *17*(4), b-141–b-164. http://www.scopus.com/inward/record.url?eid=2-s2.0-0346636333&partnerID=40&md5=b5ef518469231f711aac4c2243d1e8ff

Biswas, A., & Modak, N. (2012). A fuzzy goal programming approach for fuzzy multiobjective stochastic programming through expectation model. *Communications in Computer and Information Science*, *283 CCIS*(1), 124–135. https://doi.org/10.1007/978-3-642-28926-2_14

Biswas, A., & Pal, B. B. (2005). Application of fuzzy goal programming technique to land use planning in agricultural system. *Omega*, *33*(5), 391–398. https://doi.org/10.1016/j.omega.2004.07.003

Chalam, G. (1994). Fuzzy goal programming (FGP) approach to a stochastic transportation problem under budgetary constraint. *Fuzzy Sets and Systems*, *66*(3), 293–299. https://doi.org/10.1016/0165-0114(94)90096-5

Chanas, S., & Kuchta, D. (2002). Fuzzy goal programming – One notion, many meanings. *Control and Cybernetics*, *31*(4), 871–890.

Charnes, A., & Cooper, W. W. (1977). Goal programming and Multi-objective optimization. *European Journal of Operational Research*, *1*, 39–54.

Chhabra, Y., & Bhambri, P. (2021). Various Approaches and Algorithms for Monitoring Energy Efficiency of Wireless Sensor Networks. In *Sustainable Development Through Engineering Innovations: Select Proceedings of SDEI 2020* (pp. 761–770). Springer Singapore.

Dangwal, R., Sharma, M. K., & Singh, P. (2013). A goal programming procedure for fuzzy multi-objective linear fractional problem in vague environment using tolerance. *International Journal of Physics and Mathematical Sciences, 3*, 17–24.

Díaz-Madroñero, M., Mula, J., & Jiménez, M. (2014). Fuzzy goal programming for material requirements planning under uncertainty and integrity conditions. *International Journal of Production Research, 52*(23), 6971–6988. https://doi.org/10.1080/00207543.2014.920115

Fazlollahtabar, H., Akbari, F., & Mahdavi, I. (2013). A fuzzy goal programming for optimizing service industry market using virtual intelligent agent. *Journal of Industrial and Production Engineering, 30*(1), 20–29. https://doi.org/10.1080/10170669.2012.760493

Flavell, R. (1976). A new goal programming formulation. *Omega, 4*(6), 731–732. https://doi.org/10.1016/0305-0483(76)90099-2

Ghiani, G., Grieco, A., Guerriero, E., & Musmanno, R. (2003). Allocating production batches to subcontractors by fuzzy goal programming. *International Transactions in Operational Research, 10*(3), 295–306. https://doi.org/10.1111/1475-3995.00408

Golany, B., Yadin, M., & Learner, O. (1991). A goal programming inventory control model applied at a large chemical plant. *Production & Inventory Management Journal, 32*(1), 16–24. http://search.ebscohost.com/login.aspx?direct=true&db=bth&AN=7862877&amp%0Alang=es&site=ehost-live

Hajikarimi, A., Rahmani, K., & Farahmand, N. F. (2015). Designing a new model to improve productivity factors implementing the fuzzy goal programming method. *Indian Journal of Science and Technology, 8*(S9), 9–15. https://doi.org/10.17485/ijst/2015/v8iS9/68545

Ignizio, J. P. (1976). *Goal Programming and Extensions*. Lexington Books, Lexington, MA. https://doi.org/10.2307/3009003

Ignizio, J. P. (1985). Multiobjective mathematical programming via the multiplex model and algorithm. *European Journal of Operational Research, 22*(3), 338–346. https://doi.org/10.1016/0377-2217(85)90253-X

Ijiri, Y. (1965). *Management Goals and Accounting for Control*. Rand-McNally, Chicago, IL. https://doi.org/10.2307/3007458

Isermann, H. (1982). Linear lexicographic optimization. *OR Spektrum, 4*(4), 223–228. https://doi.org/10.1007/BF01782758

Iskander, M. G. (2006). Exponential membership function in stochastic fuzzy goal programming. *Applied Mathematics and Computation, 173*(2), 782–791. https://doi.org/10.1016/j.amc.2005.04.014

Iskander, M. G. (2015). Exponential membership functions in fuzzy goal programming: A computational application to a production problem in the textile industry. *American Journal of Computational and Applied Mathematics, 5*(1), 1–6.

Jyoti, & Mannan, H. (2016). Goal programming: an application to financial estimation of an organization/institution. *ELK Asia Pacific Journal of Finance, and Risk Management, 7*(1), 1–11.

Kaur, J., & Bhambri, P. (2019). Various DNA sequencing techniques and related applications. *International Journal of Analytical and Experimental Model Analysis, 11*(9), 3104–3111.

Kaur, J., Bhambri, P., & Sharma, K. (2019). Wheat production analysis based on NaÃve Bayes classifier. *International Journal of Analytical and Experimental Model Analysis, 11*(9), 705–709.

Kaur, K., Dhanoa, I. S., & Bhambri, P. (2020, December). Optimized PSO-EFA Algorithm for Energy Efficient Virtual Machine Migrations. In *2020 5th IEEE International Conference on Recent Advances and Innovations in Engineering (ICRAIE)* (pp. 1–5). IEEE.

Kumar, M., Vrat, P., & Shankar, R. (2004). A fuzzy goal programming approach for vendor selection problem in a supply chain. *Computers and Industrial Engineering, 46*(1), 69–85. https://doi.org/10.1016/j.cie.2003.09.010

Lee, S. M. (1972). *Goal Programming for Decision Analysis*. Auerbach, Publishers Philadelphia, Pennsylvania (Vol. 14, Issue 2).

Malik, Z. A., Kumar, R., Roy, H., & Pathak, G. (2019a). Multi-objective mathematical programming technique in the paper production. *Glimpses*, *9*(1), 380–394.

Malik, Z. A., Kumar, R., Singh, N. K., Roy, H., & Pathak, G. (2019b). Weighted goal programming approach in the bakery production planning problems. *International Journal of Management, IT & Engineering*, *7*(1), 548–556.

Mekidiche, M., Belmokaddem, M., & Djemmaa, Z. (2013). Weighted additive fuzzy goal programming approach to aggregate production planning. *International Journal of Intelligent Systems and Applications*, *5*(4), 20–29. https://doi.org/10.5815/ijisa.2013.04.02

Mohamed, R. H. (1997). The relationship between goal programming and fuzzy programming. *Fuzzy Sets and Systems*, *89*(2), 215–222. https://doi.org/10.1016/S0165-0114(96)00100-5

Naithani, V., Dangwal, R., & Kumar, A. (2016). A fuzzy goal programming approach for achieving sustainability in construction industry. *Arya Bhatta Journal of Mathematics and Informatics*, *8*(2), 253–260.

Orumie, U. C., & Ebong, D. (2014). A glorious literature on linear goal programming algorithms. *American Journal of Operations Research*, *04*(02), 59–71. https://doi.org/10.4236/ajor.2014.42007

Pal, B. B., & Moitra, B. N. (2003). Fuzzy Goal Programming Approach to Long Term Land Allocation Planning Problem in Agricultural System: A Case Study. *Proceedings of the Fifth International Conference on Advances in Pattern Recognition* (pp. 441–447), Allied Publishers Pvt. Ltd.

Pal, B. B., Moitra, B. N., & Maulik, U. (2003). A goal programming procedure for fuzzy multiobjective linear fractional programming problem. *Fuzzy Sets and Systems*, *139*(2), 395–405. https://doi.org/10.1016/S0165-0114(02)00374-3

Patel, N., Thaker, M., & Chaudhary, C. (2016). Study of some agricultural crop production planning condition through fuzzy multi-objective linear programming mathematical model. *International Journal of Science and Research (IJSR)*, *5*(4), 1329–1332. https://doi.org/10.21275/v5i4.nov162766

Petrovic, D., & Aköz, O. (2008). A fuzzy goal programming approach to integrated loading and scheduling of a batch processing machine. *Journal of the Operational Research Society*, *59*(9), 1211–1219. https://doi.org/10.1057/palgrave.jors.2602467

Ritu, P., & Bhambri, P. (2023, February 17). Software Effort Estimation with Machine Learning – A Systematic Literature Review. In Susheela Hooda, Vandana Mohindru Sood, Yashwant Singh, Sandeep Dalal, Manu Sood (Eds.), *Agile Software Development: Trends, Challenges and Applications* (pp. 291–308). John Wiley & Sons, Inc.

Rivaz, S., Nasseri, S. H., & Ziaseraji, M. (2020). A fuzzy goal programming approach to multi-objective transportation problems. *Fuzzy Information and Engineering*, *12*(2), 139–149. https://doi.org/10.1080/16168658.2020.1794498

Romero, C. (2004). A general structure of achievement function for a goal programming model. *European Journal of Operational Research*, *153*(3), 675–686. https://doi.org/10.1016/S0377-2217(02)00793-2

Sherali, H. D. (1982). Equivalent weights for lexicographic multi-objective programs: Characterizations and computations. *European Journal of Operational Research*, *11*(4), 367–379. https://doi.org/10.1016/0377-2217(82)90202-8

Sherali, H. D., & Soyster, A. L. (1983). Preemptive and nonpreemptive multi-objective programming: Relationship and counterexamples. *Journal of Optimization Theory and Applications*, *39*(2), 173–186. https://doi.org/10.1007/BF00934527

Singh, A. P., Aggarwal, M., Singh, H., & Bhambri, P. (2021). Sketching of EV Network: A Complete Roadmap. In *Sustainable Development Through Engineering Innovations: Select Proceedings of SDEI 2020* (pp. 431–442). Springer Singapore.

Toksarı, M. (2008). Taylor series approach to fuzzy multiobjective linear fractional programming. *Information Sciences*, *178*(4), 1189–1204. http://www.sciencedirect.com/science/article/pii/S0020025507002940

Tsai, K. M., You, S. Y., Lin, Y. H., & Tsai, C. H. (2008). A fuzzy goal programming approach with priority for channel allocation problem in steel industry. *Expert Systems with Applications*, *34*(3), 1870–1876. https://doi.org/10.1016/j.eswa.2007.02.034

Yimmee, R., & Phruksaphanrat, B. (2011). Fuzzy Goal Programming for Aggregate Production and Logistics Planning. *IMECS 2011 – International MultiConference of Engineers and Computer Scientists 2011*, *2*, 1082–1087.

Yu, G. F., Li, D. F., Liang, D. C., & Li, G. X. (2021). An intuitionistic fuzzy multi-objective goal programming approach to portfolio selection. *International Journal of Information Technology and Decision Making*, *20*(5), 1477–1497. https://doi.org/10.1142/S0219622021500395

Zimmermann, H. J. (1976). Description and optimization of fuzzy systems. *International Journal of General Systems*, *2*(1), 209–215. https://doi.org/10.1080/03081077508960870

Zimmermann, H. J. (1978). Fuzzy programming and linear programming with several objective functions. *Fuzzy Sets and Systems*, *1*(1), 45–55. https://doi.org/10.1016/0165-0114(78)90031-3

5 Data Analytics

Saaema Akhtar

National Institute of Technology, Warangal, India

5.1 DATA ANALYTICS

5.1.1 Introduction

The science of analysing and assessing information or data is known as data analytics (Singh et al., 2021). In order to provide final results and conclusions, data analytics relies on the application of statistics, computer programming, and research activities. Analytics is employed not only in business, but also in science, sports, and any other profession where huge amounts of data must be managed. Data analytics helps organizations to optimize performance, to perform more efficiently and to take the strategic decisions required to maximize profits.

Data analytics is the process of extracting insights from data and making data-driven decisions by employing data, statistical algorithms, and technology. It entails a wide range of actions, including:

1. Data collection: The process of acquiring information from various sources, such as databases, sensors, social media, and other outside sources.
2. Data cleaning: The process of cleaning and preparing data for analysis, which may include tasks such as removing duplicates, filling in missing information, and changing data into a format in which it can be analyzed.
3. Data exploration: The process of gaining an understanding of the structure, patterns, and relationships in data through the use of tools such as descriptive statistics, data visualization, and correlation analysis.
4. Data modelling: The process of developing models to assess data and predict future occurrences, such as statistical or machine learning models.
5. Data validation: The process of determining the quality and dependability of data and models through the use of techniques such as cross-validation, holdout sampling, and A/B testing.
6. Data interpretation: The process of analysing the outcomes of data analysis and presenting actionable insights to stakeholders.
7. Data visualization: The creation of pictorial imagery of data, including charts, graphics, and dashboards, to make data better understandable and actionable.

A wide range of areas, such as finance, healthcare, marketing, manufacturing, and human resources, can benefit from data analytics. As the development and gathering

 DOI: 10.1201/9781003383505-5

of data has increased, Big Data has become a crucial tool for organizations wanting to gain insights and make data-driven decisions.

5.1.2 History of Data Analytics

1940s	•The advent of predictive analytics, which involves conducting research on potential future outcomes
1970s	•Relational databases and non-relational databases; SQL and NoSQL are used to analyse the data in both types of databases.
1980s	•Due to the declining cost of hard drives, data and information are increasingly being stored in hard discs in data warehouses.
1989	•Business Intelligence is the act of identifying, gathering, and analysing an organization's previously stored data in order to arrive at decisions that are more beneficial to the firm as a whole.
1990s	•Data mining is the process of collecting many sets of data and analysing them by identifying patterns.
2000s	•Rise of HR Analytics

5.1.3 Types of Data Analytics

Analytics is classified into four main types:

Descriptive analytics – Which examines what actually occurred.
Diagnostic analytics – Which considers the causes of these events.
Predictive analytics – Which considers what is going to happen in the future.
Prescriptive analytics – Which considers what steps are to be taken next.

5.1.4 Phases of Development of Analytics

The traditional metrics was based on numbers that were indicated through basic statistical data. The evolution of metrics has resulted in the introduction of analytics.

The first phase of analytics was descriptive analytics. In descriptive analytics, the data of past decisions are analysed, and future decisions are modified in light of the findings (Kumar et al., 2022).

The second phase of analytics is diagnostic analysis. Once an issue with an organization has been identified during the descriptive stage, the problem will be diagnosed during this analytical step. For instance, if you visited the doctor, he would first inform you that you had a temperature then determining whether it was caused by a cold or an illness (Dhanalakshmi et al., 2022).

The third phase of development in analytics is predictive analytics. The predictive analytics focus on integration of the past and present data to forecast future data. This will help HR to make decisions accordingly.

Prescriptive analytics is the final stage of analytics. This can be observed in the more advanced level of HR analytics where high volumes of complex data sets are analysed to predict outcomes with a high level of certainty. This has resulted in organizations making more strategic planning ahead to face the challenges of the future.

5.1.5 IMPACT OF ANALYTICS ON THE CHANGING ROLE OF HR

In the past, HR analytics were used to keep track of activities and HR performance. By connecting these activities to company goals, the emphasis now is on improving the effectiveness of HR initiatives.

THEN	NOW
Functioning	Planned
Policies	Partnering
Administrative	Consultative
Function-oriented	Business-oriented
Reactive	Proactive
Activity-focused	Solution-focused

5.2 ANALYTICS IN INDUSTRIAL PROCESSES

The practise of gathering and analysing data related to human resources (HR) with the goal of enhancing organizational productivity is known as HR analytics. HR analytics assists HR managers in taking the appropriate steps to address problems within the firm. HR analysis can also be described as talent analytics, people analytics, and workforce analytics (Rani et al., 2023a).

5.2.1 STEPS INVOLVED IN ANALYTICS

1. The initial stage of the analytics process involves the systematic gathering of workforce information and the subsequent consolidation of this data into a centralized depository.
2. The second step is to create a dashboard to visualize the data to monitor various insights of HR metrics.
3. Build Analytical capabilities in the Analytical team through training in case of an absence of knowledge of Analytics.
4. Practicing HR Analytics for the data collected to get the final results and conclusion.
5. Take necessary actions to resolve issues that are determined in analytics for continuous improvement in organizational performance.

Analytics can also be used to improve industrial operations in a variety of ways, including:

1. Predictive maintenance: Organizations can forecast when maintenance is required by evaluating sensor data from industrial equipment, which can help to reduce downtime and increase equipment reliability (Kaur et al., 2019).

2. Quality control: Organizations can detect and diagnose quality concerns by evaluating sensor data from industrial processes, which can assist to enhance product quality and minimize expenses associated with rework or scrap.
3. Energy management: Organizations can find possibilities to reduce energy usage by evaluating sensor data from industrial operations, which can assist in cutting costs and enhancing environmental performance.
4. Supply Chain Optimization: Organizations can uncover inefficiencies and bottlenecks in supply chain processes by analysing data from supply chain activities, which can assist in improving delivery times and lowering costs.
5. Predictive modelling: Organizations can use predictive modelling to forecast future product demand, which can help in optimizing production schedules and inventory levels.
6. Real-time monitoring: By employing analytics to monitor industrial processes in real time, firms can immediately detect and resolve faults, improving efficiency and reducing downtime.
7. Root cause analysis: Organizations can identify the root causes of difficulties by evaluating sensor data and other data connected to industrial processes, which can assist in improving process stability and decreasing downtime.
8. Safety and compliance: Organizations can discover risks and compliance issues by evaluating data linked to safety and compliance, which can help in improving safety performance and minimizing the costs connected with fines and penalties.

Overall, analytics may be used to improve industrial processes in a variety of ways by giving insights that can assist firms in optimizing production, reducing downtime, improving quality, lowering costs, and improving environmental performance.

5.3   USES OF ANALYTICS IN HR PRACTICES OF INDUSTRIAL PROCESSES

Improving the hiring process
HR analytics helps in analysing the applications of fresh applicants to select the right people (Ritu and Bhambri, 2023). This can be done by building a prediction model which gives exact data points such as candidate demographics data, previous employment history, etc. This model can then be used in combination with the candidates' CV response to predict whether or not they are suitable for the organization.

Skills development analytics
The level of expertise and skills of the staff is crucial to the functioning of the organization (Berk et al. 2019). Due to the constant evolution of technology and work requirements, it is essential to establish and express core competency or capability demands. To meet the needs of the organization, employees must be capable of maintaining and acquiring new skills (Berk et al. 2010). The difficulties with regard to this situation can be overcome by providing a learning component that allows for the creation of customized learning programmes based on employee capabilities, job matrix identifiers, or the goals of the organization.

Once we have identified the required competencies for the entity, we may compare them to our current capabilities to identify gaps (Berk et al. 2010).

Use HR analytics to plan
Benchmarking can also be used to improve performance. Your company's capacity to incorporate data analysis results into its business strategy will be important. Multiple key performance indicators (KPIs) can be used by the HR department to determine the keys to employee retention or performance improvement. Ensure that the HR team has the appropriate personnel to analyse the vast amounts of HR data. HR analytics should assist you to plan for the future, rather than simply analysing facts.

HR data readily accessible to management
The management must be supplied with data and insights into what the staff needs to increase efficiency and perform at their peak. HR analytics will enable managers to readily acquire a valuable perspective on the attitudes and performance of the staff. By conducting an analysis of the KPIs, one can estimate the appropriate level of productive yield per worker. HR departments can easily identify the individuals who are struggling, the top performers, and the employees who are more likely to be satisfied when assigned to different tasks. This will help to identify the areas where the workforce can be optimized.

Analysis of employee turnover
Hiring and training qualified personnel is a costly and time-consuming endeavour. Researching staff turnover statistics will allow you to increase employee retention by improving your ability to forecast the future and make smarter decisions. Your HR management system is a potential source of relevant data; additionally, information obtained via work involvement, personnel satisfaction index, and through departure interviews can all play a key role.

Improving employee engagement
HR professionals seek to enhance employee engagement. Improving the sense of belonging of employees within the organization can enhance both morale and productivity. However, issues persist in identifying those factors that have the greatest impact on employees' work engagement and determining how to influence them most effectively. Information into the ways in which staffs are more involved based on quantitative variables such as recruiting, performance, remuneration, and perks can be provided by HR Analytics. This enables the HR department to examine strategies to increase operational efficiency. In addition to enhancing the company's culture and fostering a more conducive work environment, feedback provided throughout the evaluation process can also provide valuable information for this purpose.

Workforce Performance Analytics Integration
To succeed in your firm, you need competent, high-performing people. Workforce performance analytics provide an evaluation of individual employee performance and the insights necessary to identify the top and bottom performers, as well as those who may require more training or support to excel. Typically, human resources information systems are administered in silos, which makes them unavailable to other decision-makers inside the firm. There is, however, no requirement for this to be the case.

HR analytics with the organization as a whole

HR analytics provides a number of applications that can help the organization as a whole. This content cannot be understood in isolation. For instance, financial teams are currently deeply involved with human resources, yet they frequently lack the requisite data. Integrating HR and financial data can give crucial insights for improved decision-making and increased productivity.

You may want to investigate ways in which your HR software vendor may provide an HR data set to complement your Finance data set, which will be of substantial commercial value to the organization as a whole.

5.4   ANALYTIC TOOLS AND USES

5.4.1   ANALYTICS SOFTWARE APPLICATIONS

The use of analytics software assists human resource workers to collect and analyze data, as well as identifying crucial HR metrics. These technologies blend business and people data in order to determine the HR department's impact on business performance. HR analytics software is utilized by businesses to uncover inefficiencies, anticipate productivity, and optimize their use of personnel. These solutions provide organizations with the required knowledge to manage their human resources and increase their return on investment.

Different types of analytics software include the following:

1) R Studio
2) Python
3) Power BI
4) Tableau
5) Microsoft Excel
6) Visier
7) Qlik
8) SPSS
9) CPLEX optimizer

5.4.2   R AND RSTUDIO

R is a computer language that is available for free online use and is typically utilized to carry out numerical and statistical analysis. It offers a comprehensive collection of libraries for data analysis and visualization. R is by far the most popular choice as a HR analytics tool, since it is a programming language that excels in conducting analysis on massive data sets. This makes it possible to clean and analyse data sets that contain millions of rows. In addition, users are able to see the outcomes of the data analysis.

RStudio is an enhanced version of the R programming language which is capable of performing all of R's features. The user interface of RStudio comes equipped with a code editor, the R console, a workspace that is simple to navigate, a history log, and storage areas for plots and files.

5.4.3 PYTHON

Python is a general-purpose, object-oriented programming language that is available under an open-source licence. It offers a variety of libraries that can be used for the manipulation, visualization, and modelling of data. It is possible to use Python in place of R as the programming language of choice. However, R is superior when it comes to statistical analysis, has a community that is more engaged in the subject of statistics, and is better suited for the visualization of data. Python, on the other hand, is much more easy for new users to handle.

R and Python: Both R and Python are excellent programming languages for data research and visualization. They are frequently employed in advanced statistical analysis, machine learning, and data mining.

5.4.4 POWER BI

Power BI from Microsoft simplifies data aggregation, analysis, and visualization. Connecting to a wide variety of source systems is made incredibly easy by this software. Such source systems can include SQL databases that store data on people, a live Twitter feed, or Machine Learning APIs. After that, each of these one-of-a-kind data sources is included into Power BI (Chhabra and Bhambri, 2021). This straightforward aggregation method permits the combination of various data sources into a single, large database suitable for reporting and analysis. Power BI can be used to generate interactive dashboards and reports is Power BI.

5.4.5 TABLEAU

Tableau is analogous to Microsoft Power BI in that it also enables the consolidation and visualization of numerous data sources. The software, which was initially developed in 2003 as a commercialized outlet for research conducted at Stanford University, has caused quite a commotion in the realm of visualization. When it comes to the visualization of data, Tableau is the business intelligence (BI) solution that is regarded as the most efficient. It has been listed in the Gartner Magic Quadrant for each of the seven years in a row, starting in 2012 and continuing through 2019. Tableau's higher cost compared to rival Power BI is a disadvantage, however. Tableau: Tableau is a popular data visualization tool for creating interactive dashboards and reports. It can be used to investigate and display massive datasets, as well as to convey findings to stakeholders.

5.4.6 MICROSOFT EXCEL

Microsoft Excel has been the standard software for data analytics for decades. Every time we manually extract data from one of the HR systems, the outcome is a comma-separated values (CSV) file (Angrave et al., 2016). Excel can effortlessly open and edit these files. Excel features a basic interface and functionality that are straightforward to comprehend, which is a plus. Excel is therefore the most user-friendly HR analytical software. Excel is a popular data analysis, visualization, and reporting application. It has a wide range of applications, from simple data manipulation to advanced statistical analysis (Wirges & Neyer, 2022).

5.4.7 VISIER

Visier is a tool that compiles data in order to assist in providing answers to issues regarding the labour force. It integrates data from a variety of HR systems into a single HR BI tool by establishing connections to those systems.

In contrast to Tableau, Visier offers itself more as an actionable people analytics insights platform that displays trends in workforce data. Along with other aspects of human resources, it enables us to investigate the factors that contribute to people's high levels of performance and productivity (Shet et al., 2021).

5.4.8 QLIK

Similar to Visier, Qlik is a piece of software that compiles a large amount of data into one place. While Visier is a platform that extracts actionable insights from data about a workforce, Qlik is a more generic solution for gathering data and it includes several elements for dashboarding. As a result of this feature, Qlik is a great alternative for more broad purposes, involving the collection, storage, and dashboarding of data. Alongside Power BI and Tableau, Qlik has maintained its status as a leader in the Gartner Magic Quadrant for a number of years.

5.4.9 SPSS

SPSS is utilized in the process of data analysis, whereas Power BI, Tableau, and Qlik are utilized, for the most part, in the collection of data.

One of the most often used tools for HR analytics is SPSS, which is widely used in the social sciences. Because it is so simple to use, we are able to do data analysis even if we do not have a strong background in statistics (Margherita, 2022). Because SPSS is so prevalent in the social sciences, there are a lot of HR experts that are familiar with its use, particularly those individuals who enjoy examining facts. A greater number of people utilize SPSS outside of the social science industry than use SPSS itself (Mirski et al., 2017). On the other hand, the SPSS programming language is more difficult to master. The fact that SPSS is, in many respects, comparable to Excel makes the programme much simpler to employ (Rani, Pareek, Kaur, Chauhan, and Bhambri, 2023b).

5.4.10 CPLEX OPTIMIZER

There are many optimization tools made for analytics. CPLEX optimizer is one of these tools. Prescriptive analytics are often done with these tools. The goal of a prescriptive analysis is to find the best thing to do in a given situation. CPLEX Optimizer helps find the best business decisions out of all the billions of alternatives. It does this by offering data modelling that is both flexible and fast (Anand and Bhambri, 2018).

Among the other available analytical tools are the following:

SQL: SQL (Structured Query Language) is a popular computer language for managing and querying relational databases. It is capable of extracting and manipulating data from databases (Kalvakolanu & Madhavaiah, 2019).

SAS is a popular analytics software package that may be used for a variety of activities such as data management, data visualization, data mining, and statistical analysis.

Hadoop is a popular open-source software framework that can store large data sets and carry out analysis on them. It is frequently used in Big Data analytics.

Spark: Spark is a rapid, in-memory data processing engine that can be used to process large amounts of data. It is frequently used in Machine Learning and data mining.

Overall, the different analytics tools available serve a variety of different purposes based on the work at hand and the sort of data being studied. Excel and R/Python are excellent for basic data manipulation as well as complex statistical analysis. Tableau and Power BI are excellent tools for developing interactive dashboards and reports. SQL is excellent for database management and querying. Finally, SAS, Hadoop, and Spark are excellent for processing large amounts of data, data mining, and machine learning.

5.5 TWO COMPANIES THAT HAVE ADOPTED ANALYTICS

5.5.1 GOOGLE

Google has been able to completely reimagine their HR department because of the introduction of HR analytics into their company (Bhambri et al., 2020). They feel that HR analytics makes it possible to make more precise decisions on people management. Because of the significant impact that they have on a company's bottom line, these decisions are of the utmost importance. If a company's managers do not make decisions that are well informed, informed, and correct regarding their workforce, the company will not be able to attain better business outcomes. Even while the Human Resources team at Google (formerly known as People Operations) uses productivity indicators as a measurement of employee performance, it is important to note that these metrics do not tell the whole story. Google uses analytics in a novel and innovative approach by conducting regular polls with its staff in order to maintain and further improve the quality of the working environment. They make use of the feedback to enhance and better match various parts of their personnel procedures with the culture of their workplace. As a direct consequence of this, they enjoy a high level of worker involvement, as seen by an average participation rate of 90%, which demonstrates their success in increasing both business operations and morale.

5.5.2 JUNIPER NETWORKS

Juniper Networks, a provider of networking and cybersecurity solutions, is a firm that believes in the importance of introducing innovative strategies in order to keep up with the fast-changing HR industry. They are always considering the present status of HR management as well as their assumptions, and they make use of HR analytics in order to concentrate on the business results that they wish to attain. They are not afraid to give up on tried-and-true strategies or to rethink such approaches in order to achieve the best possible outcomes. Juniper Networks takes this a step further by analysing, with the help of Big Data, not only where the highest-performing employees come from but also where they go after they leave the company. This allows Juniper Networks to better understand its talent pool. The purpose of this research is to gain an understanding of the numerous career paths that are available in the various industries so that Juniper can build fresh and original tactics to recruit and retain present as well as future talent.

5.6 USES OF ANALYTICS FOR THE HR DEPARTMENT

The answer is clear, and it will help you stay competitive. Today, data is the primary source of any element of business; understanding how it works and effects your organization is critical to making the right decisions.

HR analytics tools are primarily concerned with performance metrics.
Analytics for recruiting.
The study of people.
Business intelligence in human resources.
Risk management for attrition.
Profiling of candidates.
Management of the risk of fraud.

With the proper use of HR analytics technologies, we can assure informed hiring procedures. Understanding the past and what is happening now allows you to make better judgements in the future. This allows HR managers to focus on choosing quality applicants while also expediting the hiring process. Employee performance and productivity can be reviewed on a continuous basis through evolving methods to maintain and increase employee performance and productivity. HR Analytics tools assist in determining which practises are most effective, how they can be applied across the firm, and what type of employee involvement should be employed. Significant budget modifications and budget decisions can be difficult to obtain management approval for, especially when the objective is to keep costs low. Using HR analytics technologies, HR departments can provide evidence of the impact of budget and strategy changes. Using HR analytics tools to assist HR initiatives gives management confidence that revenues will be achieved.

5.6.1 THE FUTURE OF PREDICTIVE ANALYTICS

Engaging in personnel well-being is crucial to ensure an organization's motivation, productivity, and success. The new people analytics direction attempts to measure the actions, experiences, and discussions that improve workplace success. Here are three key new breakthroughs in the realm of people analytics that businesses should consider.

1) **Correct perceptions of employee experience**
   In the same way that digital marketers use analytics to get a better understanding of their customers, businesses utilize people analytics to get a better understanding of how their employees experience the work environ-

ment (Fitz-Enz, 2022). Because telecommuting has become increasingly common in recent years, it is essential to have a streamlined approach that can provide an accurate picture of the workforce even without the need for face-to-face communication. Organizations no longer need to deal with assumptions or hypotheses when determining which workplace initiatives help employees perform better or remain with the company. People analytics collects data from the actual world to provide insight into the factors that inspire employee behaviour in the workplace.

People analytics also assists firms in determining when employees are suffering or becoming project roadblocks. This could be due to a lack of training, dissatisfaction with new work, the use of inappropriate instruments, or a loss of enthusiasm. There is also a possibility that they are coping with sluggish digital or workflow operations. The insights supplied also enable for a better knowledge of how employees manage their time as well as their tasks, meetings, and other forms of communication and documentation. These data can be used by organizations to figure out the causes of work stagnation and to identify what kinds of policy changes should be implemented.

2) **Informed, unbiased hiring processes**

More than 80% of those polled for the study published in the *Harvard Business Review* titled "HR Joins the Analytics Revolution" believe that talent-based insights are essential for determining how to proceed with business decisions. However, the typical recruitment manager does not have access to the data that would help them choose the most qualified individuals to recruit, raise, or transfer to a new role. Instead, individuals are required to strongly rely on their instinct, which contributes to the development of prejudice.

These irrational decisions hurt efforts to diversify the workforce and make it simpler to select individuals who are not compatible with the culture or who have poor performance. Not only does this strategy prohibit HR managers from approaching the best prospects, but it also makes it more challenging to keep the right personnel in their positions. The negative effects of uncovered and unresolved bias can be serious and extensive. This is due to the fact that talent acquisition is one of the pillars around which a successful company is built. The good news is that data-driven hiring, when properly implemented and managed, may be immensely effective in ensuring a smooth and bias-free hiring process. [Citation needed] [Citation needed] Analytics of people can be used by businesses to locate and fill in any shortages in their talent pools. Because of this, they are able to hire individuals based on performance, cultural compatibility, or a diversity of opinions.

- In the process of hiring new employees, HR can make use of people analytics to:
- Choose new employees hastily and cut down on the amount of time spent on the hiring procedure.
- Lessen the influence of subjectivity while boosting diversity.
- Uncover hidden growth options

- Choose potential employees who are a good fit for your organization.

3) **A digital transformation with a focus on people**
- The current environment of intense competition has pushed the topic of digital transformation to the forefront of the minds of a number of company and HR leaders. The vision of people analytics may guarantee that the approach to digitization is adapted to the accomplishments of the workforce if it is implemented properly.
- The labour procedures that impede workers, indicating that they must be mechanized.
- If the online technologies your employees use support the full extent of their work.
- If tools are causing employees to undertake redundant tasks. If so, some technologies must be incorporated in order to synchronize tasks or data.
- In situations where personnel need more training.

Predictive analytics is a branch of analytics that analyses data and makes predictions about future occurrences using statistical models, machine learning, and other approaches. Predictive analytics' future is projected to evolve in numerous ways, including:

1. Increased adoption: As organizations increasingly see the value of using data to forecast future occurrences, predictive analytics is becoming more broadly used across a wide range of industries.
2. Increased automation: Machine Learning and Artificial Intelligence (AI) techniques will be employed to automate the model development and prediction process in predictive analytics.
3. More complicated models: To improve predictions, predictive analytics models will grow more sophisticated, including more advanced approaches such as deep learning, reinforcement learning, and neural networks.
4. Greater integration with other technologies: To get insights from real-time sensor data and improve predictions, predictive analytics will be merged with other technologies such as IoT and blockchain.
5. A stronger emphasis on explainable AI: Greater weight will be placed on making predictive models more transparent and explainable, so that decision-makers can understand how predictions are formed and identify any potential biases.
6. Increased usage of streaming data: Predictive analytics will be applied to streaming data to produce real-time forecasts, allowing firms to respond swiftly to new information.
7. Increased use in decision-making: Predictive analytics will be employed more in decision-making to assist firms in making better decisions by giving insights into future trends and patterns.

Predictive analytics is predicted to become increasingly commonly used, automated, advanced, and integrated with other technologies in the future. As technology and data evolve, firms will be able to make better judgements and make more accurate predictions.

5.6.2 Integration of Analytics into Industrial Processes

Analytics integration into industrial processes can enable firms to increase the efficiency, productivity, and quality of their operations. Among the major ways analytics may be integrated into industrial operations are:

1. Predictive maintenance: Organizations can forecast when maintenance is required by evaluating sensor data from industrial equipment, which can help to reduce downtime and increase equipment reliability.
2. Process optimization: Organizations can detect inefficiencies and bottlenecks in industrial processes by evaluating sensor data from those processes. This can help to increase process efficiency and productivity.
3. Quality control: Organizations can detect and diagnose quality concerns by evaluating sensor data from industrial processes, which can assist to enhance product quality and minimize expenses associated with rework or scrap.
4. Energy management: Organizations can find possibilities to cut energy usage by evaluating sensor data from industrial operations, which can assist to reduce costs and enhance environmental performance.
5. Safety and compliance: Organizations can detect risks and compliance issues by evaluating data related to safety and compliance, which can assist to enhance safety performance and minimize costs connected with fines and penalties.
6. Real-time monitoring: By employing analytics to monitor industrial processes in real-time, firms can immediately detect and resolve faults, improving efficiency and reducing downtime.
7. Root cause analysis: Organizations can identify the root causes of difficulties by evaluating sensor data and other data connected to industrial processes, which can assist to improve process stability and decrease downtime.
8. Predictive modelling: Organizations can use predictive modelling to forecast future product demand, allowing them to optimize production schedules and inventory levels. Intelligent automation: Organizations can use analytics and AI techniques to automate repetitive and data-intensive jobs inside the industrial process, thereby increasing productivity and lowering the risk of human mistake.
9. Optimize resource allocation: By applying analytics, firms can enhance overall efficiency by optimizing the allocation of resources such as machines, human resources, and raw materials.

Overall, incorporating analytics into industrial processes can enable firms to increase efficiency, productivity, quality, and safety while lowering costs and downtime. It assists organizations in making data-driven decisions, identifying patterns and trends in data, forecasting potential challenges, and optimizing resources in order to improve overall performance.

REFERENCES

Anand, A., & Bhambri, P. (2018). Character recognition system using radial features. *International Journal on Future Revolution in Computer Science & Communication Engineering, 4*(4), 599–602.

Angrave, D., Charlwood, A., Kirkpatrick, I., Lawrence, M., & Stuart, M. (2016). HR and analytics: Why HR is set to fail the big data challenge. *Human Resource Management Journal, 26*(1), 1–11. https://doi.org/10.1111/1748-8583.12090

Berk, L., Bertsimas, D., Weinstein, A. M., & Yan, J. (2019). Prescriptive analytics for human resource planning in the professional services industry. *European Journal of Operational Research, 272*(2), 636–641. https://doi.org/10.1016/j.ejor.2018.06.035

Bhambri, P., Dhanoa, I. S., Sinha, V. K., & Kaur, J. (2020). Paddy crop production analysis based on SVM and KNN classifier. *International Journal of Recent Technology and Engineering, 8*(5), 2791–2793.

Chhabra, Y., & Bhambri, P. (2021). Various approaches and algorithms for monitoring energy efficiency of wireless sensor networks. In *Sustainable Development through Engineering Innovations: Select Proceedings of SDEI 2020* (pp. 761–770). Springer Singapore.

Davenport, T. H., Harris, J., & Shapiro, J. (2010). *Competing on Talent Analytics.* www.hbr.org

Dhanalakshmi, R., Vijayaraghavan, N., Sivaraman, A. K., & Rani, S. (2022). Epidemic awareness spreading in smart cities using the artificial neural network. In Alex Khang, Sita Rani, Arun Kumar Sivaraman (Eds.), *AI-Centric Smart City Ecosystems* (pp. 187–207). CRC Press.

Fitz-Enz, J. (2022). *Advance Praise for the New HR Analytics.* http://u.camdemy.com/sysdata/doc/f/fb30e8a98c5d9a85/pdf.pdf

Kalvakolanu, S., & Madhavaiah, C. (2019). *HR Analytics: The Emergence and Growth Higher Education View Project Management Issues View Project.* https://doi.org/10.6084/m9.figshare.13601357

Kaur, J., Bhambri, P., & Sharma, K. (2019). Wheat production analysis based on Naïve Bayes classifier. *International Journal of Analytical and Experimental Model Analysis, 11*(9), 705–709.

Kumar, P., Banerjee, K., Singhal, N., Kumar, A., Rani, S., Kumar, R., & Lavinia, C. A. (2022). Verifiable, secure mobile agent migration in healthcare systems using a polynomial-based threshold secret sharing scheme with a blowfish algorithm. *Sensors, 22*(22), 8620.

Margherita, A. (2022). Human resources analytics: A systematization of research topics and directions for future research. *Human Resource Management Review, 32*(2). https://doi.org/10.1016/j.hrmr.2020.100795

Mirski, P., Bernsteiner, R., & Radi, D. (2017). Analytics in human resource management: the OpenSKIMR approach. *Procedia Computer Science, 122,* 727–734. https://doi.org/10.1016/j.procs.2017.11.430

Rani, S., Kataria, A., Kumar, S., & Tiwari, P. (2023a). Federated learning for secure IoMT-applications in smart healthcare systems: A comprehensive review. *Knowledge-Based Systems, 2*(3), 110658.

Rani, S., Pareek, P. K., Kaur, J., Chauhan, M., & Bhambri, P. (2023b, February). Quantum machine learning in healthcare: Developments and challenges. In *2023 IEEE International Conference on Integrated Circuits and Communication Systems (ICICACS)* (pp. 1–7). IEEE.

Ritu, P., & Bhambri, P. (2023, February 17). Software effort estimation with machine learning – A systematic literature review. In Susheela Hooda, Vandana Mohindru Sood, Yashwant Singh, Sandeep Dalal, Manu Sood (Eds.), *Agile Software Development: Trends, Challenges and Applications* (pp. 291–308). John Wiley & Sons, Inc.

Shet, S. V., Poddar, T., Wamba Samuel, F., & Dwivedi, Y. K. (2021). Examining the determinants of successful adoption of data analytics in human resource management – A framework for implications. *Journal of Business Research, 131*, 311–326. https://doi.org/10.1016/j.jbusres.2021.03.054

Singh, A. P., Aggarwal, M., Singh, H., & Bhambri, P. (2021). Sketching of EV network: A complete roadmap. In *Sustainable Development through Engineering Innovations: Select Proceedings of SDEI 2020* (pp. 431–442). Springer Singapore.

Wirges, F., & Neyer, A. K. (2022). Towards a process-oriented understanding of HR analytics: Implementation and application. *Review of Managerial Science*. https://doi.org/10.1007/s11846-022-00574-0

6 Recent Advances on Deep Learning Based Thermal Infrared Object Tracking in Videos: A Survey

Aayushi Gautam, Santosh Kumar, and Swaran Singh

Chandigarh Group of Colleges, Mohali, India

6.1 INTRODUCTION

With reference to computer vision, visual object tracking is described as a deep learning mechanism where the object movement is traced by an algorithm. The algorithm is a tracker that predicts the future positions and additional appropriate information related to objects in motion inside a video sequence (Ciaparrone et al., 2020). One simple method to track is by applying a detection technique to an individual video frame; however, tracking is essential as it maintains the object identity in case of multiple targets.

Object tracking or visual object tracking (VOT) has been shown to be vital in various civilian and non-civilian applications, including surveillance, medical imaging, video analytics, Augmented Reality, traffic monitoring and so on. An immense amount of research has been carried out in target tracking during day; however, the issues relating to tracking during the night has also gained popularity over time (Liu et al., 2021). This has been made possible through the effective use of thermal imaging technology which not just allows a vision beyond dark but also acts as a power multiplier in several applications. Thermal cameras are exclusively used in video-surveillance frameworks as they can be deployed in weather circumstances where coloured cameras fail or produce poor results, such as during night and in the dark, or even during fog and rain. Thermal imaging has the ability to ensure the security of individuals and commodities in cities, at state lines, and within other monitored regions.

6.1.1 THERMAL INFRARED IMAGING

Thermal infrared (IR) imaging, also known as non-visible imaging, generally use IR cameras which contain sensors which are highly sensitive to wavelengths associated

DOI: 10.1201/9781003383505-6

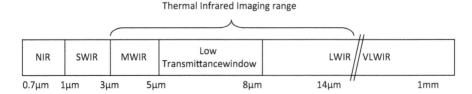

FIGURE 6.1   Infrared region in electromagnetic spectrum.

with the IR region of the electromagnetic spectrum. IR cameras detect heat emitted or replicated by the target under observation and transforms the same into heating rate, further creating an image even in low-visibility scenarios. Thermal cameras functioning in the mid-wave IR region and long-wave IR regions (Figure 6.1) rarely require supplementary heat and light sources because the sensors employed in these ranges easily record the thermal energy emitted from the object under observation. As a result, contrary to visible light cameras, they are not affected by lighting conditions, are resistant to extensive brightness fluctuations and climatic situations, and work in total darkness.

Thermal imaging sensors, however, deliver significantly fewer details in comparison to visible-light camera systems for the reason that, instead of providing the information which colour offers in the visible light band, they simply offer the observed temperature range plotted on thermograms, which usually are of significantly lesser resolution (Bourlai & Cukic, 2012). Changes in the temperature of the ambience also have an impact on the superiority of IR frames because frames are created by the heat intensity emission difference among various entities and their surroundings, therefore a greater atmospheric degree can minimize the distinction between the background and the target object. Thus, despite advances in the field, the tracking of objects in thermal video frames remains an open challenge (Dhanalakshmi et al., 2022).

6.1.2   Thermal Object Tracking

Given the initial condition of the target in the first frame, thermal infrared object tracking predicts the trajectory of the target in successive thermal IR sequences. Thermal IR frames are created by infrared radiation energy reflected into the scene. There are occasions when the appearance of a moving object in the sequence is concealed (Gautam & Singh, 2022). In such cases, when detection fails tracking works as it consists of an object's motion model and an appearance model (Bhambri et al., 2022).

Analysing and modelling the object motion is a vital element of a good tracker. Thus, a motion model which imitates the true dynamic behaviour of an entity is constructed. It predicts an object's probable position in future frames, thereby reducing the search space. A few conventional approaches have attempted to predict the motion pattern of an object; unfortunately, however, such techniques lacked the ability to anticipate rapid motion and angular variations. The majority of very precise trackers demanded a thorough comprehension of the target's visual features. More importantly, they must be able to discern between the subject and its surroundings. Visual

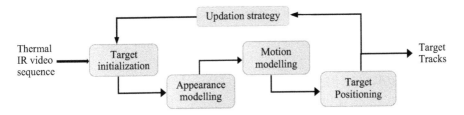

FIGURE 6.2 Major components of IR object tracking frameworks.

appearance may be adequate in single object trackers (SOT) to perform IR tracking between frames, but it is inadequate in the case of multi-object trackers (MOT). In general, all IR object trackers are made up of the segments shown in Figure 6.2.

a) *Target initialization*
 The target's initial state should always be set during this step by drawing a bounding box (BB) enclosing it. The idea is to build a BB enclosing the item in the initial video sequence, then the tracking system must estimate its location in successive frames.

b) *Appearance modelling*
 Learning procedures are used to enhance the target's visual appearance. Throughout this phase, understanding and reconstructing the visual elements associated with the moving object, such as varied viewpoints, scale disparities, and illuminations, is required.

c) *Motion modelling*
 The purpose of estimation of a motion model is to learn how to predict a zone where the subject might occur in the successive frames.

d) *Target positioning*
 The motion estimates deliver a hypothetical area in which the subject could be located, which is then inspected with the visual paradigm to determine the real target position.

Because of the scientific and industrial possibilities, infrared object tracking is gaining popularity. Although various remedies to common difficulties have been presented, it remains difficult due to features such as sudden deformations, strong occlusions, poor illumination etc. Motivated by the active research being carried on thermal imaging systems and IR MOT and SOT the major contributions of the work are as follows:

1. A comprehensive literature review which covers the recent work on thermal object tracking carried out using different deep learning models have been presented. The review has been divided in three major groups, including a review of detection-based and detection-free thermal tracking techniques, a review of single and multiple thermal objects tracking techniques and a review of object fusion based thermal tracking techniques.

2. Details of conventional and upcoming video data sets for IR tracking along with the evaluation metrics utilized to determine the detection and tracking efficiency corresponding to the model has also been investigated.

6.2   LITERATURE REVIEW

6.2.1   DETECTION-BASED AND DETECTION-FREE THERMAL TRACKING TECHNIQUES

Two principal approaches,, i.e., detection-based, and detection-free tracking (Figure 6.3) have been used to carry out thermal object tracking. In detection-based tracking using deep learning, a pre-trained detector is fed with an uninterrupted video sequence which, in turn, gives tracking trajectories based on detection proposition. The technique has been widely used as it detects the new objects and automatically terminates the disappearing one. Detection-free tracking involves the manual establishment of a predetermined number of objects in the first frame, which are then localized in subsequent frames. These trackers often fail in the cases where new objects occur in the intermediate frames.

Thermal IR frames often suffer from unwanted attributes which hinder the discriminatory features of the object of interest. Liu et al. (2017) has utilized the discriminative representation capability of a convolutional neural network (CNN) to perform thermal object tracking. An ensemble tracker based on a correlation filter having multiple convolutional layer features have been proposed. In the initial stage, a pre-trained CNN which extracts the varied features of a thermal IR object from multiple convolutional layers has been used. Further, various weak trackers corresponding to the extracted features are constructed with the help of a correlation filter. The weak trackers constructed additionally contributes to the object location response maps which have been merged to achieve better response results. Finally, an effective strategy for scale estimation has been exploited to enhance the tracking efficacy (Rani et al., 2023).

Li et al. (2019) implemented HSSNet, which is a thermal IR tracker based on a spatially ordered Siamese CNN. A Siamese CNN, which concatenates features from multiple convolutional layers, has been designed to gather the spatial and semantic information associated with the object. The network has been trained in an end-to-end manner on a visible video detection data set to acquire correlation among the matching objects. The pre-trained network is then transferred into a thermal domain to estimate the likeness between target object and its equivalent template. Eventually, the candidate which highly resembles the object being tracked has been located.

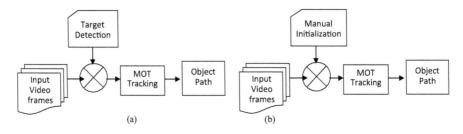

FIGURE 6.3   (a) Detection-based tracking vs (b) Detection-free tracking.

Asha & Narasimhadhan (2017) presented an IR object tracking technique which combines both generative and discriminative mechanisms. The discriminative approach utilizes AdaBoost classifier and a Kernelized Correlation Filter (KCF) to obtain the optimized locations. Of all the optimized locations, the best object location has been found using linear search technique and scale estimation has been performed using a Lucas-Kanadehomography approximation. Liu et al. (2021) achieved robust thermal object tracking using a multilayer Siamese network. Various pattern similarities have been computed to understand global semantics and local structural similarity associated with the object. The similarities act in a complementary fashion to one another, thereby enhancing the discriminative ability of the network to handle distractors (Singh et al., 2019). To integrate the structural and semantic similarities, an effective ensemble network based on relative entropy has been designed. The network, while training, adaptively learns the structural likeness and semantic weights (Kumar et al., 2022).

El Ahmar et al. (2022) introduced a new data set to perform multi-object tracking (MOT). Object tracking based on detection has been performed using transfer learning. The weights trained on ImageNet datasets have been transferred to the thermal object dataset and the efficacy of the process has been studied. To perform MOT post-detection, the ByTrack technique has been utilized, in which similarity in motion is used for feature association. Leira et al. (2021) studied a detection and tracking system for unmanned aerial vehicles (UAVs) which could be used in maritime tracking frameworks. The framework supported real-time object tracking supported by situational responsiveness on the surface of the sea. The onboard computer could georeference each target detection in order to estimate the position of the detected entities in a local north-east coordinate frame by using Machine Learning (Ritu and Bhambri, 2023). A tracking algorithm employed a Kalman filter and a uniform velocity motion model to track and estimate the position and velocity of the object based on position measurements obtained automatically by the object detection algorithm. In addition, a global nearest-neighbor method has been used to perform data association.

Krišto et al. (2020) investigated automatic tracking inside thermal frames using CNN models originally trained for RGB sequence. Faster R-CNN, Cascaded R-CNN, SSD and YOLOv3 are chosen to train for the person class belonging to a thermal data set without any actual changes in the original model. Based upon the experimentations, YOLOv3 served the base model and captured enough shape features for accurate IR object detection and tracking. X. Yu et al. (2017) presented a detection-based tracking framework which exploited online structural learning. The training of the classifier has been performed using Fourier techniques and an optimized tracking mechanism boosted the overall speed of the tracker. An effective representation of feature has been accomplished by combining motion features and histogram of gradients (HoG). Xu et al. (2010) proposed a novel forward-looking IR technique for thermal object tracking. To validate the reliability and effectiveness of the approach, a real Forward Looking Infrared (FLIR) imagery acquired from a steadily moving platform has been employed. A stationary object is recognised and tracked from a platform in motion in one of the sequences and a moving target is recognised and tracked from a manoeuvring platform in another sequences (Singh et al., 2021). Spatio-temporal intensity prediction algorithms have been used to detect objects in motion in the video frames. This data has

TABLE 6.1

Comparison of Existing Detection- Free and Detection Based Thermal Tracking Techniques

Paper	Findings	Data set	Type
Xu et al. (2010)	Spatio-temporal intensity prediction procedures used to perform detection and tracking	FLIR sequence	Detection-based tracking
Liu et al. (2017)	Ensemble tracker (MCFTS) based on correlation filter having multiple convolutional layer features.	VOT-TIR 2015 VOT-TIR 2016	Detection-free tracking
Asha and Narasimhadhan (2017)	Tracker based on combination of generative and discriminative techniques. AdaBoost and KCF and linear search utilized for final estimations.	17 IR sequences from LTIR dataset	Detection-free tracking
Yu et al. (2017)	Online structural learning-based tracking framework. Motion features and HoG features combined for effective tracking	VOT-TIR 2015 VOT-TIR 2016	Detection-based tracking
Li et al. (2019)	Tracker based on hierarchical spatially aware Siamese CNN (HSSNet). Both spatial and semantic information of object extracted.	VOT-TIR 2015 VOT-TIR 2016	Detection-free tracking
Krišto et al. (2020)	YOLOv3 used as detector to acquire initial bounding boxes, tracking performed via transfer learning.	VOT-TIR 2015, FLIR, OTCVBS	Detection-based tracking
Liu et al. (2021)	Tracker based on multi-layer Siamese network and ensemble network based on relative entropy. Enhanced discriminative abilities.	VOT-TIR 2015 PTB-TIR	Detection-free tracking
Leira et al. (2021)	Real-time detection and tracking system for UAVs based on Kalman filtering.	Self-acquired dataset	Detection-based tracking
El Ahmar et al. (2022)	MOT performed using transfer learning from ImageNet and fine tuning on ADAS.	FLIR-ADAS	Detection-based tracking

been further used as a seed to figure out the position and scale of the object in the image space. The comparison summary of above discussed techniques for thermal object tracking has been shown in Table 6.1.

6.2.2   SINGLE AND MULTIPLE THERMAL OBJECTS TRACKING TECHNIQUES

One way to categorize thermal object tracking techniques is by classifying them into single object tracking (SOT) and multi-object tracking (MOT). The trackers associated with SOT, tracks only one object, which has been initialized in the first frame even in presence of many objects in the same frame. However, in MOT all the targets occurring inside the frame are traced over time. Zulkifley & Trigoni (2018) improved the tracking potential of the FCNN-based tracker which predicted and traced the location of a single object by employing better scoring scheme and comprehensive approach for sampling. As a result, a multiple-model FCNN has been developed, which updates a small collection of fully connected layers on top of a pre-trained CNN (Chugh et al., 2021). The potential target locations are determined using a two-stage sampling method that integrates stochastically dispersed samples and aggregated foreground contour details. A total score combining appearance similarity, anticipated location, and model dependability has been used to select the best sample. To boost training accuracy even further, the samples are created using a sequence of adaptive variations based on the trustworthiness of the tracker outputs. Kadim et al. (2020) proposed a single object tracker which utilized deep learning to model the appearance of object at night.

A pre-trained CNN in conjunction with fully connected layers has been utilized which is trained in an online fashion during tracking to account for changes in appearance as the object travels. To determine the best configuration for tracking at night, diverse learning hyper-parameters associated with optimization function, learning rate, and training sample ratio have been tested. Zhang et al. (2019) discussed the problems faced during CNN-based tracking involving a limited labelled data set. To deal with the problem, frame-to-frame translation model has been proposed. The model enabled the conversion of readily available labelled RGB data to the corresponding thermal IR data. The use of both paired as well as unpaired frame translation models has also been investigated. The approach generated a huge labelled data set of synthetic thermal IR sequences which could be used for end-to-end optimum feature training to further perform tracking.

Huang et al. (2022) tackled the poor tracking performance caused due to a limited annotated data set by proposing an unsupervised deep-correlation thermal object tracking approach. Motivated by the front-reverse tracking uniformity of vigorous trackers, a novel strategy for unsupervised learning of a lightweight feature extraction network for TIR pictures has been investigated. To build the network, a Siamese correlation filter framework has been used which has been trained using quality-sensitive consistency loss per sample.

El Ahmar et al. (2022) presented a new data set for tracking multiple objects containing ground truth annotations along with images for both RGB and matching thermal IR images. The performance of TOOD and VFNET object detector has been compared separately on thermal as well as RGB frames associated with the ADAS-FLIR thermal data set. The effectiveness of transferring the weights trained on an RGB data set on to its thermal counterpart has also been investigated (Kumar, 2022). A multi-object detection-based approach that functions on thermal frames and enhances the association of data by applying active cut-off threshold on predicted bounding box has also been proposed. Kim et al. (2017) focused on the significance of VOT in the construction of a smart livestock management system. Behavioural patterns inferred from animal trajectories have the potential to provide a relevant information about the estrus cycle, disease prognosis, and so on, and thus the authors proposed a single thermal sensor-based animal tracking mechanism.

The central idea of the proposed approach is to depict the animals in the foreground by simply thresholding a thermal frame as a topographic surface, which has been extremely useful for determining the object boundary even in circumstances when they overlapped. The results of segmentation produced from morphological processes applied on the topographical surface have been further utilized for constantly updating the central position of the animal. In thermal IR tracking, the function of tracker is to track a specific object of high importance (Kumar et al., 2021).

TABLE 6.2

Comparison of Existing SOT and MOT Techniques for Thermal Objects

Paper	Findings	Dataset	Type
Kim et al. (2017)	Single-thermal sensor-based livestock management framework	Self-acquired data set	MOT
Zulkifley and Trigoni (2018)	Enhanced FCNN-based tracker using comprehensive sampling technique and scoring mechanism.	VOT-TIR 2016	SOT
Zulkifley (2019)	Siamese network and full CNN combined to form IR object tracker	VOT-TIR 2016	MOT
Zhang et al. (2019)	Frame-to-frame translation model for enhancing the labelled dataset.	VOT-TIR 2017	SOT
Kadim et al. (2020)	Online single object tracking algorithm.	Self-acquired dataset	SOT
Huang et al. (2022)	Deep-correlation unsupervised thermal object tracking framework	VOT-TIR 2015, VOT-TIR 2017	SOT
El Ahmar et al. (2022)	Active cut-off-threshold for detection-based-tracking	Thermal variant of ADAS	MOT

CNN-based trackers, which perform well on RGB frames, often fail in the case of thermal frames due to a lack of texture information and a similarity in the heating maps of two nearby objects. Thus, to eliminate the problems Zulkifley (2019) proposed a two-stream CNN tracker which combined Siamese network and full CNN in manner that each network contained a set of identical models to deal with varied changes in target appearance. To lessen the computational load, the convolutional layers are shared among both CNN streams. By superimposing the normalized scores of the two streams, a uniform dense score-map has been created. The comparison summary of above discussed single object tracking and multi-object tracking techniques for thermal objects has been shown in Table 6.2.

6.2.3 FUSION-BASED THERMAL TRACKING TECHNIQUES

Wang et al. (2021) studied the problems faced during thermal tracking in adverse situations by learning the multimodal features. Based on short-term historical data and a correlation filter, an RGBT object tracking method has been proposed. A multi-layer CNN is used to extract information from a primary object bounding box. The target has been traced individually for RGB as well as thermal modalities. Reverse tracking is then performed in both modalities. The discrepancy calculated between each pair served as an indicator of tracing efficiency for each modality. Considering the temporal continuity of frame sequence and to attain the strong fusion of dissimilar source data, the previous information has been fused into the trained weights. The experimentation has been carried out on three self-acquired RGBT data sets.

Leykin et al. (2007) presented a pedestrian classifier and a fusion tracker for coloured thermal cameras. The tracker creates a multi-modal distribution of temperatures and colours as a background model, which is a particle filter. The particle filter performs a series of reversible transformations which samples the probability space to maximize the posterior probability corresponding to the scene. A pedestrian classifier centred on periodic gait analysis after acquiring the position and measurements of moving objects is used. To distinguish people from other objects in motion such as cars, a symmetrical double helical structure in human gait has been used, which can subsequently be examined using the Frieze Group theory. The tracking results demonstrated the robustness of the framework to illumination noise and other atmospheric disturbances.

The thermal frame is often less susceptible to noisy effects; however its degree of distinguishability varies depending on the environmental changes. The solution to this has been obtained by the cognitive fusion of two different modalities. Yan et al. (2018) presented an effective approach to rationally track as well as detect saliency targets inside thermal videos. Foreground recognition in visual and thermal frames began with the extraction of a contextual information, proceeded by dual-phase background removal. While dealing with obstruction or overlaps, deductive frontward and inverse tracking have been used to distinguish discrete objects when the foreground identification failed. A publicly accessible colour-thermal standard database for target tracking and categorization in and beyond the perceptible band has been used to assess the suggested approach. T. Yu et al. (2019) proposed a vigorous tracker (RCCF-TIR), which is built using adaptive feature fusion and continuous correlation filters. An Efficient Convolution Operators framework was used initially to construct the new track. Further, the framework is equipped with an optimal set of features for TIR tracking. Finally, a novel feature fusion technique that utilized the average value of peak-to-correlation energy has been used. Experimental results on PTB-TIR and VOT-TIR 2016 indicated the tracking robustness and the accuracy of the proposed tracker.

6.2.4   BENCHMARK THERMAL DATA SETS

Experimental data is mandatory for the development and testing of any computational technique. The performance of any method can only be evaluated in reference to current knowledge. Benchmark data sets with known and verified outcomes are required for this purpose. In recent years, many benchmark data sets have been developed for thermal object tracking, which are discussed below.

(i) *BIRDSAI*:
   BIRDSAI, which stands for benchmarking IR dataset for surveillance with aerial intelligence, consists of thermal IR video sequence containing animals and humans captured under various challenging circumstances such as motion blur, scale discrepancies, camera spins, background clutter, etc. (Bondi et al., 2020). It contains 48 actual aerial TIR sequences of varied lengths that have been meticulously annotated with items such as humans and animals and their corresponding motions. The data set was acquired by the Air Shepherd, which is a conservational organization, while conducting daily flights of a fixed-wing UAV over the national parks of Southern Africa (Figure 6.4).

(ii) *CAMEL*:
   The CAMEL data set is an IR frame sequence for tracking and detection, which consists of 26 videos acquired in IR and visible domains (Gebhardt & Wolf, 2018). Ground-truth bounding boxes are included in the data set, along

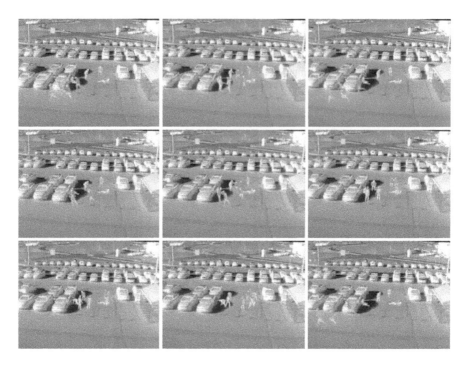

FIGURE 6.4   Frames from BIRDSAI data set.

with annotation classes, such as person, bike, car, motorbike, dog etc. Further-more, most of the IR data provided is captured from a still camera. A total of 43,022 frames are present, which were taken at very different times of day.

(iii) *LLVIP*:

The LLVIP data set is a low-light vision visible-IR paired data set contain-ing 33,672 frames (16 836 pairs), the majority of which are acquired in low-light environmental conditions, and all the frames are aligned perfectly in the spatial domain (Jia et al., 2021). All the frames are captured from a binocular camera which has both an IR and a visible light sensor. Each pair of frames is recognized and resized to maintain the same field in terms of view and dimensions. The high spatial alignment of frames makes them ideal for frame fusion and frame-to-frame translation.

(iv) *PTB-TIR*:

For the evaluation of the IR pedestrian tracker, Liu et al. (2020) developed a thermal IR pedestrian tracking data set that was comprised of 60 manu-ally annotated thermal sequences. For attribute-based analysis, each string included nine characteristic labels. Various attributes, such as thermal cross-over, occlusion, background clutter, illumination variation, low-resolution and motion blur, have been taken into account (Figure 6.5).

(v) *LTIR*:

For the short-term tracking of a single object in the IR domain, Berg et al. (2015) proposed a thermal IR data set as per VOT protocol. The benchmark

FIGURE 6.5   Frames from PTB-TIR data set.

contains a novel LTIR data set comprising of 20 IR sequences obtained from various sources and annotated in the VOT Challenge format. Sequences for the data set were gathered from seven diverse perspectives utilizing eight distinct categories of sensors. The range of the resolutions is from 320x240 to 1920x480 pixels, with certain sequences offering both 8-bit and 16-bit pixel values.

(vi) *VOT-2015*:

For evaluating the performance of short duration single IR object trackers, VOT-2015 is the first widely used benchmark (Felsberg et al., 2015). The data set considered a single sensor camera capturing a single object for a short duration and primarily consisting of an LTIR data set with 8-bit sequences. The major reason for restricting 16-bit LTIR frames is that many approaches are unable to deal with 16-bit data. Instead of illumination variation and colour changes associated with the object, dynamic and temperature deviations have been incorporated.

FIGURE 6.6   Frames from FLIR thermal data set.

(vii) *FLIR*:

The data set contains completely marked thermal and perceptible band frames that can be used to construct object detection systems with the help of convolutional neural networks (CNNs) (Bhambri et al., 2020). Consisting of 26,442 completely annotated images, it has 520,000 bounding box annotations belonging to 15 diverse object categories. A total of 7,498 video sequences are recorded at a frequency of 24Hz and containing pre-AGC frames in 16-bit format (Figure 6.6).

(viii) *OTCVBS*:

For assessing and testing the novel tracking and detection algorithms, OTCVBS is one of the most widely accessible standard data sets. The data set includes video sequences and images captured in and beyond the visible band and is open to researchers involved in all the international computer vision societies (Chhabra and Bhambri, 2021). In order to capture the data set, a camera was positioned on the rooftop of an eight-story structure. This consisted of a 300D IR sensor core with a 75mm lens. Among the frequently used databases belonging to OTCVBS data set are the OSU thermal pedestrian database, the Iris thermal and visible face database, the terravic weapon IR database, the terravic motion IR database, the OSU colour-thermal database and so on (Figure 6.7).

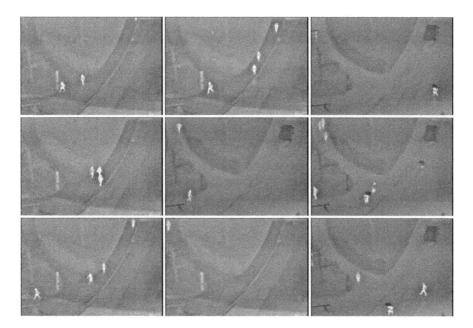

FIGURE 6.7   Frames from OTCVBS thermal data set.

6.3   PERFORMANCE METRICS

New strategies and frameworks are constantly being established, and futuristic tracking and recognition systems are emerging. One of the most critical aspects in developing an effective framework is assessing the effectiveness of that model. Different metrics are often used to estimate the performance of the model, and these measures are termed as performance metrics or evaluation metrics. Thus, in this section, performance metrics have been roughly characterized into target detection performance metrics and target tracking performance metrics.

6.3.1   DETECTION PERFORMANCE METRICS

Because numerous approaches to MOT make use of the detection-based tracking strategy, they frequently test both detection and tracking performance. Target detection metrics are thus used in MOT methods and use different parameters for evaluation. The most widely used detection performance metrics are:

a) *Precision*:
   This refers to the model's precision in detecting only relevant objects and is the ratio of true positives to total detections recorded by the model. Mathematically, this is given as Eq. (6.1). Here, TP stands for true positive and FP stands for false positives. A good model has both high precision and high recall.

$$P = \frac{\text{TP}}{\text{TP} + \text{FP}} \qquad (6.1)$$

b) *Recall*:

It is the potential of the framework to identify every single useful case, i.e., all the actual BBs (Eq. 6.2). It is the proportion of exact constructive judgments out of every possible actual judgement (Padilla et al., 2020).

$$R = \frac{TP}{TP + FN} \tag{6.2}$$

c) *Intersection over union (IoU)*:

This is a measurement founded on Jaccard's Index, which is a similarity coefficient between two sets of information. IoU estimates the overlapped region between the predicted BB and the actual BB divided by union area between the two (Eq. 6.3).

$$IoU = \frac{area\left(B_P \cap B_A\right)}{area\left(B_P \cup B_A\right)} = \frac{Overlapped\ area}{Union\ area} \tag{6.3}$$

On comparing the IoU with respect to some threshold t, the detection is classified as right or wrong. If IoU is greater that t the recognition is taken right else if IoU is less than t, it is taken wrong.

d) *Precision recall curve (PR)*:

The precision recall (PR) curve is a bartering representation of precision value and recall value at various levels of confidence. Precision and recall for an efficient framework remain high despite the confidence score fluctuations. If the confidence score of the detector is such that the false positive corresponding to it is low, the associated precision value will be high. A robust object detector is one whose precision remains high with an increase in its recall value, implying that even if the confidence cut-off shifts, recall as well as precision score will remain higher. As a result, a large area under curve (AUC) indicates higher precision as well as strong recall.

e) *Average precision* (AP):

In practical scenarios, the PR graph is frequently a zig-zagging curve, making accurate calculation of the corresponding AUC difficult. This is avoided by modifying the PR plot prior to AUC computation to eliminate the zig-zagging tendency. One of the ways to do so is by using 11-point interpolation in which the PR plot is revised by taking the maximal exactness scores in a set containing 11 uniformly spread-out levels of recall explicitly, 0, 0.1, 0.2, 0.3....1.0 as given by Eq. 6.4

$$AP@11 = \frac{1}{11}\sum_{x \in X} Y_{interp}(x) \tag{6.4}$$

where, $X = [0, 0.1, 0.2, 0.3.... 1.0]$ which signifies the recall values. Thus, average precision is defined as the value computed by using the maximal value of precision $Y_{interp}(x)$ having recall score of value higher than X.

f) *Mean average precision* (mAP):
   This metric evaluates the correctness of the target detections across various categories in each data set. It is computed as the average of AP across all the categories and is given as Eq. 6.5

$$\text{mAP} = \frac{1}{M} \sum_{x=1}^{M} \text{AP}_x \qquad (6.5)$$

where, x indicated the xth class and M denotes the sum of all the classes being assessed.

g) *Localization recall precision* (LRP):
   The widely used AP metric and PR curve are often unable to distinguish between various PR curves and lack the ability to directly measure the accuracy of localization associated with each BB. To cope up with the issues, Oksuz et al. (2018) proposed a novel metric LRP error which comprise of components associated with object localization, FN and FP rates and is computed as Eq. 6.6

$$\text{LRP}(M, Ns) = \frac{1}{Z_{TP} + Z_{FP} + Z_{FN}}$$
$$\sum_{x=1}^{Z_{TP}} \frac{1 - \text{IoU}(M_x, N_{Mx})}{1 - \tau} + Z_{FN} + Z_{FP} \qquad (6.6)$$

Here, M is the set of actual BBs, N is the set of estimated BBs, s denotes score threshold having value between 0 and 1, τ denotes IoU cut-off valued between 0 and 1, and Z_{TP}, Z_{FP}, Z_{FN} are the number of true positive, false positives and false negatives respectively.

6.3.2 Tracking Performance Metrics

Performance metrics used to compare various object tracking algorithms must exhibit two substantial properties. Firstly, they must address all the false negatives, identity switches, false positives, deviations, and fragmentations. Second, they must be monotonic and should have differentiable error types. The metrics must include data on the performance of tracker for each of the five major error categories. Some commonly used tracking performance metrics are discussed below:

(a) *Track-mAP*:
   Track-mAP compares estimates to the ground truth along a trajectory. It requires a track similarity score to be calculated between the trajectories and a threshold, with trajectories being paired only if the track similarity score is above the threshold. If TP_{tr} is the true positive trajectory, FP_{tr} is the false positive trajectory, GT_{tr} is the ground truth trajectory and g is the index, then precision and recall are given by (Eq. 6.7) and (Eq. 6.8) as

$$P_g = \frac{\left| \text{TP}_{\text{tr}} \right|_g}{g} \tag{6.7}$$

$$R_g = \frac{\left| \text{TP}_{\text{tr}} \right|_g}{\left| \text{GT}_{\text{tr}} \right|} \tag{6.8}$$

The monotonically decreasing interpolated precision is given as (Eq. 6.9)

$$\text{IntP}_g = \max\left(\text{Ph}\right) \text{such that } h \geq g \tag{6.9}$$

The track mAP score is finally calculated as the integral of IntP_g created by plotting IntP_g against R_g for all values of g.

(b) *Multi-object tracking accuracy (MOTA)*:
   This metric is the most characteristic measure which matches the maximum with human vision judgements. In MOTA, strong associations are calculated using identity switch and matching is performed at the detection stage (Luo et al., 2021). It measures three tracking errors which includes identity switch, false negative and false positive and is calculated as (Eq. 6.10)

$$\text{MOTA} = 1 - \frac{\left| \text{FP} \right| + \left| \text{IDsw} \right| + \left| \text{FP} \right|}{\left| \text{GTdet} \right|} \tag{6.10}$$

(c) *Multi-object tracking precision (MOTP)*:
   MOTP calculates the correctness of localization by averaging the intersection across all accurately matched estimates and their ground truths. Given by (Eq. 6.11), it primarily evaluates the detector localization accuracy and hence delivers little insight about the true performance of the corresponding tracker.

$$\text{MOTP} = \frac{1}{\left| \text{TP} \right|} \sum_{\text{TP}} Y \tag{6.11}$$

It aggregates the similarity score, Y, across all the TPs. MOTP and MOTA assessment criteria address intuitive tracking system attributes such as precision in localization, accuracy in detection of objects, selecting the threshold value, and tracking objects over time consistently.

(d) *Identification metrics (IDF1)*:
   This is utilized as a secondary measure on MOT Challenge as it emphasizes quantifying correlation accuracy over detection accuracy. To determine the

trajectories present, IDF1 performs a one-to-one mapping between the sets of estimated tracks and actual tracks. The ratio of successfully recognized detections to the aggregate of actual and estimated detections is defined as IDF1 (Eq. 6.12). The Hungarian algorithm chooses which trajectory is to be matched in order to minimize the summation of false positive IDs and false negative IDs.

$$
\text{IDF1} = \frac{\left|\text{ID}_{tp}\right|}{\left|\text{ID}_{tp}\right| + 0.5\left|\text{ID}_{fn}\right| + 0.5\left|\text{ID}_{fp}\right|} \tag{6.12}
$$

An improved IDF1 score reflects the overall distinct object number in a scene rather than providing information on effective detection and association. Also, it does not assess the accuracy of tracker localization.

(e) *Higher-order tracking accuracy (HOTA):*
A single amalgamated metric which estimates recognition, association along with localization is HOTA metric. In this, a one-to-one mapping between the estimated detections and true detections using IoU value or Jaccard Index given by (Eq. 6.13) is performed, along with a spatial similarity evaluation to penalize any missed or additional predictions.

$$
\text{Jaccard Index} = \frac{\text{TP}}{\text{TP} + \text{FP} + \text{FN}} \tag{6.13}
$$

In order to optimize the matching score obtained from one-to-one mapping, the Hungarian algorithm is utilized.

(f) *Average multi-object tracking accuracy (AMOTA):*
MOTA, MOTP along with IDS and F1 score belonging to CLEAR metrics, assumes that all entity paths have the same confidence, i.e. s = 1, which is an invalid hypothesis since many FP trajectories have low confidence values. Using a singular confidence level for evaluations demands substantial efforts from an individual and inhibits users from comprehending the full range of accuracy of an object tracking system. To address these issues, Weng et al. (2020) proposed two integral MOT metrics, AMOTA and AMOTP, which averages the performance of MOTP and MOTA across multiple confidence levels.

AMOTA is calculated by integrating MOTA scores obtained from all the observed recall scores and is given by (Eq. 6.14), where x denotes a specific recall value and M denotes various confidence levels.

$$
\text{AMOTA} = \frac{1}{M} \Sigma \left(1 - \frac{\text{FN}_{x+}\text{IDS}_x + \text{FP}_x}{N_{gt}} \right) \tag{6.14}
$$

6.4   CONCLUSION AND FUTURE SCOPE

This chapter has considered recent techniques which have utilized various deep learning models to perform object tracking during night in thermal IR video sequences. Infrared effects on acquisition sensors often cause non-uniformity in thermal imaging systems. IR imaging in real time is also hampered by the deficiency of texture information, colour patterns, shape information, the high percentage of dead pixels, and very unclear pixel values. Diverse treatments for the same have come up depending upon the area of application. One key challenge in IR MOT is that the performance of an MOT approach is strongly dependent on object detectors. The commonly used detection-based tracking paradigm is based on a detector which generates detection theories to guide the tracking method. A similar technique might provide tracking results with considerable performance changes if various sets of detection theories were used while the remaining components were fixed. Some methods work well in particular thermal sequences. However, when extended to other circumstances, they might not always give satisfactory outcomes. This problem can be caused by modifications in camera vision or camera position, i.e. whether it is dynamic or static.

For accurate thermal object tracking, a powerful observation model associated with the deep learning model developed to perform object detection can considerably enhance the tracking performance. More study is needed to formulate and model the object association utilizing deep neural networks. The modules, such as attention mechanism and Long Short-Term Memories (LSTMs), can also be employed to achieve enhanced tracking results.

REFERENCES

Asha, C. S., & Narasimhadhan, A. V. (2017). Robust infrared target tracking using discriminative and generative approaches. *Infrared Physics & Technology*, *85*, 114–127. https://doi.org/10.1016/j.infrared.2017.05.022

Berg, A., Ahlberg, J., & Felsberg, M. (2015). A thermal object tracking benchmark. *2015 12th IEEE International Conference on Advanced Video and Signal Based Surveillance (AVSS)*, 1–6. https://doi.org/10.1109/AVSS.2015.7301772

Bhambri, P., Aggarwal, M., Singh, H., Singh, A. P., & Rani, S. (2022). Uprising of EVs: Charging the future with demystified analytics and sustainable development. In Vikram Bali, Vishal Bhatnagar, Joan Lu, Kakoli Banerjee (Eds.), *Decision Analytics for Sustainable Development in Smart Society 5.0: Issues, Challenges and Opportunities*, 37–53. Springer Nature Singapore.

Bhambri, P., Dhanoa, I. S., Sinha, V. K., & Kaur, J. (2020). Paddy crop production analysis based on SVM and KNN classifier. *International Journal of Recent Technology and Engineering*, *8*(5), 2791–2793.

Bondi, E., Jain, R., Aggrawal, P., Anand, S., Hannaford, R., Kapoor, A., Piavis, J., Shah, S., Joppa, L., Dilkina, B., & Tambe, M. (2020). *BIRDSAI: A Dataset for Detection and Tracking in Aerial Thermal Infrared Videos*. 1747–1756. https://openaccess.thecvf.com/content_WACV_2020/html/Bondi_BIRDSAI_A_Dataset_for_Detection_and_Tracking_in_Aerial_Thermal_WACV_2020_paper.html

Bourlai, T., & Cukic, B. (2012). Multi-spectral face recognition: Identification of people in difficult environments. *2012 IEEE International Conference on Intelligence and Security Informatics*, 196–201. https://doi.org/10.1109/ISI.2012.6284307

Chhabra, Y., & Bhambri, P. (2021). Various approaches and algorithms for monitoring energy efficiency of wireless sensor networks. In *Sustainable Development Through Engineering Innovations: Select Proceedings of SDEI 2020*, 761–770. Springer Singapore.

Chugh, H., Gupta, S., & Garg, M. (2021). Image retrieval system – An integrated approach. *IOP Conference Series: Materials Science and Engineering, 1022*(1), 012040. https://doi.org/10.1088/1757-899X/1022/1/012040

Ciaparrone, G., Luque Sánchez, F., Tabik, S., Troiano, L., Tagliaferri, R., & Herrera, F. (2020). Deep learning in video multi-object tracking: A survey. *Neurocomputing, 381*, 61–88. https://doi.org/10.1016/j.neucom.2019.11.023

Dhanalakshmi, R., Anand, J., Sivaraman, A. K., & Rani, S. (2022). IoT-based water quality monitoring system using cloud for agriculture use. In Pankaj Bhambri, Sita Rani, Gaurav Gupta, Alex Khang (Ed.), *Cloud and Fog Computing Platforms for Internet of Things*, 183–196. Chapman and Hall/CRC.

El Ahmar, W. A., Kolhatkar, D., Nowruzi, F. E., AlGhamdi, H., Hou, J., & Laganiere, R. (2022). Multiple object detection and tracking in the thermal spectrum. *2022 IEEE/CVF Conference on Computer Vision and Pattern Recognition Workshops (CVPRW)*, 276–284. https://doi.org/10.1109/CVPRW56347.2022.00042

Felsberg, M., Berg, A., Hager, G., Ahlberg, J., Kristan, M., Matas, J., Leonardis, A., Cehovin, L., Fernandez, G., Vojir, T., Nebehay, G., & Pflugfelder, R. (2015). *The Thermal Infrared Visual Object Tracking VOT-TIR2015 Challenge Results*, 76–88. https://www.cv-foundation.org/openaccess/content_iccv_2015_workshops/w14/html/Felsberg_The_Thermal_Infrared_ICCV_2015_paper.html

Gautam, A., & Singh, S. (2022). Neural style transfer combined with EfficientDet for thermal surveillance. *The Visual Computer, 38*(12), 4111–4127. https://doi.org/10.1007/s00371-021-02284-2

Gebhardt, E., & Wolf, M. (2018). CAMEL dataset for visual and thermal infrared multiple object detection and tracking. *2018 15th IEEE International Conference on Advanced Video and Signal Based Surveillance (AVSS)*, 1–6. https://doi.org/10.1109/AVSS.2018.8639094

Huang, Y., He, Y., Lu, R., Li, X., & Yang, X. (2022). Thermal infrared object tracking via unsupervised deep correlation filters. *Digital Signal Processing, 123*, 103432. https://doi.org/10.1016/j.dsp.2022.103432

Jia, X., Zhu, C., Li, M., Tang, W., & Zhou, W. (2021). *LLVIP: A visible-infrared paired dataset for low-light vision*, 3496–3504. https://openaccess.thecvf.com/content/ICCV2021W/RLQ/html/Jia_LLVIP_A_Visible-Infrared_Paired_Dataset_for_Low-Light_Vision_ICCVW_2021_paper.html

Kadim, Z., Zulkifley, M. A., & Hamzah, N. (2020). Deep-learning based single object tracker for night surveillance. *International Journal of Electrical and Computer Engineering (IJECE), 10*(4), 3576. https://doi.org/10.11591/ijece.v10i4.pp3576-3587

Kim, W., Cho, Y. B., & Lee, S. (2017). Thermal sensor-based multiple object tracking for intelligent livestock breeding. *IEEE Access, 5*, 27453–27463. https://doi.org/10.1109/ACCESS.2017.2775040

Krišto, M., Ivasic-Kos, M., & Pobar, M. (2020). Thermal object detection in difficult weather conditions using YOLO. *IEEE Access, 8*, 125459–125476. https://doi.org/10.1109/ACCESS.2020.3007481

Kumar, P., Banerjee, K., Singhal, N., Kumar, A., Rani, S., Kumar, R., & Lavinia, C. A. (2022). Verifiable, secure mobile agent migration in healthcare systems using a polynomial-based threshold secret sharing scheme with a blowfish algorithm. *Sensors, 22*(22), 8620.

Kumar, S. (2022). Influence of processing conditions on the mechanical, tribological and fatigue performance of cold spray coating: A review. *Surface Engineering, 38*(4), 324–365. https://doi.org/10.1080/02670844.2022.2073424

Kumar, S., Handa, A., Chawla, V., Grover, N. K., & Kumar, R. (2021). Performance of thermal-sprayed coatings to combat hot corrosion of coal-fired boiler tube and effect of process parameters and post-coating heat treatment on coating performance: A review. *Surface Engineering*, *37*(7), 833–860. https://doi.org/10.1080/02670844.2021.1924506

Leira, F. S., Helgesen, H. H., Johansen, T. A., & Fossen, T. I. (2021). Object detection, recognition, and tracking from UAVs using a thermal camera. *Journal of Field Robotics*, *38*(2), 242–267. https://doi.org/10.1002/rob.21985

Leykin, A., Ran, Y., & Hammoud, R. (2007). Thermal-visible video fusion for moving target tracking and pedestrian classification. *2007 IEEE Conference on Computer Vision and Pattern Recognition*, 1–8. https://doi.org/10.1109/CVPR.2007.383444

Li, X., Liu, Q., Fan, N., He, Z., & Wang, H. (2019). Hierarchical spatial-aware Siamese network for thermal infrared object tracking. *Knowledge-Based Systems*, *166*, 71–81. https://doi.org/10.1016/j.knosys.2018.12.011

Liu, Q., He, Z., Li, X., & Zheng, Y. (2020). PTB-TIR: A thermal infrared pedestrian tracking benchmark. *IEEE Transactions on Multimedia*, *22*(3), 666–675. https://doi.org/10.1109/TMM.2019.2932615

Liu, Q., Li, X., He, Z., Fan, N., Yuan, D., & Wang, H. (2021). Learning deep multi-level similarity for thermal infrared object tracking. *IEEE Transactions on Multimedia*, *23*, 2114–2126. https://doi.org/10.1109/TMM.2020.3008028

Liu, Q., Lu, X., He, Z., Zhang, C., & Chen, W.-S. (2017). Deep convolutional neural networks for thermal infrared object tracking. *Knowledge-Based Systems*, *134*, 189–198. https://doi.org/10.1016/j.knosys.2017.07.032

Luo, W., Xing, J., Milan, A., Zhang, X., Liu, W., & Kim, T.-K. (2021). Multiple object tracking: A literature review. *Artificial Intelligence*, *293*, 103448. https://doi.org/10.1016/j.artint.2020.103448

Oksuz, K., Cam, B. C., Akbas, E., & Kalkan, S. (2018). *Localization Recall Precision (LRP): A New Performance Metric for Object Detection*, 504–519. https://openaccess.thecvf.com/content_ECCV_2018/html/Kemal_Oksuz_Localization_Recall_Precision_ECCV_2018_paper.html

Padilla, R., Netto, S. L., & da Silva, E. A. B. (2020). A survey on performance metrics for object-detection algorithms. *2020 International Conference on Systems, Signals and Image Processing (IWSSIP)*, 237–242. https://doi.org/10.1109/IWSSIP48289.2020.9145130

Rani, S., Kataria, A., Kumar, S., & Tiwari, P. (2023). Federated learning for secure IoMT-applications in smart healthcare systems: A comprehensive review. *Knowledge-Based Systems*, 110658.

Ritu, P., & Bhambri, P. (2023, February 17). Software effort estimation with machine learning – A systematic literature review. In Susheela Hooda, Vandana Mohindru Sood, Yashwant Singh, Sandeep Dalal, Manu Sood (Eds.), *Agile Software Development: Trends, Challenges and Applications*, 291–308. John Wiley & Sons, Inc.

Singh, A. P., Aggarwal, M., Singh, H., & Bhambri, P. (2021). Sketching of EV network: A complete roadmap. In *Sustainable Development Through Engineering Innovations: Select Proceedings of SDEI 2020*, 431–442. Springer Singapore.

Singh, S., Sharma, M., Khosla, D., Palta, P., Gupta, A. K., Sharma, T., & Goyal, S. (2019). A novel approach for deblurring colored images using blind deconvolution algorithm. *2019 5th International Conference on Signal Processing, Computing and Control (ISPCC)*, 108–113. https://doi.org/10.1109/ISPCC48220.2019.8988325

Wang, Y., Wei, X., Tang, X., Shen, H., & Zhang, H. (2021). Adaptive fusion CNN features for RGBT object tracking. *IEEE Transactions on Intelligent Transportation Systems*, 1–10. https://doi.org/10.1109/TITS.2021.3073046

Weng, X., Wang, J., Held, D., & Kitani, K. (2020). 3D multi-object tracking: A baseline and new evaluation metrics. *2020 IEEE/RSJ International Conference on Intelligent Robots and Systems (IROS)*, 10359–10366. https://doi.org/10.1109/IROS45743.2020.9341164

Xu, J., Ikram-Ul-Haq, Chen, J., Dou, L., & Liu, Z. (2010). Moving target detection and tracking in FLIR image sequences based on thermal target modeling. *2010 International Conference on Measuring Technology and Mechatronics Automation*, 715–720. https://doi.org/10.1109/ICMTMA.2010.459

Yan, Y., Ren, J., Zhao, H., Sun, G., Wang, Z., Zheng, J., Marshall, S., & Soraghan, J. (2018). Cognitive fusion of thermal and visible imagery for effective detection and tracking of pedestrians in videos. *Cognitive Computation*, *10*(1), 94–104. https://doi.org/10.1007/s12559-017-9529-6

Yu, T., Mo, B., Liu, F., Qi, H., & Liu, Y. (2019). Robust thermal infrared object tracking with continuous correlation filters and adaptive feature fusion. *Infrared Physics & Technology*, *98*, 69–81. https://doi.org/10.1016/j.infrared.2019.02.012

Yu, X., Yu, Q., Shang, Y., & Zhang, H. (2017). Dense structural learning for infrared object tracking at 200+ frames per second. *Pattern Recognition Letters*, *100*, 152–159. https://doi.org/10.1016/j.patrec.2017.10.026

Zhang, L., Gonzalez-Garcia, A., van de Weijer, J., Danelljan, M., & Khan, F. S. (2019). Synthetic data generation for end-to-end thermal infrared tracking. *IEEE Transactions on Image Processing*, *28*(4), 1837–1850. https://doi.org/10.1109/TIP.2018.2879249

Zulkifley, M. A. (2019). Two streams multiple-model object tracker for thermal infrared video. *IEEE Access*, *7*, 32383–32392. https://doi.org/10.1109/ACCESS.2019.2903829

Zulkifley, M. A., & Trigoni, N. (2018). Multiple-model fully convolutional neural networks for single object tracking on thermal infrared video. *IEEE Access*, *6*, 42790–42799. https://doi.org/10.1109/ACCESS.2018.2859595

7 Heuristics to Secure IoT-based Edge Driven UAV

Hemant Kumar Saini
Chandigarh University, SAS Nagar, India

Kusumlata Jain
Manipal University, Jaipur, India

7.1 INTRODUCTION

The increased desire to connect smart devices to the internet, the Internet of Things (IoT) has emerged. These IoT devices sense the outside world and quickly disseminate the information over the internet. Each IoT device is granted a unique IP address, facilitating the direct sharing of sensitive information that is of the utmost significance for security purposes.

In contemporary times, there has been a notable increase in the growth rates of the unmanned aerial vehicle (UAV) population through various sectors pertaining to the youth demographic. UAV are incorporated into numerous modern IoT applications. This growing number of UAV generates a large amount of Big Data. However, processing this large data at several edges is becoming a new critical challenge. According to a recent Cisco report more than 70 billion applications, organizations and government sectors were predicted to become connected by 2025 (Ara et al., 2017). Over the course of the past few years the use of new autonomous vehicles has spread to almost every industrial sector. Due to the flexibility and portability of this technology, this has attracted various IoT applications with superior functionality, which have made it responsive to scalable architecture. One such proven case was observed during the COVID-19 pandemic. UAVs have made a significant contribution to the continuation of modernization, such as smart homes, smart cultures, the so-called smart industries (Industry 4.0) and smart traffic. Since transmission protocols are now under development for the identification and motility of the UAV in order to allow it to contribute in a critical fashion to the communication network which will guarantee improved reliability, primarily these protocols provide the more flexible stretchy transmission service in the susceptible locations where no connectivity was available. The use of IoT sensors has facilitated the seamless integration of UAVs inside the peripheries of ad hoc networks. Although the centralized systems are easy to deploy, they are constrained by the high failure risks since the data can be easily leaked and there are also delays in accessing the data. Due to the latency observed in data processing, IoT devices are experiencing delays. Locally oriented approaches have arisen as a means of addressing the aforementioned concerns.

DOI: 10.1201/9781003383505-7

However, it is imperative to exercise caution in the ownership and management of IoT devices to increase their efficiency. Accordingly, UAVs have been deployed at network edges to store and process the data from IoT ecosystems. Considering the energy consumption in fixed architecture, UAVs have proved to be the best solution since they have ultra-low latency and flexible support in Big Data processing enhancing versatility and concealing large data with better transport. By leveraging the integration of UAVs and IoT at the periphery, it is possible to identify optimal unexpected settings, such as forested landscapes. Moreover, this combination aids the traditional fixed edge system in a cheaper way, but the computation would be adapted by the distance travelled by UAVs (Rani et al., 2021).

But when the IoT hardware devices are fastened to the edges, the device will be physically secure. It is not possible solely with software, hardware alone will be insufficient to secure the overall network. It is mandatory to use the corrective measure for the edge security, but also evolve the approach that requires the more and more flexible design and architecture. Blockchain is one approach to maintaining safety levels for the edges of IOT-driven UAVs (Fotouhi et al., 2020). The UAVs store their data in a chain of blocks so that if any one block is hijacked, the others will remain secure. Government agencies now also participate in the 5G infrastructure to deploy such architecture, meaning that UAVs are increasingly under their control. Despite the existence of a potential solution, UAVs located at the periphery continue to have challenges related to network performance (Ritu and Bhambri, 2022).

Since the IoT has become increasingly ubiquitous in today's technology, this has led to the development of the new concept of UAV-compatible IoT edges. Furthermore, the security concern expressed by the government has served as a catalyst for the proposal of heuristics aimed at enhancing security measures. In addition, the objective of fostering a sustainable economy has been incorporated into our government's agenda. This chapter explores the architecture of UAV-driven contours in the IoT ecosystem making use of different security improvements. However, no aspect of security has been measured yet. In this chapter, several surveys reveal the critical challenges at the edges and drive the IoT heuristics. This chapter primarily examines the practical and contemporary necessity for investigating in edged UAVS, with a specific focus on how AI-based paradigms excel in enhancing the autonomy of edged networks. (Rachna et al., 2022).

7.2   IMPACT OF THE IoT DRIVEN EDGE

It has been observed that the edges within the Internet of Things (IoT) ecosystem are increasingly functioning as service stations. Consequently, a significant challenge arises in terms of resource allocation for data provision from these edges. The performance delays associated with this process can have a detrimental impact on delay-sensitive applications. He has outlined an A3C (Asynchronous Advantage Actor-Critic) method for a delay-sensitive algorithm to alleviate the delays. Another study (Rachna et al. 2022) finds the new role for edges to cut the load of central cloud computing, in which the deep learning-based edge computing system pre-processes the necessary data at the edge of the edge processing layer.

This is then sent to the cloud, which will reduce the computational overheads as well as meaning that the data are transmitted without delays. In this way, it enhances the quality of service by a number of UAVs connected to various locations....

Sangwan et al. (2021) declares that the cloud computing is not yet up to the mark with regard to coping with the new technology of IoT, which has connected the complete world over the internet with real-time applications such as gadgets, smart devices, UAVs etc. Accordingly, it proposed a virtualization concept which will separately decouple the hardware with different paradigms and can run many virtual components on the same hardware. This will integrate several virtualization techniques, and develop new edge-based architecture.

In another contribution, Bhambri et al. (2021) proposes a situation where the action-dependent heuristic and critical Q-learning is fabricated. This uses the reinforcement learning classifier, which includes policy iteration (PI) and value iteration (VI) to sustain the performance of the edges. This methodology is suitable for benchmarking the performance edge (Sangwan et al., 2021). The IoT survives just about anywhere in the world. And this sustain the largest growth in terms of sensorized data where the IoT traffic loads this data to the clouds via last edge points (Bhambri et al., 2021). But this process produces the latency in data processing and the other risk concerns their security at the edges. This is important because the edges are nothing but types of hardware, which can easily be compromised. This leads to the introduction of a new and innovative research idea of transferring the processing burden to the edges that reduces the economy to the center that is subject to vulnerability. The proliferation of UAVs within the framework of the IoT can be attributed to the global shift toward miniaturization. Henceforth, there are a number of increasing challenges. An integration of IoT with this new edge approach transforms the society in innumerable ways, including the following:

- It helps ensure the quality of medical care through the establishment of more intelligent data centers.
- The purpose of power harvesting pertains to the current emerging trends in IoT ecosystems, which aim to facilitate the reduction of power consumption in edge processing.
- UAVs use intelligent transportation to reduce fuel consumption and create the world of driverless transportation.
- Another field is that of smart data-driven agriculture which empowers the farmers in planting and lowering agricultural expenses which impact the ecosystem.
- The concept of Digital Twin encompasses a virtual representation that serves to enhance and facilitate the execution of a business strategy.
- Using the IoT analytics tracked from the edges in distributed data centers where data from "things" is being generated.

7.3   CURRENT IoT MARKET TRENDS SUPPLYING UAV EDGES

The current markets get the data driven at the edges with the UAV, which is the most revolutionary technology. The advent of driven drone technology has enabled the development of driverless and extremely mobile drones, which has, in turn, led to a growing market demand for data processing capabilities. However, this trend also raises concerns via data security, as the reliance on edge computing introduces potential vulnerabilities.

The Growing IoT-Enabled Edge Device. In the survey of allied Markey IoT generates the economy to about \$9,096.00 million in 2020 which will be increased to approximately \$59,633.0 million by 2030, by which time nearly the entire world will have integrated into automation and intelligence. One example of this productive approach led to 60% more data breaches at IBM in 2021. These data breaches can be prevented by the proactive prevention of attacks. The global emergence of pandemics has led to a significant shift toward cloud computing, making the relevance of edge computing increasingly difficult to overlook due to its substantial impact.

7.4 ARCHITECTURE OF THE IoT EDGE

Peripheral computing is the main technique which can treat the data at its end and then transport it to the central area. Edges are to be sufficiently secured so that data should not be breached. But with the integration of IoT with the devices, the devices are now vulnerable to internet and consumer privacy is at risk. While creating ubiquitous clouds, there is a push into on-board computing outside the network that is more focused on the security challenges involved. These edges run the Docker (software component) based applications with the intelligent IoT acoustic analytics to capture the data. Mainly underlying in a business model where the IoT edges better understand the public assets and decide wisely (Rani et al., 2023). This enables UAV edges, which involves distributed architecture where the integration of IT infrastructure converges with operation technology. They work harmoniously and connects edge devices.

In Figure 7.1, a high-level layout of edge computing architecture is depicted which includes various layers such as:

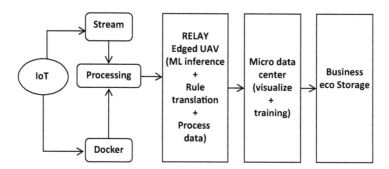

FIGURE 7.1   UAV based edge architecture.

- Edge devices: IoT has been integrated into unmanned vehicles analyses inference in real time. With the perspective of economic growth, however, it has limited computational resources.
- Edge servers: UAV edges are installed by the servers to deploy the apps so that it can maintain a pulse on the plethora of UAVs, and if some inferencing is still needed, then the data are shared to these servers for further analysis. These are supported in various remote locations, such as factory, retail shop, hotel, distribution center, or banks.
- Edge Cloud: With the advent of 5G technology, cloud computing is suddenly expanding across the globe. Telecom industries make their own edge networks and thus reduce the latency and bandwidth with the network models for the analysis.

7.5   SECURITY CHALLENGES TO UAV EDGES

To combat the attacks it is necessary to first identify the attack surfaces; one way for detection to occur is the threat modeling, in which the solution team tries to find the vectors in the designing (Fan et al., 2013). When the threat detection process is implemented, it can be attenuated by a security model. With the IoT baseline architecture, there are four typical threat areas: (1) devices, (2) field gateways, (3) cloud gateways, and (4) services. Each zone required a different scenario to protect as such; the device zone needs to be safe from physical tampering.

While UAV-based edges in comparison to the typical cloud-based era, UAVs devour physical access. Given that the IoT-UAV is not deployed at the centers, these locations present an open vulnerability for data centers, as the vehicle can be readily compromised, leading to potential negative impact on the data. Furthermore, a loophole has been observed as a result of the present use of commodity technology in these instances. Since everyone concentrated mainly on the strategies implemented by the invaders. But this is limited to skills. To properly get the exploited vehicle one must find the nefarious attackers who spoof malicious code and inject their own data into edge devices. By means of the implanted code, the process of retrieving the identity from the aircraft is facilitated.

Another approach of compromising the devices at the software level where the invader tamper the edge by signing the code against the trusted which will authenticate them by siphoning off the attack. Henceforth, the traffic path should be encrypted and secured. One final case involves the plain data residing on the edges which is to be encrypted. Because it is not safe to totally depend on the hardware for security. The world of interconnected IoT is particularly complex in nature and intruders try to gain the advantage of the adversary, which might have catastrophic consequences. Some such attacks include the Mirai botnet exploit the IoT devices; again, in August 2019 Microsoft attackers exploited printers, and video-encoders; finally, in December 2021 Microtik routers were exploited. With the growing pervasion of IoT operations, mostly data carried over the two internets at the edge devices like mobile, sensors etc. Since they are fairly inexpensive, they are utilized for various purposes of communication at edges. This chapter also develops the pitfalls and security risks in IoT integration technology with on-board drones and various countermeasures to solve them.

7.6 PITFALLS IN IoT EDGES

Most pitfalls occurred due to the high volume of transmissions through the devices which are not updated according to emerging technology and some are challenging due to manufacturer policies that make devices without any policy at low costs. Challenges of this kind included:

- Not every manufacturer follows security policy.
- Software updates are not installed on time.
- The proliferation of the market makes it impossible to patch up all devices, with older ones being particularly vulnerable.
- Very few IoT security standards are tailored for IoT devices.

The newly supported IoT-edged UAVs have encountered several obstacles. One significant challenge is the limited availability of Internet connectivity at the edges, resulting in a luck of updates for these UAVs. Additionally, the deployment of these UAVs has been hindered by civic activities, particularly in terms of adequate planning. These limitations have led to security vulnerabilities (Granjal and Silva, 2020). Since it is not supervised in any manner so the edge devices as UAV hardware can be easily susceptible to attacks (Ali et al., 2018).

There are numerous ways in which the above challenges can be tackled. One is to adapt the standard security protocol at edges; traffic monitoring can also be enforced. In the following sections, we will discuss some of the case studies for security approaches.

AAIoT: Standards-Based IoT Security. At present, there are no such endorsements for the confidential in IoT applications. Recently, an internet engineering task force (IETF) designed a protocol, which thus termed Authentication and Authorization for Constrained Environments (ACE), but it is also unable to deal with tactical scenarios (Bhambri et al., 2022). For such compatibility an "Authentication and Authorization for IoT Devices (AAIoT)" moderated, which bridges the two gaps of the old ACE protocol: (1) bootstrapping client and device credentials; and (2) authorization revocation for compromised devices.

Bootstrapping of Credentials (Lehong, 2019). Due to the heterogeneity of IoT devices credentials will be exchanged between the devices which is again a risk of impersonation by any device as a human attacker can impersonate the device in the network adhere to exchange the credentials. In order to enhance the security of a nine-coded QR code created by each device for credit exchange, it is advisable to employ a pairing mechanism with a pre-shared key (PSK) as described within the QR code. This approach ensures a higher level of security (Roman et al. 2018b).

Agreement Revocation. Another concept of the ACE protocol is agreement revocation, which allows devices to be paired in the same way as in bootstrapping through a one-time authentication procedure (Bhambri et al., 2023). However, if the IoT enables UAV, it does not receive any calls for a long time and eventually disconnects, posing a new problem in identifying the edge device in the network (Yuchang et al., 2021). When a device is not monitored and becomes compromised, and the edges are then activated on demand by extending the timer, it is critical to prevent all other

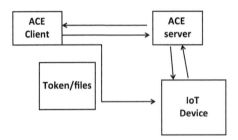

FIGURE 7.2   Token based architecture of the AAIoT prototype.

devices from connecting to the compromised device. To defend against such a scenario, ACE is followed by token-based revocation, as shown in Figure 7.2.

In a similar vein, KalKi, a runtime enforcement IoT security strategy, was developed despite the fact that adding new IoT devices to the mix of already existing ones
would raise the likelihood of further unlatched vulnerabilities. The chance of malicious code being embedded in the gadget during production would be a supply chain
risk, but many commonplace devices, including the UAV, may be dealt with in the
public sphere for quick replies. The KalKi platform was made available as a defence
against outside threats.

A more flexible and secure SDN-based interface between hardware and the network is KalKi. The definitions of a policy are updated to take use of its flaws and
vulnerabilities in order to provide this protection. The KalKi system has the ability to
be customized to reflect new vulnerabilities and recognizes threats (Echeverría et al.,
2020).

To maintain security for various modes in normal, suspicious, and under-attack
states, it features many µboxes. In addition, it is adaptable enough to use various
architectures to counter threats and simple enough to scale to a number of edge
devices without any deterioration in performance.

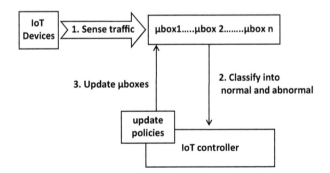

FIGURE 7.3   Defending mechanism of KalKi: (a) Monitoring sensor-based data, (b) µboxes
analysis of traffic, (c) policies µboxes updating devices to secure device, and (d) µboxes updates
the security postures on demand are the mechanisms of the SDN-based Kalki platform.

7.7 VARIOUS IoT EDGE ROLE APPLICATIONS

UAVs explores the majority of the areas where IoT devices have been used to improve performance.

7.7.1 AUTONOMOUS VEHICLES

UAVs cover almost all tasks in this environment. They rely on the prime edges in real time to be safe and reliable. However, the mobility and Internet connectivity of IoT-enabled vehicles might pose challenges when transmitting the data they generate to the cloud without any significant delays that may compromise safety. The volume of data that these vehicles amass is staggering.

7.7.2 SMART CITIES

At the moment, cutting-edge devices such as UAVs are becoming increasingly common. This edge supports the hotspots for transforming the data publicly by adjusting real-time ground conditions (Gao et al., 2019). This has become one of the most significant methods for detecting network congestion and rerouting traffic. Furthermore, these edge devices provide instant responses in civic areas where power grids and public infrastructure are required to sustain real human life.

7.7.3 STRONGER SECURITY

The environment employs these edges to increase security through video surveillance and biometric scanning when data is needed in real time with authorizations, since the edges in both commercial and consumer aspects can be strengthened (Sun et al. 2019). When optical technology is used in any company to secure the entrances to rooms or entire buildings, the records of employees' biometrics are held at the edge nodes.

7.7.4 HEALTHCARE

Medical information from various healthcare systems, from numerous medical devices, and from patients themselves has been taken into account. Yet all of this data is processed at various edges, which reduces congestion and investigates storage possibilities. In this situation an IoT-based UAV device evaluates the data so as to decide which should be kept and which should be thrown away. As an illustration, consider cardiac equipment, where the edge device could gather the data and compare it to the standard data, quickly alerting the user if anything abnormal was noted. Real-world success stories show that medical robotic surgery can be employed where it will be used most creatively.

7.7.5 MANUFACTURING AND INDUSTRIAL PROCESSES

The data on each connected device must be transferred to the centralized server because the industrial IoT links a significant number of devices in manufacturing facilities (Anand and Bhambri, 2018). Yet, within this setting, transmitting data to the centralized server has a considerable cost impact on computation. The idea of edge computing was introduced to the program to reduce power processing computing since data traversal is considerably more expensive (Gubbi et al., 2013). Also, with the new integration of IoT cars at the edges, numerous projects in the areas of smart manufacturing, intelligent operation, and energy improvements in plants and production units have been carried out (McSherry & Talwar, 2007).

7.8   THE BEST HEURISTICS TO SECURE UAVS AT EDGES

Security is necessary in IoT devices to ensure the protection of the data that is transferred between the edges and the IoT devices (Bhambri et al., 2020). Secure socket layer (SSL) and transport layer security (TLS) are used by hypertext transfer protocol (HTTP) to secure communication over the internet. Because TLS is linked to TCP, it supports authentication, integration, confidentiality, and so on, whereas Datagram Transport Layer Security (DTLS) supports the same security (M. Du et al., 2018). With the increased vulnerability potential, the Institute of Electrical and Electronics Engineers (IEEE) declares that edge processing is more secure than central processing. IEEE recommends the prevention of malicious attacks at the edges, which are safer than the core network. To keep your data secure, you must understand how to use IoT devices at the edge (Nia and Jha, 2016). The following are among the techniques for persuading the security edge:

i.   *End-To-End Encryption*: Since the IoT ends with a number of endpoints that might be vulnerable, the sensitive data has to be encrypted with a key that must be kept protected.
ii. Because technology is constantly evolving and one cannot predict every future change, the compatibility constraint of software components, which could increase security, includes the compatibility of software components for future trends.
iii. Since IoT moves into every place, there will be a need for an extra encryption policy, which is a key or token kept in safe hardware or software that should not be connected to the internet. Through such means, it can be ensured that there are fewer chances of compromising the keys. Keys can be of any combination, such as biometric, password, etc. (Michailidis and Vouyioukas, 2022).
iv. An edge device such as a UAV should run only the particular services that are necessary, leaving behind the unnecessary ones. Because protected applications can securely communicate over the internet within their own environment they can only do so for the purposes for which they were designed. Here, the IoT UAVs are not interacting with any other platform. Monolithic solutions are deployed to secure the edges with physical security features (He et al., 2018).
v.   *Edge protection vulnerabilities*: Because end users' data, which is collected from various ubiquitous sources, requires protection, it is necessary to achieve differential privacy, k-anonymity (Kewei Sha et al., 2020), and

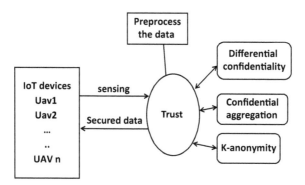

FIGURE 7.4   Edge-based privacy-preserving design.

privacy-preserving aggregation at the end edges. In this scenario, IoT devices first query for the data, then the edges process them and respond, supplying the IoT applications with privacy-preserved data, as illustrated in Figure 7.4.

A lightweight privacy-preserving data aggregation (LPDA) plan is organized at the end point (Ranaweera et al., 2021), where the IoT-assisted UAV devices process the data with a Message Authentication Code (MAC), which is a one-way secure function. Once the connected devices are validated by comparing the aMAC codes, they are aggregated into the environment.

The next step was to use cryptographic techniques such as homomorphism Paillier encryption, the Chinese Remainder Theorem (CRT) (Bithas et al., 2019), and one-way hash chain techniques to solve false data reports in the IoT environment. Furthermore, to understand privacy preservation, the LDPA incorporated differential privacy techniques (Mehta et al., 2020).

Similarly, the Output Perturbation (OPP) method outperforms the Object Perturbation (OJP) method, where the Laplacian random noise was not marked up to date to obtain the correct output value (Lu et al., 2017), and the OJP yields significantly improved solitude results. Moreover, a privacy-aware scheduling algorithm based on edge computing was proposed (Roman et al., 2018a). The deployment focuses on executing various tasks with varying privacy settings on various servers (Kumar et al., 2022).

vi. Enterprises must ensure that any change in the technical component will result in vulnerability, so they must update their patches, the information of which must be shared among the owners in order to maintain supply chain management (SCM) procedures (Ansari and Sun, 2016).

vii. Establish a high level of confidence in the IoT security chain, where the framework includes the devices, gateways, and appliances, which need to be updated with patches and adapted to new changes (Kothandaraman et al., 2022). According to the Internet Consortium's security framework, the trust chain includes:

  a) To ensure the system's security, there should be no unauthorized disclosures or alterations that would destroy the information.

b) To make the system safe, the IoT devices should run without posing any threats.

c) The assurance of the device's availability is referred to as reliability.

d) Resilience should be achieved while providing an automatically altered solution when the fault process occurs.

viii. AWS IoT Greengrass (Sodanapalli et al., 2021) is a smart handle integrated module that includes Machine Learning classifiers to filter malicious traffic, authorization modules for device pairing, and an access module for validating data and analyzing the vulnerability in a protected manner.

ix. Since the intruders are working to find the vulnerabilities, it is necessary to patch all the edge devices as soon as the vulnerability is found to stop the attacker's entry.

x. Since the multiple edged UAV devices are communicating in an unencrypted way due to the overheads involved in such synchronization, this should be transferred over the cryptographic mechanism, where the entropy of attacks would be dropped by the encryption key.

xi. A novel secure heuristic of famous public key cryptography, RSA (Rivest–Shamir–Adleman), is used to encrypt the data at edged UAVs where they use the public key of the receiver UAV, which becomes more secure when the data received is decrypted with its own private key. Pseudo-random number generators (PRNG) were used to generate the key with large sizes but were not sufficient; hence the Trusted Platform Module (TPM) (Sharma et al., 2019) is integrated to secure the source of entropies (keys, certificates, device passwords, entropy, etc.).

xii. Due to the conversion of cryptographic functions, however, the communication suffers from latency issues in the network; hence, the cryptographic function was being replaced by the real-time PRINCE algorithm.

xiii. Multi-factor authorization has been adapted with the combination of authentication procedures, soft tokens, phone verification, etc. to more effectively thwart the attacks.

xiv. Use automated AI holistic approaches to analyze anomalous behavior in sensed data logs. Snort and YARA are the most commonly used security monitoring tools when a mobility-based device, such as an UAV, requires additional security.

xv. The various edge points are separated on the basis of different functionalities by instituting network segregation, so that an attacker's penetration, if invoked at one edge, cannot penetrate the entire network.

xvi. Another paradigm ensures the validation of the secured edge device, which is typically mobile, such as UAVs. When the device boots to detect flight, it must validate the kernel signature using the TPM that stored the signatures. If an edge point is attacked, the signatures will not match.

7.9 CONCLUSION

The IoT world is increasing tremendously with the proliferation of edge-based UAV devices. Due to the proliferation of easily available UAVs, which can be purchased relatively cheaply, the risk of attacks widens. To reduce the risk of penetrations in the future, all manufacturers, network defenders, ISPs, security researchers, and cyber security zones will have to collaborate in a secure ecosystem. As the world is connected through IoT, the attackers have also developed their infrastructure for their forthcoming attacks for espionage purposes. Attackers try either to degrade the legitimate services or to compromise the data. Therefore, different heuristics are needed to be deployed, which help in signing the devices with the validated mechanism and determining when these might be compromised. To mitigate the risks, various encryption strategies have been deployed, which are the subject of discussion. Nevertheless, IoT-enabled UAV-edged devices are becoming a new way to attack the IoT ecosystem, which opens the way to new realistic challenges.

REFERENCES

Ali Z, Hossain MS, Muhammad G, Ullah I, Abachi H, Alamri A (2018).Edge-centric multi-modal authentication system using encrypted biometric templates, *Future Generation Computer Systems*, 85: 76–80.

Anand A, Bhambri P (2018). Character recognition system using radial features, *International Journal on Future Revolution in Computer Science & Communication Engineering*, 4(4), 599–602.

Ansari N, Sun X (2016). Edge IoT: Mobile edge computing for the internet of things, *IEEE Commun. Mag*. 2016, 54: 22–29.

Ara A., Al-Rodhaan M., Tian Y., Al-Rodhaan A (2017). A secure privacy-preserving data aggregation scheme based on bilinear ElGamal cryptosystem for remote health monitoring systems, *IEEE Access*, 5: 12601–12617.

Bhambri P, Dhanoa IS, Sinha VK, Kaur J (2020). Paddy crop production analysis based on SVM and KNN classifier, *International Journal of Recent Technology and Engineering*, 8(5): 2791–2793.

Bhambri P, Singh M, Dhanoa IS, Kumar M (2022). Deployment of ROBOT for HVAC duct and disaster management, *Oriental Journal of Computer Science and Technology*, 15, 1–8.

Bhambri P, Singh M, Jain A, Dhanoa IS, Sinha VK, Lal S (2021). Classification of gene expression data with the aid of optimized feature selection, *Turkish Journal of Physiotherapy and Rehabilitation*, 32: 3.

Bhambri P, Singh S, Sangwan S, Devi J, Jain S (2023). Plants recognition using leaf image pattern analysis, *Journal of Survey in Fisheries Sciences*, 10(2S): 3863–3871.

Bithas PS, Michailidis ET, Nomikos N, Vouyioukas D, Kanatas AG (2019). A survey on machine-learning techniques for UAV-based communications, *Sensors*, 19(23): 5170.

Du M, et al (2018). Big data privacy preserving in multi-access edge computing for heterogeneous internet of things, *IEEE Communications Magazine*, 56(8): 62–67.

Echeverría S et al. (2020). Kal Ki: A software-defined IoT security platform, *IEEE 6th World Forum on Internet of Things (WF-IoT)*, New Orleans, LA, USA, 2020, pp. 1–6. DOI: 10.1109/WF-IoT48130.2020.9221050.

Fan CI, Huang SY, Lai YL (2013). Privacy-enhanced data aggregation scheme against internal attackers in smart grid, *IEEE Transactions on Industrial Informatics*, 10: 666–675.

Fotouhi M, Bayat M, Das AK, Far HAN, Pournaghi SM, Doostari MA (2020). A lightweight and secure two-factor authentication scheme for wireless body area networks in healthcare IoT, *Computer Networks*, 177: 107333.

Gao JF, Cui YH, Luo SL, Jiao LL (2019). Reasearch on information system controllability evaluation, *Netinfo Security*, 8: 67–75.

Granjal EM, Silva JS (2020). End-to-end transport-layer security for internet-integrated sensing applications with mutual and delegated ECC public-key authentication, *IEEE Ifip Networking Conference*, pp. 1–9.

Gubbi J, et al (2013). Internet of things (Iot): A vision, architectural elements, and future directions future gener, *Computer System*, 29(7): 1645–1660.

He D., Chan S., Guizani M. (2018). Security in the Internet of Things supported by mobile edge computing, *IEEE Communications Magazine*, 56(8): 56–61.

Kewei Sha T Yang A, Wei W, Davari S (2020). A survey of edge computing-based designs for IoT security, *Digital Communications and Networks*, 6(2): 195–202.

Kothandaraman D, Manickam M, Balasundaram A, Pradeep D, Arulmurugan A, Sivaraman AK, ... & Balakrishna R (2022). Decentralized link failure prevention routing (DLFPR) algorithm for efficient Internet of Things, *Intelligent Automation & Soft Computing*, 34(1), 132–156.

Kumar R, Rani S, Awadh MA (2022). Exploring the application sphere of the internet of things in industry 4.0: A review, bibliometric and content analysis, *Sensors*, 22(11): 4276.

Lehong H (2019). *Hype Cycle for the Internet of Things*, Stamford: Gartner Inc.

Lu R, Heung K, Lashkari A, Ghorbani AA (2017). A lightweight privacy-preserving data aggregation scheme for fog computing-enhanced iot, *IEEE Access*, 5: 3302–3312.

McSherry F, Talwar K (2007). Mechanism design via differential privacy, *Proceedings of 48th Annual IEEE Symposium on Foundations of Computer Science (FOCS'07)*.

Mehta P, Gupta R, Tanwar S (2020). Blockchain envisioned UAV networks: Challenges, solutions, and comparisons, *Computer Communications*, 151: 518–538.

Michailidis ET, Vouyioukas D (2022). A review on software-based and hardware-based authentication mechanisms for the internet of drones, *Drones*, 6(2): 41.

Nia AM, Jha NK (2016). A comprehensive study of security of internet-of-things. *IEEE Transactions on Emerging Topics in Computing*, 5(4): 586–602.

Rachna R, Bhambri P, Chhabra Y (2022). Deployment of distributed clustering approach in WSNs and IoTs. In *Cloud and Fog Computing Platforms for Internet of Things* (pp. 85–98). Boca Raton, FL: Chapman and Hall/CRC.

Ranaweera P, Jurcut AD, Liyanage M (2021). Survey on multiaccess edge computing security and privacy, *IEEE Communications Surveys and Tutorials*, 23(2): 1078–1124.

Rani S, Kataria A, Kumar S, Tiwari P (2023). Federated learning for secure IoMT-applications in smart healthcare systems: A comprehensive review, *Knowledge-Based Systems*, 65(6), 110658.

Rani S, Kataria A, Sharma V, Ghosh S, Karar V, Lee K, Choi C (2021). Threats and corrective measures for IoT security with observance of cybercrime: A survey, *Wireless Communications and Mobile Computing*, 2021: 1–30.

Ritu K, Bhambri P (2022). A CAD System for Software Effort Estimation, Paper presented at the *International Conference on Technological Advancements in Computational Sciences*, pp. 140–146. IEEE. DOI: 10.1109/ICTACS56270.2022.9988123.

Roman R, Lopez J, Mambo M, (2018b). Mobile edge computing Fog et al: A survey and analysis of security threats and challenges, *Future Generation Computer Systems*, 78: 680–698.

Roman R, Rios R, Onieva J (2018a). Lopez immune system for the internet of things using edge technologies, *IEEE Internet of Things Journal*, 178, 1–8.

Sangwan YS, Lal S, Bhambri P, Kumar A, Dhanoa IS (2021). Advancements in social data security and encryption: A review, *NVEO-Natural Volatiles & Essential Oils Journal| NVEO*, 8(4), 15353–15362.

Sharma N, Sultana HP, Singh R, Patil S (2019). Secure hash authentication in IoT based applications, *Procedia Computer Science*, 165: 328–335.

Sodanapalli S, et al. (2021). Recent advances in edge computing paradigms: Taxonomy benchmarks and standards for unconventional computing, *IJFC*, 4(1): 37–51.

Sun X, Ng DWK, Ding Z, Xu Y, Zhong Z (2019). Physical layer security in UAV systems: Challenges and opportunities, *IEEE Wireless Communications*, 26(5): 40–47.

Yuchang L, Bhagya NS, Kijun H (2021). Algorithmic implementation of deep learning layer assignment in edge computing based smart city environment, *Computers & Electrical Engineering*, 89: 106909.

8 Phased.js: Automated Software Deployment and Resource Provisioning and Management for AI

P. Ushashree

Geethanjali College of Engineering and Technology, Hyderabad, India

Archana Naik, Anurag Verma, and Anshuman Priyadarshini

NITTE Meenakshi Institute of Technology, Bangalore, India

8.1 INTRODUCTION

Artificial Intelligence (AI) is useful in decision-making, since its application means that the system can mimic the actions of the human brain through a process of automation to carry out the assignment (Shekhar, 2019). In the early phases of development, programmers generally have no idea with regard to the process of backend server. Even if they know about the development of a local host application it is an entirely different prospect for them to convert it to a production build application. The main problem for programmers that arises here is that "they know what to do" but "they don't know how to do" (Singh et al., 2021).

We have a range of technology, such as Amazon EC2 and the Google compute engine (Shaik et al., 2018), which have many configurations and dependencies for different applications used by programmers. EC2 has its own administration panel which gives the status of the application, but this is very hard to understand until you go through the associated documentation. Accordingly, it is more usual, when logging real-time data from the live application, for developers to use bash script to log it to a single file (Karakostas, 2014).

Due to the high learning curve involved in the deployment of technology faced by new learners, they encounter many problems in learning the techniques and fail to make an accurate determination of the resources to provision (Huang et al., 2017). In this respect the main idea now advanced is to remove that dependency on learning and to provide a user-friendly platform for developers to easily go through the steps of deployment (Kumar et al., 2022). The research conducted focuses on the automation of the deployment process and the development of a logging interface. This was achieved through and examination of three key studies: "Survey of Automated Software Deployment for Computational and Engineering Research", "RWELS: A Remote Web Event Logging System", and "Automating Application Deployment in Infrastructure Clouds" (Bose et al., 2021).

Cloud services require a very good understanding of dependency and configuration and beginner developers find it hard to read through all the documentation (Jabeen et al., 2021). For experienced developers, it is a repetitive and annoying task to do the same configurations on every application and to go through the documentation from time to time (Rachan et al., 2021). This waste of one's time is thought to be excessive due to the necessary extensive searching on the internet for solutions (Rani et al., 2023). Experiencing an unfamiliar framework can also cause problems for developers and it can provide barriers to development. Boilerplate code unavailability is another issue. Debugging, no logging feature, not being able to identify server crashes, security issues, basic automation, central app manager are the issues that need to be handled (Microsoft Azure, 2023).

Cloud computing and AI each play a crucial role in today's world. Combined, these two approaches help to reduce the amount of human effort and provide efficient results. The proposal is to provide an automation of the deployment of AI applications over the cloud. As we are aware, storage is one of the major concerns in the design of any application. In this respect, the flexibility of AI on the cloud can be a huge advantage.

The primary objective of this project is to provide developers with a one-click controller that will handle all the applications for user developers and make both resource provisioning and deployment easier (Amazon Web Services, 2023).

The end application will be fruitful for both beginners and experienced developers if the process is already automated. This outcome will benefit time management since it means that multiple collaborators can work on different branches through the use of Phased.js. Better code monitoring will be there for users to monitor their deployed servers. In addition, there will be file handling with less memory operations. Server crash issues can also be addressed through this system, since these are usually the result of memory outflow.

As the world is evolving through increasing automation and the introduction of AI and ML in our daily lives is quite evident, there is a need for a platform that helps developers to easily deploy and monitor their application (Babu et al., 2021). As mentioned earlier, the learning curve for new developers is so high, meaning that we want to decrease it to such an extent that the time consumption is less and is also more fruitful for both end users and programmers. The framework that we are developing is the one-shot click system for all the issues that we talked about. This will give the user a better development environment (Minnen et al., 2018) and an easily deployable platform (Vijayalakshmi et al., 2021).

8.2 LITERATURE SURVEY

In the present world, cloud computing is getting demand for platforms such as distributed systems. Cloud Infrastructure As A Service (IaaS) provides Virtual Machines (VM) on demand but does not provide the necessary tools to manage it once they have been fixed for a given application or server. The work in Automating App deployment in infrastructure clouds (Juve and Deelman, 2011) provides a survey on how to make the deployment and management of the cloud services automatic and identify areas for research.

In the present world, cloud computing is becoming an increasingly essential platform for distributed systems. The authors in Benson et al. (2016), provide a survey of software deployment on cloud platforms. It is noted that there are many challenges in the deployment of multi-cloud platforms, such as constraints on configuration and managing dependencies. There are also many management tools for application automation, each of which have their own strengths.

Remote Web Event Logging System (RWELS) (Shah et al., 2008): In the present world, event logs are an important data source in identifying the problems in websites for app deployers and maintainers. This approach presents a web-based application for client-server, RWELS for logging user interface events and storing in the text files when a user interacts with the website. This logging system automatically stores log events without the user's interaction and attention. RWELS is easily configurable and allows users to filter event logs. A user can select some events log every page on the website. The event logs are transferred through HTTP to the server, where all the event logs are stored as text files. User sessions logs on the app can be logged in a unique fashion.

Kikuchi (2015) proposes the architecture design and benefits of designing scalable apps on the cloud server. It also revels the efficient use of load balancer and stateless client management. In addition, it considers how microservices are more scalable than monolithic types of applications.

Toffetti et al. (2017) proposes a novel arch of cloud native applications, which enables scalable and resilient self-managing apps in the cloud. The current approach has intrinsic limits that prevent the apps to be self-sustainable and self-scalable as a great deal of human intervention is required, along with manual coding.

Xu et al. (2017) proposes a log model tool for declaratively-cloud applications using Kubernetes logs. It reads the logs generated by Kubernetes and provides potential suggestions. There are many real-world Kubernetes problems, which are identified as potential bugs.

CELAR is an Automated application elasticity platform that enables cloud developers to build efficient, high-performance services by flexibly managing the use of available resources (Giannakopoulos et al., 2014). When a surge in the number of users occurs, in order to meet their demands service providers must provide an environment that can help them deploy applications quickly. In other contributions, the work in Yu et al. (2013) proposed a private cloud tool kit and Yokoyama and Yoshioka (2012) introduced a method that manages the cluster as service deployments called dodai-deploy.

Ocone et al. (2019) proposed an analysis which places an emphasis the policies of scaling to be used by auto-scalers. Canali and Lancellotti (2012) has given an outline about the virtual machines in cloud data centers and their automated classification. Lu et al. (2013) proposed a method that investigates the requirement for the service to delineate its connections and display the test cases and apprehend the crucial features of the service. Durairajan and Sundararajan (2013) discussed a strategy for deploying interoperable service management over cloud.

The work presented by Deshmukh and Khandagale (2017), provides the study of software deployment, in the application development environment. The environment involves multiple code changes, and the use of applications, on multiple servers.

Danielsson et al. (2021) presents the quicker and easier deployment of web-based applications on cloud platforms. Quinton et al. (2014) developed a model to automatically select the suitable cloud environment to deploy. The work provides a scalable model to deal with dynamic changes in the cloud environment. Finally, the tool developed in Chen et al. (2013) provides the virtualization and management tools for constructing dynamic and virtual machines for the application.

8.3   AUTOMATED PROVISIONING ARCHITECTURE

The main objective of this system is to develop an automated one-click controller that will provision all the AI-driven web applications for developers and make it easy to carry out resource provisioning and deployment on cloud platforms. The deployment service needs to be automated (Wang et al., 2019a). The load balancing task to be taken care of during the deployment, considering the type of applications that needs to be deployed. In order to automate the deployment, it is necessary to benchmark the type and size of the application. Resource provisioning is performed by looking into the needs of the application and the available resources. The scripts required for the application's configuration are then created using a middleware program (Bhambri et al., 2021).

The proposed system will be of great use to both technical and non-technical users if the entire process is automated. Multiple collaborators can work on multiple branches with the use of Phased.js, with a provision of monitoring the applications on the deployed servers. Applications are managed with less memory consumption and server crash issues can also be handled efficiently (Paoletti et al., 2018).

The architecture for Automated Provisioning is depicted in Figure 8.1.

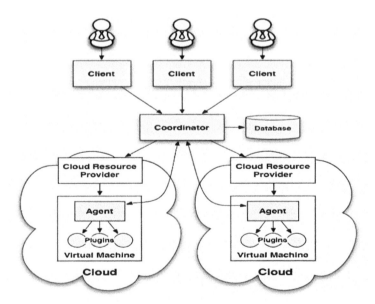

FIGURE 8.1   Automated provisioning architecture.

8.4 METHODOLOGY

The proposed system creates a simple and minimal application which assists users in deployment procedure and introduces an auto resource allocation to the process. The web application will run locally on the host machine (which runs on a PhasedJS framework) and allows users to manage and deploy their applications on the production server (PaaS such as Heroku, AWS, Azure etc.).

Many processes work together cooperatively under the hood to achieve this task. Since Phased JS is based on NodeJS, every script runs asynchronously, which reduces CPU overheads and mean that the deployment becomes smoother. Since different applications have different memory requirements, PhasedJS automatically analyzes target applications for memory usage and sets a threshold before deployment. This ensures that the target application does not exceed the memory limit. Also, before deployment PhasedJS attaches a logger and a couple of bash scripts for target application scaling. The logger logs useful console statements to the end user for further debugging live applications.

In Figure 8.2 Phased Js Architecture is illustrated. The PhasedJS creates a package which includes user app, logger, scaling scripts and other helper bash scripts, which then is sent to the cloud platform for deployment.

Figure 8.3 summarizes in detail the dataflow design of the proposed architecture. This is called cloud orchestration, which means using multiple tools, processes, and API to combine and automate successful deployment of the target application. The coordination takes place in an orchestration layer which governs and controls all the deployed apps in one platform. The bash script creates a process called Master Process, which itself creates error handles and worker processes. A worker process takes care of an http request and a web socket connection. The master process automatically carries out the allocation of CPU and memory to the worker process. This allows the target application to scale and use memory within the target limit (Tanwar et al., 2022).

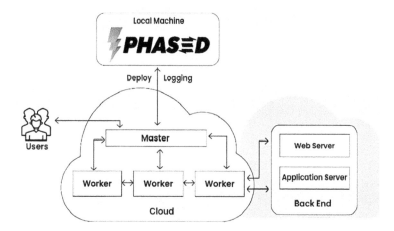

FIGURE 8.2 Phased.JS architecture.

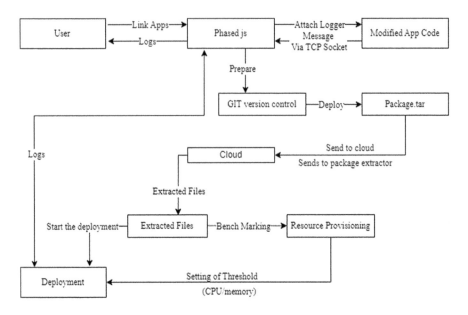

FIGURE 8.3   Phased.Js data flow design.

8.5   IMPLEMENTATION

By using express framework and other scripting languages, the proposed system enables developers to deploy lightweight applications to the cloud.

Making a local app scalable:

```
cluster = require('cluster')
os = require('os')
expressServer =require('./app.js')
/*check if current process is master*/
if cluster.isMaster then {
    print "Master <process.pid> is running"
    /*get the number of cpu cores*/
    cpuCount = os.cpus().length
  /*create a worker for each cpu core*/
    for(i = 0; i < cpuCount; i++){
        cluster.fork()
    }
}
else {
    /*not a master  process, so we'll just spawn the express
  server */
    expressServer()
    print "Worker <process.pid> started"
}
/*cluster API*/
/*create a new process if a worker dies*/
```

```
Cluster on 'exit' => callback(worker){

    print "Worker ${worker.id} died"

    print "Starting a new worker"
    cluster.fork()
})
```

The approach applied here in PhasedJS is the pre-benchmarking done on the deployed application and compressed to make it compatible for deployment. The manual process of git version control is automated and the extra steps such as commit and push to git remote branches are completely removed and the deployment is completely done on any local git repository. Our PhasedJS was able to successfully deploy several applications made using react, angular, flask, next, go, etc. using resource provisioning and bash scripts which were used to automate the manual steps.

Figures 8.4, 8.5 and 8.6 are sample benchmarks of the application deployed on the server using which the threshold is determined.

```
error count:  0
stats {
  totalElapsed: 1427.4177999999374,
  main: {
    meter: {
      mean: 703.4816926979545,
      count: 1000,
      currentRate: 703.4841176501527,
      '1MinuteRate': 0,
      '5MinuteRate': 0,
      '15MinuteRate': 0
    },
    histogram: {
    meter: {
      mean: 509.12841797015807,
      count: 100,
      currentRate: 509.18519167257637,
      '1MinuteRate': 0,
      '5MinuteRate': 0,
      '15MinuteRate': 0
    },
    histogram: {
      min: 5.292101000086404,
      max: 76.99290099996142,
      sum: 1404.4281950006261,
      variance: 64.21468493167306,
      mean: 14.044281950006262,
      stddev: 8.01340657471422,
      count: 100,
      median: 12.189549500006251,
      p75: 14.632149999961257,
      p95: 27.125300000054985,
      p99: 76.52816498996201,
      p999: 76.99290099996142
    }
  }
}
```

FIGURE 8.4   Sample benchmark1.

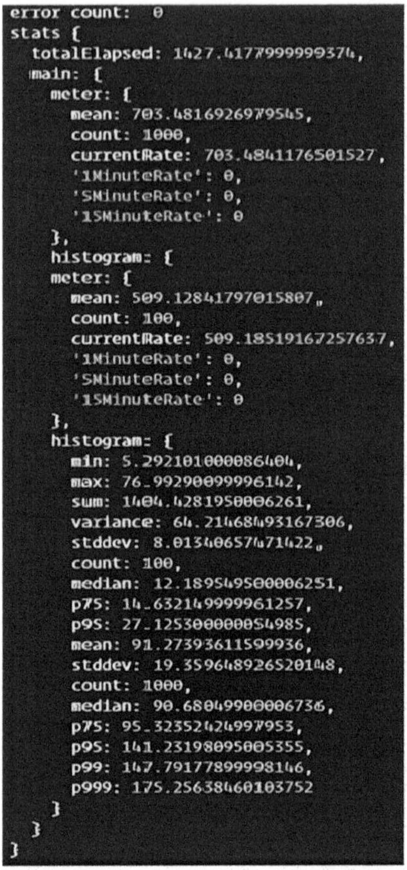

```
error count:  0
stats {
  totalElapsed: 1427.4177999999374,
  main: {
    meter: {
      mean: 703.4816926979545,
      count: 1000,
      currentRate: 703.4841176501527,
      '1MinuteRate': 0,
      '5MinuteRate': 0,
      '15MinuteRate': 0
    },
    histogram: {
    meter: {
      mean: 509.12841797015807,
      count: 100,
      currentRate: 509.18519167257637,
      '1MinuteRate': 0,
      '5MinuteRate': 0,
      '15MinuteRate': 0
    },
    histogram: {
      min: 5.292101000086404,
      max: 76.99290099996142,
      sum: 1404.4281950006261,
      variance: 64.21468493167306,
      stddev: 8.01340657471422,
      count: 100,
      median: 12.189549500006251,
      p75: 14.632149999961257,
      p95: 27.125300000054985,
      mean: 91.27393611599936,
      stddev: 19.359648926520148,
      count: 1000,
      median: 90.68049900006736,
      p75: 95.32352424997953,
      p95: 141.23198095005355,
      p99: 147.79177899998146,
      p999: 175.25638460103752
    }
  }
}
```

FIGURE 8.5 Sample benchmark2.

Sequences of commands executed after the app is sent to target server:

```
#!/bin/bash
tar -C /"$1" -xvf myApp.tar &&
node benchmark.js &&
node setThreshold.js &&
npm install &&
npm start
```

Figure 8.7 depicts the experimental setup of Phased Js

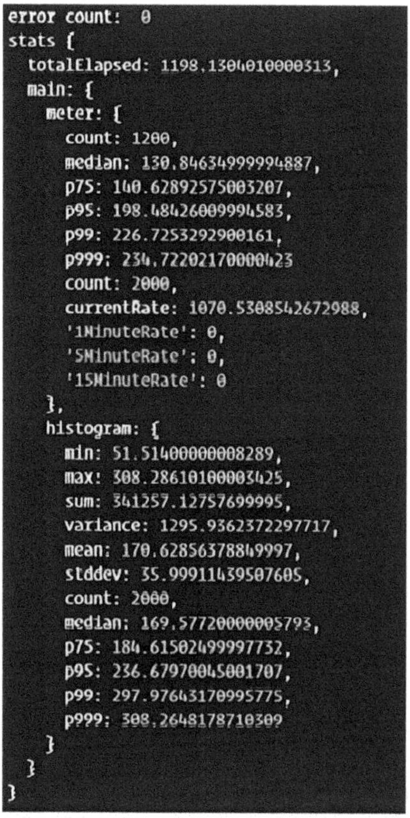

```
error count:  0
stats {
  totalElapsed: 1198.1304010000313,
  main: {
    meter: {
      count: 1200,
      median: 130.84634999994887,
      p75: 140.62892575003207,
      p95: 198.48426009994583,
      p99: 226.7253292900161,
      p999: 234.72202170000423
      count: 2000,
      currentRate: 1070.5308542672988,
      '1MinuteRate': 0,
      '5MinuteRate': 0,
      '15MinuteRate': 0
    },
    histogram: {
      min: 51.51400000008289,
      max: 308.28610100003425,
      sum: 341257.12757699995,
      variance: 1295.9362372297717,
      mean: 170.62856378849997,
      stddev: 35.99911439507605,
      count: 2000,
      median: 169.57720000005793,
      p75: 184.61502499997732,
      p95: 236.67970045001707,
      p99: 297.97643170995775,
      p999: 308.2648178710309
    }
  }
}
```

FIGURE 8.6   Sample benchmark3.

FIGURE 8.7   Phased.js UI.

8.6   RESULTS AND DISCUSSION

AI-based applications are taken to act as the test cases used for testing the phased Js setup. These applications were chosen to highlight various statistical parameters and memory usage to manually deploy an application on the cloud and using a proposed automated system.

The metrics such as CPU usage, memory usage, resource allocation are measured using both manual and proposed systems. The results achieved are shown in the form of tables provided in Tables 8.1 and 8.2. The AI-based applications were chosen based on various parameters. We had taken some heavy applications to be deployed by PhasedJS.

TABLE 8.1
Time Comparison Table

Application	Automated Time With Phased.js (seconds)	Manual Time Without Phased.js (seconds)
DownTube	79	900
Fertilizer recommendation	50	600
Test case App (self-deployment)	30	300

TABLE 8.2
Relative Usage by Using Phased.js

Applications	Memory Usage	CPU Usage
DownTube	1.3×	2×
Fertilizer Recommendation	1.3×	1.7×

Powered by – Phased.js

My App Name

C:\Users\hhxgdoihgopxh

One Click – Deploy, Start, Stop, Prepare

79:43

[Prepare] [Deploy] [Attach Logger]

Deployed!!

FIGURE 8.8   Result of Application 1 deployed using Phased.Js.

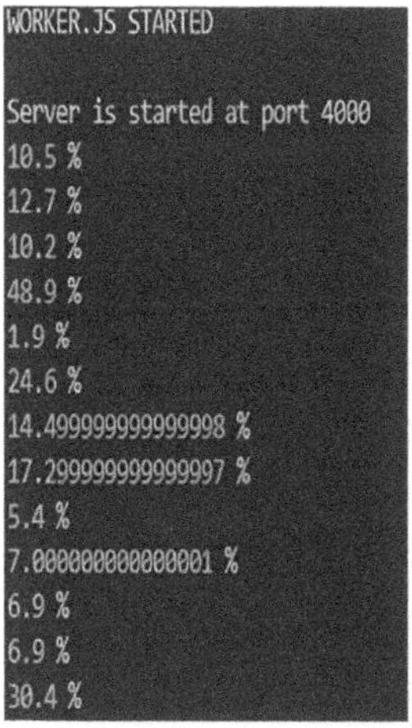

FIGURE 8.9   App statistics.

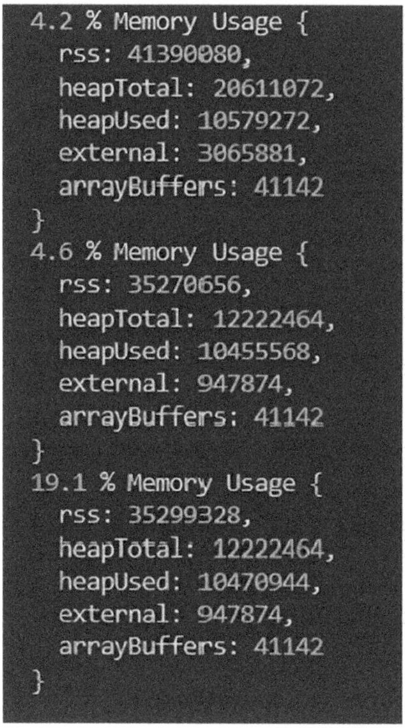

FIGURE 8.10   App memory usage.

8.6.1   APPLICATION 1: DOWNTUBE: YOUTUBE VIDEO/AUDIO DOWNLOADER

DownTube is an AI-based application that helps to download video/audio content present in YouTube. The application has been deployed using automated system name Phased Js and the time taken is presented in Figure 8.8.

```
52.92 %
59.157 %
68.60699999999999 %
59.535 %
63.882000000000005 %
57.644999999999996 %
58.211999999999996 %
69.17399999999999 %
81.08099999999999 %
58.967999999999996 %
58.211999999999996 %
52.353 %
51.597 %
52.92 %
53.109 %
```

FIGURE 8.11   Manual app statistics.

Apart from the time taken to deploy the application, various other statistical parameter values are also recorded for the application when deployed using Phased Js. The recorded results, such as memory usage, RSS, Heaptotal, Heapused, External, and Array buffers are displayed in Figures 8.9 and 8.10.

In manual deployment it's clear that, without proper optimization and resource provisioning, the application CPU usage is much more than when compared with the automated one. By analyzing the results yielded from both manual and automated systems, it is evident that the CPU usage is approximately 2x as compared to the manual approach. The memory usage is also high (on idle condition i.e. when server was not receiving any requests). We compared these data and found that PhasedJS optimized the memory usage by 1.3x (in both idle and multiple parallel incoming requests). AI-based application DownTube has been deployed manually and the results retrieved for statistical parameters and memory usage is displayed in Figures 8.11 and 8.12, respectively.

Since PhasedJS has optimized the app config, the CPU usage is relatively less when compared with the manual method.

8.6.2   APPLICATION 2: FERTILIZER RECOMMENDATION

The Fertilizer Recommendation system is one of the heavy-based AI applications that has been designed to recommend an appropriate fertilizer for a specific crop and season. This application has also been deployed both using the proposed system of PhasedJs and manually.

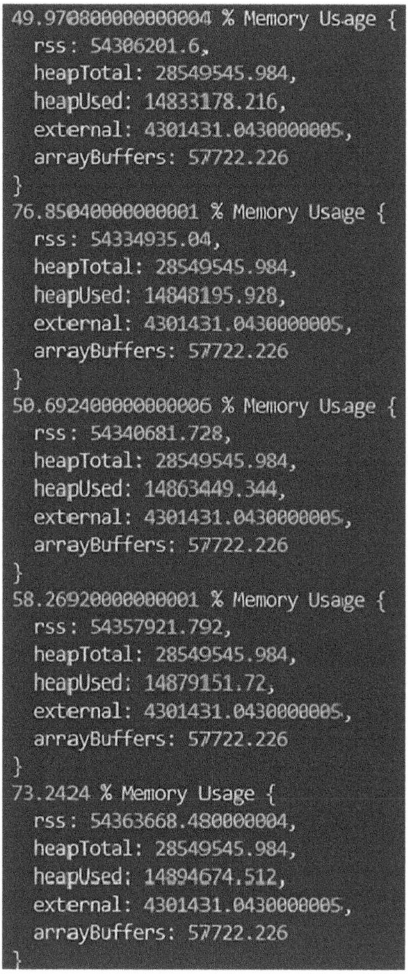

```
49.9708000000000004 % Memory Usage {
  rss: 54306201.6,
  heapTotal: 28549545.984,
  heapUsed: 14833178.216,
  external: 4301431.0430000005,
  arrayBuffers: 57722.226
}
76.85040000000001 % Memory Usage {
  rss: 54334935.04,
  heapTotal: 28549545.984,
  heapUsed: 14848195.928,
  external: 4301431.0430000005,
  arrayBuffers: 57722.226
}
50.6924000000000006 % Memory Usage {
  rss: 54340681.728,
  heapTotal: 28549545.984,
  heapUsed: 14863449.344,
  external: 4301431.0430000005,
  arrayBuffers: 57722.226
}
58.26920000000001 % Memory Usage {
  rss: 54357921.792,
  heapTotal: 28549545.984,
  heapUsed: 14879151.72,
  external: 4301431.0430000005,
  arrayBuffers: 57722.226
}
73.2424 % Memory Usage {
  rss: 54363668.480000004,
  heapTotal: 28549545.984,
  heapUsed: 14894674.512,
  external: 4301431.0430000005,
  arrayBuffers: 57722.226
}
```

FIGURE 8.12   Manual app memory usage.

The results in Figure 8.13 show that the automated system approximately reduced memory usage by 1.3× times and CPU usage by 1.7× times. The manual deployment of the application had higher values of memory and CPU usage. Figure 8.14 displays a snap of the results using the manual method without optimization and resource provisioning.

A comparison of the proposed system and manual deployment has been undertaken for the two AI-based applications: Downtube and Fertilizer Recommendation system. Table 8.1 depicts the performance of the automated system in comparison to the manual deployment.

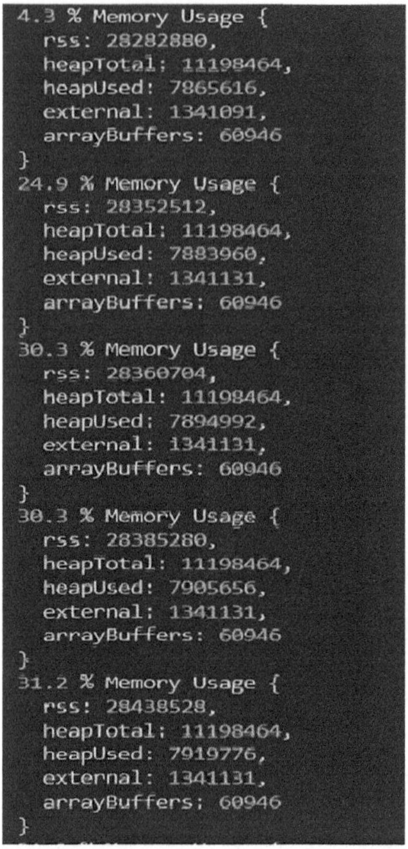

```
4.3 % Memory Usage {
  rss: 28282880,
  heapTotal: 11198464,
  heapUsed: 7865616,
  external: 1341091,
  arrayBuffers: 60946
}
24.9 % Memory Usage {
  rss: 28352512,
  heapTotal: 11198464,
  heapUsed: 7883960,
  external: 1341131,
  arrayBuffers: 60946
}
30.3 % Memory Usage {
  rss: 28360704,
  heapTotal: 11198464,
  heapUsed: 7894992,
  external: 1341131,
  arrayBuffers: 60946
}
30.3 % Memory Usage {
  rss: 28385280,
  heapTotal: 11198464,
  heapUsed: 7905656,
  external: 1341131,
  arrayBuffers: 60946
}
31.2 % Memory Usage {
  rss: 28438528,
  heapTotal: 11198464,
  heapUsed: 7919776,
  external: 1341131,
  arrayBuffers: 60946
}
```

FIGURE 8.13   Automated using Phased.Js.

Table 8.2 displays metrics such as the memory usage and CPU usage comparison of both manual and proposed systems. The results displayed show that both the CPU and the memory usage is low in PhasedJs.

8.7   CONCLUSION

The PhasedJS provides an overview of how web automation and deployment will help developers to easily manage and debug their AI applications. The ability to automatically make the target application scalable and allocate resources according to the needs of the user application. This revolutionary framework will also help to deploy many AI applications on the same server with minimal load and better performance. Logs and the packages are encrypted over the air using RSA1024, which ensures application shareable data is highly secure. At the root level, this framework has been designed to deploy the AI-based application to all kinds of users who do not have

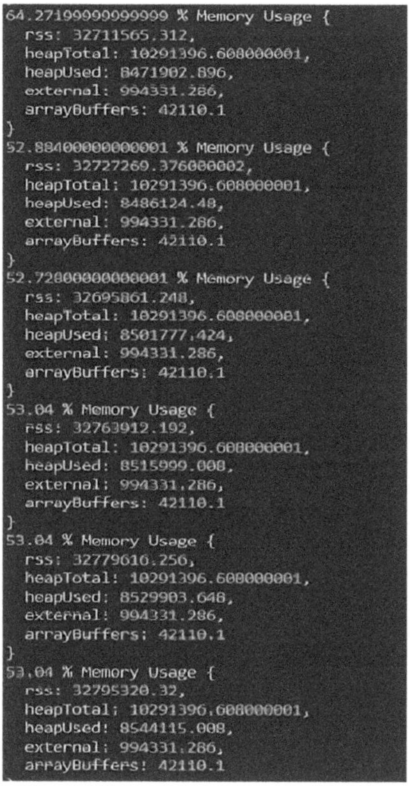

FIGURE 8.14   Manual without Phased.Js.

knowledge of deployment and manage their applications very easily as it will eliminate all the repetitive tasks and will help them to focus on their innovation better.

REFERENCES

Amazon Web Services (AWS) (2023). https://aws.amazon.com/

Babu, G. C. N., Gupta, S., Bhambri, P., Leo, L. M., Rao, B. H., & Kumar, S. (2021). A semantic health observation system development based on the IoT sensors. *Turkish Journal of
Physiotherapy and Rehabilitation*, 32(3), 1721–1729.

Benson, J. O., Prevost, J. J., & Rad, P. (2016, April). Survey of automated software deployment
for computational and engineering research. In *2016 Annual IEEE Systems Conference
(SysCon)* (pp. 1–6). IEEE.

Bhambri, P., Singh, M., Jain, A., Dhanoa, I. S., Sinha, V. K., & Lal, S. (2021). Classification of
the gene expression data with the aid of optimized feature selection. *Turkish Journal of
Physiotherapy and Rehabilitation*, 32(3), 1158–1167.

Bose, M. M., Yadav, D., Bhambri, P., & Shankar, R. (2021). Electronic customer relationship
management: Benefits and pre-implementation considerations. *Journal of Maharaja
Sayajirao University of Baroda*, 55(01(VI)), 1343–1350.

Canali, C., & Lancellotti, R. (2012, September). Automated clustering of VMs for scalable cloud monitoring and management. In *SoftCOM 2012, 20th International Conference on Software, Telecommunications and Computer Networks* (pp. 1–5). IEEE.

Chen, H. S., Wu, C. H., Pan, Y. L., Yu, H. E., Chen, C. M., & Cheng, K. Y. (2013, December). Towards the automated fast deployment and clone of private cloud service: the Ezilla toolkit. In *2013 IEEE 5th International Conference on Cloud Computing Technology and Science* (Vol. 1, pp. 136–141). IEEE.

Danielsson, P., Postema, T., & Munir, H. (2021). Heroku-based innovative platform for web-based deployment in product development at axis. *IEEE Access*, 9, 10805–10819.

Deshmukh, S. N., & Khandagale, H. P. (2017, April). A system for application deployment automation in a cloud environment. In *2017 Innovations in Power and Advanced Computing Technologies (i-PACT)* (pp. 1–4). IEEE.

Durairajan, S., & Sundararajan, P. (2013, October). Portable service management deployment over cloud platforms to support production workloads. In *2013 IEEE International Conference on Cloud Computing in Emerging Markets (CCEM)* (pp. 1–7). IEEE.

Giannakopoulos, I., Papailiou, N., Mantas, C., Konstantinou, I., Tsoumakos, D., & Koziris, N. (2014, October). Celar: Automated application elasticity platform. In *2014 IEEE International Conference on Big Data (Big Data)* (pp. 23–25). IEEE.

Huang, F., Li, H., Yuan, Z., & Li, X. (2017, May). An application deployment approach based on hybrid cloud. In *2017 IEEE 3rd International Conference on Big Data Security on Cloud (Big Data Security), IEEE International Conference on High Performance and Smart Computing (HPSC), and IEEE International Conference on Intelligent Data and Security (IDS)* (pp. 74–79). IEEE.

Jabeen, A., Pallathadka, H., Pallathadka, L. K., & Bhambri, P. (2021). E-CRM successful factors for business enterprises case studies. *Journal of Maharaja Sayajirao University of Baroda*, 55(01(VI)), 1332–1342.

Juve, G., & Deelman, E. (2011, November). Automating application deployment in infrastructure clouds. In *2011 IEEE Third International Conference on Cloud Computing Technology and Science* (pp. 658–665). IEEE.

Karakostas, B. (2014, September). Towards autonomic cloud configuration and deployment environments. In *2014 International Conference on Cloud and Autonomic Computing* (pp. 93–96). IEEE.

Kikuchi, S. (2015, December). Prediction of workloads in incident management based on incident ticket updating history. In *2015 IEEE/ACM 8th International Conference on Utility and Cloud Computing (UCC)* (pp. 333–340). IEEE.

Kumar, P., Banerjee, K., Singhal, N., Kumar, A., Rani, S., Kumar, R., & Lavinia, C. A. (2022). Verifiable, secure mobile agent migration in healthcare systems using a polynomial-based threshold secret sharing scheme with a blowfish algorithm. *Sensors*, 22(22), 8620.

Lu, H., Shtern, M., Simmons, B., Smit, M., & Litoiu, M. (2013, June). Pattern-based deployment service for next generation clouds. In *2013 IEEE Ninth World Congress on Services* (pp. 464–471). IEEE.

Microsoft Azure (2023). https://azure.microsoft.com/en-in/

Ocone, L., Rak, M., & Villano, U. (2019, June). Benchmark-based cost analysis of auto scaling web applications in the cloud. In *2019 IEEE 28th International Conference on Enabling Technologies: Infrastructure for Collaborative Enterprises (WETICE)* (pp. 98–103). IEEE.

Quinton, C., Romero, D., & Duchien, L. (2014). Automated selection and configuration of cloud environments using software product lines principles. *2014 IEEE 7th International Conference on Cloud Computing* (pp. 144–151). DOI: 10.1109/CLOUD.2014.29.

Rachna, R., Chhabra, Y., & Bhambri, P. (2021). Various approaches and algorithms for monitoring energy efficiency of wireless sensor networks. In Harvinder Singh, Puneet Pal Singh Cheema, Prashant Garg (Eds.), *Lecture Notes in Civil Engineering* (Vol. 113, pp. 761–770). Springer, Singapore.

Rani, S., Pareek, P. K., Kaur, J., Chauhan, M., & Bhambri, P. (2023, February). Quantum machine learning in healthcare: Developments and challenges. In *2023 IEEE International Conference on Integrated Circuits and Communication Systems (ICICACS)* (pp. 1–7). IEEE.

Shah, I., Al Toaimy, L., & Jawed, M. (2008). RWELS: A remote web event logging system. *Journal of King Saud University-Computer and Information Sciences*, 20, 1–11.

Shaik, B., Vallarapu, A., Shaik, B., & Vallarapu, A. (2018). *Google Cloud. Beginning PostgreSQL on the Cloud: Simplifying Database as a Service on Cloud Platforms*, 133–167. https://doi.org/10.1007/978-1-4842-3447-1 https://link.springer.com/book/10.1007/978-1-4842-3447-1

Shekhar, S. S. (2019). Artificial intelligence in automation. *Artificial Intelligence*, 3085(06), 14–17.

Singh, M., Bhambri, P., Lal, S., Singh, Y., Kaur, M., & Singh, J. (2021). Design of the effective technique to improve memory and time constraints for sequence alignment. *International Journal of Applied Engineering Research (Netherlands)*, 6(02), 127–142.

Tanwar, R., Chhabra, Y., Rattan, P., & Rani, S. (2022, September). Blockchain in IoT networks for precision agriculture. In *International Conference on Innovative Computing and Communications: Proceedings of ICICC 2022* (Vol 2, pp. 137–147). Springer Nature Singapore.

Toffetti, G., Brunner, S., Blöchlinger, M., Spillner, J., & Bohnert, T. M. (2017). Self-managing cloud-native applications: Design, implementation, and experience. *Future Generation Computer Systems*, 72, 165–179.

Vijayalakshmi, P., Shankar, R., Karthik, S., & Bhambri, P. (2021). Impact of work from home policies on workplace productivity and employee sentiments during the Covid-19 pandemic. *Journal of Maharaja Sayajirao University of Baroda*, 55(01(VI)), 1314–1331.

Xu, J., Chen, P., Yang, L., Meng, F., & Wang, P. (2017, November). Logdc: Problem diagnosis for declaratively-deployed cloud applications with log. In *2017 IEEE 14th International Conference on e-Business Engineering (ICEBE)* (pp. 282–287). IEEE.

Yokoyama, S., & Yoshioka, N. (2012, June). Dodai-deploy: Fast cluster deployment tool. In *2012 IEEE 19th International Conference on Web Services* (pp. 681–682). IEEE.

Yu, H. E., Pan, Y. L., Wu, C. H., Chen, H. S., Chen, C. M., & Cheng, K. Y. (2013, December). On-demand automated fast deployment and coordinated cloud services. In *2013 IEEE 5th International Conference on Cloud Computing Technology and Science* (Vol. 2, pp. 252–255). IEEE.

9 Robust Image Enhancement Technique to Automatically Enrich the Visibility of Satellite Captured Snaps

M. R. Dileep, A. V. Navaneeth, and Vidyadevi G. Biradar
Nitte Meenakshi Institute of Technology, Bengaluru, India

Madhwaraj Kango Gopal
New Horizon College of Engineering, Bengaluru, India

9.1 INTRODUCTION

There are wide categories of imageries available in the globe used for various applications, viz., medical research, surveillance systems, psychological analysis, the digital processing of images and many more (Bakshi et al., 2021a). Among a number of applications, DSM/DTM imagery applications play a major role in object identification, object detection and the analysis of the data. These multi-resolution images have minute and unique features incorporated within them. Processing these images is a challenging task (Sumathi et al., 2021). By using cutting-edge techniques in terms of feature extraction, blurring (such as the use of de-blurring techniques), morphological operations (such as dilation and erosion, open and close and so on), there are various applications in real time which are coming into existence. Some of the applications perform with high accuracy while others are less effective (Rana et al., 2021). Furthermore, the analysis of performance is on the base of parameters viz., execution time, accuracy level and response time.

Hyper-spectral images are special types of images which are used in confined applications (Bhambri, 2021). Usually, these kind of images are utilized in taking geographical pictures, configuring geographical specifications and many more (Bakshi et al., 2021b). The unique feature of hyper-spectral images lies in their efficiency to represent each pixel within the image with a certain band of spectrum. These spectrums are directly related to the intensity or wavelength associated with

DOI: 10.1201/9781003383505-9

the amount of light, reflected from the objects which are captured from geo-spectral cameras (Puri et al., 2022).

In this chapter, the core objective is the enhancement of images., These are considered as an input, and may be any one (or a combination) of hyper-spectral images, SOR images or DSM/DTM images (Kataria et al., 2022). Irrespective of the type of images, the algorithm has to functionally perform at its best as per the model (Bhambri, 2020). The model involves the incorporation of AI-oriented concepts such as ANN, deep neural networks and fuzzy systems with the combination of mathematical framework such as n-Sigma controls (Kuzhaloli et al., 2020).

The following sections of the chapter are as follows: section 9.2 contains a literature survey; section 9.3 has a database analysis; and section 9.4 offers a proposed methodology. Following this, the proposed algorithm is briefly sketched out in section 9.5; linkages to multidisciplinary approaches are listed in section 9.6. Finally, the conclusion is drawn in section 9.7 and future enhancements are outlined in the last section.

9.2   LITERATURE SURVEY

A large amount of previous work has been done in the area of image processing. The techniques of image processing have been used in a wide variety of fields. These have been involved in the image processing area of satellite images where they are widely employed in the analysis of collected groups of images which contain a range of different aspects. The ways in which an image or collection of images are processed may involve concepts such as boundary value analysis, color corrections, brightness and hue corrections, image compression, the reconstruction of images, and many other more modern techniques.

Rahman Md and Mohamed Hamada (2019) have made a study of loss-less image compression methods which provides a state-of-the-art survey in which the study was conducted in a broad manner related to the real-time applications. In another contribution, Ayoob khan et al. (2019) has designed the work on Prediction-based Lossless Image Compression in which a methodology of lossless image compression was implemented. Similarly, Hussain Abir Jaafar et al. (2018) has conducted a comparative study on image compression techniques. It is a study which gives a detailed methodology and a broad discussion on aspects on lossless and lossy algorithms. Another research group, has demonstrated a method involving combined autoregressive and graded priors for educated copy density, which gives a unique method of image compression. Johnston et al. (2018) has worked on enhanced lousy appearance firmness with preparing and spatially adaptive bit rates for recurrent networks. Sibaruddin et al., (2018) has made a series of research experiments on an assessment of pixel-based and object-based image classification techniques in extracting information from UAV imagery data. Ghamisi et al. (2018) invented a novel approach on innovative boundaries in spectral-spatial hyperspectral image taxonomy. This approach explores the up-to-date improvements which are founded on calculated morphology, Markov random fields, segmentation, sparse representation, and deep learning.

Mercedes et al. (2018) has described a method involving deep convolutional neural networks for fast hyper-spectral image classification. Li Ying et al. (2018) has made a survey on the study of the classifier – deep learning for remote sensing image classification. This study has demonstrated a unique method of classification. Jin et al. (2019) have explored the concept on learning deep CNNs for impulse noise removal in images, which demonstrates various uses of CNN. Mishra et al., (2019) has described a detailed study on the involuntary de-noising of close-range hyper spectral imageries by a wavelength-specific shearlet-based image noise reduction method. Higaki et al. (2019) has made a detailed analysis on the Development of imageries excellence at CT and MRI using deep learning technique. Fan et al. (2019) did a brief review of image de-noising techniques. Owotogbe et al. (2019) studied various models on the Edge Detection Techniques on Digital Images. This study represents a broad review on wide aspects of edge detection techniques. Wang et al. (2019a) has presented a novel approach on the edge detection of infrared images which demonstrates different methodologies for edge detection techniques. Westreich et al. (2019) has worked in detail on an innovative approach to image stromal flesh and evaluate its morphological topographies through polarized light near a tumor microenvironment prognostic signature. Samadi et al. (2019) has worked on the study of alteration discovery in SAR images using a deep belief network. This novel approach is based on morphological images. Kandala et al. (2019) demonstrated a method towards the achievement of a real-time heartbeat classification technique. This approach explains an evaluation of nonlinear morphological features and a voting method. Wang et al. (2019b) has conducted a brief study on morphological division examination and texture-based provision vector machines cataloging mice liver fibrosis microscopic images. Dileep and Danti (2018) made a detailed articulation on predicting human age based on morphological features through the use of neural networks.

Drawing on these earlier studies, the work which has been carried out in this chapter focuses on an image enhancement technique for satellite images, and it involves three distinct phases: image compression, image categorization, and image enhancement. In each phase, the satellite images are processed with advanced methodologies for gathering sectional outcomes, and will be further processed by subsequent stages for the final outcome.

9.3 DATABASE ANALYSIS

The experiments can be conducted using one of two types of databases.

9.3.1 INDIGENOUS DATABASE

The image dataset prepared in-house. The images are captured through high-definition cameras and drones. Then all the images are standardized into 3D matrix conversion of $256 \times 256 \times 256$ dimensions. The below images are samples of an experimental imagery data set (Figure 9.1).

FIGURE 9.1 Indigenous database.

9.4 PROPOSED METHODOLOGY

This chapter outlines the design and development of a framework using cutting-edge techniques in advanced digital image processing. This chapter outlines a process of image processing, which enhances the images, leading to greater clarity and visibility. In this process, various phases are involved as listed below:

- *Preliminary Phase*: An effective compression of images for further processing results in the optimum utilization of the memory space.
- *Secondary Phase*: The categorization of the images.
- *Tertiary Phase*: An efficient enhancement of the images for high-quality visibility.

The architecture of the proposed framework is represented in Figure 9.2.

9.4.1 PRELIMINARY PHASE

Modern developments in IT-related technology have resulted in the generation of enormous quantities of information each second (Singh et al., 2021). Consequently, it is almost inevitable that the quantity of information deposited and transmitted is probably likely to rise steeply in future. These types of data can be in a variety of different forms: video, audio, image, numeric and so on (Rani et al., 2023). When the data is of type image, the image enhancement techniques play a major role in various areas of technology as such images take up a great deal of memory. In performing enhancement techniques on images, various pre-processing activities are required (Paoletti et al., 2018). The first step among the pre-processing activities is the image compression technique. In this technique, high-resolution images such

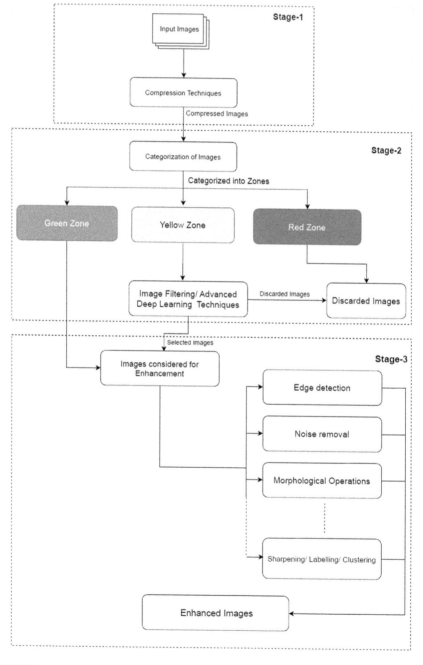

FIGURE 9.2 Architecture of the proposed framework.

as Hyper-Spectral Images and SOR Images are used as an input and can be suitably compressed for standard size using various algorithms (Ayoobkhan et al., 2019; Dileep and Danti, 2018; Fan et al., 2019).

$$\text{Data Compression Ratio}\left(\text{DCR}\right) = \text{Original File Size} / \text{compressed file size} \quad (9.1)$$

$$\text{Percentage Savings} = \left(1 - 1 / \text{DCR}\right) \times 100\% \quad (9.2)$$

The image solidity practises are approximately categorized in dual groups viz.

9.4.1.1 Lossless Compression Techniques

The novel data is flawlessly restored after the flattened data in lossless compression. It uses all of the info in the true images during compression, resulting in an image that is similar to the original image when decompressed (Ayoobkhan et al., 2019).

Among the Lossless Compression Techniques are:

- bzip2
- Finite State Entropy
- Huffman coding
- Lempel-Ziv compression
- Prediction by partial matching
- Run-length encoding

9.4.1.2 Lossy Compression Techniques

The reconstruction of an image using lossy compression is only an approximation of the original data. Some data is lost as a result of this technique (Fan et al., 2019). The most common application of this technology is in the area of multimedia. Among the Lossy Compression Techniques are:

- Predictive coding
- Transform coding

As the Lossy Compression Technique results in the loss of data (Dileep and Danti, 2018), Lossless Compression Technique is considered in the proposed project, which can be able to retain even the minute features of the image in compressed form for further processing (Figure 9.3).

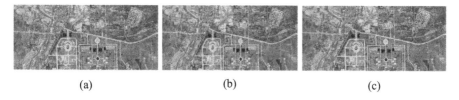

(a)   (b)   (c)

FIGURE 9.3 Lossy and lossless compression techniques (a) original image, (b) lossless compression, (c) lossy compression.

(a)   (b)

FIGURE 9.4   Pre-processing stages (a) compressed image, (b) transformed image.

9.4.2   SECONDARY PHASE

In the Secondary Phase of the process, all the compressed images are considered for further processing of categorization (Minnen et al., 2018). Here, in Stage-2, the images are pre-processed and then filtered based on their clarity and visibility. Based on the complexity of the image, this is then converted into ether grayscale or black & white (Figure 9.4).

To identify the properties of the image (Contrast, Blur, Noise, Artefact and Distortion, etc.), various pre-processing techniques are available, namely,

- regionprops() method in matlab.
- img.shape, img.size, img.dtype and many more properties in python.
- glFrustum(), glLoadIdentity() and many more methods in openGL.

The parameters to be considered to define the simplicity and discernibility of the imageries are the combination of Contrast, Blur, Noise, Artefact and Distortion.

For image filtration purposes, various commonly used techniques are available. These are stated below (Minnen et al., 2018; Owotogbe et al., 2019).

9.4.2.1   Strength Alterations and Spatial Filtering
- Histogram equalization
- Linear spatial filters, correlation, convolution
- Smoothing (linear) spatial filters
- Sharpening linear spatial filters using the Laplacian

9.4.2.2   Sifting in the Regularity Domain
- 1D and 2D continuous and discrete Fourier transforms
- Convolution theorem
- Properties of the Fourier transform
- Sieving in the incidence field (flattening and improving, low-pass and high-pass filtering)
- The Laplacian in the frequency domain, enhancement
- Homomorphic filtering
- Band Reject and Band Pass Filters

9.4.2.3 Image Filtering Techniques

Along with a couple of these common image filtering techniques, it is planned to incorporate various mathematical approaches to categorize the images. Among the approaches available are the following:

- n-Sigma Control limit
- Grouping Technique
- Spatial Classification
- Temporal Classification

Of the above mathematical approaches, the n-Sigma control limit is the most popularly/significantly used method (Jin et al., 2019). In this method, the boundaries are defined based on the properties of images which are used to define the clarity and visibility (Maddipati et al., 2020). The compressed images are given as inputs to n-Sigma controls, which compares the properties of image with the fixed boundary values and categorizes them into three classes as shown in Figure 9.5. Zonal representations are then given as shown in Figure 9.6.

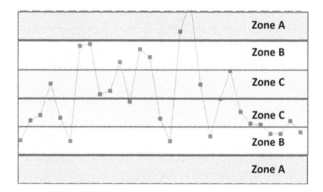

FIGURE 9.5   Pictorial representation of n-sigma control limits.

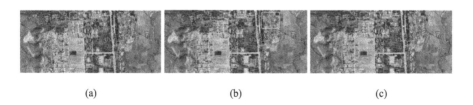

(a) (b) (c)

FIGURE 9.6   Zonal representation (a) green zone image, (b) yellow zone image, (c) red zone image.

9.4.3 TERTIARY PHASE

In the Tertiary Phase, the visibility and clarity of the filtered images taken from Stage-2 will be improvised by the process of enhancement techniques. Here, initially, the original compressed image will be passed through the high pass filter, which leads to the extraction of high frequency components, and generates the scaled version of the image. Then, this scaled version will be added to the original compressed image results in an enhanced version of the image as the final outcome. During this enhancement process, the edge detection, the noise removal process and the morphological operations will be implemented (Figure 9.7).

The various edge detection techniques which can be considered are listed below:

- Sobel
- Canny
- Prewitt

The various noise removal algorithms which can be considered are listed below:

- Linear Filters
- Non-Linear Filters

The various morphological operations which can be considered are listed below:

- Dilate
- Erosion
- Compliment
- Intersection
- Union

Along with the listed methods, additional techniques can be adopted for the better vision of the image. These techniques include:

- Sharpening
- Labelling
- Clustering

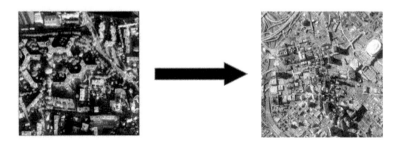

FIGURE 9.7   Filtering process.

9.5   PROPOSED ALGORITHM

The algorithm to enrich the visibility of satellite captured snaps is as follows:

Input: Query Image I.
Output: Enhanced Image E_i.
  Step 1: Input all n images I_n to compressor C. Where $n = 1, 2, 3$……… and
    I is an Image.
  Step 2: Compress all Images I_n to C_n. Where C_n is the Compressed Image
    and $n = 1, 2, 3$….. Using equation (1) and calculate the percentage of
    compression using equation (2) in Preliminary Phase.
  Step 3: Pre-process the image for noise removal and apply filter for the
    assessment of clarity and visibility. Images are then converted to
    Grayscale or Black & White.
  Step 4: Impose n-Sigma Control limit on images and categorize the images
    into Zone-A (Red), Zone-B (Yellow) and Zone-C (Green) respectively.
  Step 5: Superimpose Scaled Version S_n on C_n of the images of Zone-B and
    Zone-C respectively leads to the Enhanced Version of the Image E_i as
    final outcome.

9.6   RESULTS AND DISCUSSIONS

The proposed intelligent system takes satellite captured images as input. These
images are then trained using AI learning mechanisms to realise the structures,
objects and geographical orientations. The features are extracted and processed and
morphological operations are carried out on those features. During processing, as an
intermediate phase, the scaled version of the image is produced (Chauhan and Rani,
2021). Then, this scaled version will be added to the original compressed image,
which results in the production of an enhanced version of the image as the simulated
model of final outcome as shown in Figure 9.8.

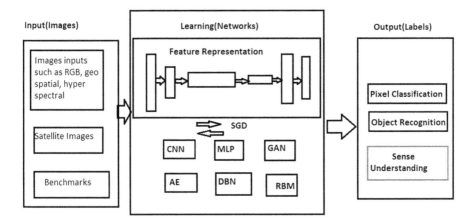

FIGURE 9.8   Simulation model.

9.7   LINKAGES TO MULTIDISCIPLINARY APPROACHES

This chapter establishes linkages to various applications of the multidisciplinary applications are listed below:

- This process bridges the gaps that exist between the objects depicted in photos with incomplete details and the desired level of detail in fully rendered images.
- An effective memory utilization technique is adopted in the proposed methodology.
- An efficient categorization model is adopted, which can be applied within multidisciplinary applications.

9.8   CONCLUSION

The work in this current chapter outlines a process for the processing of images in various stages, resulting in the enrichment of visibility of satellite captured snaps. The proposed work will also be able to accept images in a range of different formats and is able to process them according to required criteria. The algorithm proposed in the chapter consists of discrete stages, namely, the removal of noise, and the implementation of morphological operations for the processing of the images. It is also observed that in this current work, because of the utilization of advanced mathematical and image processing models, the rapid processing of output is achieved. The observational remarks and comparative analysis between various methodologies considered and the proposed model is reflected in Table 9.1 and graphically represented in Figure 9.9.

Overall, in this chapter an attempt has been made to meet the modern trend requirements with a combination of different novel approaches and efficient mathematical concepts so as to produce a state-of-the-art technique in the enhancement of clarity of images.

TABLE 9.1
Existing Methods v/s Proposed Method

Sl.no	Existing Methods	Success Rate (%)
1	Joint autoregressive and hierarchical priors for learned image compression (Ghamisi et al., 2018)	84
2	Comparison of pixel-based and object-based image classification techniques in extracting information from UAV imagery data (Hussain et al., 2018)	82
3	Change detection in SAR images using deep belief network: a new training approach based on morphological images (Sibaruddin et al., 2018)	88
4	Morphological segmentation analysis and texture-based support vector machines classification on mice liver fibrosis microscopic images (Wang et al., 2019b)	89
5	Proposed Method	91

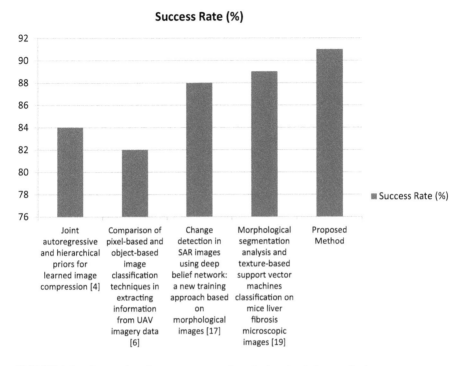

FIGURE 9.9 Comparison between proposed method and existing methods.

9.9 FUTURE WORK

In the present model, the architecture has been built with respect to the images which are captured by satellites for the purpose of analysis, study, monitoring, socio-technical applications and forecasting solicitations. In this work, the contributions are very specific and limited to geospatial aspects. In the proposed framework, the enhancement of pictures is improved using state-of-the-art approaches along with unique mathematical models for the purpose of improving image clarity and visibility.

Apart from the applications of the proposed architecture, a wide range of applications can incorporate this framework. Among the major fields where this system can be utilised are medical imaging, defence systems, agriculture and disaster management systems. The efficiency, accuracy and appropriateness of this architecture has been found to be ideal for use in real-time systems.

REFERENCES

Ayoobkhan, M. U. A., Chikkannan, E., Ramakrishnan, K., & Balasubramanian, S. B. (2019). Prediction-based lossless image compression. In *International Conference on ISMAC in Computational Vision and Bio-Engineering* (pp. 1749–1761). Springer, Cham.

Bakshi, P., Bhambri, P., & Thapar, V. (2021a). A review paper on wireless sensor network techniques in Internet of Things (IoT). *Wesleyan Journal of Research*, *14*(7), 147–160.

Bakshi, P., Bhambri, P., & Thapar, V. (2021b). A review paper on wireless sensor network techniques in Internet of Things (IoT). In *Proceedings of the International Conference on Contemporary Issues in Engineering & Technology*.

Bhambri, P. (2020). Green compliance. In S. Agarwal (Ed.), *Introduction to Green Computing* (pp. 95–125). AGAR Saliha Publication. ISBN: 978-81-948141-5-3.

Bhambri, P. (2021). Electronic evidence. In Kamal Gulati, Narinder Kumar Bhasin (Eds.), *Textbook of Cyber Heal* (pp. 86–120). AGAR Saliha Publication. ISBN: 978-81-948141-7-7.

Chauhan, M., & Rani, S. (2021). COVID-19: A revolution in the field of education in India. *Learning How to Learn Using Multimedia*, 23–42.

Dileep, M. R., & Danti, A. (2018). Human age and gender prediction based on neural networks and three sigma control limits. *Applied Artificial Intelligence*, *32*(3), 281–292.

Fan, L., Zhang, F., Fan, H., & Zhang, C. (2019). Brief review of image denoising techniques. *Visual Computing for Industry, Biomedicine, and Art*, *2*(1), 1–12.

Ghamisi, P., Maggiori, E., Li, S., Souza, R., Tarablaka, Y., Moser, G., … & Benediktsson, J. A. (2018). New frontiers in spectral-spatial hyperspectral image classification: The latest advances based on mathematical morphology, Markov random fields, segmentation, sparse representation, and deep learning. *IEEE Geoscience and Remote Sensing Magazine*, *6*(3), 10–43.

Higaki, T., Nakamura, Y., Tatsugami, F., Nakaura, T., & Awai, K. (2019). Improvement of image quality at CT and MRI using deep learning. *Japanese Journal of Radiology*, *37*(1), 73–80.

Hussain, A. J., Al-Fayadh, A., & Radi, N. (2018). Image compression techniques: A survey in lossless and lossy algorithms. *Neurocomputing*, *300*, 44–69.

Jin, L., Zhang, W., Ma, G., & Song, E. (2019). Learning deep CNNs for impulse noise removal in images. *Journal of Visual Communication and Image Representation*, *62*, 193–205.

Johnston, N., Vincent, D., Minnen, D., Covell, M., Singh, S., Chinen, T., … & Toderici, G. (2018). Improved lossy image compression with priming and spatially adaptive bit rates for recurrent networks. In *Proceedings of the IEEE Conference on Computer Vision and Pattern Recognition* (pp. 4385–4393).

Kandala, R. N., Dhuli, R., Pławiak, P., Naik, G. R., Moeinzadeh, H., Gargiulo, G. D., & Gunnam, S. (2019). Towards real-time heartbeat classification: evaluation of nonlinear morphological features and voting method. *Sensors*, *19*(23), 5079.

Kataria, A., Agrawal, D., Rani, S., Karar, V., & Chauhan, M. (2022). Prediction of blood screening parameters for preliminary analysis using neural networks. In *Predictive Modeling in Biomedical Data Mining and Analysis* (pp. 157–169). Academic Press.

Kuzhaloli, S., Devaneyan, P., Sitaraman, N., Periyathanbi, P., Gurusamy, M., & Bhambri, P. (2020). IoT based Smart Kitchen Application for Gas Leakage Monitoring [Patent application number 202041049866A]. India.

Li, Y., Zhang, H., Xue, X., Jiang, Y., & Shen, Q. (2018). Deep learning for remote sensing image classification: A survey. *Wiley Interdisciplinary Reviews: Data Mining and Knowledge Discovery*, *8*(6), e1264.

Mercedes, L., Gil, L., & Bernat-Maso, E. (2018). Mechanical performance of vegetal fabric reinforced cementitious matrix (FRCM) composites. *Construction and Building Materials*, *175*, 161–173. https://doi.org/10.1016/j.conbuildmat.2018.04.171

Minnen, D., Ballé, J., & Toderici, G. D. (2018). Joint autoregressive and hierarchical priors for learned image compression. *Advances in neural information processing systems*, *31*, 1–13.

Mishra, P., Karami, A., Nordon, A., Rutledge, D. N., & Roger, J. M. (2019). Automatic denoising of close-range hyperspectral images with a wavelength-specific shearlet-based image noise reduction method. *Sensors and Actuators B: Chemical*, *281*, 1034–1044.

Owotogbe, J. S., Ibiyemi, T. S., & Adu, B. A. (2019). Edge detection techniques on digital images – A review. *International Journal of Innovative Science and Research Technology*, *4*, 329–332.

Paoletti, M. E., Haut, J. M., Plaza, J., & Plaza, A. (2018). A new deep convolutional neural network for fast hyperspectral image classification. *ISPRS Journal of Photogrammetry and Remote Sensing*, *145*, 120–147.

Puri, V., Kataria, A., Solanki, V. K., & Rani, S. (2022, December). AI-based botnet attack classification and detection in IoT devices. In *2022 IEEE International Conference on Machine Learning and Applied Network Technologies (ICMLANT)* (pp. 1–5). IEEE.

Rahman, M. A., & Hamada, M. (2019). Lossless image compression techniques: A state-of-the-art survey. *Symmetry*, *11*(10), 1274.

Rana, R., Chhabra, Y., & Bhambri, P. (2021). Design and development of distributed clustering approach in wireless sensor network. *Webology*, *18*(1), 696–712.

Rani, S., Pareek, P. K., Kaur, J., Chauhan, M., & Bhambri, P. (2023, February). Quantum machine learning in healthcare: Developments and challenges. In *2023 IEEE International Conference on Integrated Circuits and Communication Systems (ICICACS)* (pp. 1–7). IEEE.

Samadi, F., Akbarizadeh, G., & Kaabi, H. (2019). Change detection in SAR images using deep belief network: a new training approach based on morphological images. *IET Image Processing*, *13*(12), 2255–2264.

Sibaruddin, H. I., Shafri, H. Z. M., Pradhan, B., & Haron, N. A. (2018, June). Comparison of pixel-based and object-based image classification techniques in extracting information from UAV imagery data. In O. O. Elutade, I. A. Obisesan, O. E. Omotayo, O. A. Ajayi-Odoko, T. A. Olaogun (Eds.), *IOP Conference Series: Earth and Environmental Science* (Vol. 169, No. 1, p. 012098). IOP Publishing.

Singh, Y. S., Lal, S., Bhambri, P., Kumar, A., & Dhanoa, I. S. (2021). Advancements in social data security and encryption: A review. *Natural Volatiles & Essential Oils*, *8*(4), 15353–15362.

Sumathi, N., Thirumagal, J., Jagannathan, S., Bhambri, P., & Ahamed, I. N. (2021). A comprehensive review on bionanotechnology for the 21st century. *Journal of the Maharaja Sayajirao University of Baroda*, *55*(1), 114–131.

Wang, B., Chen, L. L., & Zhang, Z. Y. (2019a). A novel method on the edge detection of infrared image. *Optik*, *180*, 610–614.

Wang, Y., Shi, F., Cao, L., Dey, N., Wu, Q., Ashour, A. S. & Wu, L. (2019b). Morphological segmentation analysis and texture-based support vector machines classification on mice liver fibrosis microscopic images. *Current Bioinformatics*, *14*(4), 282–294.

Westreich, J., Khorasani, M., Jones, B., Demidov, V., Nofech-Mozes, S., & Vitkin, A. (2019). Novel methodology to image stromal tissue and assess its morphological features with polarized light: Towards a tumour microenvironment prognostic signature. *Biomedical Optics Express*, *10*(8), 3963–3973.

10 Implementation of FIR Filter and the Creation of Custom IP Blocks

Gampa Nikhitha, Pusa Vineela, Polishetty Gayatri, and Dharmavaram Asha Devi

Sreenidhi Institute of Science and Technology, Hyderabad, India

10.1 INTRODUCTION

By definition, a signal is anything that sends information. In everyday life, signals are used to collect numerous kinds of data (Devadutta et al., 2020). These might include data such as audio, video, etc. During the collection of these signals, noise is also added (Schafer & Oppenheim, 1975). To minimize noise, the concept of filters is introduced (Bhatt & McCain, 2005). The idea of filters is introduced to reduce noise. Two forms of signal processing exist: analogue and digital channel coding. Due to benefits, including cost-effectiveness, accuracy, easy storage, and processing, digital processing is chosen over analogue processing (Prabhu & Elakya, 2012). A filter is fundamentally a circuit that modulates a signal associated with positive in a deliberate and intended way (Patel et al. 2016). The goals of filtering are to boost a signal's strength (for example, by eliminating noise) or to extract information from signals (Zheng & Wei 2018). As stated above, the two main types of filters are analogue filters and digital filters (Kaur et al. 2020). An algorithm that can be used in hardware or software is called a digital filter. These usually operate on digitalized analogue signals that have been in the user's browser (Ruan et al. 2009). They are recommended in many instances over analogue filters, such as lossless encoding, noise treatment, quality control unit, etc. (Kolawole et al. 2015). In contrast to FIR filters, which have a limited pulse width, IIR filters have feedback. Accordingly, FIR filters are more dependable than IIR filters (Sangram et al. 2017). For linear phase applications, they are used (Rani et al., 2021). Three blocks make up the majority of the proposed FIR filter: blocks that add, multiply, or delay events. A carry select adder has been used for an adder block. A Booth Multiplier has been used for the multiplier block, while a flipflop has been used for the delay block (Fan et al. 2014). Given the rigid hardware architecture and limited resources, such as MAC units, memory blocks, hardware accelerators, etc., congestion prohibits the use of DSP processors for faster-transfer DSP applications (Devi & Rani 2019). The re-configurability of FPGAs, on the other hand, enables the creation of specialized hardware for a variety of DSP applications (Devi & Vlcek 2012). A specified FIR filter uses the 15-tap direct form low-pass FIR

DOI: 10.1201/9781003383505-10

filter with the lowest latency and power consumption, concentrating on the ongoing necessities of digital signal analysis (Rai et al. 2018). The adder to choose is decided by the applications. Adders are used in the majority of Finite Impulse Response (FIR) filters and message transfer applications (Govekar & Amonkar 2017). The Carry Skip adder is one of the quickest ripple carry adders used frequently in Digital Image Processing applications (Bhambri et al., 2020a). The performance of the adder was evaluated by looking at the power consumption, latency, and area of several carry choose adders for 8 bit and 16 bit (Kaur et al., 2022).

10.1.1 Motivation

We were inspired to work on something valuable and adaptable due to the growing number of uses for Field Programmable Gate Arrays (Bali et al., 2023). In order to design something that can be utilized for more applications, we looked at the range of signal processing and filtering techniques, which have a wealth of knowledge available but relatively few implementations (Rani et al., 2023).

10.1.2 Project Statement

Because the FIR filter has so many uses, constructing a FIR filter with a low delay and power consumption would increase its effectiveness. FPGA implementation of high-performance FIR filter is suited for the aforementioned requirements are the formulation of the problem (Singh et al., 2020).

10.1.3 Scope of the Project

By altering the filter's position in the chain and its number of taps, the FIR filter can be further customized for a certain application (Rana et al., 2020). It can be applied to biological applications to remove noise from signals such as ECG, EEG, and EOG (Sharma and Bhambri, 2020). It can be used in signal processing to remove noise from speech, audio signals, and other signals (Kaur and Bhambri, 2020).

10.1.4 Objective of the Project

- To design and analyze the FIR Filter.
- To verify the custom IP.
- To utilize very efficient adders and multipliers, develop the FIR filter in Verilog HDL.
- To verify and establish the functionality of the FIR filter.
- To introduce a RTL-level tutorial on custom IP block creation.

10.2 LITERATURE REVIEW

This section provides a succinct description of the linked articles that have been published.

J. F. Sayed, B. H. Hasan, B. Muntasir, M. Hasan and F. Arifin (2021): This study introduces a FIR filter, a fundamental filter in DSP applications, for the 45 nm technology node. The performance of several adders, including the hybrid 1-bit adder, ripple carry adder, half adder, and so forth, as well as that of bit D-flip-flops, including the 2-bit DFF and the 5-bit DFF, and FIR filters, are all compared in this work. Additionally, it compares several 2×2 Vedic multipliers and includes the Vedic multiplier in its calculations. The circuit's performance may be enhanced by the suggested technology, but the circuit's complexity is increased by using pass transistor and transmission gate logic.

A. S. Thakur and V. Tiwari (2018): This study proposes a FIR filter based on a sophisticated combining of the Vedic exponent with common logic. Four 8×8 basic Vedic multipliers are used in the construction of the complicated Vedic multiplier. The basic 8-bit Vedic multiplier is constructed using the Common Boolean Logic Adder. In comparison to other adders, the designed complex Vedic multiplier using CBL adder has a shorter delay (25.204 ns) and consumes 43095 less LUTs. Additionally, In Xilinx 14.2, the suggested design was put into practice software and written in VHDL.

S. Nagaria, A. Singh and V. Niranjan (2018): This study proposes that a number of parameters have been examined between two distinct multipliers, the Booth Multiplier and the matrix converter, have indeed been used in this study to suggest the FIR filter. The array multiplier (303), as well as the delay, are both smaller than the number of LUTs employed (232). For array multipliers and Booth Multipliers, respectively, the bond IOB utilization rate is 39% and 66%. The Xilinx 14.7 ISE tools and the Verilog HDL visual identity were used to develop the suggested filters. According to the results of this study, a Booth Multiplier significantly decreases a FIR filter's chip size without increasing power dissipation, which accelerates the system.

R. Balakumaran and E. Prabhu (2016): In this research, a hybrid carry look-ahead adder (CLA), a modified Booth Multiplier, and a novel structural design for the CLA are proposed. MAC processing, power use, and area performance are all strong points of the suggested hybrid CLA. The MAC table comparison takes into account variables such as the total latency, the number of LUTs, and the number of slices. When compared to the suggested MAC, the current MAC (34.35 ns) is slower (27.31 ns). This paper also discusses reversible logic architecture, which optimizes complexity and data redundancy. The suggested design was put into practice and synthesized using the Xilinx ISE tool.

B. Lamba and A. Sharma (2018): This review study compares various multipliers according to their various performance metrics. There are contrasts between the modified Wallace multiplier, the modified Wallace tree multiplier, the array multiplier, and the modified Booth Multiplier. This study provides a thorough analysis of multipliers' performance by taking factors like speed, area, power consumption, etc. Through this paper's observations, we learn that Booth Multipliers use less power and perform very quickly.

S. Sarkar, S. Sarkar and J. Mehedi (2018): This research compares different discrete components and suggests a hybrid adder. Propagation delay, area on chip, and power consumption are utilized as comparison metrics. Included in this is the creation and presentation of a hybrid adder that fuses together CSA and CIA. It displays the efficiency of the hybrid adder, which propagates nearly twice as quickly as the traditional adder. Verilog HDL is used to process all adder findings, and Xilinx 17.7 ISE is used for all programming.

Dharmavaram Asha Devi and L. Sai Sugun (2018): An engineer's duty is to lower the cost and boost the performance of embedded systems because that is the world in which we live. Making our own intellectual properties (IPs) is one of several ways to accomplish this. Real-time clocks are essential elements in the development of real-time embedded systems. Additionally, technology has advanced significantly, from 180 nm to 28 nm and beyond. As a result, IPs are in high demand in the relevant technology nodes.

Deepika, and Nidhi Goel (2016): This study proposes the implementation of a FIR filter-based on a reconfigurable MAC unit. A reconfigurable MAC unit was built with a Booth Multiplier and a carry look-ahead adder. The proposed design is created using Xilinx ISE 14.3 and Verilog HDL. The planned MAC unit uses 0.242 watts of electricity and has a 3.27 ns delay.

Kaur et al. (2020): In order to increase system speed, it is recommended to use the HDL language while designing a FIR filter. As a result, the suggested architecture offers faster performance at a reduced cost, and low hardware also offers high operating frequency without compromising performance.

10.3   DESIGN AND IMPLEMENTATION OF AN FIR FILTER

Convolution can be used to create an FIR filter in Verilog. Any n-tap filter, including 2-tap, 4-tap, 8-tap, and 16-tap filters, may be created using the convolution approach. The power spectrum h and the input signal x can be converted to form the equation of an FIR filter.

$$y(n) = \sum_{k=-\infty}^{\infty} x(k)k(n-k)$$

This formula is the same as the formula for the convolution of the two signals.

An impulse response filter (FIR), used in digital signal processing, has a defined period and eventually approaches zero. IIR filtration, which might provide individual responses and actively respond, are frequently contrasted with this. Before everything hits zero, an algebraic discretization period FIR filter's input impedance appropriately calls for Probability 1 observations. Active filters, which occur in time domain, discrete time, conventional, digitized, and other forms, are the most common type of filters used in software. Each filter's function is to let through AC components while preventing DC components. Filters are used in signal conditioners. Phone service are the clearest indicator of a filter since they narrow the spectrum of frequencies to a level far below what humans can hear (Figure 10.1).

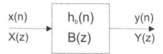

FIGURE 10.1   FIR filter.

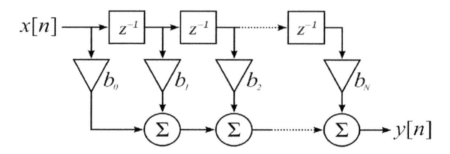

FIGURE 10.2   Basic block diagram of FIR filter.

Filters come in a variety of forms, including transfer function, high-pass filter, quality factor, and BSF. An LPF is used to filter out high frequencies since it only permits low-frequency signals to pass through to its output. An LPF makes it simple to regulate the audio signal's highest frequency range (Bhambri et al., 2020b). Only frequency components below a predetermined threshold are rejected by the LPF, which is a significant difference from an HPF. The output waveform of a precisely defined FIR filter of Nth order lasts for N plus one samples before zeroing off. A time-domain system's outcome y is created by superposition of the original signal and the response of the system (b) (x).

The output of a precisely defined FIR filter is the weighted average of the present value and a specified number of previous values in the input. The equation below (Figure 10.2) describes the method and defines the output vector $y[n]$ in terms of the initial series $x[n]$. The FIR filter is primarily composed of three blocks. Blocks that compound, delay, or add events. To shorten the delay of the filters, we use efficient adders and multipliers.

Due to their simplicity of use, reliability, and top performance, FIR filters are frequently employed in a variety of applications, including biomedical, communication, and control. For many situations where it is necessary to reduce computational needs, its simplicity makes it appealing. By removing the chosen frequencies from the incoming signal, filters play a crucial role in the elimination of undesired signal or noise from the original input signal. They gained enormous popularity as a result of the development of digital signal processing.

10.3.1   BOOTH MULTIPLIER

Multiplication is the fundamental mathematical operation utilized in nearly all applications requiring digital signal processing (DSP). Addition can be viewed as a chain

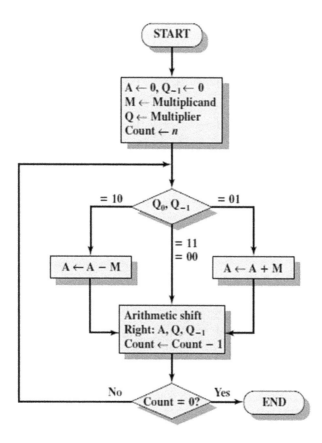

FIGURE 10.3 Flow chart of Booth algorithm.

of successive additions. For portable battery-powered entertainment devices, energy-efficient multiplication circuit design is required. Utilizing the hardware heavily increases the multiplier's speed. As a result, it is vital to develop a multiplier that is both fast and small in size (Figure 10.3).

10.3.2 CARRY SELECT ADDER

The sum of different N binary values is produced using the carry select adder, an algebraic combinational and sequential circuit, together with a 1-bit carry. However, unlike the ripple carry adder, the carry chooses adder's architecture prohibits it from spreading the carry via as many full adders. This suggests that adding two numbers should proceed more quickly.

Figure 10.4 is a block diagram of the basic component of a block size for the carry-select adder is 4. The carry-in determines which carry and sum bits will be generated by multiplexing two 4-bit ripple-carry adders. The preferred outcome is obtained by selecting which shockwave multiplexer has the correct statement by using the exact carry-in since one ripple-carry adder assumes a carry-in of 0 while the other assumes a carry-in of 1.

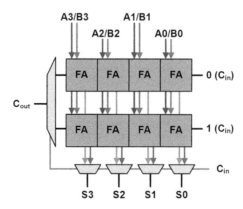

FIGURE 10.4   Block diagram of carry select adder.

10.3.3   Delay Block

D-Flip Flop is a delay unit in an FIR filter that produces delay. A signal postponement of one sample is provided by the unit delay. For one sample clock cycle, a sample value is kept in a memory slot before being made accessible as input to the following unit operation. The period of time it takes for a gate's output to shift from one value to zero is referred to as the fall delay. By using the delay control, you can simply extend the time between when the emulator meets a statement and when it really executes it. There are three values that can be set for each sort of delay: minimum, maximum, and type.

10.4   CREATION CUSTOM IP BLOCKS

Figure 10.5 shows the IP packaging and usage flow:

To connect to the Zynq PS, we will build a straightforward custom AXI IP block that multiplies two numbers. Two 16-bit unsigned values will be fed into the multiplier, and the result will be output as one 32-bit unsigned number. The two 16-bit inputs, divided into lower and upper 16 bits, will be contained in a single 32-bit write to the IP block. The outcome of multiplying the two 16-bit inputs will be contained within a single 32-bit read from the peripheral.

10.5   EXPERIMENTAL RESULTS

Figure 10.6 shows the FIR filter output. The given input frequency is 400 kHz, so that the output is distorted due to the cut-off frequency which is less than the given input signal.

Since the FIR filter is a finite-length impulse response filter, the signal that results from a specific input signal is made up of impulses spaced equally apart in line with the waveform of the input signal.

From Figure 10.7 we observed the RTL schematic, which consists of adder blocks and logic gates.

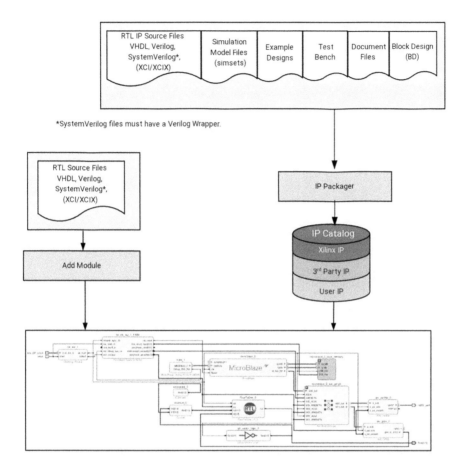

| RTL IP Source Files VHDL, Verilog, SystemVerilog*, (XCI/XCIX) | Simulation Model Files (simsets) | Example Designs | Test Bench | Document Files | Block Design (BD) |

*SystemVerilog files must have a Verilog Wrapper.

RTL Source Files VHDL, Verilog, SystemVerilog*, (XCI/XCIX)

IP Packager

Add Module

IP Catalog
Xilinx IP
3rd Party IP
User IP

MicroBlaze

RTL

FIGURE 10.5 IP packaging and usage flow.

From Figure 10.8 we observed that the ZYNQ Processing system is created. The M_AXI_GPO_ACLK Pin is connected to the slowest_sync_clk. The inter connect_ aresetn[0:0] is connected to the ARESETN pin.

In Figure 10.9 we observed the various design IP pins of the FIR filter. In this figure, Fixed Input/Output pins, Double data rate address pins, Clock pin and Reset pin are used. This design is generated from the RTL schematic.

Figure 10.10 shows that the total onchip power utilized is 1.691 w, that the junction temperature is 44.5 degree celsius and that the dynamic power utilized is 92% and the device static utilized is 8%.

10.5.1 COMPARISON

The difference between the existing model and the proposed model is shown in Table. 10.1. Comparing the new FIR filter with a Booth Multiplier to the existing FIR filter, a significant reduction in the number of LUTs and slices was achieved.

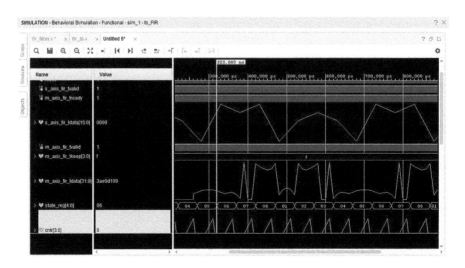

FIGURE 10.6 Simulation results of fir filter.

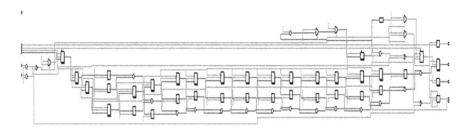

FIGURE 10.7 RTL schematic.

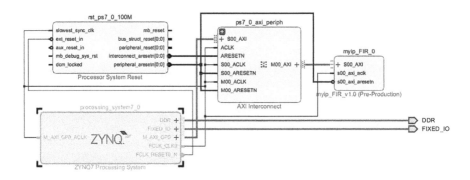

FIGURE 10.8 Creation of custom IP block and verification in SDK environment.

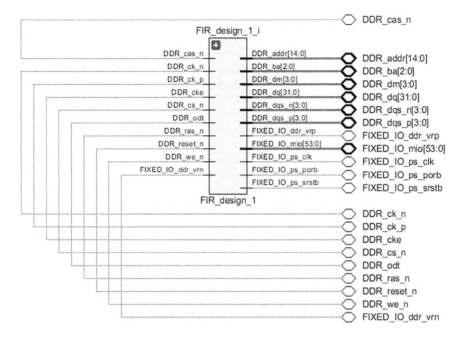

FIGURE 10.9 FIR design IP pins.

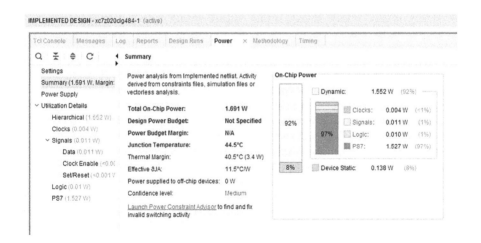

FIGURE 10.10 Power report.

10.6 APPLICATIONS

1. Linear Predictive coding
2. Linear Interpolation
3. Hilbert Transform
4. Speech Analysis

TABLE 10.1

Comparison of the New FIR Filter with the Existing FIR Filter

Parameters	Existing FIR Filter with Booth Multiplier	Proposed FIR Filter with Booth Multiplier and CSA
Number of LUTS	232	176
Number of Slices	1146	9
Number of bonded IOBs	44	48

5. Radar Application
6. Multirate Signal Processing
7. Medical applications like ECG Signals, EOG Signals.

10.7 CONCLUSION

This chapter, shows the development of a low pass filter with a specific pass band frequency, a stop band frequency utilizing Booth's Multiplier, and a carry select adder for maximum performance with minimal logic usage. Depending upon the specific situation, this 15-tap filter may need to be tweaked further. In applications such as signal processing and communications, the filter's order and coefficients can be modified to meet the requirements of the particular application.

10.8 FUTURE SCOPE

As this field of study is so vast, this work can only serves as an introduction. We can continue to work on it in a variety of ways. By utilizing numerous effective strategies, we can try to reduce its power usage even further. In future, we can look to improve its speed. The potential for significant improvement lies in its capacity to reduce surface area, consume less energy, and enhance acceleration. As long as science and technology continue to advance, there will always be a need to create ever-simpler, easier-to-implement procedures as well as ways to carry out tasks more quickly and effectively. As a result, this sector of employment will continue to advance and expand in the years to come.

REFERENCES

Balakumaran, R., & Prabhu, E. (2016). Design of high-speed multiplier using modified Booth algorithm with hybrid carry look-ahead adder. *2016 International Conference on Circuit, Power and Computing Technologies (ICCPCT)*. doi:10.1109/iccpct.2016.7530164.

Bali, V., Bali, S., Gaur, D., Rani, S., & Kumar, R. (2023). Commercial-off-the shelf vendor selection: A multi-criteria decision-making approach using intuitionistic fuzzy sets and TOPSIS. *Operational Research in Engineering Sciences: Theory and Applications*, 12(4), 100–113.

Bhambri, P., Kaur, H., Gupta, A., & Singh, J. (2020a). Human activity recognition system. *Oriental Journal of Computer Science and Technology*, 13(2–3), 91–96.

Bhambri, P., Sinha, V. K., & Dhanoa, I. S. (2020b). Diabetes prediction with WEKA tool. *Journal of Critical Reviews*, 7(9), 2366–2371.

Bhatt, T. M., & McCain, D. (2005). "MATLAB as a development environment for FGPA design". *Proceedings of the 42nd Annual Conference on Design Automation-DAC'05*. doi:10.1145/1065579.1065737.

Deepika, & Goel, N. (2016). Design of FIR filter using reconfigurable MAC unit. *20163rd International Conference on Signal Processing and Integrated Networks (SPIN)*. doi:10.1109/spin.2016.7566710.

Devadutta, K., Bhambri, P., Gountia, D., Mehta, V., Mangla, M., Patan, R., Kumar, A., Agarwal, P. K., Sharma, A., Singh, M., & Gadicha, A. B. (2020). Method for Cyber Security in Email Communication among Networked Computing Devices [Patent application number 202031002649]. India.

Devi, D. A., & Rani, N. S. (2019). Design and implementation of custom IP for real time clock on reconfigurable device. *2019 Third International Conference on Inventive Systems and Control (ICISC)* (pp. 414–418). doi:10.1109/ICISC44355.2019.9036428.

Devi, D. A., & Sugun, L. S. (2018). Design, implementation and verification of 32-Bit ALU with VIO. *2018 2nd International Conference on Inventive Systems and Control (ICISC)* (pp. 495–499). doi:10.1109/ICISC.2018.8399122.

Devi, P., & Vlcek, M. (2012). Perfect decomposition narrow-band FIR filter banks. *IEEE Transactions on Circuits and Systems II: Express Briefs*, 59(11), 805–809. doi:10.1109/tcsii.2012.2218453.

Fan, K.Y. et al. (2014). Optimization of FIR filter design scheme based on FPGA. *Research and Exploration in Laboratory*, 33(5), 91–95. doi:10.3969/j.issn.1006-7167.2014.05.023

Govekar, D., & Amonkar, A. (2017). "Design and implementation of high speed modified Booth Multiplier using hybrid adder". *2017 International Conference on Computing Methodologies and Communication (ICCMC)*. doi:10.1109/iccmc.2017.8282661.

Kaur, J., & Bhambri, P. (2020). *Hybrid Classification Model for the Reverse Code Generation in Software Engineering*. Jalandhar: I.K. Gujral Punjab Technical University.

Kaur, K., Dhanoa, I. S., Bhambri, P., & Singh, G. (2020). Energy saving VM migration techniques. *Journal of Critical Reviews*, 7(9), 2359–2365.

Kaur, S., Kumar, R., Kaur, R., Singh, S., Rani, S., & Kaur, A. (2022). Piezoelectric materials in sensors: Bibliometric and visualization analysis. *Materials Today: Proceedings*, 4(4), 10–20.

Kolawole, Emmanuel S., Ali, Warsame H., Cfie, Penrose, Fuller‚ John, Tolliver, C., & Obiomon, Pamela (2015). Design and implementation of low-pass, high-pass and band- pass finite impulse response (FIR) filters using FPGA. *Circuits and Systems*, 6, 30–48.

Lamba, B., & Sharma, A. (2018). A review paper on different multipliers based on their different performance parameters. *2018 2nd International Conference on Inventive Systems and Control (ICISC)*. doi:10.1109/icisc.2018.8399088.

Maddipati, U., Ahemedali, S., Ramya, M. S. S., Reddy, M. D. P., & Priya, K. N. J. (2020). "Comparative analysis of 16-tap FIR filter design using different adders". *2020 11th International Conference on Computing, Communication and Networking Technologies (ICCCNT)*. doi:10.1109/ICCCNT49239.2020.9225691.

Nagaria, S., Singh, A., & Niranjan, V. (2018). "Efficient FIR Filter Design using Booth Multiplier for VLSI Applications". *2018 International Conference on Computing, Power and Communication Technologies (GUCON)*. doi:10.1109/gucon.2018.8674998

Patel, D. K., Chouksey, R., & Saxena, M. (2016). Design of fast FIR filter using compressor and carry select adder. *2016 3rd International Conference on Signal Processing and Integrated Networks (SPIN)*. doi:10.1109/spin.2016.7566739.

Prabhu, A. S., & Elakya, V. (2012). Design of modified low power Booth Multiplier. *2012 International Conference on Computing, Communication and Applications*. doi:10.1109/iccca.2012.6179166.

Rai, N. S., Shree, P., Meghana, Y. P., Chavan, A. P., & Aradhya, H. R. (2018)."Design and implementation of 16 tap FIR filter for DSP Applications". *2018 Second International Conference on Advances in Electronics, Computers and Communications (ICAECC).* doi:10.1109/icaecc.2018.8479480.

Rana, R., Chabbra, Y., & Bhambri, P. (2020). Comparison of clustering approaches for enhancing sustainability performance in WSNs: A study. In *Proceedings of the International Congress on Sustainable Development through Engineering Innovations* (pp. 62–71). ISBN 978-93-89947-14-4.

Rani, S., Kataria, A., Sharma, V., Ghosh, S., Karar, V., Lee, K., & Choi, C. (2021). Threats and corrective measures for IoT security with observance of cybercrime: A survey. *Wireless Communications and Mobile Computing, 2021*, 1–30.

Rani, S., Pareek, P. K., Kaur, J., Chauhan, M., & Bhambri, P. (2023, February). Quantum machine learning in healthcare: Developments and challenges. *2023 IEEE International Conference on Integrated Circuits and Communication Systems (ICICACS)* (pp. 1–7). IEEE.

Ruan, A. W., Liao, Y. B., & Li, J. X. (2009) An ALU-based universal architecture for FIR filters. *IEEE Proceedings of International Conference on Communications, Circuits and Systems, Milpitas* (pp. 1070–1071). July 2009.

Sangram, Patil, Prithviraj, Patil, Indrajit, Patil, Prof. Jadhav, Sachin (October 2017). Implementation of FIR filter using VLSI. *AESS Journal.* ISSN: 0975–6779.

Sarkar, S., Sarkar, S., & Mehedi, J. (2018). Comparison of various adders and their VLSI implementation. *2018 International Conference on Computer Communication and Informatics (ICCCI).* doi:10.1109/iccci.2018.8441253.

Sayed, J. F., Hasan, B. H., Muntasir, B., Hasan, M., & Arifin, F. (2021). "Design and evaluation of a FIR filter using hybrid adders and Vedic multipliers". *2022 International Conference on Robotics, Electrical and Signal Processing Techniques (ICREST).* doi:10.1109/ICREST51555.2021.9331063.

Schafer, Ronald W., & Oppenheim, Alan V. (1975). *Digital Signal Processing*, Second Edition. USA: Pearson Publishers.

Sharma, R., & Bhambri, P. (2020). *Energy Aware Bio Inspired Routing Technique for Mobile Adhoc Networks.* Jalandhar: I.K. Gujral Punjab Technical University.

Singh, G., Singh, M., & Bhambri, P. (2020). Artificial intelligence based flying car. In *Proceedings of the International Congress on Sustainable Development through Engineering Innovations* (pp. 216–227). ISBN 978-93-89947-14-4.

Thakur, A. S., & Tiwari, V. (2018). Design high speed FIR filter based on complex vedic multiplier using CBL adder. *2018 International Conference on Recent Innovations in Electrical, Electronics & Communication Engineering (ICRIEECE).* doi:10.1109/icrieece44171.2018.9.

Zheng, J., & Wei, Z. (2018). "FIR Filter Design Based on FPGA". *2018 10th International Conference on Measuring Technology and Mechatronics Automation (ICMTMA).* doi:10.1109/icmtma.2018.00016.

11 Use Cases of Blockchain in Post-Covid Healthcare

Charu Krishna, Divya Kumar, and Dharmender Singh Kushwaha

Motilal Nehru National Institute of Technology Allahabad, Prayagraj, India

11.1 INTRODUCTION

The healthcare sector comprises medical equipment and devices, hospitals, telemedicine, health insurance, clinical trials, etc. The current market in India is being driven by government initiatives such as tax benefits, e-health and incentives. The industry is growing rapidly as a result of rising cases of lifestyle diseases and the increased demand for affordable healthcare delivery systems due to increasingly expensive healthcare, technical developments, the rise of telemedicine, and the increase in health insurance (Dhanalakshmi, et al., 2022). Due to the additional legal requirements to protect patients' medical information, the healthcare industry has unparalleled security and privacy standards. Healthcare data management is required for the timely and accurate treatment of patients (Rani et al., 2022). It has evolved tremendously in line with the advancement of technology, from storing medical records on paper to using client-server architecture to storing electronic medical records (EMRs) on the cloud (Ekblaw et al., 2016).

Prior to the spread of COVID-19 (SARS-CoV-2 virus), the healthcare sector was already facing a number of difficulties due to the interoperability, privacy, and supply chain traceability issues (Singh et al., 2021a). With the ongoing pandemic, new difficulties and costs have emerged, including the need to modify supply networks to deliver the urgently required personal protective equipment (PPE), to rapidly produce and approve treatments, tests, and vaccines fast, to repatriate pharmaceutical supply chains, and to deal with rampant counterfeiting and increased false insurance claims, etc.

Issues with data, such as interoperability, transparency, error, privacy and security, legislation, and control of access to patients' medical information records, were amplified by the pandemic as it has an effect on all stakeholders in the healthcare industry (McGhin et al., 2019). For example, almost 41 million health records were compromised in 2019, with one hacking attack involving approximately 21 million records. The proprietary electronic health record (EHR) systems developed by over 700 manufacturers often need to communicate between themselves. In surveys more than 70% of top medical researchers stated they had had access to erroneous, deceptive, or incomplete information, making it difficult to make decisions. The healthcare issues include interoperability, infodemics, privacy and security, continuous patient monitoring, inadequate data for research, false insurance claims, drug counterfeiting,

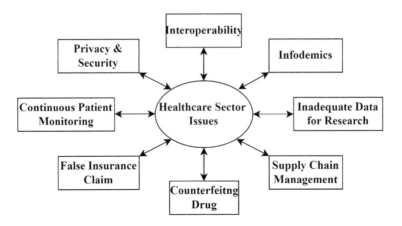

FIGURE 11.1 Healthcare sector issues.

and supply chain management (Tanwar et al., 2022). Figure 11.1 illustrates all of the various issues faced by healthcare. The healthcare industry can solve these issues with emerging technologies, such as blockchain.

11.2 BLOCKCHAIN

Blockchain is a type of distributed ledger technology. It involves an ever-increasing chain of blocks which are used to store data in the form of transactions that are immutable and stored on a distributed ledger. Each block is linked together by storing the previous block's hash to form a unique chain which cannot be corrupted. Figure 11.2, shows the basic structure of a Blockchain, which eliminates the need for central authority and the risk of single-point failure. Blockchain technology came into existence in 2008, when Satoshi Nakamoto first introduced the cryptocurrency Bitcoin (Nakamoto, 2008). Since then, many other cryptocurrencies have been introduced, such as Litecoin, ether, dogecoin, Solana, etc. Outside of the financial sector, the popularity of Blockchain has risen exponentially in various sectors, including healthcare, business, banking, land registry, supply chain management, etc. Different Blockchain platforms, such as Ethereum, Hyperledger, and IOTA, have also been introduced.

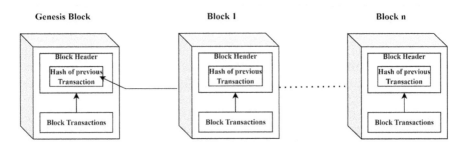

FIGURE 11.2 Blockchain structure.

11.2.1 Types of Blockchain Networks

A Blockchain network is a peer-to-peer network. They can be found in three different types: public, private, or consortium.

1. Public Blockchain networks
   A network that allows anyone to join and participate is called a public Blockchain — for instance, Bitcoin. The disadvantages of such networks include weak security, considerable computational power, and less privacy for transactions.
2. Private Blockchain networks
   A network in which one body administrates the Blockchain is known as a private Blockchain network, managing who can join and participate in a consensus protocol and managing the shared distributed ledger. Based on the use case, this can highly increase confidence and trust between stakeholders.
3. Consortium Blockchains
   A Blockchain can be maintained by multiple organizations in a consortium Blockchain network. The selected organizations govern who can access the data or execute transactions (Rani et al. 2023). This Blockchain is suitable for use cases where all participants are to be allowed and have a shared responsibility in the Blockchain.

11.2.2 Features of Blockchain Which Are Useful for the Healthcare Industry

Blockchain, a distributed ledger technology (DLT), has the capacity to empower the healthcare industry in multiple ways (Zheng et al., 2018) and research scholars from all around the world are working to create Blockchain networks for the healthcare sector (Kumar et al., 2022). As health data are sensitive personal information, the collecting, recording, and analyzing of health data is particularly delicate. In order to safeguard patient data, health data is arranged into separate silos. This means that there tends not to be uniform information exchange. A failure to share information results in incorrect and slower disease diagnoses, insecure data flows across silos, and incomplete records. The concept of employing a DLT to make the patient the sole and unique owner of their data was introduced in order to address these difficulties. The adoption of such a technology makes system interoperability possible. The following characteristics of the system make Blockchain useful for the healthcare industry:

1. *Immutability*. Immutability achieved by cryptographic hash functions does not allow data to change by malicious users, thereby increasing reliability. Once a transaction is saved on the Blockchain, it cannot be tampered with or corrupted. The current block stores the previous block's hash to be added in the chain. This maintains the chronological order of the Blockchain and makes it tamper-proof.

2. *Decentralization*. The decentralized nature of Blockchain eliminates the risk of system failures due to single-point failures or other attacks (e.g., DDoS attacks), further improving system security and reliability. Decentralized data management eliminates the need for one central authority over the overall data, giving controlled access to all stakeholders.

3. *Enhanced Security and Privacy*. Data may receive some protection from Blockchain security schemes, which include asymmetric encryption/ decryption schemes and digital signatures. Second, adding additional security measures such as access control and authentication to Blockchain increases security. Cryptographic functions are utilized to provide security to the Blockchain network. These functions are used to sign a transaction for authentication. Central point failure problems are eliminated as the network is decentralized.

4. *Transparency and Trust*. The data kept on a Blockchain is fully traceable. The decentralized consensus algorithms and asymmetric cryptographic methods (i.e., digital signature) of Blockchain implement data traceability and non-repudiation. The stakeholders now have more trust in one another. All transactions are visible to everyone in a public Blockchain network and each transaction is identified by a unique id called a transaction hash. A transaction receipt is generated after the processing of each transaction which is available publicly. The unique transaction id is used to find a record. The receipt contains details of the transactions. All the nodes have access to all the records to achieve transparency. Transparency in the system can also instill trust in institutions.

5. *Health Data Ownership*. Blockchain enables healthcare data to be patient-centric. The patient owns their data and has full control over who can have access. Letting people take control over the managing of their healthcare data. All of a patient's data is available to them anytime, anywhere.

6. *Data Availability and Robustness*. As the data is not stored at a central location but is held at all the Blockchain nodes, it is readily available. Hence a robust and resilient system is guaranteed. Every node in the Blockchain network has a copy of the entire Blockchain. Transactions are not processed on a centralized system; rather, they are verified in various locations by the network participants. The distributed nature of the Blockchain network enables it to be an egalitarian, peer-to-peer, self-reliant network.

11.3   BLOCKCHAIN APPLICATIONS IN POST-COVID-19 HEALTHCARE

Blockchain technology has the potential to revolutionize the entire healthcare sector. It provides a novel, innovative, and disruptive solution to the various problems encountered by the sector. Applications of Blockchain in the healthcare sector post-COVID include electronic medical records, automatic insurance systems, drug supply chains, data collection platforms for research, anti-infodemic systems, secure data-sharing platforms, continuous patient monitoring, contact tracing, outbreak tracking, and donation tracking (Ritu and Bhambri, 2023). Figure 11.3 lists the

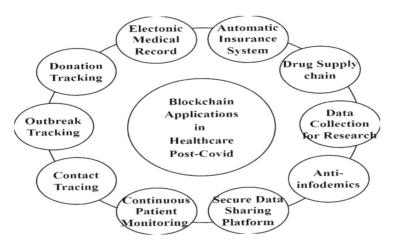

FIGURE 11.3 Blockchain applications in post-COVID-19 healthcare.

TABLE 11.1
Blockchain Use Cases in Healthcare

Blockchain Use Cases	Related Work
Electronic medical records	Ekblaw et al. (2016), Dagher et al. (2018), Dubovitskaya et al. (2017), Tanwar et al., (2020), Tang et al. (2019)
Insurance claim	Kurni and Mrunalini (2021), Amponsah et al. (2022), Ismail and Zeadally (2021)
Medical supply chain	Clauson et al. (2018), McGhin et al. (2019), Zheng et al. (2018)
Anti-infodemics	Marbouh et al. (2020)
Continuous patient monitoring	Hathalia et al. (2019) Uddin et al. (2018)
Contact tracing	Xu et al. (2020)), Singh and Levi (2020)
Outbreak tracking	Joshi (2020)
Donation tracking	Zhang (2020)

probable applications of Blockchain in the healthcare sector post-COVID. Table 11.1 records the related works corresponding to each use case of Blockchain in a medical setting. The applications of Blockchain in the medical domain are detailed below.

11.3.1 ELECTRONIC MEDICAL RECORDS SYSTEM

One of the key requisites of the medical sector is interoperability (Ekblaw et al., 2016; Dagher et al. 2018; Dubovitskaya et al., 2017; Tanwar et al., 2020; Tang et al., 2019). Interoperability is the process of disseminating data among various institutions. A centralized storage system hampers the interoperability of the records in medical institutions. A huge number of medical records are created daily and stored at a centralized location at various hospitals. These records, which are maintained at various hospitals, can be lost. The accuracy of electronic health records will improve with a focus on data management and the compatibility of multiple health systems.

More emphasis is being placed on the patient's needs in healthcare services. Health data administration can benefit greatly from the possibilities of distributed ledger technology.

11.3.2 AUTOMATIC AND TRANSPARENT INSURANCE CLAIMS

Fraudulent insurance claims in the healthcare sector are difficult to detect. Fraudsters may ask for treatment for an ailment on more than one occasion. Equally, they may forge an illness or injury to claim disability benefits from the government. There may also be a falsification of certificates on the part of healthcare professionals. All of these frauds can be handled using DLT and smart contracts. By enhancing fraud detection, health insurance, reinsurance, and claims administration, Blockchain can help make to sell and service insurance in a quicker, more efficient, and less expensive manner (Kurni and Mrunalini, 2021, Amponsah et al. 2022, Ismail and Zeadally, 2021). Lower costs and improved client experiences might be the outcome.

11.3.3 PHARMACEUTICAL SUPPLY CHAIN/COUNTERFEITING OF DRUGS

Tracking extremely valuable patents of pharmaceutical industry participants is an important Blockchain application. According to the World Health Organization (WHO), counterfeit drugs cost more than $75 million globally. Tracing the drugs using Distributed Ledger Technology is a method to minimize the trade in counterfeit drugs. Blockchain can help by enabling better transparency and traceability for products and payments (Clauson et al., 2018; McGhin et al., 2019; Zheng et al., 2018). It fast-tracks the validation process by eliminating third parties and minimizes processing and handling delays. The resulting system effectively manages and processes time, operational hazards, costs, and settlements for all stakeholders.

11.3.4 DATA COLLECTION FOR RESEARCH

Biotechnology firms work with sensitive genetic data and material that requires data integrity, privacy, and access control (Rachna et al., 2022). The dissemination of information on a common platform is highly essential for vaccine development and research. In order to respond effectively to the pandemic, the collection, accumulation, and availability of the data required for tracking the virus, administering research, and interpreting trends represent a crucial area of potential (Ritu and Bhambri, 2022). The Blockchain framework provides a foundation for novel research while enabling associations and organizations to disseminate their data with entrepreneurs, researchers, and scientists in order to test and incorporate data to form novel gadgets and solutions (Bhambri et al., 2022).

11.3.5 ANTI-INFODEMICS

The dissemination of huge amounts of information, including unreliable or misleading information on media or the physical environment during pandemic-like situations, is known as infodemics. Infodemics can cause confusion and irrational behaviors among the masses, leading to potentially devastating losses (Zheng et al., 2018). It also causes a decline in trust for health authorities and weakens the public health response. Blockchain helps in fighting endemics owing to its feature of immutability. Accurate data can be stored on the Blockchain to be circulated with the public globally. Blockchain's decentralized feature eradicates the need for an intermediary party, which can significantly cut the appearance of information manipulation and fake news and also boost the credibility of data among both the public and medical professionals. False information adds to disorder and causes both economic and emotional harm. Consequently, recording facts and news on a Blockchain eliminates their alteration and make them traceable, making it simpler to eliminate false information and data (Singh et al., 2021b).

11.3.6 A SECURE PLATFORM FOR SHARING PATIENT INFORMATION

Securely sharing electronic medical records is an important issue in the medical industry (Marbough et al., 2020). It should be done in compliance with the laws of the Health Insurance Portability and Accountability Act of 1996 (HIPAA) and the General Data Protection Regulation (GDPR). Blockchain provides a secure platform for sharing patient records.

11.3.7 CONTINUOUS PATIENT MONITORING

As the disease is highly contagious, patients are quarantined (Chhabra and Bhambri, 2021). The quarantined patients warrant regular monitoring as their condition may deteriorate suddenly. Blockchain provides a safe platform for healthcare givers to monitor the patient continuously without the need for human intervention (Hathalia et al., 2019; Uddin et al., 2018). This proves to be a boon for overburdened professionals in emergencies and saves their lives to a great extent as it reduces the risk of infection.

11.3.8 CONTACT TRACING

Contact tracing is an effective tool to prevent the transmission of a virus by recognizing, informing, and, if required, quarantining high-risk individuals. The tracing method is valuable, and smartphones contribute to the system's efficiency, but only if privacy and other concerns are handled (Xu et al. 2020, Singh and Levi, 2020). To monitor patients, governments and healthcare institutions conduct contact-tracing efforts. Nevertheless, utilizing Blockchain at each step improves the correctness and dependability of the obtained data (Bhambri et al., 2020). Blockchain networks can track patients' movements and give real-time updates regarding the afflicted regions. In order to inform the public of safe regions, it may also be used to detect areas that are virus-free. This is to note that monitoring companies can get this information by combining technologies like Artificial Intelligence and geographic information systems (GIS). Complying with quarantine requirements, Blockchain provides practical methods to safeguard communities from the growth of the pandemic.

11.3.9 OUTBREAK TRACKING

Verification and quality of data are critical in managing pandemics for recommendations based on recorded data (Joshi, 2020). To limit the transmission of this virus and preserve the integrity and quality of data, it is required and beneficial to implement tracking applications (Babu et al., 2021). The trustworthy, exact, tamper-proof, and transparent nature of the data processed on a Blockchain-based network makes it an ideal platform for coronavirus tracking. As a result, governments may provide more accurate updates on the progress of the pandemic for future planning, including anticipating the spread, setting aside potential territories, and monitoring the outbreak (Sangwan et al., 2021).

11.3.10 DONATION TRACKING

The pandemic crisis has presented humanity with formidable challenges. Several contributors have contributed supplies and financial aid to reduce the obstacles, and the entire contribution process, including storage, delivery, and distribution, may be recorded on the Blockchain ledger (Zhang, 2020). Utilizing the technology, the benefactor can authenticate the transfer of supplied money with both precision and transparency. Blockchain will reduce costs, do away with middlemen, stop the improper use of donations, and improve social organization. Assisting those facing medical or financial hardships as a result of the spread of infection is the driving force behind donation practices (Anand and Bhambri, 2018). A Blockchain-based platform called Hyperchain specializes in individually tracking donations to combat the emergence of coronavirus. By assisting healthcare organizations and governments, this website facilitates the contribution mechanism for patients and their relatives (Bose et al., 2021). The network guarantees that the contribution procedure remains consistent, traceable, and efficient (Vijayalakshmi et al., 2021). It enables a transparent platform for donors to track how their money is utilized (Jabeen et al., 2021). The Blockchain donation network guarantees that gifts reach their intended beneficiaries without the need for intermediaries to confirm proof of receipt.

11.4 CHALLENGES FOR BLOCKCHAIN TECHNOLOGY IN THE HEALTHCARE INDUSTRY

Blockchain is considered to be one of the most significant technologies of the 21st century (Bhambri et al., 2021). It has found application in several areas in less than a decade to revolutionize them for various benefits. Blockchain technology is a relatively new technology, meaning that its adoption is still in its infancy (Bhambri et al., 2023). Exploration and research are needed to overcome the challenges and obstacles faced by adopting Blockchain in the healthcare sector. The healthcare domain faces numerous challenges, as shown in Figure 11.4.

11.4.1 LACK OF STANDARDIZATION

Healthcare applications based on Blockchain have no standard implementations; hence apps from various Blockchain platforms cannot currently share a common

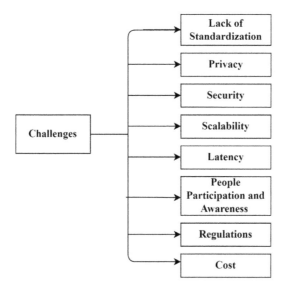

FIGURE 11.4   Challenges faced by the application of Blockchain in the healthcare industry.

workflow. The need for standardization rose as there was an increase in the adoption of Blockchain in various sectors. The inhibition in the adoption of Blockchain technology is due to a lack of uniformity. For instance, communication between Ethereum and Hyperledger fabric-based healthcare apps is not easy.

11.4.2   PRIVACY AND SECURITY

The healthcare Blockchain is at risk of being attacked by malicious organizations or government agencies. Blockchain networks have witnessed several attacks in the past (Zheng et al., 2018). By stealing the private key used to encrypt and decrypt healthcare data, unauthorized individuals may gain access to the information stored on the Blockchain.

11.4.3   SCALABILITY

Another obstacle in adopting Blockchain technology in medical settings is the scalability of Blockchain. At present, Visa handles 1700 transactions per second, for example, whereas Bitcoin and Ethereum handle 7 and 20, respectively.

11.4.4   LATENCY

The issue of speed is another one that might be problematic because processing which is dependent on Blockchains might cause a sizable delay. For instance, to complete the validation process, the validation mechanism employed in the current configuration of the Blockchain on the Ethereum platform requires the involvement of all network nodes. Processing is significantly delayed as a result, especially if there is a large quantity of data load.

11.4.5 People Participation, Awareness, and Education

Finding a way to involve people in the Blockchain-based management of their data presents another challenge. Patients, including children and the elderly, may lack the interest or capacity to contribute to the management of their data.

11.4.6 Regulation

Government regulations and cultural values have been identified as two of the biggest obstacles to the introduction of Blockchain technology. The regulatory concerns regarding Blockchain that have been expressed need to be addressed by government institutions, and the actors in the international healthcare sector will need to be very committed to the technology's cultural acceptability.

11.4.7 Cost

This includes restrictions on the amount of time, money, and money-related expenses needed to adopt Blockchain. The costs associated with implementing the dispersed Blockchain app are high. Restrictions include the time required to globally identify smart contracts, increased time, the timing of transmissions, the time needed for the data receiver to find the right data in shared storage, and longer total execution times.

11.5 CONCLUSION

As shown in this chapter, revolutionary Blockchain technology is being used increasingly in the healthcare sector, particularly for patient monitoring systems. Recent applications of distributed ledger technology in the medical business demonstrate that it is typically utilized for data distribution, electronic health record management, supply chain management, and drug prescription administration, among other applications. This chapter demonstrates that Blockchain technology can help overcome the challenges faced by the healthcare industry such as the secure dissemination of data, supply chain management, the management of electronic medical records, infodemics, etc. Regarding future research, Blockchain technology is still a relatively novel technology in the medical industry, and creative, inventive solutions can still be investigated. In conclusion, Blockchain technology has tremendous potential to change the healthcare domain so that the industry is better prepared for future calamities or pandemics.

REFERENCES

Amponsah, A. A., Adekoya, A. F., & Weyori, B. A. (2022). Improving the financial security of national health insurance using cloud-based blockchain technology application. *International Journal of Information Management Data Insights*, 2(1), 100081.

Anand, A., & Bhambri, P. (2018). Character recognition system using radial features. *International Journal on Future Revolution in Computer Science & Communication Engineering*, 4(4), 599–602.

Babu, G. C. N., Gupta, S., Bhambri, P., Leo, L. M., Rao, B. H., & Kumar, S. (2021). A semantic health observation system development based on the IoT sensors. *Turkish Journal of Physiotherapy and Rehabilitation*, 32(3), 1721–1729.

Bhambri, P., Dhanoa, I. S., Sinha, V. K., & Kaur, J. (2020). Paddy crop production analysis based on SVM and KNN classifier. *International Journal of Recent Technology and Engineering*, 8(5), 2791–2793.

Bhambri, P., Singh, M., Dhanoa, I. S., & Kumar, M. (2022). Deployment of ROBOT for HVAC duct and disaster management. oriental *Journal of Computer Science and Technology*, 15, 1–18.

Bhambri, P., Singh, M., Jain, A., Dhanoa, I. S., Sinha, V. K., & Lal, S. (2021). Classification of gene expression data with the aid of optimized feature selection. *Turkish Journal of Physiotherapy and Rehabilitation*, 32, 3.

Bhambri, P., Singh, S., Sangwan, S., Devi, J., & Jain, S. (2023). Plants recognition using leaf image pattern analysis. *Journal of Survey in Fisheries Sciences*, 10(2S), 3863–3871.

Bose, M. M., Yadav, D., Bhambri, P., & Shankar, R. (2021). Electronic customer relationship management: Benefits and pre-implementation considerations. *Journal of Maharaja Sayajirao University of Baroda*, 55(01(VI)), 1343–1350.

Chhabra, Y., & Bhambri, P. (2021). Various approaches and algorithms for monitoring energy efficiency of wireless sensor networks. In *Sustainable Development Through Engineering Innovations: Select Proceedings of SDEI 2020* (pp. 761–770). Springer Singapore.

Clauson, K. A., Breeden, E. A., Davidson, C., & Mackey, T. K. (2018). Leveraging blockchain technology to enhance supply chain management in healthcare: An exploration of challenges and opportunities in the health supply chain. *Blockchain in Healthcare Today*, 5(8), 132–142.

Dagher, G. G., Mohler, J., Milojkovic, M., & Marella, P. B. (2018). Ancile: Privacy-preserving framework for access control and interoperability of electronic health records using blockchain technology. *Sustainable Cities and Society*, 39, 283–297.

Dhanalakshmi, R., Vijayaraghavan, N., Sivaraman, A. K., & Rani, S. (2022). Epidemic awareness spreading in smart cities using the artificial neural network. In Sita Rani Khang, Arun Kumar Sivaraman (Eds.), *AI-Centric Smart City Ecosystems* (pp. 187–207). CRC Press.

Dubovitskaya, A., Xu, Z., Ryu, S., Schumacher, M., & Wang, F. (2017). Secure and trustable electronic medical records sharing using blockchain. In *AMIA Annual Symposium Proceedings* (Vol. 2017, p. 650). American Medical Informatics Association.

Ekblaw, A., Azaria, A., Halamka, J. D., & Lippman, A. (2016, August). A case study for blockchain in healthcare: "MedRec" prototype for electronic health records and medical research data. In *Proceedings of IEEE Open & Big Data Conference* (Vol. 13, p. 13).

Hathaliya, J., Sharma, P., Tanwar, S., & Gupta, R. (2019, December). Blockchain-based remote patient monitoring in healthcare 4.0. In *2019 IEEE 9th International Conference on Advanced Computing (IACC)* (pp. 87–91). IEEE.

Ismail, L., & Zeadally, S. (2021). Healthcare insurance frauds: Taxonomy and blockchain-based detection framework (Block-HI). *IT Professional*, 23(4), 36–43.

Jabeen, A., Pallathadka, H., Pallathadka, L. K., & Bhambri, P. (2021). E-CRM successful factors for business enterprises case studies. *Journal of Maharaja Sayajirao University of Baroda*, 55(01(VI)), 1332–1342.

Joshi, M. (2020). PHBC announces blockchain monitor to track virus-free zones. *Cryptopolitan*, 19 March 2020. https://www.cryptopolitan.com/phbc-blockchain-monitor-for-virus-free-zones/. Accessed 27 May 2023.

Kumar, P., Banerjee, K., Singhal, N., Kumar, A., Rani, S., Kumar, R., & Lavinia, C. A. (2022). Verifiable, secure mobile agent migration in healthcare systems using a polynomial-based threshold secret sharing scheme with a blowfish algorithm. *Sensors*, 22(22), 8620.

Kurni, M., & Mrunalini, M. (2021). Managing health insurance using blockchain technology. In *Blockchain in digital healthcare* (pp. 169–194). Chapman and Hall/CRC.

Marbouh, D., Abbasi, T., Maasmi, F., Omar, I. A., Debe, M. S., Salah, K., … & Ellahham, S. (2020). Blockchain for COVID-19: Review, opportunities, and a trusted tracking system. *Arabian Journal for Science and Engineering*, 45, 9895–9911.

McGhin, T., Choo, K. K. R., Liu, C. Z., & He, D. (2019). Blockchain in healthcare applications: Research challenges and opportunities. *Journal of Network and Computer Applications*, *135*, 62–75.

Nakamoto, S. (2008). Bitcoin: A peer-to-peer electronic cash system. *Decentralized Business Review*, 21260, 34–35.

Rachna, Bhambri, P., & Chhabra, Y. (2022). Deployment of distributed clustering approach in WSNs and IoTs. In Pankaj Bhambri, Sita Rani, Gaurav Gupta, Alex Khang (Eds.), *Cloud and Fog Computing Platforms for Internet of Things* (pp. 85–98). Chapman and Hall/CRC.

Rani, S., Bhambri, P., & Gupta, O. P. (2022). Green smart farming techniques and sustainable agriculture: Research roadmap towards organic farming for imperishable agricultural products. In Vikram Bali, Rajni Mohana, Ahmed A. Elngar, Sunil Kumar Chawla, Gurpreet Singh (Eds.), *Handbook of Sustainable Development through Green Engineering and Technology* (pp. 49–67). CRC Press.

Rani, S., Pareek, P. K., Kaur, J., Chauhan, M., & Bhambri, P. (2023, February). Quantum machine learning in healthcare: Developments and challenges. In *2023 IEEE International Conference on Integrated Circuits and Communication Systems (ICICACS)* (pp. 1–7). IEEE.

Ritu, & Bhambri, P. (2022). A CAD system for software effort estimation. *Paper presented at the International Conference on Technological Advancements in Computational Sciences* (pp. 140–146). IEEE. https://doi.org/10.1109/ICTACS56270.2022.9988123

Ritu, P., & Bhambri, P. (2023, February 17). Software effort estimation with machine learning – A systematic literature Review. In Susheela Hooda, Vandana Mohindru Sood, Yashwant Singh, Sandeep Dalal, Manu Sood (Eds.), *Agile Software Development: Trends, Challenges and Applications* (pp. 291–308). John Wiley & Sons, Inc.

Sangwan, Y. S., Lal, S., Bhambri, P., Kumar, A., & Dhanoa, I. S. (2021). Advancements in social data security and encryption: A review. *NVEO-Natural Volatiles & Essential Oils Journal| NVEO*, 8(4), 15353–15362.

Singh, A. P., Aggarwal, M., Singh, H., & Bhambri, P. (2021a). Sketching of EV network: A complete roadmap. In *Sustainable Development Through Engineering Innovations: Select Proceedings of SDEI 2020* (pp. 431–442). Springer Singapore.

Singh, G., & Levi, J. (2020). MiPasa project and IBM Blockchain team on open data platform to support Covid-19 response. *IBM, Armonk, NY*.

Singh, M., Bhambri, P., Lal, S., Singh, Y., Kaur, M., & Singh, J. (2021b). Design of the effective technique to improve memory and time constraints for sequence alignment. *International Journal of Applied Engineering Research (Netherlands)*, 6(02), 127–142.

Tang, F., Ma, S., Xiang, Y., & Lin, C. (2019). An efficient authentication scheme for blockchain-based electronic health records. *IEEE Access*, *7*, 41678–41689.

Tanwar, R., Chhabra, Y., Rattan, P., & Rani, S. (2022, September). Blockchain in IoT networks for precision agriculture. In *International Conference on Innovative Computing and Communications: Proceedings of ICICC 2022, Volume 2* (pp. 137–147). Singapore: Springer Nature Singapore.

Tanwar, S., Parekh, K., & Evans, R. (2020). Blockchain-based electronic healthcare record system for healthcare 4.0 applications. *Journal of Information Security and Applications*, *50*, 102407.

Uddin, M. A., Stranieri, A., Gondal, I., & Balasubramanian, V. (2018). Continuous patient monitoring with a patient centric agent: A block architecture. *IEEE Access*, *6*, 32700–32726.

Vijayalakshmi, P., Shankar, R., Karthik, S., & Bhambri, P. (2021). Impact of work from home policies on workplace productivity and employee sentiments during the Covid-19 pandemic. *Journal of Maharaja Sayajirao University of Baroda*, 55(01(VI)), 1314–1331.

Xu, H., Zhang, L., Onireti, O., Fang, Y., Buchanan, W. J., & Imran, M. A. (2020). Beep Trace: Blockchain-enabled privacy-preserving contact tracing for COVID-19 pandemic and beyond. *IEEE Internet of Things Journal*, 8(5), 3915–3929.

Zhang, J. (2020). Chinese startup launches blockchain platform to improve donation efficiency. *Tech in Asia*, 14.
Zheng, Z., Xie, S., Dai, H. N., Chen, X., & Wang, H. (2018). Blockchain challenges and opportunities: A survey. *International Journal of Web and Grid Services*, *14*(4), 352–375.

12 A Prediction of Telecom Customer Churn Analysis Using the I-GBDT Algorithm

P. Geetha, R. K. Kapila Vani, S. Lakshmi Gayathri, and S. Keerthana Sri

Sri Venkateswara College of Engineering, Sriperumbudur, India

12.1 INTRODUCTION

Customers in today's competitive telecom market expect high-quality service, value for money, and competitive pricing (Toderean and Beleiu, 2016). If they do not find what they are looking for, today's customers will not hesitate to switch service providers. The term for this occurrence is called churning (Liu et al., 2022). The satisfaction of customers is connected directly to customer churn. Since acquiring new customers is much more expensive than retaining existing ones, mobile carriers are changing their attention from client acquisition to customer retention (Kincaid, 2003). After years of intensive research in the subject of churn prediction, data analysis being integrated with Machine Learning was discovered to be a successful way to recognize churn. These obtain results faster and get insights that raise red flags before any damage can occur, giving businesses a chance to take preventative measures (Caigny et al., 2018). Typically, these methods are used to build models and learn from past data to predict customer churn. However, only a few of these methods tell us *why* customers churn, while the majority of them provide a result that customers may or may not churn (Rani and Gupta, 2016). Data normalization, pre-processing, feature selection, reducing class discrepancies and incomplete values, and substituting current variables with derived variables can all help in increasing the accuracy of churn prediction. Experiments conducted from the perspective of end users, as well as gathering their opinions on the network, also contribute to this improvement (Mahalekshmi and Chellam, 2022).

This helps the telecom industry retain customers more effectively. A smaller study, on the user's perspective and the quality of their experience, was conducted in contrast. In fact, user data volumes were not the sole focus of any study (Zhang et al., 2017). The relationships between Quality of Experience (QoE) and traffic characteristics for estimating this measure could assist service providers in keeping an eye on user satisfaction and taking prompt and appropriate action to address performance issues and reduce churn as well as finding the relationships in between (Perez and

DOI: 10.1201/9781003383505-12

Flannery, 2009). One of the most pressing issues facing businesses is the acquisition and retention of new customers. In order to take advantage of cross-selling opportunities, mature businesses try to keep the ones they already have instead of focusing on acquiring new ones (Chauhan and Rani, 2021).

One of the best methods to improve the value of consumers is to keep them for longer periods of time. The rise of electronic commerce in the modern era has increased the amount of information that is available (Kataria et al., 2022). As a result of greater competition brought on by the internet and the empowerment of customers who are no longer constrained by a single company's decision, customer attrition rates are anticipated to rise. In response to this threat, businesses ought to be equipped with the most efficient and effective methods for analyzing customer behavior and predicting future failure. The study, whose findings you have access to, uses Machine Learning techniques to develop a precise and reliable forecasting models for customer attrition in the pre-paid mobile phone industry (Rani, Kataria, and Chauhan, 2022).

Customers' acquisition and retention are crucial to the telecom industry's survival and profitability because of the industry's immense size, vitality, and ubiquity (Azeem et al., 2017). The newcomers place an emphasis on acquiring new customers, while the established firms place greater emphasis on maintaining existing ones. Customers may choose from a variety of products and services thanks to globalization, which helps them to choose the best services on offer. Customer retention and satisfaction are specifically correlated. Operators place a high importance on a range of customer-related approaches and analytics to ensure customer retention because the cost of gaining new customers is substantially higher than the cost of sustaining existing ones. The prediction method that should be used to identify churn is not clearly agreed upon by all researchers. Since around a decade ago, substantial churn prediction research has made extensive use of statistical and data mining techniques.

Data analytics and Machine Learning have each been proven to be efficient ways for anticipating churn. Numerous prior studies addressed the churn prediction based on call detail information, which was the basis for several Machine Learning algorithms. In order to identify churn, the work concentrated on recording service failures and disconnections. The goal of the study is to assign a "Churn Score" to a variety of customer transaction logs in order to identify early warning signs of churn. To date, customer churn has largely been studied in relation to network parameters. It is difficult to find any comprehensive analysis that addresses the issue of consumer dissatisfaction from the perspective of their level of engagement. The important and most widely used data mining method decision trees is the primary focus of this thesis on identifying churn. An excellent categorizer that uses a method similar to a flowchart to classify instances is the decision tree. Telecom operators frequently needed to analyze the steps in the process of predicting customer churn so as to determine the likely cause and justification for churn. Due to their simplicity in interpretation, visualization and analysis, decision trees can be the only option to reach this goal.

12.1.1 STATEMENT OF THE PROBLEM

The majority of businesses in the low-cost switching industries focus on customer turnover. At an estimated annual turnover rate of 30%, the telecommunications industry is the most affected by this issue. This model should have the option to recognize clients who are probably going to leave sooner rather than later. However, customer turnover is difficult to track and define because the pre-paid mobile phone market is not contractual, making it difficult to build a predictive model. In order to reach this objective, it appears that the first step in the pre-paid market segment is to define the bearing and a wedge, followed by the bearing forecast. In addition, churn data set management can enhance the performance of the model since churn data sets always contain an uncommon problem for the churn class. Public policies and the standardization of mobile communication in the competitive telecom industry make it simple for customers to switch carriers, creating a strained fluid market. Churn prediction, or figuring out which customers are most likely to stop using a service, is a very important aspect of business. Using Big Data Analytics, this study examines and analyzes customer turnover prediction using mobile data usage volumes related to environmental quality and user perspectives.

12.1.2 OBJECTIVES

In reviewing a client's characteristics, develop a model to predict the extent to which they are likely to leave information on demographics, accounts and services. In this proposed system goal is to find a data-driven solution that will allow us to lower churn rates and, as a result, boost revenue and customer satisfaction.

- To examine and analyze the prediction of customer turnover using mobile data usage volumes in connection to QoE and users' viewpoints.
- To determine how to bring the clients and their operator closer together.
- To guarantee the accuracy of the work, to produce engaging and original outcomes in the given context, and to discuss the importance of the customer churn model.
- To satisfy the customer in terms of timely response, service with a smile, continuously improve the customer experience through comparing the various algorithms
- To reduce the lost rate by analyzing the churn analysis effectively for the businesses

In this churn, the prediction system must satisfy the likely requirements, including the high level of recall and precision, execution speed, flexible forecast rates with new data, and the scalable way of positively increasing while the new data increases, to identify the concrete data while the users leaving the service.

As a result, these requirements are taken into consideration when coming up with a solution to this issue. The speed of execution and model performance requirements are the most difficult to meet. The existing algorithms may take a longer time to finish because there is a large amount of data available to construct our solutions. This proposed system uses a parallel computing strategy to overcome this disadvantage. The processing is split by the number of cores and distributed among the available cores in this manner.

12.1.3 FEATURES AND APPLICATIONS

The GUI comprises of 19 attributes, which are to be used in the prediction of customer churn. It was indicated on a row and column basis in a matrix. The rows of a matrix have features such as senior citizen, partner, internet service, tech support, monthly charges, payment method, dependence, online security, streaming TV, total charges, paperless billing, phone service, online backup, streaming movies, tenure, gender, multiple lines, device protection, contract. Similarly, the column of the matrix indicate the characteristics of the clients of a fictional telecom industry. There is an option to the predict customer churn by clicking the backend machine learning algorithms run and based on the confidence value.

Customer churn is the major challenge in this regard, being used for businesses such as global-level telecom industries and was used to improve the level of customer retention in businesses. The classification of customer churn is achieved by grouping them together into different categories. The phenomenon of churn in the context of contractual agreements encompasses both voluntary and non-voluntary instances. Voluntary churn occurs when a client willingly terminates their association with a firm. By contrast, non-voluntary churn refers to situations where a customer is unable to fulfil their financial obligations, resulting in their departure from the organization, as exemplified by the inability to pay credit card bills.

A lack of usage of the product, poor service, and finding a better deal elsewhere are among the most frequent reasons for customer churn. To precisely describe any of these reasons, domain expertise is required. Regardless of the various factors that may apply to various sectors, one thing is constant across all domains, as we have stated repeatedly: Retaining existing customers is less expensive than acquiring new ones. There could be an impact on budgets for both the company's running and marketing costs.

12.2 RELATED LITERATURE

This section gives a brief description of related research articles.

Zengyuan et al. (2022) proposed a Machine Learning approach, which is based on the PCA-Ada Boost model related to analyze the churn performance of e-commerce customers. To predict e-commerce customer turnover, this system integrates data pre-processing and ensemble-learning techniques, and it is partly connected to a proposal.

A POOH (Positioning the Optimal Occlusion Area) approach was implemented by Gucci and Mardiansyah (2020). This model enhances the detection precision while also identifying the occlusion face. Chen et al. (2015) combined the use of an Ada boost and a PCA algorithm for ultrasound image segmentation. Similarly, Zeineb and Rania (2019) proposes a method related to the classification of customers' contractual and non-contractual in traditional industries. This approach was used to identify the corners effectively.

Hughes (2005) proposes a RFM analysis-based approach for conducting a customer value assessment and identifying their status. This method was used to track and to discern the customers' purchasing behaviors during a cycle of online shopping.

Traditional Statistical Prediction methods are used to design classifiers that are less accurate and highly interpretable for small-scale data in industries such as decision trees (Kisioglu & Topcu, 2011), logistic regression (Hossain et al., 2019) and a Bayes classifier (Zacharis et al., 2018).

Even though deep learning and ensemble learning have recently been developed, they still produce less accurate predictions when dealing with massive amounts of data (Guo et al. 2017; Li et al., 2020).

Jayaswal et al. (2016) implemented an algorithm with the integration of decision tree, GBDT, and Random Forest to predict customer churn more accurately. These features will not be included in the prediction model through simple cleaning, which will lead to excessive complexity, a long training duration, and inferior predictive performance. By contrasting the PCA-AdaBoost model's performance with that of other algorithms such as SVM, logistic regression, and the AdaBoost method, its efficacy may be determined.

According to Olafsson et al. (2008), an approach to a valued customer is typically dynamic. It is possible to understand how the connection between a company and a customer varies over time by looking at the customer lifecycle, otherwise known as customer lifetime. The goal of customer relationship management is to keep customers from leaving a business by keeping them satisfied.

The strategy taken by Reinartz et al. (2005) assumes that client retention is more crucial than customer acquisition. New customers make it challenging to choose target customers with ineffective marketing strategies. Using a CRM methodology, Rygielski et al. (2002) identify important customers, forecast future behaviours, and make proactive, informed decisions. The total accuracy recorded for Bayesian networks, neural networks, and support vector machines was 99.10%, 99.55%, and 99.70%, respectively.

Recently, customer churn has become a popular issue in this field of research. This innovative and sophisticated data mining technique employs a data set of call detail records from 3333 customers, each with 21 variables, to predict customer churn and a churn-dependant variable with two classes: Yes/No. Information about their voicemail and the corresponding inbound/outbound SMS counts are among the aspects considered (Kuzhaloli et al., 2020).

In order to identify churn, artificial neural networks, decision trees, K-means clustering, and regression analysis were taken into consideration and prediction for mobile and wireless service providers using data mining techniques were discussed by Yabas and Cankaya (2013). However, decision trees were able to more precisely identify the potential corner.

According to the unified analytical technique offered by Muhammad Raza Khan and Blumenstock (2016), each client was assigned a churn score based on the likelihood that they would quit within a certain amount of time. Nonetheless, this approach creates an enormous number of covering highlights from client exchange logs and measurements that are generally prescient of client beat. These features were taken into account by a number of supervised learning algorithms that can successfully predict subscriber churn (Bhambri et al., 2020).

Xiaohang Zhang et al. (2021) looked into how network attributes affected consumer engagement and social network topologies based on customer call behaviors. The author proposes two approaches based on the phone survey statistics and the billing system of current customers using empirical data from the telecommunications industry.

12.3   SYSTEM ARCHITECTURE

Customer turnover is a key factor in moving away from business and preventing customer attrition (Sumathi et al., 2021). Therefore, customer retention is an important factor, being less expensive than acquiring new customers. In this proposed system, we take the Telco Customer churn data set from IBM sample data sets through Kaggle. Predicting the corners in the telecom industry is to defend the churn and churner from non-corners (Rana et al., 2021). An example was provided whereby a data set consisting of two million customers was utilized. The cutomers were classified taking into account numerical, ordinal and categorical features. Additionally, the data set contained information pertaining to network usage, subscriptions and interactions with call centres (Bhambri, 2020).

In the Knowledge Discovery in Databases (KDD) process of decision tree analysis, diverse patterns are extracted from different databases. The monthly/weekly data volumes, along with the characteristics of the consumers and their recent history, are taken into account during the data pre-processing (Devadutta et al., 2020). There are two ways to analyze the data, namely statistical analysis and decision tree analysis. The statistical way of analyzing the customers in telecom companies to optimize the resources of a network, to improve the service and to reduce the customer churn. In statistical analysis, this involved calculating the mean, standard deviation, variance, standard error and confidence interval. In the decision tree way of analyzing the customers based on the likely steps, data acquisition, data preparation, data pre-processing, data extraction, and the final decision are among various possibilities (Singh et al., 2020).

In the proposed system, the data set employed is a telco customer churn dataset that first goes through the data preparation process in which the missing values are

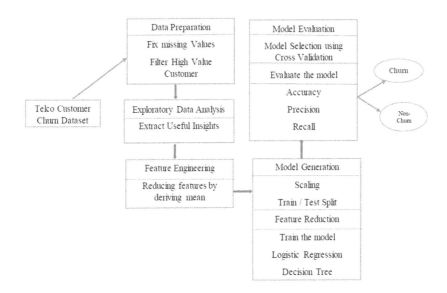

FIGURE 12.1   System architecture.

first fixed and then the high-value customers are filtered. Then the exploratory data analysis is performed, which helps in extracting the useful insights. Using the extracted information feature, data manipulation is performed whereby the features are reduced by means. This process is followed by model generation, which includes scaling, train/test split, feature reduction, and the model is then trained using various algorithms such as logistic regression, decision tree. The I-GBDT algorithm is chosen by applying a cross-validation algorithm and its estimated using valuation metrics likely to find accuracy, to find precision, to estimate recall. The optimal results are derived from the I-GBDT model. Window OS, the Python – Flask micro web framework, the XGBoost Open Source Library, and the Pickle –Python Object Structure are all employed to implement the proposed system (Singh et al., 2021). The data set contains the customer details. Likely information includes the Login and service history, Account information, and Demographic information (Bhambri et al., 2021).

12.3.1 ALGORITHM OF I-GBDT

1. Data preparation
    a. Prepare the data set for the customer (customer id and total charges) based on numerical and categorical values.
2. Exploratory data analysis
    a. Remove the duplicates and to perform univariate and bivariate analysis
    b. Generate the bar plot which shows the percentage of observations (Yes/No).
    c. Generate the histogram to evaluate the influence of each independent variable.
3. Feature Engineering
    a. Extracting the features of the data into the .my-GBDT model.
    b. Measures the mutual dependency between two variables based on entropy.
    c. Higher degree of dependency shows to predict the target of the independent variable.
    d. Transformations made by Pandas & alternative implementation by Scikit-Learn.
    e. Label encoding – to convert categorical to numerical values.
    f. One-hot Encoding – to create a column will set the level of categorical value.
4. Model Generation
    a. Using the Scikit-Learn preprocessing package.
    b. Normalize the data within the range then speed up the calculations.
    c. Build a model based on the training set and testing sets to evaluate the performance.
    d. In this model, create X to store the independent attributes of the data set, Y to store the target variable churn.
    e. Churn rate = (Users at the beginning of the period – Users at end of period) / Users at beginning of period.

5. Model Evaluation
   a. Perform hyper-parameter tuning and validation.
   b. Generate the confusion matrix or error matrix to evaluate the model by examining the observations that are correctly/incorrectly.
   c. Confusion matrix composed of 2 × 2 elements likely, the True Positive (TP), True Negative (TN), False Positive (FP) and False Negative (FN).
   d. Evaluates accuracy, accuracy and recall measures.
   e. Predict Churn/Non-Churn.

In preparing the data, there are 21 columns and 7043 observations within the data set. The data set appears to be devoid of zero values; however, we see that the Total Charges segment has been wrongly recognized as an article. The total amount billed to the customer is shown in this column, which makes this a numeric variable. We have to convert that column into a numerical data type for further analysis. Despite the fact that the Monthly Fee is not zero for these records, observations do have a duration of 0. These observations are removed from the data set because they appeared to conflict with this information.

In this exploratory data analysis, the data was pre-processed to remove duplicates, dropping null values as the percent of null value was low. BW techniques are used to include univariate and bivariate analysis to draw inferences about the correlation between turnover and different features of the data (Bakshi et al., 2021).

The percentage of observations that correspond to each class of the response variable is shown using a bar plot: yes and no. Due to the fact that neither class constitutes the majority of the 33 observations, this data set is an imbalanced data set. This imbalance will result in a significant amount of false negatives during modelling. The impact of each independent categorical variable with the result can be examined by means of standard stacked bar charts. Because each column in a normalized stacked bar plot has the same height, it is useless in comparing total numbers; notwithstanding, it is ideal for looking at how the reaction variable changes across all gatherings of a free factor.

In contrast, evaluate the effect of each independent numerical variable on the result using histograms (Rachna et al., 2021). The data set is not balanced, as mentioned previously. To correctly compare the two distributions, generate a probability density function for each class with a density equal to True.

The BW inferences include:

- Customers who pay electronically are most likely to leave.
- Customers who sign a long-term agreement are more likely to do leave than those who sign a short-term agreement.
- Customers without any access to technical support are more likely to quit. Compared with other citizens, the elderly are less likely to leave their contract.

The importance of the various functions of the data set, and the functionalities of the I-GBDT algorithm, are measured by Scikit-learn with the Pandas library.

Model generation is carried out with the help of Scikit-learn preprocessing packages. When creating a model, the step consists of splitting the data into two groups: raining sets and test sets. The model is built by the I-GBDT algorithm with the aid of

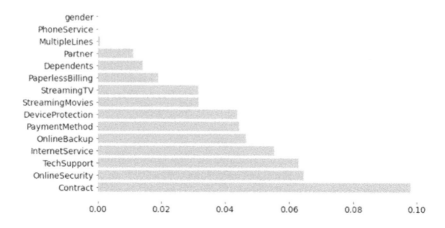

FIGURE 12.2 Important features of dataset.

the training package. The test set, which is used to assess how well the model is presented, involves tests that are not a part of the developing experience. To ensure an impartial assessment, it is essential to use unseen data in order to evaluate the model's quality. First, to create an X variable to store the individual attributes of the dataset. To store only the destination variable (Churn), and also create a variable called y. Next, sklearn. model_selection. train_test_split in the package may be used to create both training and test sets.

The number of observations that are correctly and wrongly categorized using the confusion matrix, also known as the confusion matrices, is used to evaluate the I-GBDT model. The expected classes are in each row of the matrix, and the real classes are in each column. Except for the diagonal, the confusing matrix will contain all zeros in a perfect ranking. Each of the components contributes to the misclassification of the principal oblique address. The perplexing matrix facilitates the examination of patterns of misclassification, keeping in mind the underlying principles.

The confusion matrix has four individual metrics that can be found based on the information: True Positive (TP), True Negative (TN), False Positive (FP) and False Negative (TN).

12.4 RESULTS AND DISCUSSION

12.4.1 EVALUATION MEASURES

The important measure is precision, which is calculated by dividing the true positives by all that have been predicted to be positive. The precision is the preferable one than recall.

$$precision = \frac{TP}{TP + FP}$$

The second metric recall is computed by dividing the real positives by everything that should have been predicted as positive.

$$recall = \frac{TP}{TP + FN}$$

The F1 measures harmonic mean of precision and recall, more accurately, the model's performance.

$$F1 = \frac{2 * precision * recall}{precision + recall}$$

The high accuracy is predicting who will churn which is computed between the observed values to the predicted values.

$$accuracy = \frac{TP + TN}{TP + TN + FP + TN}$$

The examining results were analyzed to compare the performance of different sizes of training/testing telecom industry data.

The I-GBDT results of evaluation metrics performance are,

The evaluation metrics associated with the various Machine Learning Algorithms likely, XG Boost, Ada Boost, Random Forest, and Decision Tree with I-GBDT algorithm are shown in Table 12.1.

The I-GBDT algorithm comparatively high accuracy and high recall while testing 20% data with 80% training data set of Telecom data in Kaggle.

The churn prediction results of confusion matrix are,

Prediction	XG Boost/ Ada Boost		Decision Tree		Random Forest		Gradient Boost Decision Tree (I-GBDT)	
	FALSE	TRUE	FALSE	TRUE	FALSE	TRUE	FALSE	TRUE
FALSE	1234	330	1395	346	1381	281	1423	227
TRUE	150	399	153	214	167	279	178	162

	Precision	Recall	F1-score	Support
0	0.96	0.88	0.92	534
1	0.91	0.97	0.94	646
Accuracy			0.93	1180
Macro avg	0.94	0.93	0.93	1180
Weighted avg	0.93	0.93	0;93	1180

FIGURE 12.3 Evaluation metrics performance of I-GBDT with state-of-the-art approaches.

TABLE 12.1

Comparison with Other Approaches

Algorithm	Accuracy (%)	Recall (%)	Precision (%)	F-Measure
XGBoost	89	86	85	58
Ada-Boost	84	86	81	85
Random Forest	85	83	82	79
Decision Tree	76	79	80	81
I-GBDT	93	88	96	92

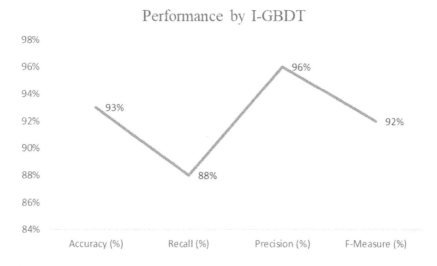

FIGURE 12.4   Performance by I-GBDT.

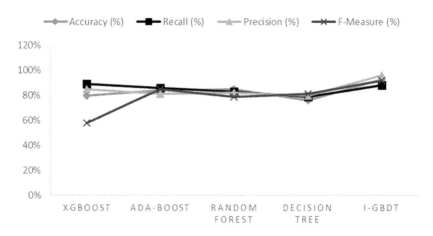

FIGURE 12.5   Comparison of churn prediction results of ML algorithms.

12.5 CONCLUSION AND FUTURE SCOPE

In this telecom industry, the key factor of churn prediction is related to CRM for the retaining of customers and making increased profits. By doing a comparative analysis, we aim to evaluate the performance of different Machine Learning algorithms, XG-Boost, Ada-Boost, DT, RF, in comparison with I-GBDT which is an integration of Gradient Boost and decision tree algorithms. The implementation of I-GBDT is expected to yield superior outcomes. Future efforts will be bolstered by the optimization of system performance enhanced in terms of the speed, accuracy and effectiveness, hence improving the mitigation of losses and the optimization of the objective function.

REFERENCES

Azeem, M., Usman, M., & Fong, A. C. M. (2017). A churn prediction model for prepaid customers in telecom using fuzzy classifiers. *Telecommunication Systems*, 66(4), 603–614.

Bakshi, P., Bhambri, P., & Thapar, V. (2021). A review paper on wireless sensor network techniques in Internet of Things (IoT). *Wesleyan Journal of Research*, 14(7), 147–160.

Bhambri, P. (2020). Green compliance. In S. Agarwal (Ed.), *Introduction to green computing* (pp. 95–125). AGAR Saliha Publication. ISBN: 978-81-948141-5-3.

Bhambri, P., Kaur, H., Gupta, A., & Singh, J. (2020). Human activity recognition system. *Oriental Journal of Computer Science and Technology*, 13(2–3), 91–96.

Bhambri, P., Singh, M., Jain, A., Dhanoa, I. S., Sinha, V. K., & Lal, S. (2021). Classification of the GENE expression data with the aid of optimized feature selection. *Turkish Journal of Physiotherapy and Rehabilitation*, 32(3), 1158–1167.

Caigny, A. D., Coussement, K., & Koen, W. (2018). A new hybrid classification algorithm for customer churn prediction based on logistic regression and decision trees. *European Journal of Operational Research*, 269(2), 760–772.

Chauhan, M., & Rani, S. (2021). COVID-19: A revolution in the field of education in India. *Learning How to Learn Using Multimedia*, 23–42.

Chen, K., Hu, Y. H., & Hsien, Y. C. (2015). Predicting customer churn from valuable B2B customers in the logistics industry: A case study. *Information Systems and E-Business Management*, 13(3), 475–494.

Devadutta, K., Bhambri, P., Gountia, D., Mehta, V., Mangla, M., Patan, R., Kumar, A., Agarwal, P. K., Sharma, A., Singh, M., & Gadicha, A. B. (2020). Method for Cyber Security in Email Communication among Networked Computing Devices [Patent application number 202031002649]. India.

Gucci, D. O. D. R., & Mardiansyah, Y. (2020). IMPLEMENTASI LEMBAR PENILAIAN POTENSI BAHAYA BERDASARKAN FRAMEWORK PENILAIAN POTENSI BAHAYA IDEACM DI INDUSTRI MENGGUNAKAN PENDEKATAN ERGONOMI MAKRO (STUDI KASUS: PT XYZ). *Journal Rekayasa Sistem Industri*, 6(1), 45–50.

Guo, C., Pleiss, G., Sun, Y. & Weinberger, K.Q. (2017). On Calibration of Modern Neural Networks. Proceedings of the 34th International Conference on Machine Learning. *Proceedings of Machine Learning Research*, 70, 1321–1330. Available from https://proceedings.mlr.press/v70/guo17a.html

Hossain, M. A., Quaresma, R., & Rahman, M. H. (2019). Investigating factors influencing the physicians' adoption of electronic health record (EHR) in healthcare system of Bangladesh: An empirical study. *International Journal of Information Management*, 44, 76–87. https://doi.org/10.1016/j.ijinfomgt.2018.09.016

Hughes, A. M. (2005). *Strategic database marketing*. McGraw-Hill Pub. Co.

Jayaswal, P., Tomar, D., Agarwal, S., & Prasad, B. R. (2016). An ensemble approach for efficient churn prediction in telecom industry. *International Journal of Database Theory and Application*, 9(8), 211–232.

Kataria, A., Agrawal, D., Rani, S., Karar, V., & Chauhan, M. (2022). Prediction of blood screening parameters for preliminary analysis using neural networks. In Sudipta Roy, Lalit Mohan Goyal, Valentina Emilia Balas, Basant Agarwal, Mamta Mittal (Eds.), *Predictive modeling in biomedical data mining and analysis* (pp. 157–169). Academic Press.

Khan, M. R., & Blumenstock, J. E. (2016). Machine learning across cultures: Modeling the adoption of financial services for the poor. In *2016 ICML Workshop on #Data4Good: Machine Learning in Social Good Applications*, New York, NY, USA.

Kincaid, J. (2003). *Customer relationship management: Getting it right*. NJ: Prentice-Hall.

Kisioglu, P., & Topcu, Y. I. (2011). Applying Bayesian Belief Network approach to customer churn analysis: A case study on the telecom industry of Turkey. *Expert Systems with Applications*, 38(6), 7151–7157. https://doi.org/10.1016/j.eswa.2010.12.045

Kuzhaloli, S., Devaneyan, P., Sitaraman, N., Periyathanbi, P., Gurusamy, M., & Bhambri, P. (2020). IoT based Smart Kitchen Application for Gas Leakage Monitoring [Patent application number 202041049866A]. India.

Li, Qing, Huaige Zhang, & Xianpei Hong (2020). Knowledge structure of technology licensing based on co-keywords network: A review and future directions. *International Review of Economics & Finance*, 75, 267–268. https://doi.org/10.1016/j.iref.2021.03.018

Liu, Rencheng, Ali, Saqib, Bilal, Syed Fakhar, Sakhawat, Zareen, Imran, Azha, Almuhaimeed, Abdullah, Alzahrani, Abdulkareem, & Sun, Guangmin, (2022). An intelligent hybrid scheme for customer churn prediction integrating clustering and classification algorithms. *MDPI Applied Sciences*, *12*, 9355.

Mahalekshmi, A., & Chellam, G. H. (2022). Analysis of customer churn prediction using machine learning and deep learning algorithms. *International Journal of Health Sciences*, 6(S1), 11684–11693.

Olafsson, S., Li, X., & Wu, S. (2008). Operations research and data mining. *European Journal of Operational Research*, 187, 1429–1448.

Perez, M. J., & Flannery, W. T., (2009). A study of the relationships between service failures and customer churn in a telecommunications environment. In *PICMET '09 - 2009 Portland International Conference on Management of Engineering Technology*, 2009, pp. 3334–3342.

Rachna, Chhabra, Y., & Bhambri, P. (2021). Various approaches and algorithms for monitoring energy efficiency of wireless sensor networks. In *Lecture notes in civil engineering*, Vol. 113, pp. 761–770. Springer Singapore.

Rana, R., Chhabra, Y., & Bhambri, P. (2021). Design and development of distributed clustering approach in wireless sensor network. *Webology*, 18(1), 696–712.

Rani, S., & Gupta, O. P. (2016). Empirical analysis and performance evaluation of various GPU implementations of Protein BLAST. *International Journal of Computer Applications*, 151(7), 22–27.

Rani, S., Kataria, A., & Chauhan, M. (2022). Cyber security techniques, architectures, and design. In *Holistic approach to quantum cryptography in cyber security* (pp. 41–66). CRC Press.

Reinartz, W., Thomas, J., & Kumar, V. (2005). Balancing acquisition and retention resources to maximize profitability. *Journal of Marketing*, 69(1), 63–79.

Rygielski, C., Wang, J., & Yen, D. (2002). Data mining techniques for customer relationship management. *Technology in Society*, 24(4), 483–502.

Singh, G., Singh, M., & Bhambri, P. (2020). Artificial intelligence based flying car. In *Proceedings of the International Congress on Sustainable Development through Engineering Innovations*, pp. 216–227. ISBN 978-93-89947-14-4.

Singh, M., Bhambri, P., Dhanoa, I. S., Jain, A., & Kaur, K. (2021). Data mining model for predicting diabetes. *Annals of the Romanian Society for Cell Biology*, 25(4), 6702–6712.

Sumathi, N., Thirumagal, J., Jagannathan, S., Bhambri, P., & Ahamed, I. N. (2021). A comprehensive review on bionanotechnology for the 21st century. *Journal of the Maharaja Sayajirao University of Baroda*, 55(1), 114–131.

Toderean, & Beleiu, H. (2016). Methods for churn prediction in the prepaid mobile telecommunications industry. In *2016 International Conference on Communications (COMM)*, 2016, pp. 97–100.

Yabas, U., & Cankaya, H. C., (2013). Churn prediction in subscriber management for mobile and wireless communications services. In *2013 IEEE Globecom Workshops (GC Wkshps)*, 2013, pp. 991–995.

Zacharis, K., Messini, C. I., Anifandis, G., Koukoulis, G., Satra, M., & Daponte, A. (2018). Human Papilloma Virus (HPV) and fertilization: A mini review. *Medicina (Kaunas)*, 54(4), 50. https://doi.org/10.3390/medicina54040050

Zeineb, A., & Rania, H. K. (2019). Forecast bankruptcy using a blend of clustering and MARS model: Case of US banks. *Annals of Operations Research*, 281(1–2), 27–64.

Zengyuan, Wu, Lizheng, Jing, Wu, Bei, & Jin, Lingmin (2022). A PCA-AdaBoostmodel for E-commerce customer churn prediction. *Annals of operations research*. Springer Nature.

Zhang, H., Demirer, R., & Pierdzioch, C. (2017). On the short-term predictability of stock returns: A quantile boosting approach. *Finance Research Letters*, 22(3), 35–41.

Zhang, X., Gao, T., Fang, L., Fackler, S., Borchers, J. A., Kirby, B. J., … Takeuchi, I. (2021, November 17). Chiral Spin Bobbers in Exchange-Coupled Hard-Soft Magnetic Bilayers. arXiv preprint, arXiv:2111.09183.

13 Deployment of Machine Learning and Deep Learning Algorithms in Industrial Engineering

Hutashan Vishal Bhagat and Manminder Singh

Sant Longowal Institute of Engineering and Technology, Sangrur, India

13.1 INTRODUCTION

Industrial engineering is defined as the engineering branch that considers the design, analysis and control of production and service operations within a system. The advent of the Internet of Things (IOT) and Artificial Intelligence (AI) in industries makes the manufacturing processes more optimal. Today, the deployment of numerous Machine Learning (ML) and deep learning (DL) techniques in distinct industrial processes help to increase productivity and efficiency, improve quality, reduce industrial waste and optimize industrial workflows. AI helps industrial engineers to increase overall productivity in the automation of distinct industrial processes such as designing, manufacturing, defect detection etc. There are several sequential operations in a production line and continuous monitoring of the production line is required to make sure the product is of high quality. Manual monitoring of the production line is a tedious task for industrial engineers, hence ML models are deployed that take into consideration the data sets generated by the distinct production-line procedures to enhance quality control, risk evaluation and cost-cutting (Kang et al., 2020). DL techniques give the benefit of product designing by taking into consideration distinct evaluation metrics (manufacturability, cost-effectiveness, quality, etc.) that cannot be achieved using traditional techniques. This chapter discusses distinct models based on ML and DL techniques that are utilized in industrial engineering in the following sections (Arunachalam et al., 2022).

13.2 INDUSTRY 4.0

The 4th industrial revolution is another name for Industry 4.0, which focused primarily on cyber-physical transformation in the manufacturing process (Lemstra and de Mesquita, 2023). It includes the optimal way to organize the industrial resources, processes and societal patterns to sense, predict and interact with the physical environment. The production line is the main concern of industrial engineers to increase

DOI: 10.1201/9781003383505-13

productivity. There exist several data-driven techniques to solve the problems concerned with production lines. ML models are proven to be efficient in the analysis of complex systems and provide solutions to the problems concerned with manufacturing. To understand the applications of ML and DL techniques in industrial engineering processes, the concept of manufacturing lines and their attributes are covered in the next section.

13.2.1 PRODUCTION LINES

In present-day manufacturing industries, the production lines are considered to be the backbone of all units. The key idea of the production line is to automate the distinct set of processes in the production phase of the product. The authors (Lemstra and de Mesquita, 2023) define production lines as manufacturing or assembly processes that undergo several sequential processes (manufacturing or assembly processes, fault detection, etc.) to make the desired end product. In the manufacturing process, the raw material needs to go through the production line which further passes through distinct working stations to produce the end product. The components form distinct production lines which are assembled through the assembly production line to make a complex end product (Rani, Bhambri, and Chauhan, 2021). The assembly production lines tend to be used in both the automobile industries and the large equipment industries (Bhagwan and Evans, 2023).

A production line can be categorized into five major categories, viz., *a) Job-Shop b) Batch c) Repetitive d) Continuous* and *e) Mass production*. The authors (Bierbooms, 2012) defined the four major characteristics of the production line for ease of categorization and these characteristics are discussed in turn as follows.

- *Production Volume*: Depending upon the type of manufacturing products, there can be variations in the size and volume of the production line. It can have either a low volume or a high volume according to the type of product manufacturing (Banerjee et al., 2022). The cycle time of a low production line is comparatively longer because of the continuous interventions of humans and the lower degree of automation in the production process. For example, a luxury car manufacturing industry has a job-shop production line which has a low volume. In contrast, machinery in the high production line is less flexible and requires less intervention from humans, resulting in high throughput. For example, a paper-manufacturing or food-processing industry requires less customization; as a result, such industries have high-volume production lines that run at high speed without human intervention (Bauza et al., 2018).
- *Workstation arrangement*: Depending upon the type of complexity within an industry, the workstation can be either single-server or multi-server in nature. In a single-sever workstation, a single machine is capable enough of handling the whole manufacturing process of the industry and, hence, the machine setup is simple, but the reliability is highly uncertain (Rani, Arya, and Kataria, 2022). In a multi-server workstation, several machines in parallel are utilized to carry out the production process. The multi-server

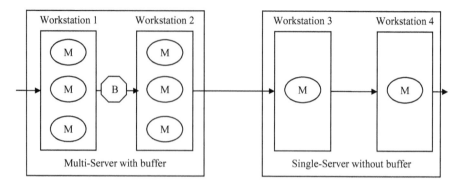

FIGURE 13.1   Conceptual model of production line.

workstations have high throughput, but they have complex machinery set-ups (Ling, et al., 2022).

- **Buffers:** A buffer in industrial engineering is defined as a pipeline or con-veyor belt that assists in the easy transportation of products/goods from one working station to another. Furthermore, a buffer also provides storage to synchronize the cycle time variations among the distinct working stations of an industry. The key advantage of the buffer is that the downstream working station does not stop, even if there is a failure in the upstream working sta-tions (Chang et al., 2019).

- **Process type:** The processes within a production line can be either discrete or continuous. The discrete production line has processes of varied cycle times. Depending upon the availability of storage in the downstream buf-fer, a machine needs to stop when the downstream buffer is fully occupied and restarts working when the downstream buffer is emptied (Alsawafy and Selim, 2022). This concept is known as Booking After Services (BAS). In a continuous production line, the congestion between the upstream and downstream buffer is removed by adjusting the cycle time of the working machines and, hence, there exists a non-stop production flow in a continu-ous production line (Jelsch et al., 2022).

Figure 13.1 shows the model that conceptualizes the working of the production line with multi-server with buffer and single-server without buffer workstations. In this section, the key components, characteristics, workflow and conceptualized model explaining the working of the production line are discussed. In Section 13.3 below, the distinct applica-tions of machine learning techniques in industrial engineering are discussed.

13.3   APPLICATIONS OF ML TECHNIQUES IN INDUSTRIAL ENGINEERING

The introduction of ML techniques in Industry 4.0 resulted in the improvement of manufacturing processes. The data availability, high-performance computing and tre-mendous storage units have made the ML models able to provide solutions for the distinct challenges in the manufacturing process of the industry (Usuga Cadavid et al., 2020). Cycle time prediction is a complicated problem for industrial engineers in the case of complex manufacturing setups. A simulation model for the discrete events on a production line in order to predict the cycle time by utilizing the genetic programming and effective process time are used by the authors (Can and Heavey, 2016). This model improves control and planning processes in manufacturing systems.

The authors (Wang et al., 2018) used predictive ML techniques based on SVMs (Support Vector Machines) and AMPSO (Adaptive Mutation Particle Swarm Optimization) for the prognosis of strip crowns in the hot-strip rolling process. The proposed AMPSO-SVR model results in a new technique and optimal shape finding in the hot-strip rolling method. The authors (Golkarnarenji et al., 2019) used ML models to predict the mechanical properties of carbon fibers. The proposed ML model is based on the Support Vector Regression (SVR) and ANN. A limited training data set is considered for training the model.

A critical quality indicator for cement clinkers in rotary cement kilns is the amount of free lime (f-CaO). For the majority of time, the cement clinker's f-CaO amount is measured in a lab offline because of the unavailability of hardware sensors. The authors (Liu et al., 2020) proposed a soft-sensor technique ESVM (SVM Ensemble), based on ML, to predict free lime amount during the production process of cement. Another soft sensor developed by the authors (Mulrennan et al., 2018) is responsible for properly estimating the yield stress by utilizing an instrumented slit die for an extruded Polylactide (PLA) sheet inline at the extrusion process. The yield stress is then predicted, utilizing ML techniques, for the extruded PLA sheet by using the data gathered from the slit die sensors. By decreasing machine downtime and improving the energy efficiency of the process, the proposed technique results in lower scrap rates and production costs.

In the manufacture of vehicle bodies, the fixtures used to fasten the panels together during the joining processes are typically hard constructions that demand a laborious hand setup process. Different adjustment modules are created at the Fraunhofer IWU which satisfy various necessities for the automation of the adjustment process and shorten the ramping-up periods (Sharma et al., 2020). Produced components are tested against an adjustment database due to strict quality criteria. The measured values and the expertise of the template specialists used for the precise location for each clamping point is determined by applying the mathematical algorithms and contemporary AI techniques developed by the authors (Fritzsche et al., 2017).

The fundamental requirement of the manufacturing system is to diagnose and forecast the fitness value of the distinct machines over the production line for automotive components (Bhambri et al., 2020). Great amounts of Big Data from the production line can now be captured easily and can be stored in large volumes because of the Internet of Things (IoT) technology. The advancement of AI has made it possible to effectively mine large amounts of data. The authors (Luo and Wang, 2018) proposed an ML model to detect the fitness condition of the machines through utilizing the data generated by the different machines in response to the industrial demand for health self-diagnosis for car manufacturing lines. To replicate the machines' long-term health state, the PID control parameters of the motors are split. The proposed model of the correlation between the large data trend and the machine's diagnostic score is trained using three different ANN techniques. The proposed model is more effective in terms of speed and precision for machine fitness status diagnosis and prediction than the traditional empirical analysis.

Architecture is intended to figure out the issue of human–machine interaction in manufacturing, which is related to digital-twin modeling on both the Cyber-Physical (C-P) and Human-Cyber sides, is the Digital-twin visualization architecture. Although there is a lot of research and a range of applications in this area, there is not sufficient focus on lightweight architecture and services that are useful throughout their entire lifecycle. To have flexible manufacturing systems (FMS), architecture of digital-twin visualization is proposed by the authors (Fan et al., 2021). Experimental findings demonstrate the effectiveness of the proposed GHOST (geometry (G)-history (H)-ontology (O)-snapshot (S)-topology (T)) strategy in several facets of the FMS lifecycle.

Nowadays, majority of the e-commerce warehouses now deploy autonomous mobile robotic machines to increase efficiency, save energy and overcome the human errors. The robots, the other important resources and activities in a warehouse, are under the management of the Robotic-Mobile-Fulfillment System (RMFS). The authors (Bolu and Korçak, 2021) proposed a centralized task management method that is dynamically responsive to the centralized system. A cutting-edge process conversion method that creates process from a batch of orders and offers a significant pile-on value is proposed. Then, taking into account the position of robots and pods, the use of totes, and the age of the tasks, an adaptive heuristic strategy for the assignment of produced tasks to robots is proposed. The outcomes give an idea of creating an efficient smart warehousing system.

13.4 APPLICATIONS OF DL TECHNIQUES IN INDUSTRIAL ENGINEERING

The treads are the most important part of the tire in terms of predicting the average lifespan. The authors (Lihao and Yanni, 2018) utilized the data obtained from different parameters such as rotating speed, air pressure and main current as an input to the Convolution Neural Network (CNN) model of DL to detect fault and diagnosis for tire tread lines (Dhanoa and Bhambri, 2020). The proposed model outperforms the traditional models based on the Back propagation neural network, decision tree and logistic regression.

Chemical mechanical polishing is a very common process in automobile industries. The prediction of material removal rate (MRR) is a critical measure in determining the quality of a product. The authors proposed a data-driven approach that is based on the Deep Belief Network (DBN) and different polishing parameters are utilized to find the relation with MRR (Wang and Yang, 2017).

The motors are considered to be the most important parts in industrial operations because of their stability, low cost, and robust performance. The shutdown of a whole production line due to a motor failure may result in significant financial loss. The diagnosis of motor faults must be precise, trustworthy, and efficient (Potluri et al., 2019). Currently, the area of motor fault diagnostics is receiving considerable attention as it is thought to be very promising in terms of ensuring safe motor operations. A Long Short-Term Memory (LSTM) neural network, which has the ability to acquire meaningful data from raw information without the use of feature engineering, and is therefore a unique fault detection approach for three-phase asynchronous motors, is proposed by the authors (Xiao et al., 2018). Other classification techniques, such as LR, SVM, MLP, and basic RNN, are evaluated and their results are compared. The proposed technique, according to the results, achieves a high degree of accuracy in fault diagnosis.

An emulsion explosive is an anti-water industrial explosive that was developed at the end of the 1960s. Emulsion explosives have a number of benefits, including strong explosion and water resistance performance, accessibility to a variety of raw materials, low production costs, and minimal environmental contamination. Emulsion explosives have emerged as a prominent focus in in the industry in recent years, being widely employed in various applications. Since the emulsifier is an important element in the creation of emulsion explosives, it is important to track and analyze its operational status. The authors (Wang et al., 2017) proposed a data-driven design to create a fault diagnosis system. Through the use of sensors, the system gathers data on emulsifiers. The fault diagnostic model of the emulsifier is built using the signal acquired after transmission to the PLC module, then utilizing the host computer software, in order to achieve the function of fault updating, online monitoring, and alarm recording.

Through a variety of sensors, a significant volume of real-time quality data is gathered in the manufacturing process. The majority of process data, however, are high-dimensional, nonlinear, and highly correlated, making it challenging to model the process profiles and limiting the use of traditional statistical process control techniques. The authors (Liu et al., 2019) proposed a real-time quality monitoring and diagnosis system based on a deep-belief network (DBN) for manufacturing process profiles, which is motivated by its potent capacity to extract the key aspects of input data. An experiment based on simulation is utilized to prove the effectiveness of the proposed recognition model for the manufacturing process, and the performance is assessed using an actual example of the injection moulding process. The outcomes demonstrate that the proposed DBN model performs better than competing approaches (Kaur and Bhambri, 2020).

In production line testing, electric motor fault detection plays a crucial role and it is often carried out by skilled operators. Numerous techniques for automatically finding defects are proposed in the literature in recent years. By utilizing a novel detection method based on deep auto-encoders, the authors (Principi et al., 2019) proposed an unsupervised approach for diagnosing defects in electric motors. In the proposed technique, accelerometers are used to collect vibration signals, which are then processed to generate LogMel coefficients as features. The outcomes demonstrated that the one-class support vector machine (OCSVM) algorithm is outperformed by all auto-encoder-based methods.

The reduction in the maintenance expenses of the production systems is largely achieved through the Fault Detection and Diagnosis (FDD) data of rotating machinery. The question of how to increase FDD accuracy is one that is still up for debate. The authors (Jalayer et al., 2021) come up with a novel feature-engineering technique that integrates the Fast Fourier Transform, Continuous Wavelet Transform and statistical characteristics of raw signals in order to fully utilize signals and show all the defect features. A unique Convolutional Long Short-Term Memory (CLSTM) to comprehend and categorize the multi-channel array inputs is proposed. To assess the performance of the multi-domain feature set in various DL architectures, the authors conduct a sensitivity analysis on the input channels, where CLSTM demonstrates its superiority in comprehending the feature set (Kaur et al., 2020).

13.5   CHALLENGES

Although industrial engineers have come up with several new ideas and techniques to improve the overall workflow of the industry, there are still a number of challenges (Sharma and Bhambri, 2020). The critical challenges to Industry 4.0 are discussed below.

a) *Inability to implement or embrace a new business model*
To compete on the world stage, present-day industries demand a highly specialized and flexible environment. In this regard, industries must embrace fresh business strategies. Because of the excessive amount of data collected throughout the manufacturing process, the collaboration of many systems results in the data into the Big Data space. Enterprise productivity is increased through the use of industrial Big Data analytics. Big Data's ability to predict future events gives project planners a firm basis on which to build. It is difficult for data analysts to build appropriate techniques for implementing/adopting new business strategies because not all new aspects will necessarily be implementable and only certain events (out of millions) are interesting (Khan et al., 2017).

b) *Inadequate current data quality*
The other important criterion for the implementation of new industrial features of Industry 4.0 is data quality. A large volume of data is generated (Big Data) because of the interconnection of several machines, sensor devices, industrial equipment, and facilities in Industry 4.0. The higher management may use the Big Data at their disposal to put Industry 4.0's technologies into effect for a sustainable future. In the absence of high-quality data, this would have been unachievable (Santos et al., 2017).

c) *Coordination and collaboration issues*
To have a good understanding of corporate policy, there must exist collaboration and transparency among the members within an industrial unit to adopt the new industrial principles (Industry 4.0) (Pfohl et al., 2017). There must be a proper communication mechanism between the different industrial units and this can only be possible if there exists compatibility of software and hardware, and standard interfaces, and there must be good coordination and collaboration with suppliers. Data synchronization in order to gain better synchronization with manufacturers is also necessary (Duarte and Cruz-Machado, 2017).

d) *Legal issues*
In the era of Industry 4.0, distinct machines, sensor devices, buildings, and people interact with one another through a cyber-physical network. The connection may have some complex legal ramifications. Legal considerations are made to be available using contemporary technological routines and methods for the welfare of the industries. In the present day, Industry 4.0 comes up with a data-driven business model that takes into consideration data privacy and security issues (Müller et al., 2017).

e) *Financial concerns*
Enterprises in Industry 4.0 take into consideration the financial constraints as a big hindrance to the growth in terms of need of heavy machinery, the latest equipment, basic amenities, and eco-friendly process innovations (Nicoletti, 2018).

13.6 CONCLUSION

Industry 4.0 tries to implement cyber-physical transformation in the manufacturing and production processes of various industries. The conceptual model of the production line in a manufacturing industry is briefly explained and the distinct problems concerned with the production line are discussed in this chapter. Depending upon the end-product produced by a manufacturing unit, the distinct categories of production lines are also explained. The four major characteristics of a production line within a manufacturing unit to have maximum throughput are explained in this chapter.

ML and DL techniques have a wide range of applications in manufacturing industries which help industrial engineers to have optimal workflow within the manufacturing unit. The AMPSO-SVR machine learning model is considered to be the most accurate model for forecasting strip-crowns during the hot strip-rolling process. In addition, the SVR model along with ANNs is used to determine the various properties of carbon fibre. In the production of cement, the ESVM model of ML is utilized to predict free lime content in the cement. In the area of e-commerce, centralized task management based on Machine Learning is utilized to deploy autonomous robots in the warehouse. In automobile industries, a data-driven approach based on DBN is utilized for the process of chemical mechanical polishing.

In addition to all these applications, there are still some challenging areas discussed in this chapter for Industry 4.0 that can be considered by industrial engineers as future projects.

REFERENCES

Alsawafy, O. G., & Selim, S. Z. (2022). Analysis of a discrete production workstation. *Computers & Operations Research*, *137*, 105532. https://doi.org/10.1016/j.cor.2021.105532

Arunachalam, P., Janakiraman, N., Sivaraman, A. K., Balasundaram, A., Vincent, R., Rani, S., … & Rajesh, M. (2022). Synovial sarcoma classification technique using support vector machine and structure features. *Intelligent Automation & Soft Computing*, *32*(2), 34–43.

Banerjee, K., Bali, V., Nawaz, N., Bali, S., Mathur, S., Mishra, R. K., & Rani, S. (2022). A machine-learning approach for prediction of water contamination using latitude, longitude, and elevation. *Water*, *14*(5), 728.

Bauza, M. B., Tenboer, J., Li, M., Lisovich, A., Zhou, J., Pratt, D., & Knebel, R. (2018). Realization of industry 4.0 with high speed CT in high volume production. *CIRP Journal of Manufacturing Science and Technology*, *22*, 121–125. https://doi.org/10.1016/j.cirpj.2018.04.001

Bhagwan, N., & Evans, M. (2023). A review of industry 4.0 technologies used in the production of energy in China, Germany, and South Africa. *Renewable and Sustainable Energy Reviews*, *173*, 113075. https://doi.org/10.1016/j.rser.2022.113075

Bhambri, P., Sinha, V. K., & Dhanoa, I. S. (2020). Diabetes prediction with WEKA tool. *Journal of Critical Reviews*, *7*(9), 2366–2371.

Bolu, A., & Korçak, Ö. (2021). Adaptive task planning for multi-robot smart warehouse. *IEEE Access*, *9*, 27346–27358. https://doi.org/10.1109/ACCESS.2021.3058190

Can, B., & Heavey, C. (2016, December). A demonstration of machine learning for explicit functions for cycle time prediction using MES data. In *2016 Winter Simulation Conference (WSC)* (pp. 2500–2511). IEEE. https://doi.org/10.1109/WSC.2016.7822289

Chang, P. C., Lin, Y. K., & Chiang, Y. M. (2019). System reliability estimation and sensitivity analysis for multi-state manufacturing network with joint buffers–A simulation approach. *Reliability Engineering & System Safety*, *188*, 103–109. https://doi.org/10.1016/j.ress.2019.03.024

Dhanoa, I. S., & Bhambri, P. (2020). Traffic-aware energy efficient VM migrations. *Journal of Critical Reviews*, *7*(19), 177–183.

Duarte, S., & Cruz-Machado, V. (2017, July). Exploring linkages between lean and green supply chain and the industry 4.0. In *International Conference on Management Science and Engineering Management* (pp. 1242–1252). Springer, Cham. https://doi.org/10.1007/978-3-319-59280-0_103

Fan, Y., Yang, J., Chen, J., Hu, P., Wang, X., Xu, J., & Zhou, B. (2021). A digital-twin visualized architecture for flexible manufacturing system. *Journal of Manufacturing Systems*, *60*, 176–201. https://doi.org/10.1016/j.jmsy.2021.05.010

Fritzsche, R., Richter, A., & Putz, M. (2017). Automatic adjustment of car body fixtures using artificial intelligence. *Procedia Cirp*, *62*, 600–605. https://doi.org/10.1016/j.procir.2016.06.075

Golkarnarenji, G., Naebe, M., Badii, K., Milani, A. S., Jazar, R. N., & Khayyam, H. (2019). A machine learning case study with limited data for prediction of carbon fiber mechanical properties. *Computers in Industry*, *105*, 123–132. https://doi.org/10.1016/j.compind.2018.11.004

Jalayer, M., Orsenigo, C., & Vercellis, C. (2021). Fault detection and diagnosis for rotating machinery: A model based on convolutional LSTM, Fast Fourier and continuous wavelet transforms. *Computers in Industry*, *125*, 103378. https://doi.org/10.1016/j.compind.2020.103378

Jelsch, M., Roggo, Y., Mohamad, A., Kleinebudde, P., & Krumme, M. (2022). Automatic system dynamics characterization of a pharmaceutical continuous production line. *European Journal of Pharmaceutics and Biopharmaceutics*, *180*, 137–148. https://doi.org/10.1016/j.ejpb.2022.09.010

Kang, Z., Catal, C., & Tekinerdogan, B. (2020). Machine learning applications in production lines: A systematic literature review. *Computers & Industrial Engineering*, *149*, 106773. https://doi.org/10.1016/j.cie.2020.106773

Kaur, J., & Bhambri, P. (2020). *Hybrid classification model for the reverse code generation in software engineering*. I.K. Gujral Punjab Technical University.

Kaur, K., Dhanoa, I. S., Bhambri, P., & Singh, G. (2020). Energy saving VM migration techniques. *Journal of Critical Reviews*, *7*(9), 2359–2365.

Khan, M., Wu, X., Xu, X., & Dou, W. (2017, May). Big data challenges and opportunities in the hype of Industry 4.0. In *2017 IEEE International Conference on Communications (ICC)* (pp. 1–6). IEEE. https://doi.org/10.1109/ICC.2017.7996801

Lemstra, M. A. M. S., & de Mesquita, M. A. (2023). Industry 4.0: A tertiary literature review. *Technological Forecasting and Social Change*, *186*, 122204. https://doi.org/10.1016/j.techfore.2022.122204

Lihao, W., & Yanni, D. (2018, November). A fault diagnosis method of tread production line based on convolutional neural network. In *2018 IEEE 9th International Conference on Software Engineering and Service Science (ICSESS)* (pp. 987–990). IEEE. https://doi.org/10.1109/ICSESS.2018.8663824

Ling, S., Li, M., Guo, D., Rong, Y., & Huang, G. Q. (2022). Assembly Workstation 4.0: Concept, framework and research perspectives for assembly systems implementation in the Industry 4.0 era. *IFAC-PapersOnLine*, *55*(2), 420–426. https://doi.org/10.1016/j.ifacol.2022.04.230

Liu, X., Jin, J., Wu, W., & Herz, F. (2020). A novel support vector machine ensemble model for estimation of free lime content in cement clinkers. *ISA Transactions*, *99*, 479–487. https://doi.org/10.1016/j.isatra.2019.09.003

Liu, Y., Zhou, H., Tsung, F., & Zhang, S. (2019). Real-time quality monitoring and diagnosis for manufacturing process profiles based on deep belief networks. *Computers & Industrial Engineering, 136*, 494–503. https://doi.org/10.1016/j.cie.2019.07.042

Luo, R. C., & Wang, H. (2018, August). Diagnostic and prediction of machines health status as exemplary best practice for vehicle production system. In *2018 IEEE 88th Vehicular Technology Conference (VTC-Fall)* (pp. 1–5). IEEE. https://doi.org/10.1109/VTCFall.2018.8690710

Müller, J., Dotzauer, V., & Voigt, K. I. (2017). Industry 4.0 and its impact on reshoring decisions of German manufacturing enterprises. In Christoph Bode, Ronald Bogaschewsky, Michael Eßig, Rainer Lasch, Wolfgang Stölzle (Ed.), *Supply management research* (pp. 165–179). Springer Gabler, Wiesbaden. https://doi.org/10.1007/978-3-658-18632-6_8

Mulrennan, K., Donovan, J., Creedon, L., Rogers, I., Lyons, J. G., & McAfee, M. (2018). A soft sensor for prediction of mechanical properties of extruded PLA sheet using an instrumented slit die and machine learning algorithms. *Polymer Testing, 69*, 462–469. https://doi.org/10.1016/j.polymertesting.2018.06.002

Nicoletti, B. (2018). The future: Procurement 4.0. In *Agile procurement* (pp. 189–230). Palgrave Macmillan. https://doi.org/10.1007/978-3-319-61085-6_8

Pfohl, H. C., Yahsi, B., & Kurnaz, T. (2017). Concept and diffusion-factors of industry 4.0 in the supply chain. In Michael Freitag, Herbert Kotzab, Jürgen Pannek (Eds.), *Dynamics in logistics* (pp. 381–390). Springer. https://doi.org/10.1007/978-3-319-45117-6_33

Potluri, S., Tiwari, P. K., Bhambri, P., Obulesu, O., Naidu, P. A., Lakshmi, L., Kallam, S., Gupta, S., & Gupta, B. (2019). Method of Load Distribution Balancing for Fog Cloud Computing in IoT Environment [Patent number IN201941044511].

Principi, E., Rossetti, D., Squartini, S., & Piazza, F. (2019). Unsupervised electric motor fault detection by using deep autoencoders. *IEEE/CAA Journal of Automatica Sinica, 6*(2), 441–451. https://doi.org/10.1109/JAS.2019.1911393

Rani, S., Arya, V., & Kataria, A. (2022). Dynamic pricing-based E-commerce model for the produce of organic farming in India: A research roadmap with main advertence to vegetables. In *Proceedings of Data Analytics and Management: ICDAM 2021, Volume 2* (pp. 327–336). Springer Singapore.

Rani, S., Bhambri, P., & Chauhan, M. (2021, October). A machine learning model for kids' behavior analysis from facial emotions using principal component analysis. In *2021 5th Asian Conference on Artificial Intelligence Technology (ACAIT)* (pp. 522–525). IEEE.

Santos, M. Y., Oliveira e Sá, J., Costa, C., Galvão, J., Andrade, C., Martinho, B., ... & Costa, E. (2017, April). A big data analytics architecture for industry 4.0. In *World Conference on Information Systems and Technologies* (pp. 175–184). Springer. https://doi.org/10.1007/978-3-319-56538-5_19

Sharma, R., & Bhambri, P. (2020). *Energy aware bio inspired routing technique for mobile adhoc networks*. I.K. Gujral Punjab Technical University.

Sharma, R., Bhambri, P., & Sohal, A. K. (2020). Mobile adhoc networks. *Journal of Composition Theory, 13*(2), 982–985.

Usuga Cadavid, J. P., Lamouri, S., Grabot, B., Pellerin, R., & Fortin, A. (2020). Machine learning applied in production planning and control: A state-of-the-art in the era of industry 4.0. *Journal of Intelligent Manufacturing, 31*(6), 1531–1558. https://doi.org/10.1007/s10845-019-01531-7

Wang, P., Gao, R. X., & Yan, R. (2017). A deep learning-based approach to material removal rate prediction in polishing. *Cirp Annals, 66*(1), 429–432. https://doi.org/10.1016/j.cirp.2017.04.013

Wang, Y., & Yang, R. (2017, October). Fault diagnosis system of emulsifier based on neural network theory. In *2017 Chinese Automation Congress (CAC)* (pp. 3087–3091). IEEE. https://doi.org/10.1109/CAC.2017.8243305

Wang, Z. H., Liu, Y. M., Gong, D. Y., & Zhang, D. H. (2018). A new predictive model for strip crown in hot rolling by using the hybrid AMPSO-SVR-based approach. *Steel Research International*, 89(7), 1800003. https://doi.org/10.1002/srin.201800003

Xiao, D., Huang, Y., Zhang, X., Shi, H., Liu, C., & Li, Y. (2018, October). Fault diagnosis of asynchronous motors based on LSTM neural network. In *2018 Prognostics and System Health Management Conference (PHM-Chongqing)* (pp. 540–545). IEEE. https://doi.org/10.1109/PHM-Chongqing.2018.00098

14 Simulation Analysis of AODV and DSDV Routing Protocols for Secure and Reliable Service in Mobile Adhoc Networks (MANETs)

Gurjeet Singh
Guru Kashi University, Bathinda, India

Pankaj Bhambri
Guru Nanak Dev Engineering College, Ludhiana, India

14.1 INTRODUCTION

A mobile ad hoc network is an unstructured group of mobile nodes (which also serve as routers) linked by a wireless connection as depicted in Figure 14.1. Since the nodes are movable, the network architecture changes both dynamically and unexpectedly (Sharma & Patheja, 2012). The lack of a central administrative infrastructure prevents the direct application of the conventional routing techniques used in wired networks to these networks (Singh et al., 2021).

In future, wireless network interfaces and mobile devices will be a crucial component of both infrastructured and unstructured mobile networks (Bose et al., 2021). The most widely used infrastructured mobile network uses a IEEE 802.11 controller (Quy et al., 2019b; Quy et al., 2022). In this network, a mobile node talks with a stationary ground station, resulting in a wireless connection that can only go one hop (Jabeen et al., 2021). By contrast, as a multi-hop network without infrastructure, MANET allows nodes to connect with one another, either directly or indirectly, by way of intermediary nodes (Vijayalakshmi et al., 2021; Alhaidari et al., 2021). As a result, every node in a MANET essentially performs the role of a mobile router taking part in the routing protocol necessary for choosing and maintaining the routes (Babu et al., 2021).

DOI: 10.1201/9781003383505-14

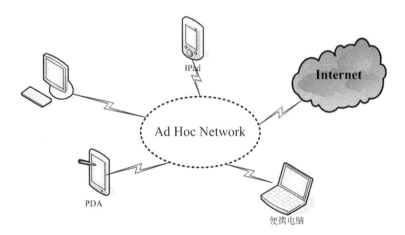

FIGURE 14.1   A mobile ad hoc network.

14.2   MANET ROUTING PROTOCOLS

The ad hoc routing protocol's job is to regulate node choices made when sending packets between devices in MANET (Bhambri et al., 2023; Anchugam &
Thangadurai, 2015). A node has no knowledge of the network topology when it joins
or attempts to join. It learns the topology by proclaiming its presence or receiving
signals from nearby nodes. The implementation of the routing protocol affects the
route discovery process in a network. Every time an envelope must be sent to a destination reached by several nodes, the Routing Protocol is also required (Bhambri
et al., 2022; Ibrahim et al., 2022). Because nodes in mobile ad hoc networks might
move unpredictably, joining or leaving the network, the routing methods for wired
networks cannot be employed. This implies that a path that is ideal at one point in
time might not be appropriate at another.

14.2.1   AODV Routing Protocol

The ad hoc on-demand distance vector (AODV routing protocol routes are only
known to the station as the next hop and destination pair; they are established as
needed in the routing database of AODV.

14.2.2   Destination Sequenced Distance Vector Protocol (DSDV)

The DSDV routing protocol has been enhanced to overcome the count to infinity
problem. Every node keeps a routing table with entries for each additional node in
the network. Each node keeps track of the shortest hops required to send a packet
to its destination via its neighbours, and it selects that neighbour as the subsequent
node (Quy et al., 2018). It is a proactive protocol; therefore any time the topology changes or at regular intervals, the nodes send their routing tables to their
close neighbours (Ritu & Bhambri, 2022). The sequence number of a node must
be increased when sending an update message (Quy et al. 2019a). A broadcast

message can be received by a node at any time from its locality. It contrasts the fields for the sequence number and hop count of the incoming message in its routing table with the relevant entry (Mahmoud et al., 2015). The node changes its routing database with distances being recalculated using the updated sequence number and hop count if there is a discrepancy between the two. In response to Route ERRor (RERR) warnings, DSDV invalidates all routes that include broken links in their routing database. These routes receive an unlimited metric and an increased sequence number right away (Jamal et al., 2022).

14.2.3 Comparison between AODV and DSDV Protocols

The AODV and DSDV routing protocols differ in a few ways. Firstly, unlike DSDV, AODV only updates routing information when it is necessary to do so. It does not routinely update the routing data. By contrast, DSDV will upgrade the nodes' routing table on every occasion. Every node frequently shifts positions. There is no recurrent updating in AODV. There is no cycle topology in DSDV; instead, routing information propagates continuously. DSDV has a significantly lower packet delivery latency than on-demand protocols. When compared to table-driven protocols, AODV has a higher first-packet delivery time. There is a route to every other neighbour node in DSDV that is not present in AODV.

14.2.4 Simulation Environment

NS-2 is free, open source, and supports a variety of networks, including wired networks, wireless ad hoc modes, an managed wireless modes. NS-2 is used for simulation. Additionally, NS-2 is more realistic than other simulators due to its vast model library, effective simulation design, and its ability to produce good results (Bhambri et al., 2021). It is an object-oriented tool command language and C++ discrete event simulator. It is appropriate for evaluating various protocols, traffics, and creating new protocols. Both the NS-wireless and Excel applications visually represent the performance indicators by monitoring the movements and occurrences of the nodes inside the simulated network. The NS-2 software also provides a visual depiction of the network, shown in Figure 14.2.

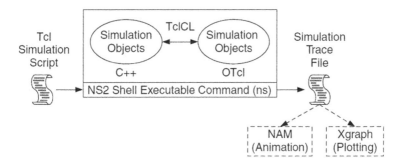

FIGURE 14.2   Architecture of NS-2.

14.2.5 Performance Metrics

Packet delivery ratio, packet loss, throughput, and average end-to-end delay were all factors taken into account in the development of this model (E2E).

14.2.5.1 Packet Delivery Ratio (PDR)

The PDR is the percentage of datagram created by CBR sources that were successfully delivered to the locations they were intended for. The service quality of the routing protocol is improved by a higher delivery ratio. The calculation of the Packet Delivery Ratio is shown in Equation (14.1)

$$\text{Packet Delivery Ratio} = \frac{\text{Received packets}}{\text{Sent packets}} \times 100 \qquad (14.1)$$

14.2.5.2 Packet Loss

The MAC layer, as well as the network layer, may experience mobility-related packet loss (Ritu and Bhambri, 2023). Here, network layer packet loss is the main focus. When a packet reaches the network layer and a viable path to the receiver is identified. In the absence of a route, the packet is buffered. When a packet needs to be buffered but the buffer is already full, the packet is dropped. It can also be dropped when the buffer time is too long. Packet loss is determined as shown in Equation (14.2):

$$\text{PER} = \text{Total Packet Sent} - \text{Total Packet received} \qquad (14.2)$$

14.2.5.3 Average End to End delay

It comprises retransmission delays at the MAC, interface queue queuing, and data packet buffering during route discovery (Sangwan et al., 2021). It is the interval of time between the source node's packet sending and the destination node's packet receiver.

14.2.5.4 Throughput

The ratio of total data sent from a transmitter to a receiver is known as throughput (Ritu and Bhambri, 2022). The throughput measures how quickly the most recent communication is delivered to the recipient. Bits per second, or bytes (byte/sec or bit/sec), are used to measure throughput. In every network, a high throughput is the only option.

14.2.6   Simulation Parameter

TABLE 14.1
Simulation Parameter

Parameter	Value
Number of nodes	15, 25, 35, 45, 55
Simulated Period	55s
Internet Size	500 m × 500 m
Size of a Pack	55 bytes
Vitality of Nodes	1000 J
Simulator	NS-2
Antenna Type	Omni directional
MAC Type	IEEE802.11
Agent	TCP
Routing Protocol	AODV & DSDV

14.2.7   Simulation Results

In this concept, a rectangular region of 500*500 unit squares has a number of randomly distributed networks. Awk was used to manage the trace files generated by the simulations of the AODV and DSDV protocols. Packet delivery ratio, throughput, packet loss, and end-to-end delay values were plotted on graphs. These values were found in Tables 14.2–14.4.

14.2.7.1   Packet Delivery Ratio

Figures 14.3–14.5 display the Packet Delivery Ratio for various numbers of nodes operating at various speeds based on the findings in Tables 14.2–14.4. At 5 m/s,

TABLE 14.2
Speed of 5 m/s

	PDR[%]		Packet loss		E2E [ms]		Throughput [kbps]	
# Nodes	AODV	DSDV	AODV	DSDV	AODV	DSDV	AODV	DSDV
15	100	5.66	0	3082	6.13	4.13	544.11	30.81
25	98.71	28.5	42	2336	20.39	4.02	537.13	155.06
35	90.85	2.75	299	3177	25.19	4.13	494	28.2
45	69.12	34.04	1009	2155	55.58	4.16	376.06	185.21
55	98.04	3.49	64	3153	34.33	4.16	533.44	37.72

TABLE 14.3
Speed of 10 m/s

# Nodes	PDR[%]		Packet loss		E2E [ms]		Throughput [kbps]	
	AODV	DSDV	AODV	DSDV	AODV	DSDV	AODV	DSDV
15	100	24.15	0	2478	6.13	4	544.11	131.4
25	99.91	28.34	5	2323	6.14	4.02	543.44	157.22
35	90.85	33.09	299	3102	25.19	4.13	494.3	91.75
45	98.13	24.4	152	1537	24.84	4.05	518.76	288.12
55	94.89	24.92	787	1380	24.84	5.46	413.01	267.56

TABLE 14.4
Speed of 15 m/s

# Nodes	PDR[%]		Packet loss		E2E [ms]		Throughput [kbps]	
	AODV	DSDV	AODV	DSDV	AODV	DSDV	AODV	DSDV
15	100	23.15	534.10	132.4	6.12	4.32	0	2468
25	98.85	27.9	544.45	147.22	4.55	4.83	5	2313
35	91.85	5.03	484.3	92.75	25.09	4.02	289	3103
45	94.35	51.85	517.66	289.13	43.14	4.24	142	1527
55	74.91	48.13	412.02	257.46	51.53	4.25	789	1370

OADV achieves an average of 81.34% and DSDV 14.88%. The values fall from 86.75% to 82.39 in OADV as the speed varies from 10 m/s to 15 m/s, they increase from 16.98% to 22.04% in DSDV. PDR drops as the number of nodes grows because more packets are discarded due to collisions as a result of network congestion. PDR is greater for AODV. The best performance is indicated by the highest PDR value (Rachna et al., 2022).

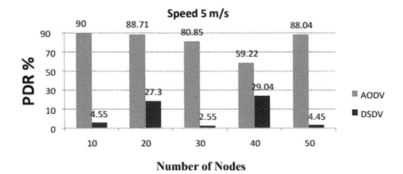

FIGURE 14.3 PDR on Speed of 5m/s.

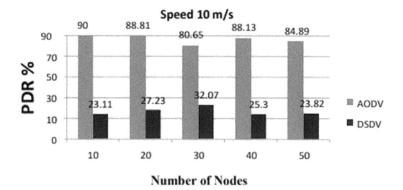

FIGURE 14.4   PDR on Speed of 10m/s.

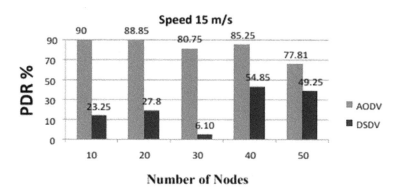

FIGURE 14.5   PDR on Speed of 15m/s.

14.2.7.2   Packet Loss

The Packet Delivery Ratio versus various numbers of nodes at various speeds is depicted in Figures 14.6–14.8 based on the observations of Tables 14.2–14.4. DSDV loses packets at a higher rate than AODV: at 5 m/s, AODV loses 292 packets compared to DSDV's 2880, at 10 m/s, AODV loses 84 packets compared to DSDV's 2482, and at 15 m/s, AODV loses 248 packets compared to DSDV's 2264. As network congestion grows and more packets are discarded due to collisions, loss decreased as the number of nodes increased.

14.2.7.3   End to End Delay

The average E2E Delay for various numbers of nodes operating at various speeds is depicted in Figures 14.9–14.11 based on findings from Tables 14.2–14.4. The average AODV delay is reduced at 10 nodes and reaches its maximum delay at 40 nodes. As node density increases, post-route setup calculation requirements decrease, requiring less time. Semi-fixed values are used in DSDV. In the simulation situations, it was observed that the DSDV routing protocol exhibits a lower end-to-end delay when compared with the AODV routing protocol. On average, the OADV was

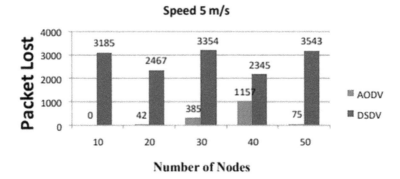

FIGURE 14.6   Packet Lost on Speed of 5m/s.

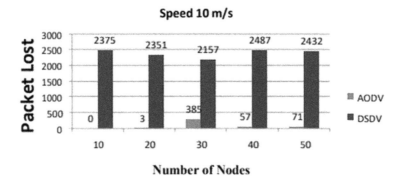

FIGURE 14.7   Packet Lost on Speed of 10m/s.

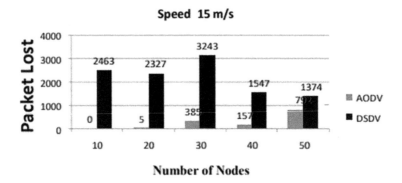

FIGURE 14.8   Packet Lost on Speed of 15m/s.

delayed by 29.32 seconds and the DSDV delayed by 5.12 seconds at 5 m/s, 27.42 seconds and 5.33 seconds at 10 m/s, and 27.12 seconds and 5.31 seconds at 15 m/s. The AODV's hop-by-hop routing strategy results in a substantial end-to-end delay. However, DSDV tiny delay values don't make sense when considering packet delivery ratio because it has less packet delivery ratio and high packet loss.

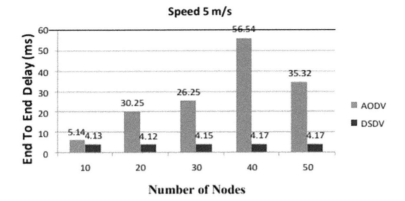

FIGURE 14.9 End to End Delay on Speed of 5m/s.

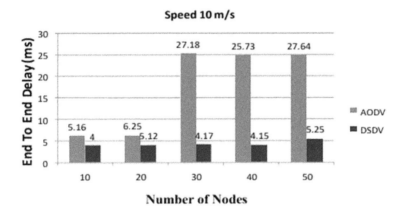

FIGURE 14.10 End to End Delay on Speed of 10m/s.

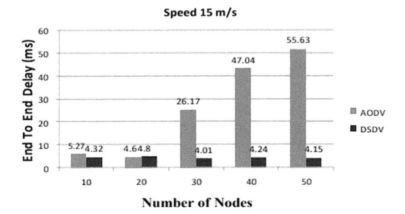

FIGURE 14.11 End to End Delay on Speed of 15m/s.

14.2.7.4 Throughput

The PDR with different number of nodes at various speeds is shown in Figures 14.12–14.14 based on the observations of Tables 14.2–14.4. AODV has a higher throughput than DSDV. AODV has 597 kbps and DSDV has 97.4 kbps at 5 m/s. It is 545.97 kb/s in AODV and 147.93 kb/s in DSDV at 10 m/s. Additionally, the average at 15 m/s is 525.98 kb/s in AODV and 240.84 kb/s in DSDV. Throughput suffers while utilizing the DSDV routing protocol since it is a table-driven protocol and needs additional control required to keep the route open to all other nodes. Because each node maintains a routing database, there is no need to send the entire route through the network, giving the AODV routing protocol the maximum throughput.

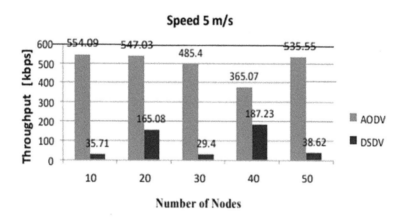

FIGURE 14.12   Throughput on Speed of 5m/s.

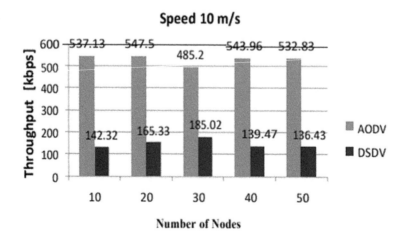

FIGURE 14.13   Throughput on Speed of 10m/s.

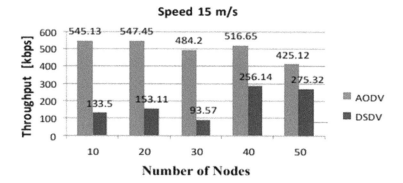

FIGURE 14.14   Throughput on Speed of 15m/s.

14.3   CONCLUSION

The simulation findings show that AODV's packet delivery ratio (PDR) is superior to DSDV's PDR. In AODV, it is superior in 5m/s by 86.5%, in 10m/s by 79.8%, and in 15m/s by an average of 65.26%. AODV has a higher throughput than DSDV. AODV outperforms DSDV at 5 m/s by 92.4%, while also being 82% better than DSDV on average at 10 and 15 m/s AODV. Due to its hop-by-hop routing mechanism, AODV achieves significant E2E delay. DSDV, however, experiences high packet losses than AODV on average at speeds of 5 m/s, 10 m/s, and 15 m/s. DSDV experiences 86.9% and 85.5% more packet losses than AODV respectively. Despite having a better throughput and PDR with a mobility speed of 5m/s for both sources, AODV uses more energy (38.2% more to be exact) and lower packet losses. In both locations with a 5m/s speed AODV uses an average of 68.2% more energy than DSDV.

REFERENCES

Alhaidari, F., Almotiri, S. H., Ghamdi, M. A., Khan, M. A., Rehman, A., Abbas, S., Khan, K. M., & Rahman, A. (2021). Intelligent software-defined network for cognitive routing optimization using deep extreme learning machine approach. *Computers, Materials & Continua*, vol. 67, no. 1, 1269–1285.

Anchugam, C.V., & Thangadurai, K. (July 2015). Detection of black hole attack in mobile adhoc networks using ant colony optimization – Simulation analysis. *Indian Journal of Science and Technology*, vol. 8(13).

Babu, G. C. N., Gupta, S., Bhambri, P., Leo, L. M., Rao, B. H., & Kumar, S. (2021). A semantic health observation system development based on the IoT sensors. *Turkish Journal of Physiotherapy and Rehabilitation*, vol. 32, no. 3, 1721–1729.

Bhambri, P., Singh, M., Dhanoa, I. S., & Kumar, M. (2022). Deployment of ROBOT for HVAC duct and disaster management. *Oriental Journal of Computer Science and Technology*, vol. 15, 1–18.

Bhambri, P., Singh, M., Jain, A., Dhanoa, I. S., Sinha, V. K., & Lal, S. (2021). Classification of gene expression data with the aid of optimized feature selection. *Turkish Journal of Physiotherapy and Rehabilitation*, vol. 32, 3.

Bhambri, P., Singh, S., Sangwan, S., Devi, J., & Jain, S. (2023). Plants recognition using leaf image pattern analysis. *Journal of Survey in Fisheries Sciences*, vol. 10, no. 2S, 3863–3871.

Bose, M. M., Yadav, D., Bhambri, P., & Shankar, R (2021). Electronic customer relationship management: Benefits and pre-implementation considerations. *Journal of Maharaja Sayajirao University of Baroda*, vol. 55, no. 01(VI), 1343–1350.

Ibrahim, N. M., Gabr, D. G. I., Rahman, A., Dash, S., & Nayyar, A. (2022). A deep learning approach to intelligent fruit identification and family classification. *Multimedia Tools and Applications*, vol. 6, no. 7, 76–87.

Jabeen, A., Pallathadka, H., Pallathadka, L. K., & Bhambri, P. (2021). E-CRM successful factors for business enterprises case studies. *Journal of Maharaja Sayajirao University of Baroda*, vol. 55, no. 01(VI), 1332–1342.

Jamal, M., Zafar, N. A., Rahman, A., Musleh, D., Gollapalli, M., & Chabani, S. (2022). Modeling and verification of aircraft takeoff through novel quantum nets. *Computers, Materials and Continua*, vol. 72, no. 2, 3331–3348.

Mahmoud, T. M., Aly, A., & Makram, O. (January 2015). A modified AODV routing protocol to avoid black hole attack in MANETs. *International Journal of Computer Applications*, vol. 109, no. 6, 876–888.

Quy, V. K., Ban, N. T., & Han, N. D. (2018). An advanced energy efficient and high performance routing protocol for MANET in 5G. *Journal of Communications*, vol. 13, no. 12, 743–749.

Quy, V. K., Ban, N. T., & Han, N. D. (2019a). A high performance routing protocol for multimedia applications in MANETs. *Journal of Communications*, vol. 14, no. 4, 267–274.

Quy, V. K., Hung, L. N., & Han, N. D. (2019b). CEPRM: A cloud-assisted energy-saving and performance-improving routing mechanism for MANETs. *Journal of Communications*, vol. 14, no. 12, 1211–1217.

Quy, V. K., Nam, V. H., Linh, D. M., et al. (2022). Communication solutions for vehicle ad-hoc network in smart cities environment: A comprehensive survey. *Wireless Personal Communications*, vol. 122, 2791–2815.

Rachna, Bhambri, P., & Chhabra, Y. (2022). Deployment of Distributed Clustering Approach in WSNs and IoTs. In Pankaj Bhambri, Sita Rani, Gaurav Gupta, Alex Khang (Eds.), *Cloud and Fog Computing Platforms for Internet of Things* (pp. 85–98). Chapman and Hall/CRC.

Ritu, & Bhambri, P. (2022). A CAD System for Software Effort Estimation. *Paper presented at the International Conference on Technological Advancements in Computational Sciences* (pp. 140–146). IEEE. DOI: 10.1109/ICTACS56270.2022.9988123.

Ritu, P., & Bhambri, P. (2023, February 17). Software Effort Estimation with Machine Learning – A Systematic Literature Review. In Susheela Hooda, Vandana Mohindru Sood, Yashwant Singh, Sandeep Dalal, Manu Sood (Eds.), *Agile Software Development: Trends, Challenges and Applications* (pp. 291–308). John Wiley & Sons, Inc.

Sangwan, Y. S., Lal, S., Bhambri, P., Kumar, A., & Dhanoa, I. S. (2021). Advancements in social data security and encryption: A review. *NVEO-Natural Volatiles & Essential Oils Journal|NVEO*, vol. 8, no. 4, 15353–15362.

Sharma, S., & Patheja, P. S. (2012). Improving AODV routing protocol with priority and power efficiency in mobile ad hoc WiMAX network. *International Journal of Computer Technology and Electronics Engineering (IJCTEE)*, vol. 2, no. 1, 67–89. ISSN 2249-6343.

Singh, M., Bhambri, P., Lal, S., Singh, Y., Kaur, M., & Singh, J. (2021). Design of the effective technique to improve memory and time constraints for sequence alignment. *International Journal of Applied Engineering Research (Netherlands)*, vol. 6, no. 02, 127–142.

Vijayalakshmi, P., Shankar, R., Karthik, S., & Bhambri, P. (2021). Impact of work from home policies on workplace productivity and employee sentiments during the Covid-19 pandemic. *Journal of Maharaja Sayajirao University of Baroda*, vol. 55, no. 01(VI), 1314–1331.

15 Landmine Detection and Classification Based on Machine Learning Algorithms

T. Kalaichelvi and S. Ravi

Pondicherry University, Puducherry, India

15.1 INTRODUCTION

Landmine detection is a serious issue in many countries around the world, and the condition can become a natural disaster. The landmines used are either anti-personnel (AP) or anti-tank (AT) in nature. Anti-personnel landmines are buried beneath the ground, while anti-tank landmines are always on the surface (Hussein and Waller, 2000). Approximately 110 million landmines are buried in over 80 countries worldwide ("Facts About Landmines – Minesweepers," Minesweepers, 2019. https://Landminefree.Org/Facts-about-Landmines/, n.d.). The impact of landmines extends to deaths and injuries caused by the explosives. Landmines also affect the social and economic growth and environmental status of the people in affected areas. Thus, the detection and safe removal of landmines is necessary. Safe detection involves a non-touch detection method that uses signals from explosive materials. Landmine detectors use a variety of sensors to detect them, which include biological, metal detectors (MD), ground-penetrating radar (GPR), infrared cameras, chemical, acoustic, optical, and nuclear (Kasban et al., 2010). Of all these, MD and GPR are the most common method used for detecting landmines.

Metal detectors operated by humans emit the current and measure the reflected signal of explosives from the subsurface field (Rani, Bhambri, and Chauhan, 2021). This sends an alarm signal in the presence of metallic objects in the subsurface. This means that it generates more false alarms in the presence of metallic clutter and also that non-metallic objects are undetected (Takahashi et al., 2011). Automated wireless metal detectors (Robo-Pi) detect landmines, reducing the risk of humans coming into direct contact with landmines and proving less effective in detecting non-metallic mines (Ghareeb et al., 2017). By contrast, GPR communicates radar waves from a surface antenna and records the reflected wave through a receiving antenna. The electromagnetic wave's velocity changes as it passes through the subsurface because of the physical properties of the materials (Banerjee et al., 2022). A GPR generates the data from the subsurface material by measuring velocity changes and the time radar signal movement (Conyers, 2018). This work

DOI: 10.1201/9781003383505-15

uses GPR and other sensor data to detect buried landmines and explosives under the ground surface. This technique is widely used in landmine detection systems because of their security and humanitarian benefits. It mainly detects landmines in smaller targets (under 10 cm in diameter). It penetrates subsurface depths from 15 cm to 30 cm using the L-band range in 12 GHz with Ultra-Wideband (UWB) transmission (Giovanneschi et al., 2013). Clutters, such as inhomogeneous soil, antenna ringing, and surface roughness, can impede the detection of targets. When using GPR to locate landmines, it is critical to distinguish between natural and manufactured clutter under the subsurface. The most common materials used to make landmines are plastics, which do not react with radar and are difficult to identify due to the relatively low dielectric contrast (Sato et al., 2004).

Landmines are detected, classified, and cleared using a variety of techniques (Gupta, Rani, and Pant, 2011). Landmine detectors help to locate the buried landmine's actual position and to understand the technology used in the landmines. Landmine detection systems also identify the landmine's size, shape, burial depth, and casing material of explosives. The feature extraction strategy transforms the unique GPR data features into the grouping of perceptions to classify landmines and other objects. Several image segmentations, clutter reduction, and classification strategies, such as manual and automated ones, can rapidly increase the capacity for handling images based on features retrieved from the subsurface object through sensors. Finally, the classification algorithm separates the landmine and non-mine objects.

This chapter presents the Machine Learning algorithms and their applications with examples. It also reviews and analyses the different algorithms used to classify landmines and the challenges faced during landmine detection caused by the various types of landmines, the detection requirements, and the terrain. Furthermore, the chapter discusses the suitability of different classifiers used for landmine detection with accuracy, probability detection, and false alarm rates. Finally, the chapter proposes the classification architecture used for landmine detection.

15.2   MACHINE LEARNING TYPES WITH ALGORITHMS, APPLICATIONS, AND EXAMPLES

Machine Learning (ML) enables a system to learn from data, automatically improving the performance of experiences and predicated things without being explicitly programmed (Mohssen Mohammed and Muhammad Badruddin Khan, n.d.). The learning system consists of learning from existing data, building a model, and using new data to predict the output. The output's accuracy depends on the amount of data, as the larger the volume of data the easier it proves to create a more accurate model. Many use cases are available to understand the importance of ML easily and quickly. Figure 15.1 shows the different types of machine-learning algorithms (Ayon Dey, 2016).

The supervised Machine Learning technique allows an algorithm to learn and map the input to a separate output. Depending on classification or regression strategy, it can predict new unseen data (Abraham, 2013). The classification problem uses labeled data in two or more classes and indicates the outcome based on training. It

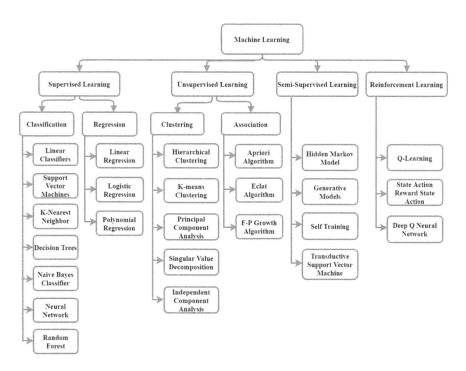

FIGURE 15.1 Types of Machine Learning algorithms. (Mohssen Mohammed, Muhammad Badruddin Khan, n.d.)

consists of many algorithms to classify the data set, such as identifying an email message as spam or not (Osisanwo et al., 2017). A regression algorithm helps to recognize the association between dependent and independent variables. For instance, a regression model used to forecast a given business's sales revenue depend on different data. An unsupervised Machine Learning algorithm works with unlabeled data, including clustering or association. A clustering technique groups unlabeled data according to either their similarities or dissimilarities. Image recognition, segmentation, and data analysis use these techniques. Association uses various rules to identify relations among variables in a dataset. Semi-supervised learning (SSL) uses supervised and unsupervised learning data. Reinforcement learning concerns the agent's probability of taking action in an environment of the maximum to long-term reward. The diagrams below illustrate several Machine Learning algorithms.

15.2.1 Support Vector Machine

The most frequently used classification technique under supervised Machine Learning is the Support Vector Machine (SVM). SVM creates a boundary line to separate two data classes in a dimensional space (Singh et al., 2021a). The most suitable decision boundary is the hyperplane. Adding new data to a support vector assigns it to the most appropriate class by the extreme case. Figure 15.2 displays the phases in the Support Vector Machine algorithm (Bhambri, 2021).

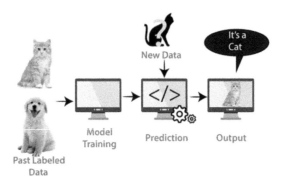

FIGURE 15.2 Support vector machine algorithm. (Support Vector Machine (SVM) Algorithm – Javatpoint, n.d.)

KNN Classifier

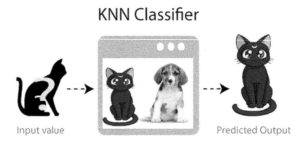

FIGURE 15.3 K-nearest neighbors algorithm. (K-Nearest Neighbor (KNN) Algorithm for Machine Learning – Javatpoint, n.d.)

15.2.2 K-NEAREST NEIGHBORS

One supervised Machine Learning method that classifies and predicts new data created on the available data is the K-Nearest Neighbors (KNN) algorithm. The training data set creation for KNN is the immediate neighborhood. It is quick to implement, but has a significant drawback of increased computation time when data usage grows.

Landmines are classified using KNN frameworks based on their nearest neighbors to separate and organize clutter. Figure 15.3 shows the process of the K-Nearest Neighbors Algorithm.

15.2.3 HIDDEN MARKOV MODEL

Semi-supervised learning through the Hidden Markov Model (HMM) determines any random process of probabilistic characteristics from one node to another (Bakshi et al., 2021). HMM accepts the sequence of inputs and produces an output of the same length. It observes the hidden states of Markov chains. Whenever a Markov process X contains hidden states Y, the HMM solidifies them. The history of X cannot influence probability distribution during that particular period. Figure 15.4 shows an HMM for weather forecasting.

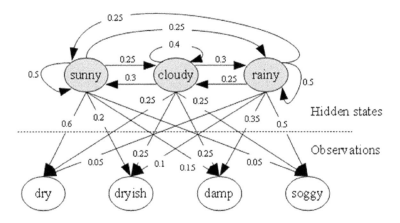

FIGURE 15.4   HMM for weather forecasting. (Nguyen, 2016.)

15.3   LANDMINE DETECTION AND CLASSIFICATION TECHNIQUES USING MACHINE LEARNING ALGORITHMS

The Least Mean Square (LMS) pre-screening is used for anomaly recognition and finding signatures similar to landmines. Translation-invariant features were extracted from the identified regions of interest (ROI) using edge histogram descriptor (EHD) assigned the confidence value for accurate detection using probabilistic KNN (Frigui and Gader, 2009). Ultra-Wideband synthetic aperture radar (UWB SAR) identified the suspected area through space-wavenumber processing. The efficient features were retrieved using the sequential forward floating selection (SFFS) and classified using a fuzzy hypersphere support vector machine (FHSSVM) (Rachna et al., 2021). Equation (15.1) calculated the risk based on the number of misclassified landmines and clutter (N_L, N_C) and the risk of misclassification of landmines and clutter (R_L, R_C) (Jin and Zhou, 2010).

$$\text{Risk} = N_L R_L + N_C R_C \tag{15.1}$$

The multiple instance learning (MIL) approach groups several features from various sensors. A linear classifier is a type of Machine Learning algorithm that is used to classify data into different categories based on a linear decision boundary. The calculation of SumMemship was performed in a mapped feature space using Equation (15.2), and a Relevance Vector Machine (RVM) classifier was calculated in sparse mapped space using Equation (15.3), where the probability of alarm is p_{ik} and sparse Bayesian weight is W_k. The Edge histogram Descriptor (EHD) retrieved the edge features in cross- and down-track dimensions (Andrew Karem, 2011).

$$Conf_i = \sum_{k=1}^{K} p_{ik}{}^M \tag{15.2}$$

$$Conf_i = \sum_{k=1}^{K} \left(W_k * p_{ik} \right) \Big/ \sum_{k=1}^{K} W_k \tag{15.3}$$

A multi-stream discrete Hidden Markov Model (MSDHMM) included a stream-related weighting segment created to fuse the multiple modalities. The EHD and Gabor feature calculated a stream relevance weight using Baum Welch (BW) and minimum classification error (MCE). Distance-based MSDHMM structure (λ) referred to in Equation (15.4), where π, A, and B are state prior, transition and observation probabilities, and W-relevance weight, respectively. Probability-based MSDHMM b_{ij} was calculated using Equation (15.5), relevance weights w_{ijk} and partial stream probability b_{ijk} in each state i, symbol j, and stream k (Missaoui et al., 2011).

$$\lambda = \left(\pi, A, B, W \right) \tag{15.4}$$

$$b_{ij} = \sum_{k=1}^{L} w_{ijk} b_{ijk} \tag{15.5}$$

The multi-stream continuous Hidden Markov Model (MSCHMM) used a maximum likelihood estimation (MLE)-based BW algorithm and the MCE to identify the state and component level of stream relevance weights (Oualid Missaoui et al., 2013). Multiple Hidden Markov Model (HMM) was used to develop the ensemble Hidden Markov Model (eHMM). GPR images were analyzed using B-Scan signatures to extract EHD and Gabor features. HMM was used to identify the similarity between observed sequences in a cluster by log-likelihood-based similarity and path mismatch (Anis Hamdi, 2015).

Based on Multiple-instance HMM (MiHMM), they developed an HMM sequence from the alarm area. Discrete and HOG features were extracted from GPR data and tested on synthetic/landmine data sets (Manandhar et al., 2015). A forward-looking ground penetrating radar (FLGPR) uses stepped frequency for sensing and filtered back projection to create images of subsurface objects. A Machine Learning classification algorithm was trained with features around each selected location. With the help of Bag-of-Visual-Words (BOV) and Fisher Vector (FV) feature learning methods, k-means algorithms discriminate between landmines and non-mines in FLGPR data. (Camilo et al., 2016).

The context-based classification used various classifiers based on the measure of the context. It took a variable length of sequences using a mixer of experts (ME) and a mixture of the HMM Experts (MHMME) model to decompose the data into several contexts (Yuksel and Gader, 2016). The data from the A-Scan images were normalized and classified using one-class support vector machines (OCSVMs), where the kernel Radial Basis Function (RBF) was measured using Equation (15.6) through x_i and x_j (Tbarki et al., 2017).

$$K_{(RBF)} = e^{-\left(\frac{\|x_i - x_j\|^2}{2\sigma^2} \right)} \tag{15.6}$$

A supervised Machine Learning classifier investigated the problem of keypoint utilization and introduced a PatchSelect method for selecting training and testing data with a better performance than other strategies. GPR-based Buried Threat Detection (BTD) used the raw data with EHD and Histogram of Gradients (HOG) features for Random Forest (RF) and SVM (Reichman et al., 2018). The Prony method extracts the Complex Natural Resonance (CNR) and normalizes the extracted feature. The reflected and reconstructed signals were identical. The Multiclass Support Vector Machine (MC-SVM) evaluated the technique with the highest accuracy and sensitivity using the Equations (15.7)–(15.9) compared to KNN, ANN, and DT (Khalaf et al., 2018).

$$\text{Accuracy} = \frac{\left(\text{TP} + \text{TN}\right)}{\left(\text{TP} + \text{TN} + \text{FP} + \text{FN}\right)} \tag{15.7}$$

$$\text{Sensitivity} = \frac{\left(\text{TP}\right)}{\left(\text{TP} + \text{FN}\right)} \tag{15.8}$$

$$\text{Specificity} = \frac{\left(\text{TN}\right)}{\left(\text{TN} + \text{FP}\right)} \tag{15.9}$$

The channels were pre-processed in a down-track direction to highlight abnormalities. The HOG and SVM methods are applied in the cross-track to identify the locations of interest in a 2-D GPR image. Energy feature methods excluded non-mine targets, and weight judgment methods confirmed the landmine targets. Equation (15.10) depicted $\alpha(x, y)$ based on gradient images (Shi et al., 2018).

$$\alpha\left(x, y\right) = \tan^{-1} \frac{G_y\left(x, y\right)}{G_x\left(x, y\right)} \tag{15.10}$$

The clutter removal process used recursive algorithms, such as linear predictive coding (LPC) and recursive least squares (RLS). Improvised explosive devices (IEDs) were classified using an SVM algorithm (Gutierrez et al., 2019). The objective was to arrange the window of GPR radiograms into two classes using neural networks RBF with a multi-objective genetic algorithm (MOGA). MOGA detected hyperbola structures in GPR images (Harkat et al., 2019).

A wavelet decomposition (WD) with skewness and kurtosis removed the clutter (Rani and Gupta, 2016). The kurtosis Gaussianity test resulted in a high-peak signal-to-noise ratio (PSNR). The neural networks (NN) approach detect buried objects automatically (Singh, 2019). Both learning technologies and data analysis use deep learning today. Landmine features extracted through first-order grayscale statistics (FOS) and second-order grayscale statistics (SOS) using Narrow Infra-Red (NIR) Thermal Sensor (TS) images. The features of the landmine were selected using a filter, wrapper, and combined embedded method. ANN, DT, SVM, and KNN classification results were compared separately and connected with fusion to a convolutional neural network (CNN). The performance in identifying larger-size landmines improved, and smaller landmines decreased with the Deep Learning (DL) methodology (Silva et al., 2019).

The twin vector of the B-Scan GPR image generated twin gray statistics sequences (TGSS) for the hyperbola classification of landmines (Yuan et al., 2019). Combining local decision-making (LDM) with cooperative decision-making (CDM) was used to identify IEDs. The accuracy of CDM was improved using artificial intelligence approaches, such as a fuzzy decision support system (FDSS) and a feed-forward Artificial Neural Network (ffANN). For identifying the True Positive Rates (TPR) and False Positive Rates (FPR) calculations were made using Equations (15.11) and (15.12) (Florez-Lozano et al., 2020).

$$TPR = \frac{TP}{TP + FN} \tag{15.11}$$

$$FPR = \frac{FP}{FP + TN} \tag{15.12}$$

A metal detector (MD) detected the sound responses from the presence of a landmine to build a database (Sumathi et al., 2021). The signature matrix (SM) and derivative maps (DM) feature extraction methods extracted the derivative image from MD signals. Then the image was classified with Machine Learning algorithms such as Linear Discriminant Analysis (LDA), Bagging, Quadratic Support Vector Machine (Q-SVM), Boosting, and CNN (Rana et al., 2021). Using Equation (15.13), Q-SVM depicted the polynomial kernel with second degree, where x and y are feature vectors and $c \geq 0$ for the free parameter (Safatly et al., 2021). OCSVM detected the thin debonding from the air and ground-coupled data of GPR, which differs from reference data. The performance of the OCSVM model computed Dice Score using a confusion matrix (Todkar et al., 2021).

$$k(x, y) = \left(x^T y + c\right)^2 \tag{15.13}$$

15.4   DISCUSSION ON CLASSIFICATION ALGORITHMS USED FOR LANDMINE DETECTION

The necessity of landmine detection is increasing due to the danger of buried landmines which costs people's lives and environmental development. The discussion includes the type of image sensors, methods, and classifiers applied to detect and classify landmines. Table 15.1 shows the different image sensors, techniques, and classifiers used for landmine detection with merits, demerits, and evaluation metrics. Numerous recent research publications have described automated algorithms for detecting and classifying landmines (Singh et al., 2021b). This chapter briefly discusses the methods for

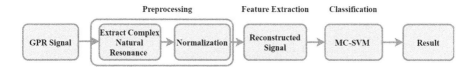

FIGURE 15.5 The Prony method of Multi Class-Support Vector Machine-based target detection algorithm. (Khalaf et al., 2018.)

identifying and classifying buried explosive objects from the subsurface and compares the best classification techniques commonly applied in Machine Learning through GPR images. The confidence value is assigned based on classification algorithms, such as SVM, KNN, HMM, and RF methods, when the landmine is present at a particular point of the subsurface area. Several classification models are trained and tested on GPR images in A-Scan (1D), B-Scan (2D), and C-Scan (3D) data sets of explosive objects from the subsurface (Bhambri et al., 2021).

Different versions of SVM classifiers are used in the articles (Jin and Zhou, 2010; Andrew Karem, 2011; Camilo et al., 2016; Tbarki et al., 2017; Reichman et al., 2018; Khalaf et al., 2018; Shi et al., 2018; Gutierrez et al., 2019; Todkar et al., 2021). Among these modified versions of the SVM algorithm, the Prony method of MC-SVM has given the best accuracy and sensitivity at 99.94% and 98.97%, respectively. This method detected only AP landmines. Figure 15.5 shows a Multi Class-Support Vector Machine-based target detection algorithm (Khalaf et al., 2018).

In addition, the SVM classifier used with the HOG method has given 95% probability detection with 0.017 FAR. The test collected data from different sites, including gravel, sand, grassland, and clay. The HOG method was tested and detected only AT landmines. This method retrieved characteristics from all three directions from cross-track, down-track, and depth directions, confirming the target location on the time slice using weight judgment. Figure 15.6 shows the process of a three-direction-based target detection algorithm (Shi et al., 2018).

The KNN algorithm was used by Frigui and Gader (2009) and Yuan et al. (2019) to classify landmines. A possibility KNN classifier was used with the EHD method for feature extraction and LMS for pre-screening. It achieved 90% probability detection with a low false alarm rate. It principally detected AT landmines (Frigui and Gader, 2009). Furthermore, KNN was used with the TGSS method to identify landmines with 63.37% accuracy. The data set included 32 x 32-pixel GPR B-scan images. The technique produced a dimension-reduction performance for different imbalance ratios (Yuan et al., 2019).

HMM is used in Missaoui et al. (2011), Oualid Missaoui et al. (2013), Anis Hamdi (2015), Manandhar et al. (2015), and Yuksel and Gader (2016) in different combinations.

eHMM proposed a continuous and discrete version of HMM, and each shared the common data attributes. The ensemble method produced 94% probability detection and fi% FAR. Figure 15.7 shows the process of the ensemble Hidden Markov Model of landmine detection (Anis Hamdi, 2015).

The discrete and continuous-based multi-stream HMM was implemented in Missaoui et al. (2011) and Oualid Missaoui et al. (2013) with Baum Welch and

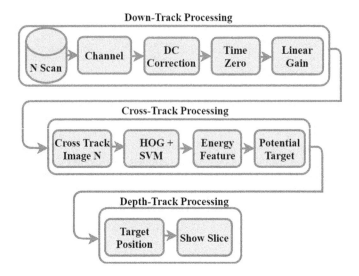

FIGURE 15.6   The process of a three-direction-based target detection algorithm. (Shi et al., 2018.)

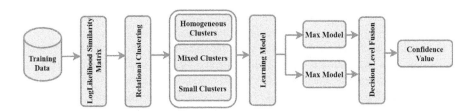

FIGURE 15.7   Ensemble Hidden Markov Model for landmine detection. (Anis Hamdi, 2015.)

minimum classification error and produced probability detection greater than 0.5 and 75%, respectively, based on stream relevance weight. The MSCHMM method detected both AT and AP landmines.

NN, CNN, and ANN were used by Singh (2019), Silva et al. (2019), and Florez-Lozano et al. (2020). The model for the kurtosis Gaussianity test produced a clutter-reduced image with high PSNR. Figure 15.8 illustrates the target detection using wavelet-based clutter reduction and a neural network classifier (Singh, 2019). Multispectral images produced 97% accuracy using the CNN approach. This method detected both AP and AT landmines. But the performance increased only for detecting AT landmines. Figure 15.9 displays the process of landmine detection using multispectral images (Silva et al., 2019).

The MOGA model produced a high-performance and low-complexity result with CNN, SVM, and Viola-Jones (Harkat et al., 2019). Figure 15.10 displays wavelet-based clutter reduction and target detection using a neural network classifier. Table 15.1 presents a comparative analysis of landmine detection methods and techniques using ML algorithms.

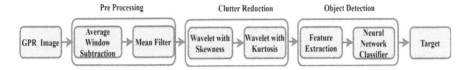

FIGURE 15.8 Target detection using wavelet-based clutter reduction and neural network classifier. (Singh, 2019.)

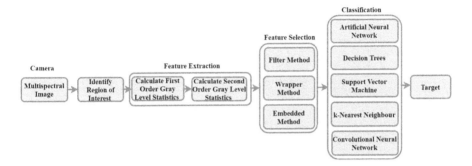

FIGURE 15.9 Landmine detection using multispectral images. (Silva et al., 2019.)

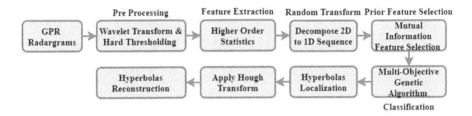

FIGURE 15.10 Wavelet-based clutter reduction and target detection using neural network classifier. (Harkat et al., 2019.)

The development of landmine detection algorithms and techniques has improved the performance of various evaluation metrics, including the probability of detection, accuracy (Acc), false alarm rate (FAR), receiver operating characteristic (ROC), and dice score (Ds) at reduced FAR achieved the highest accuracy.

15.5   CONCLUSION AND FUTURE PERSPECTIVES

Landmines are buried by terrorists and detected by military personnel using various sensors (Bhambri, 2020). This work aims to find landmines using sensors and integrate Machine Learning algorithms simultaneously. Multiple sensors are used to collect data, and algorithms will be evaluated by analyzing metrics generated from the data. GPR sensor data is used primarily and processed using Machine Learning-based classification algorithms (Kuzhaloli et al., 2020). The GPR images created a database for selecting features based on surrogate mines and non-mines,

TABLE 15.1

A Comparative Analysis of Landmine Detection Methods and Classification Techniques Using Machine Learning Algorithms

Author	Image	Methods	Classifier	Merits	Demerits	Metrics
Frigui and Gader (2009)	GPR	LMS, EHD	KNN	EHD used fuzzy techniques to distinguish accurate detections from false alarms	Factors appear to be influenced by geography and the environment	Pd - 90%
Jin and Zhou (2010)	UWB SAR	SFFS	FHSSVM	Showed improvement in the performance of identifying anti-tank mines	Impossible to achieve a low FAR	Pd - 0.7
Andrew Karem (2011)	GPR	MIL, EHD, SumMemship	RVM	MIL approach performed well in multi-sensor fusion at different resolutions	More suitable only in significant intra-class variations	Pd - 90%, FAR - 0.008
Missaoui et al. (2011)	GPR	BW, MCE	MSDHMM	Stream relevance weights used for the various components of each state	Streams must include different feature extraction methods and sensors	Probability-based -75%
Oualid Missaoui et al. (2013)	GPR	BW, MCE	MSCHMM	MSCHMM improved the discriminative power and the classification accuracy	Sequential training could replace batch-mode training	Pd >= 0.5
Anis Hamdi (2015))	GPR	Decision Level Fusion	eHMM	Identified the coherent HMM mixture model to define the multiple properties of the data	eHMM used only single-layer ANN	Pd - 94%, FAR - 10%
Manandhar et al. (2015)	GPR	MIL, Variational Bayes	MiHMM	Tractable and computationally efficient using variational Bayes	Improved parameter estimation requires Markov Chain Monte Carlo inference	Pd - 0.7 FAR-0.5
Camilo et al. (2016)	GPR	BOV feature learning	Linear SVM	FV showed improved performance with BOV in multiple object classification	Filters learned from the BOV only in HH polarization	Pd - 0.6 FAR - 0.02
Yuksel and Gader, 2016	MD, EMI	ME	MHMME	MHMME showed better performance than ME and HMM	Classification becomes a problem in the absence of contextual data	Mean - 0.73 SD - 0.02

Tbarki et al. (2017)	GPR	MC-SVM	OCSVM	OCSVM based on RBF kernel handled well on unbalanced data	OCSVM based on polynomial kernel was worthless	AUC (RBF Kernel) -89.24%
Reichman et al. (2018)	GPR	RF, PatchSelect	SVM	Keypoint utilization had a significant impact on a landmine detection	Prediction of keypoint was a difficult task in A-Scan images	FAR - 0.005
Khalaf et al. (2018)	GPR	Prony	MC-SVM	The MC-SVM achieved the highest accuracy and sensitivity	The frequency level is low	Acc - 99.94%
Shi et al. (2018)	GPR	HOG	SVM	Target detected using all three directions in sand and gravel	It was more challenging to process big data in real-time	Sens -98.97%
Gutierrez et al. (2019)	GPR	RLS, LPC	SVM	The SVM effectively discriminates and detects targets as IEDs or non-IEDs	Field setup configuration needed to reduce soil-clutter reflection	Pd - 95%
Harkat et al. (2019)	GPR	CNN, SVM	MOGA	The online execution of MOGA was much faster than the remaining models	Time-consuming process	FAR - 0.017
Singh (2019)	GPR	Skewness, Kurtosis	NN	WD with kurtosis outperformed in removing clutter in the soil	The method failed to locate the plastic target	Acc - 87.02%
Silva et al. (2019)	TS, NIR	ANN, DT SVM, KNN	CNN	The performance increased for AT mines and decreased for AP mines	Decision Trees alone achieved the worst performance	FPR -10.53%
Yuan et al. (2019)	GPR	TGSS	RoF, K-NN	Showed good robustness and dimension reduction for different imbalance ratios	Data sets trained using a small number of samples	Acc - 89%
Florez-Lozano et al. (2020)	GPR, TS, VS, IR, UV	LDM, CDM	ffANN, FDFS	The system detected IEDs of any shape, material, and type with high accuracy	TS and GPR sensors perform less well than cameras	FP - 7%, FN - 21%
Safatly et al. (2021)	MD	SM, DM	Bagging, CNN Boosting,	Accurately classify the buried objects	Extend the database with more samples	TN - 86%
Todkar et al. (2021)	GPR	GprMax	OCSVM	OCSVM method performed better with air Coupled	OCSVM used only smaller learning datasets	Acc - > 97%

employing reference signatures taken from the homogeneous medium. For training data samples, these feature selections are considered for the classifier, resulting in improved accuracy. The performance of landmine-buried objects depends on their type, the soil's contents, and the soil's nature. Machine learning has separate segmentation, feature extraction, and classification process techniques. Future work will incorporate deep learning (DL) to automate segmentation, feature extraction, and classification. DL uses neural networks with multiple layers, each extracting one or more unique features in an image. The performance of deep learning models for image classification has improved significantly in recent years. Deep learning architectures for image classification often achieve the highest accuracy rates, including AlexNet, CSAERNet, VGGNet, ResNet, GoogLeNet, Squeeze Net, Shuffle Net, DenseNet, etc.

REFERENCES

Abraham, R. S. A. (2013). Comparison of supervised and unsupervised learning algorithms for pattern classification. *International Journal of Advanced Research in Artificial Intelligence*, 2(2), 34–38.

Andrew Karem, H. F. (2011). A multiple instance learning approach for landmine detection using ground penetrating radar. *2011 IEEE International Geoscience and Remote Sensing Symposium*, Vancouver, BC, Canada. (pp. 878–881).

Anis Hamdi, H. F. (2015). Ensemble hidden Markov models with application to landmine detection. *EURASIP Journal on Advances in Signal Processing*. https://doi.org/10.1186/s13634-015-0260-8

Ayon Dey. (2016). Machine learning algorithms: A review. *International Journal of Computer Science and Information Technologies*, 7(3), 1174–1179. https://doi.org/10.21275/ART20203995

Bakshi, P., Bhambri, P., & Thapar, V. (2021). A review paper on wireless sensor network techniques in Internet of Things (IoT). *Wesleyan Journal of Research*, 14(7), 147–160.

Banerjee, K., Bali, V., Nawaz, N., Bali, S., Mathur, S., Mishra, R. K., & Rani, S. (2022). A machine-learning approach for prediction of water contamination using latitude, longitude, and elevation. *Water*, 14(5), 728.

Bhambri, P. (2020). Green compliance. In S. Agarwal (Ed.), *Introduction to Green Computing* (pp. 95–125). AGAR Saliha Publication. ISBN: 978-81-948141-5-3.

Bhambri, P. (2021). Electronic evidence. In Kamal Gulati, Narinder Kumar Bhasin (Eds.), *Textbook of Cyber Heal* (pp. 86–120). AGAR Saliha Publication. ISBN: 978-81-948141-7-7.

Bhambri, P., Singh, M., Jain, A., Dhanoa, I. S., Sinha, V. K., & Lal, S. (2021). Classification of the GENE expression data with the aid of optimized feature selection. *Turkish Journal of Physiotherapy and Rehabilitation*, 32(3), 1158–1167.

Camilo, J. A., Malof, J. M., & Collins, L. M. (2016). A feature learning approach for classifying buried threats in forward looking ground penetrating radar data. *Detection and Sensing of Mines, Explosive Objects, and Obscured Targets XXI*, 9823, 98231I. https://doi.org/10.1117/12.2223117

Conyers, L. B. (2018). Ground penetrating radar. In *The Encyclopedia of Archaeological Sciences*. John Wiley & Sons, Inc. https://doi.org/10.1002/9781119188230.saseas0272

"Facts About Landmines - Minesweepers," (n.d.). *Minesweepers, 2019.* https://landminefree.org/facts-about-landmines/

Florez-Lozano, J., Caraffini, F., Parra, C., & Gongora, M. (2020). Cooperative and distributed decision-making in a multi-agent perception system for improvised land mines detection. *Information Fusion*, 64 (September 2019), 32–49. https://doi.org/10.1016/j.inffus.2020.06.009

Frigui, H., & Gader, P. (2009). Detection and discrimination of land mines in ground-penetrating radar based on edge histogram descriptors and a possibilistic K-nearest neighbor classifier. *IEEE Transactions on Fuzzy Systems*, *17*(1), 185–199. https://doi.org/10.1109/TFUZZ.2008.2005249

Ghareeb, M., Bazzi, A., Raad, M. and Abdulnabi, S. (2017). Wireless Robo-Pi for landmine detection. *2017 First International Conference on Landmine: Detection, Clearance and Legislations (LDCL)* (pp. 1–5). https://doi.org/10.1109/LDCL.2017.7976932

Giovanneschi, F., Gonzalez-Huici, M. A., & Uschkerat, U. (2013). A parametric analysis of time and frequency domain GPR scattering signatures from buried landmine-like targets. *Detection and Sensing of Mines, Explosive Objects, and Obscured Targets XVIII, 8709* (November 2014, p. 870914). https://doi.org/10.1117/12.2015804

Gupta, O., Rani, S., & Pant, D. C. (2011). Impact of parallel computing on bioinformatics algorithms. In *Proceedings 5th IEEE International Conference on Advanced Computing and Communication Technologies* (pp. 206–209).

Gutierrez, S., Vega, F., Gonzalez, F. A., Baer, C., & Sachs, J. (2019). Application of polarimetric features and support vector machines for classification of improvised explosive devices. *IEEE Antennas and Wireless Propagation Letters*, *18*(11), 2282–2286. https://doi.org/10.1109/LAWP.2019.2934691

Harkat, H., Ruano, A. E., Ruano, M. G., & Bennani, S. D. (2019). GPR target detection using a neural network classifier designed by a multi-objective genetic algorithm. *Applied Soft Computing Journal*, *79*, 310–325. https://doi.org/10.1016/j.asoc.2019.03.030

Hussein, E. M. A., & Waller, E. J. (2000). Landmine detection: The problem and the challenge. *Applied Radiation and Isotopes*, *53*(4–5), 557–563. https://doi.org/10.1016/S0969-8043(00)00218-9

Jin, T., & Zhou, Z. (2010). Ultrawideband synthetic aperture radar unexploded ordnance detection. *IEEE Transactions on Aerospace and Electronic Systems*, *46*(3), 1201–1213. https://doi.org/10.1109/TAES.2010.5545183

Kasban, H., Zahran, O., Elaraby, S. M., El-Kordy, M., & Abd El-Samie, F. E. (2010). A comparative study of landmine detection techniques. *Sensing and Imaging*, *11*(3), 89–112. https://doi.org/10.1007/s11220-010-0054-x

Khalaf, M. W., Elsherbeni, A. Z., El-Hefnawi, F. M., Harb, H. M., & Bannis, M. H. (2018). Feature extraction and classification of buried landmine signals. *2018 IEEE Antennas and Propagation Society International Symposium and USNC/URSI National Radio Science Meeting, APSURSI 2018 - Proceedings* (vol. 2, 1175–1176). https://doi.org/10.1109/APUSNCURSINRSM.2018.8609023

K-Nearest Neighbor(KNN) Algorithm for Machine Learning - Javatpoint. (n.d.). Retrieved November 11, 2022, from https://www.javatpoint.com/k-nearest-neighbor-algorithm-for-machine-learning

Kuzhaloli, S., Devaneyan, P., Sitaraman, N., Periyathanbi, P., Gurusamy, M., & Bhambri, P. (2020). IoT Based Smart Kitchen Application for Gas Leakage Monitoring [Patent application number 202041049866A]. India.

Manandhar, A., Torrione, P. A., Collins, L. M., & Morton, K. D. (2015). Multiple-instance hidden markov model for GPR-based landmine detection. *IEEE Transactions on Geoscience and Remote Sensing*, *53*(4), 1737–1745. https://doi.org/10.1109/TGRS.2014.2346954

Missaoui, O., Frigui, H., & Gader, P. (2011). Landmine detection with ground-penetrating radar using multistream discrete hidden Markov models. *IEEE Transactions on Geoscience and Remote Sensing*, *49*(6 PART 1), 2080–2099. https://doi.org/10.1109/TGRS.2010.2090886

Mohammed, Mohssen, Khan, Muhammad Badruddin, Bashier, E. (n.d.). *Machine learning algorithms and applications*. CRC Press. https://doi.org/10.1201/9781315371658

Nguyen, L. (2016). Tutorial on hidden Markov model. *Special Issue "Some Novel Algorithms for Global Optimization and Relevant Subjects", Applied and Computational Mathematics (ACM)*, *6*(4–1), 16–38. https://doi.org/10.11648/j.acm.s.2017060401.12

Osisanwo, F. Y., Akinsola, J. E. T., Awodele, O., Hinmikaiye, J. O., Olakanmi, O., & Akinjobi, J. (2017). Supervised machine learning algorithms: Classification and comparison. *International Journal of Computer Trends and Technology, 48*(3), 128–138. https://doi. org/10.14445/22312803/ijctt-v48p126

Oualid Missaoui, H. F., Frigui, H, & Gader, P. (2013). Multi-stream continuous hidden Markov models with application to landmine detection. *EURASIP Journal on Advances in Signal Processing, 6*(3), 43–56.

Rachna, Chhabra, Y., & Bhambri, P. (2021). Various approaches and algorithms for monitoring energy efficiency of wireless sensor networks. In *Lecture Notes in Civil Engineering* (Vol. 113, pp. 761–770). Springer.

Rana, R., Chhabra, Y., & Bhambri, P. (2021). Design and development of distributed clustering approach in wireless sensor network. *Webology, 18*(1), 696–712.

Rani, S., Bhambri, P., & Chauhan, M. (2021, October). A machine learning model for kids' behavior analysis from facial emotions using principal component analysis. In *2021 5th Asian Conference on Artificial Intelligence Technology (ACAIT)* (pp. 522–525). IEEE.

Rani, S., & Gupta, O. P. (2016). Empirical analysis and performance evaluation of various GPU implementations of protein BLAST. *International Journal of Computer Applications, 151*(7), 22–27.

Reichman, D., Collins, L. M., & Malof, J. M. (2018). On choosing training and testing data for supervised algorithms in ground-penetrating radar data for buried threat detection. *IEEE Transactions on Geoscience and Remote Sensing, 56*(1), 497–507. https://doi. org/10.1109/TGRS.2017.2750920

Safatly, L., Baydoun, M., Alipour, M., Al-Takach, A., Atab, K., Al-Husseini, M., El-Hajj, A., & Ghaziri, H. (2021). Detection and classification of landmines using machine learning applied to metal detector data. *Journal of Experimental and Theoretical Artificial Intelligence, 33*(2), 203–226. https://doi.org/10.1080/0952813X.2020.1735529

Sato, M., Hamada, Y., Feng, X., Kong, F.-N., Zeng, Z., & Fang, G. (2004). GPR using an array antenna for landmine detection. *Near Surface Geophysics, 2*(1), 7–13. https://doi. org/10.3997/1873-0604.2003011

Shi, X., Song, Z., & Wang, C. (2018). *A Real-time Method For Landmine Detection Using Vehicle Array GPR*. Water. https://www.mdpi.com/2073-4441/14/5/728

Silva, J. S., Guerra, I. F. L., Bioucas-Dias, J., & Gasche, T. (2019). Landmine detection using multispectral images. *IEEE Sensors Journal, 19*(20), 9341–9351. https://doi. org/10.1109/JSEN.2019.2925203

Singh, M., Bhambri, P., Dhanoa, I. S., Jain, A., & Kaur, K. (2021a). Data mining model for predicting diabetes. *Annals of the Romanian Society for Cell Biology, 25*(4), 6702–6712.

Singh, N. S. V. (2019). Decluttering using wavelet based higher order statistics and target detection of GPR images. *Sensing and Imaging*. https://doi.org/10.1007/s11220-018-0223-x

Singh, Y. S., Lal, S., Bhambri, P., Kumar, A., & Dhanoa, I. S. (2021b). Advancements in social data security and encryption: A review. *Natural Volatiles & Essential Oils, 8*(4), 15353–15362.

Sumathi, N., Thirumagal, J., Jagannathan, S., Bhambri, P., & Ahamed, I. N. (2021). A comprehensive review on bionanotechnology for the 21st century. *Journal of the Maharaja Sayajirao University of Baroda, 55*(1), 114–131.

Support Vector Machine (SVM) Algorithm - Javatpoint. (n.d.). Retrieved November 10, 2022, from https://www.javatpoint.com/machine-learning-support-vector-machine-algorithm

Takahashi, K., Preetz, H., & Igel, J. (2011). Soil properties and performance of landmine detection by metal detector and ground-penetrating radar – Soil characterisation and its verification by a field test. *Journal of Applied Geophysics, 73*(4), 368–377. https://doi. org/10.1016/j.jappgeo.2011.02.008

Tbarki, K., Ben Said, S., Ksantini, R., & Lachiri, Z. (2017). Landmine detection improvement using one-class SVM for unbalanced data. *Proceedings – 3rd International Conference on Advanced Technologies for Signal and Image Processing, ATSIP 2017* (pp. 1–6). https://doi.org/10.1109/ATSIP.2017.8075597

Todkar, S. S., Baltazart, V., Ihamouten, A., Dérobert, X., & Guilbert, D. (2021). One-class SVM based outlier detection strategy to detect thin interlayer debondings within pavement structures using ground penetrating radar data. *Journal of Applied Geophysics, 192.* https://doi.org/10.1016/j.jappgeo.2021.104392

Yuan, D., An, Z., & Zhao, F. (2019). Gray-statistics-based twin feature extraction for hyperbola classification in ground penetrating radar images. *Procedia Computer Science, 147,* 567–573. https://doi.org/10.1016/j.procs.2019.01.215

Yuksel, Seniha E., & Gader, P. D. (2016). Context-based classification via mixture of hidden Markov model experts with applications in landmine detection. *IET Computer Vision,* 873–883. https://doi.org/10.1049/iet-cvi.2016.0138

16 Application of Queuing Technique in an Educational Institute Canteen: A Case Study

Jagdeep Singh and Prem Singh

Guru Nanak Dev Engineering College, Ludhiana, India

16.1 INTRODUCTION

Waiting time in queues is a significant present-day problem faced by peoples, particularly in locations such as businesses, colleges, offices, hospitals, canteens, book store, libraries, banks, post offices, gas pumps, cinemas, music halls etc. They also wait fora telephone operator to answer, for a traffic signal to change, for the before noon mail to be delivered, and in numerous other similar situations (Hira, 2007).

The main causes of queuing problems are:

- *Overburden*: Due to large interest in the facilities, there is an occurrence of overabundance of waiting time. So we state that there are a deficient number of service facilities.
- *Demand*: Due to little demand, there is an excessive amount of idle facility. Which we can say about a large number of services.

In either case, the issue might be either a scheduled arrival or give a legitimate number of services, or both, in order to get an optimal stability among the expense related to waiting time and idle time.

In the college cafeteria or canteen students expect a definite level of service; however, the owner of the canteen attempts to reduce the costs to the lowest level possible while still maintaining the essential service level. This study exhibits the optimization between the waiting time and the service rendered. The fundamental qualities of a waiting time period phenomenon are entities reach, at standard or sporadic interval of time, at a particular point called the service center. Such might include lorries arriving at a stocking location, students arriving at a cafeteria, peoples entering a theatre, ships arriving a port, letters arriving on the secretary's desk etc. all these items are named entries or the arrival of the clients (Chawla, 2005).

At least one service channel or facility station or service facility is gathered at the service center. If the facility station in a certain region is unoccupied or

DOI: 10.1201/9781003383505-16

unavailable, the incoming clients will be attended to. If not, will customers stay in queue until the service arrives? When the service to the client has been completed, they leave the service line (Rao, 1978). We have a waiting line issue whenever customers are using a service facility and either the customers or the facilities must wait. At this point it may be useful to outline definitions of some of the terms which we will draw upon in this chapter:

1. Customer (Students in this case): The incoming clients that needs some services to be completed. In different cases, the clients may be peoples, automobiles, or parts etc.
2. Queue (Waiting line): The numbers of clients waiting to be serviced. The waiting line does not include the clients being served.
3. Service channel: The method or skill, which is carrying out to the client as services. This might be single-channel or multi-channel. This service channel is represented by the symbol c.

The following section outlines the structure of a queuing classification.

16.1.1 STRUCTURE OF A QUEUING CLASSIFICATION

A queuing system is composed of seven key components:

1. Arrival or input distribution
2. Departure or output distribution
3. Service channel
4. Service discipline
5. The maximum numbers of customer permitted in the system
6. Calling sources of population
7. Client behaviors

16.1.1.1 Input or Arrival Distribution

This shows the quantity of clients lands at the service facility. Entrances may also be communicated with using the inter-arrival time, which is the interval between two consecutive arrivals (Taha, 2021). Entrances might be isolated by an equivalent interval of time, by inconsistent yet certainly identified intervals of time or by an inconsistent interim of time whose possibilities are identified, termed as irregular/random factors/variables respectively.

The frequency at which clients land to be adjusted is termed the arrival rate i.e. the quantity of clients showing up per unit of time. At the point when the arrival rate is random, the clients land in no sensible example or request after some time. This speaks to most cases in the business world.

At the point when arrivals are haphazard, we need to identify the probability distribution depicting arrivals, indicating the time among arrivals. The arrivals are regularly best depicting by the poison distribution. The mean estimation of the arrival rate is given by λ.

16.1.1.2   Service (Departure) Distribution

It shows the pattern wherein the quantity of clients leaves the service facility. Departure may likewise be given by the service or inter-departure time, which is the time between two progressive services.

On the off-chance that service time is arbitrarily circulated, we need to discover what probability distribution best portrays their behavior. In cases when service time exhibits a random nature, researchers in executive positions have determined that it is most accurately represented by the exponential probability distribution. Consequently, the study of waiting queue behavior becomes relatively more straightforward and practical to develop and implement.

The quantity of service served per unit of time provided by one service channel is referred to as the service rate. This rate accepts the service channel to be constantly occupied, with no inactive time permitted. The mean estimation of the service rate is given by μ. In business issues, more instances of a uniform service rate will be found than of uniform arrival rates.

16.1.1.3   Service Channels

The waiting line may only have one service channel. Arriving customers can form one line and be served, just as in a specialist's centre. The framework may be the number of service channels, which might be masterminded in parallel, in an arrangement or an intricate mix of both. When the system has only one server, it was referred to as a one-server model. By contrast, when the system had multiple parallel channels, each with their own server, it was referred to as a multi-server model.

Occasionally, a few service stations may be combined into one consequent service station: for instance, a few ticket offices in a performance center may send all the ticket owners to a solitary ticket collector at the entry of the theater. Then again, a single service station may scatter clients between a few stations that come after it; for instance, an inquiry assistant in a workplace.

16.1.1.4   Service Discipline

The standard by which clients are chosen from the service's waiting line is known as service discipline or order of facility. The best well-known approach is a 'first-come-first-served' basis, in this clients are attended in the order of their arrival. This might be observed, for example, at cinema box offices, train stations, commercial banks, and so on. As in a large warehouse, the most recently arrived items are removed first. Still, other disciplines incorporate haphazard and priority. Priority is said to occur when a newly arrived client is picked for service in front of different clients who are already in the queue. A unit is said to have pre-emptive priority on the off-chance that it simply goes to the head of the waiting line, dislodging any unit previously being served when it arrives. Given that the request for service isn't identified with the service time, it doesn't influence the waiting line size or normal waiting time, yet it does impact the time a distinct client needs to wait. The service discipline, in this manner, influences the induction of conditions utilized for examination. In this content, just the most widely recognized service discipline 'first come first served' will be accepted for further exchange.

16.1.1.5   The Maximum Number of Clients Permitted in the System

The maximum number of clients permitted in the system can be either limited or boundless. In certain facilities, only a limited number of clients are permitted in the system. Any clients who turn up subsequently are not permitted to enter the system, unless the numbers queueing turn out to be less than the permitted limit.

16.1.1.6   Population/Calling Source

The arrival of the clients relies on the basis which creates them. On the off-chance that only a couple of potential clients are present, the calling source is called limited/finite. In the event that there is a substantial quantity of potential clients, beyond 41 or 51, it is commonly assumed to be unbounded or infinite. There is as yet an alternative standard for arranging the source as limited or unlimited. A limited/finite source occurs when an entrance influences the probability of entrance of upcoming clients. For example, when considering apparatus repair a backup of N operating devices can be considered a finite resource. Before any apparatus stops working, it turns into a client and henceforth cannot create any additional call until it is restored. An unbounded/infinite source is said to exist when the entrance of a client does not influence the entrance rate of probable upcoming clients.

16.1.1.7   Client's Behavior

The client's behavior plays a crucial role in the analysis of waiting lines. A client is said to have baulked if he decides not to join the queue for the reason that it is too long. Similarly, a client is deemed to have reneged if he chooses to join the line but eventually becomes impatient and quits it. Customers are considered to be jockeying for position when there are at least two parallel lines and they switch from one line to the next.

16.1.2   FUNCTIONAL FEATURES OF A QUEUING/WAITING LINE SYSTEM

Examination of a waiting system contains a study of its various functional features. Among these are the following:

1. Length of Queue (Lq) – Avg. number of clients in the line waiting to acquire the service. This eliminates the clients being served.
2. Length of System (Ls) – Avg. number of clients in the system containing those waiting as well as those being served.
3. In the queue waiting time (Wq) – Avg. time that a client has to spend in the waiting line to get service.
4. In the system total time (Ws) – Avg. total time consumed by the clients in the system from the instant they reach until they leave the system. This is taken to be time to wait + the service time. It is also called traffic intensity.
5. Utilization factors (ρ) – This is the amount of time a service provider really devotes to the clients. It is also called traffic intensity.

16.1.3 Queuing Models Representation by Kendall's

D.G. Kendall (1953) and later A. Lee (1966) presented valuable representation for queuing models. The comprehensive representation can be articulated as

$$(a / b / c) : (d / e / f),$$

Where

- a: Arrival distribution
- b: Departure or service time distribution
- c: Number of parallel service channels in the system
- d: Service discipline
- e: Queuing discipline
- f: Max. No. of consumers permitted in the system

The given conservative codes are commonly applied to substitute the notation a, b and d:

Notations for 'a' and 'b' notation

M: Markovian (Poisson) arrival or departure
E_k: Erlangian or gamma inter-arrival or service time distribution with parameters k,
GI: General independent arrival distribution
G: General departure distribution
D: Deterministic inter-arrival or service times

Notation for 'd'

FCFS: First come, first service
LCFS: Last come, first service
SIRO: Service in random order
GD: Deterministic inter-arrival rate

16.1.4 Classifications of queuing models

There are three types of queuing model as shown in Figure 16.1.

16.2 BACKGROUND

Abolnikov et al. (2007) analyzed difficult stochastic framework with a solitary server that works in two similar positions. The researcher utilized and improved strategies for change examination for multivariate random walks to examine the waiting line methods. It empowered us to arrive at closed-form functional for the procedures and connected random parts. Uses were found in PC organizing and working systems investigation.

Nobel and Moreno (2008) considered a single-server waiting line model with retrials in discrete time. The periodicity situation and the producing capacity of the

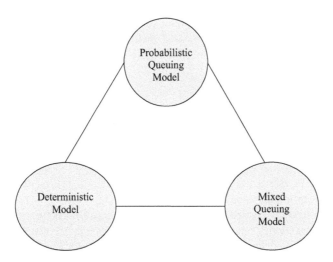

FIGURE 16.1 Classification of queuing models.

joint balance conveyance of the number of works/jobs in orbit and the leftover service time of the activity in service are determined. From the producing capacity, a few presentation measures were reasoned, similar to the normal orbit size. Additionally, the occupied time frame and the no. of works/jobs attended through a bustling period were talked about.

Pazgal and Radas (2008) examined client basic decision-making while waiting in the queue. The goal of the examination was to decide if individuals appear to pursue the targets gave by the waiting theory or whether mental expenses and impression of time nullify these targets. The researcher utilized a computerized examination where members face unequivocal money-related prizes and punishments for their choices in a between-subjects, completely crossed structure with two trial factors – clock information, and data about anticipated queuing time, each at two levels, absence and presence. The outcomes that appeared by giving clock time had no effect on basic conclusion.

Akbari et al. (2016) written about joining weighted linear prediction method and M/M/1 waiting line theory to improve the vitality effectiveness of cloud data centers. The objective is to recreate the impact of different remaining burdens on the vitality utilization of the cloud system utilizing CloudSim or comparative programming.

Malipatil et al. (2017) studied a toll plaza on a four-lane separated main road having two-way driving (N–S and S–N) is assessed employing waiting line theory. Factors such as road traffic volume, space-mean speed, and time progress are communicated in one-hour interim periods. If there should be an occurrence of N–S movement, watched recurrence and hypothetical recurrence are discovered to be equivalent, demonstrating the proposed Poisson dispersion to be the genuine populace distribution.

In their study, Oluwadare et al. (2019) utilized a waiting queue system and regression analysis to investigate the organizational structure and performance of the Federal University of Technology, Akure (FUTA). Traffic information streams were taken over a time of about a month using a Wireshark catching instrument at various vital areas in the grounds. The analyst built up an observational model that recognized factors that essentially decide network traffic. The model could help organize overseers to screen, design and enhance the nature of service.

16.3 PROBLEM FORMULATION

Queuing theory is a generally accepted and essential tool to improve the decision-making in manufacturing and service organizations. Given increasing globalization and the presence of international competitors in the market, the scenario of these organizations is also changing. Literature reviews reveal that the study on toll plaza was carried out to assess the queue. To date, however, much less study has been reported on institutional canteens.

The present study is carried out to exhibit the optimization between the waiting time as well as the service rendered in college canteen. The data collected during the peak or rush hours, i.e., from 10: 00 a.m. to 12:p.m. and from 11:45 am to 1:45 pm and divided these hours in six divisions, each of 20 minutes duration. From that data, various parameters, i.e, the average time a student spends in the canteen, the average waiting time of a student in the waiting line, and the utilization rate etc., were also observed.

16.4 METHODOLOGY

The research methodology used for the current research work is depicted in Figure 16.2.

In the college cafeteria or canteen students expect a certain level of service whereas the owner of canteen giving service facility attempts to keep the costs least while giving the required service. This study exhibits the optimization between the waiting time and the service rendered.

There are two main factors, the arrival rate as well as the departure rate, that should be noted meticulously. Two tables were prepared, one for arrivals and other for departures. The time for the arrivals as well as for the departure have been observed. The data were observed during the peak or rush hours, as outlined earlier. Observations for undertaken over a period of two days. It has been noted that there

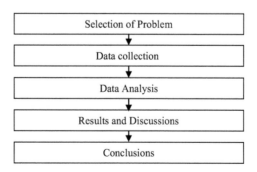

FIGURE 16.2 Research methodology.

were three people serving at the canteen counters and they were receiving respective salaries of 5000, 3000 & 2000 INR per month. This is predominantly a self-service canteen, with one person on the cash counter, while the other two are involved in serving students. After acquiring this data, first the arrival and then the departure rate, the mean of the two is calculated.

16.5 RESULTS & DISCUSSION

16.5.1 MEAN ARRIVAL RATE (λ) FOR TIME INTERVAL 10:00 A.M. TO 12:00 P.M.

The mean arrival rate of students who were visited the canteen in stipulated time is shown in Table 16.1.

From Table 16.1 it has been observed that the mean arrival rate (λ) = 14.05/6 = 2.34

16.5.2 MEAN DEPARTURE RATE (M) FOR TIME INTERVAL 10:00 A.M. TO 12:00 P.M.

The mean departure rate of students who visited the canteen in the stipulated time is shown in Table 16.2.

TABLE 16.1
Mean Arrival Rate of Students in the Canteen

S. No.	No. of Students Arrive in the Canteen	Time Interval From	To	Arrival Rate (λ)
1	2 + 4 + 3 + 1 + 4 + 1 + 2 + 2 + 1 + 2 + 1 + 2 + 3 + 3 + 2 + 1 + 1 + 1 + 2 + 3 + 2 + 1 + 2 + 1 + 2 = 49	10:00 a.m.	10:20 a.m.	2.45
2	2 + 3 + 1 + 1 + 1 + 2 + 2 + 1 + 1 + 2 + 1 + 4 + 6 + 1 + 1 + 2 + 1 + 5 + 3 + 2 + 2 + 2 + 2 + 2 + 221 + 1 + 3 + 1 + 3 = 59	10:20 a.m.	10:40 a.m.	2.59
3	1 + 1 + 3 + 1 + 3 + 1 + 1 + 1 + 1 + 2 + 1 + 1 + 1 + 1 + 1 + 2 + 3 + 3 + 3 + 1 + 2 + 2 + 1 + 1 + 3 = 42	10:40 a.m.	11:00 a.m.	2.1
4	1 + 2 + 2 + 1 + 1 + 2 + 2 + 1 + 4 + 1 + 1 + 1 + 2 + 1 + 2 + 2 + 1 + 1 + 2 + 3 + 2 + 3 + 1 = 38	11:00 a.m.	11:20 a.m.	1.9
5	4 + 3 + 2 + 2 + 1 + 3 + 3 + 1 + 1 + 3 + 4 + 1 + 2 + 4 + 3 + 2 + 1 + 5 + 2 + 3 + 1 + 1 = 51	11:20 a.m.	11:40 a.m.	2.55
6	5 + 1 + 4 + 2 + 4 + 3 + 1 + 1 + 2 + 1 + 2 + 2 + 2 + 1 + 1 + 2 + 2 + 2 + 2 + 2 + 3 + 1 + 3 + 2 + 2 + 1 + 2 = 59	11:40 a.m.	12:00 p.m.	2.8
		Total time: 120 minutes		14.05

TABLE 16.2
Mean Departure Rate of Students in the Canteen

S. No.	No. of students departure from the canteen	Time Interval		Departure Rate (μ)
		From	To	
1	$1 + 1 + 2 + 2 + 2 + 2 + 2 + 6 + 2 + 2 + 2 = 24$	10:00 a.m.	10:20 a.m.	1.2
2	$2 + 2 + 4 + 4 + 1 + 2 + 2 + 4 + 1 + 2 + 2 + 2 + 5 + 2 + 3 + 1 + 2 + 2 = 41$	10:20 a.m.	10:40 a.m.	2.05
3	$1 + 1 + 1 + 2 + 2 + 3 + 2 + 1 + 2 + 2 + 5 + 1 + 2 + 1 + 9 + 1 + 1 = 37$	10:40 a.m.	11:00 a.m.	1.85
4	$3 + 4 + 3 + 1 + 2 + 2 + 4 + 1 + 2 + 1 + 1 = 23$	11:00 a.m.	11:20 a.m.	1.15
5	$3 + 1 + 2 + 2 + 1 + 1 = 10$	11:20 a.m.	11:40 a.m.	0.5
6	$4 + 1 + 4 + 1 + 2 + 1 + 1 + 2 + 2 + 2 + 2 + 3 + 2 + 4 + 4 + 3 + 1 + 2 + 2 + 2 = 45$	11:40 a.m.	12:00 p.m.	2.25
		Total time: 120 minutes		9.0

From Table 16.2 it has been observed that the mean departure rate (μ) = 9/6 = 1.5.

16.5.3 QUEUING THEORY PARAMETERS

Various parameters of queuing theory for the mean arrival rate (λ) = 2.34, mean departure rate (μ) = 1.5 and service channels counters = c are shown in Table 16.3.

From each parameter of queuing theory it has been observed that for two service centers the service facility is optimized for the time interval 10: 00 a.m. to 12:00 p.m.

16.5.4 MEAN DEPARTURE RATE (M) FOR TIME INTERVAL 11: 45 A.M. TO 01:45 P.M.

The mean departure rate of students who were visited the canteen in stipulated time is shown in Table 16.4.

TABLE 16.3
Parameters of Queuing Theory

S. No.	Parameters	Values	
		When c = 3	When c = 2
1	Po = Probability of having no students in the canteen	0.18	0.14
2	Ls = Avg. no. of students in the canteen	2.27	1.9
3	Lq = Avg. no. of students waiting to be served	0.67	0.3
4	Ws = Avg. time a student spends in the canteen	0.59 hrs	0.13 hrs
5	Wq = Avg. waiting time for a student	0.28 hrs	0.25 hrs
6	P = Utility factor	0.52	0.78

TABLE 16.4
Mean Departure Rate of Students in the Canteen

S. No.	No. of Students Departure from the Canteen	Time Interval From	Time Interval To	Departure Rate(μ)
1	$2+2+2+2+2+2+1+2+1+3+2+3+$ $2+1 = 27$	11:45 a.m.	12:05 p.m.	1.35
2	$1+1+1+1+1+2+2+1+5+4+2+3+$ $2+1+2+1+1+4+2+2+1+2 = 42$	12:05 p.m.	12:25 p.m.	2.1
3	$2+1+2+3+2+2+2+2+3+1+3 = 25$	12:25 p.m.	12:45 p.m.	1.25
4	$2+1+1+2+2+6+3+2+3+1+1+2+$ $2 = 28$	12:45 p.m.	01:05 p.m.	1.4
5	$1+3+2+4+1+3 = 14$	01:05 p.m.	01:25 p.m.	0.7
6	$1+3+3+2+4+3+1+1+3+1+1+2+$ $1 = 26$	01:25 p.m.	01:45 p.m.	1.3
			Total time: 120 minutes	8.1

TABLE 16.5
Parameters of Queuing Theory

S. No.	Parameters	Values When c = 3	Values When c = 2
1	Po = Probability of having no students in the canteen	0.42	0.19
2	Ls = Avg. no. of students in the canteen	1.43	1.6
3	Lq = Avg. no. of students waiting to be served	0.28	0.44
4	Ws = Avg. time a student spends in the canteen	0.92 hrs	0.28 hrs
5	Wq = Avg. waiting time for a student	0.18 hrs	0.13 hrs
6	P = Utility factor	0.39	0.57

From Table 16.4 it has been observed that mean departure rate $\mu = 8.1/6 = 1.35$.

16.5.5 QUEUING THEORY PARAMETERS

Various parameters of queuing theory for the mean arrival rate (λ) = 1.56, mean departure rate (μ) = 1.35 and service channels counters = c are shown in Table 16.5.

From the each parameter of queuing theory it has been observed that for two service centers the service facility is optimized for the time interval 11: 45 a.m. to 01:45 p.m.

16.6 SUMMARY OF CHAPTER

Queuing theory is a generally accepted and essential tool to improve decision-making in manufacturing and service organizations. Given increasing globalization and the presence of international competitors in the market, the scenario of these organizations is also changing. The objective of the research was to investigate the waiting lines problems in the college canteens. Queues are common phenomena, which we detect regularly in our day-to-day life. The fundamental qualities of a waiting line phenomenon are that units arrive, at standard or sporadic interims of time, at a given point called the service center. The "queuing or waiting lines" may be either schedule arrival or the delivery of an appropriate quantity of services, or both, so as to attain an optimal stability among the cost related to the waiting time and idle time. In the college cafeteria or canteen, students expect a definite level of facility; however, the owner of the canteen delivering service facility attempts to spend as little as possible while delivering the essential service. The present study is carried out to optimize the balance between the waiting time as well as the service rendered in the college canteen. The data was collected during the peak or rush hours. From that data various parameters, i.e, the average time a student spends in the canteen, the average waiting time of a student in the queue, and the utilization rate etc. have also been observed. It has been observed that queuing theory plays a vital role in the decision-making of various waiting line problems. From the study, it has been concluded that currently the owner of the canteen have three service providers and has to pay a salary of Rs. 71 per hour to each of them. On the basis of the analysis it was observed that the owner has to employ only two service providers in order to optimize the cost, while the owner can save Rs.21 per hour. The scope of the present research work was limited to one canteen only, but it could be expanded to other canteens and also to other sections of the college such as the accounts department and broader student services. With the implementation of queuing theory, there will be both time and cost savings. Waiting line theory is a very easy and user-friendly tool which may help the decision-maker to make appropriate business policies in future. With this, the business will grow and achieve new milestones in the world.

REFERENCES

Abolnikova L., Agarwal R. P. and Dshalalow J. H. (2007). Random walk analysis of parallel queuing stations, *Mathematical and Computer Modelling*, 27, 452–468.

Akbari E., Cung F., Patel H. and Razaque A. (2016). Incorporation of Weighted Linear Prediction Technique and M/M/1 Queuing Theory for Improving Energy Efficiency of Cloud Computing Datacenters, *IEEE Long Island Systems, Applications and Technology Conference (LISAT)*, 12, 55–60.

Chawla V.K. (2005). *Operation Research*, Kalayani publications, New Delhi.

Hira D. S. (2007). *Operations Research*, S. Chand publications, New Delhi.

Malipatil N., Avati S. I., Vinay H. N. and Sunil S. (2017). Application of queuing theory to a Toll Plaza-A case study, *Conference of Transportation Research Group of India (CTRG-2019)*, 45, 343–354.

Nobel R. and Moreno P. (2008). A discrete-time retrial queuing model with one server, *European Journal of Operational Research*, 189, 1088–1103.

Oluwadare S. A., Agbonifo O. C. and Babatunde A. T. (2019). Network Traffic analysis using queuing model and regression technique, *Journal of Information*, 5, 16–26.

Pazgala A. I. and Radas S. (2008). Comparison of customer balking and reneging behavior to queuing theory predictions: An experimental study, *Computers & Operations Research*, 35, 2537–2548.

Rao S. S. (1978). *Optimization-Theory and Practice*, Wiley Eastern Ltd., New Delhi.

Taha H. A. (2001). *Operation Research: an Introduction* (sixth ed.), Macmillan publishing co., New York.

17 IoT-Based Driver Drowsiness Detection and Alerting System Using Haar Cascade and Eye Aspect Ratio Algorithms

R. Sathya, D. Sai Surya Harsha, G. Pavan Sundar Reddy, and M. Gopala Krishna

SRM Institute of Science and Technology, Chennai, India

17.1 INTRODUCTION

The Driver Drowsiness Detection and Alerting system refers to in-vehicle systems that monitor driver and/or vehicle behavior. These systems keep an eye on the driver's performance and alert or stimulate them if they exhibit signs of impairment. It alerts drivers when they start to feel sleepy. There are many approaches employed, including eye monitoring, physiological movement, and the lane position of the car [1]. These tools, which come as standard in all cars, can only alert a motorist that he or she is drowsy. It is the driver's responsibility to take a break and to make sure that the break is long enough to allow them to refocus [2]. The technology is unable to evaluate the driver's break quality. After a pause, though, the system will continue to track the driver's behavior and notify them once again if fatigue is found [3]. It is anticipated that the warnings will provide drivers the motivation they need to take a rest. Road accidents can happen for a number of reasons, and one of those reasons is drowsy driving. When the driver didn't get enough sleep, this generally occurs [4]. The body performs less effectively when it is fatigued. Drivers may suffer serious injuries or even die. According to the National Highway Traffic Safety Administration's assessment, in 2013 drowsy driving contributed to 800 fatalities, 40,000 injuries, and 70,000 collisions [5].

17.1.1 OBJECTIVE

The main objective of this model is to detect whether or not the driver is in a drowsy state. The target of this system is to help the drivers to no to get through any accidents [6].

Only the driver's drowsiness can be detected by the system. It is the driver's responsibility to take a break and to make sure that the break is long enough to allow him to focus again [7]. In the previous work the technique used was EEG, it resulted that the spatial resolution of EEG is minimal compared to the Haar Cascade method [8, 9].

17.1.2 SCOPE OF THE CHAPTER

The main idea is to provide a system which is embedded inside the vehicle that constantly monitors the drivers and alerts them when they have their eyes closed for a certain minimum number of seconds [10–12]. Since there would be chances where driver would not wake even after the system has alerted him/her, as a safety measure a unit has been included in this system that triggers if an accident takes place and alerts with the current location [13].

17.2   RELATED LITERATURE

Below are some implementations on the discussed issue.

Mohsen Babaeian and Mohammad [14] have used biomedical signal analysis, which is based on machine learning in order to detect the drowsiness of the driver. Two different frequencies were analyzed and found out that EEG signals, since they are not stationary, perform better than wavelets. Umit Budak and Varun Baja [15] used three feature extraction methods to characterize the drowsiness of the driver; these features were then classified individually. Frequency features from first and deep features from second feature extraction procedure were extracted. In J. Rajevenceltha, V. Anjana and Vilas H. Gaidhane [16], the face is detected using linear binary patterns and histogram of oriented gradients (HOG) algorithm is later used to extract the features. The performance of the system is tested in different lighting conditions [17].

Chamaporn Chianrabutra, Chamaiporn Sukjamsri, Theekapun Charoenpong and Wisaroot Tipprasert [4], performed four stages i.e., face, mouth, eyes and yawn detection [18]. An infrared camera was used for analysis and accuracies were obtained for each stage. Next, in Hongyi Li, Feng You, Haiwei Wang, Xialong Li, Yunbo Gong [19] the SVM classifier is trained and the state of the eyes is decided based on the results of the testing phase. Face features of the driver were obtained from live video using DCCNN that bypasses the process of artificial feature extraction. In Chao Zhang, Shui Yu, Xiaopei Wu and Xi Zheng [20], drowsiness is detected by the parallel detection of yawn, blink and blood volume pulse signals.

Federico Geude-Fernandez, Juan Ramos-Castro, Miguel A. Garcia-Gonzalez and Mireya Fernandez-Chimeno [21] found that respiratory rate variability had been analyzed. Based on this analysis, a novel method had been proposed to monitor the driver's drowsiness. 15 test cases have been conducted and an algorithm known as TEDD has been used for identifying the driver's fight against drowsiness [22–26].

In Alexey Kashevnik, Anton Shabaev, Nikolay Shilov and Vladimir Parfenov [27], readings of the features of the driver's face are taken from the front camera of the smartphone and these readings are classified into both online and offline modes. A reference model for recognition of facial features has been proposed. In their article, Bijay Guragain, Chunwu Wang, Nicholas Wilson and Shubha Majumder [28], analyzed feature extraction based on waveband power using PSD estimation. They showed that these features provide useful information about the change in power of the frequency bands of EEG. Two bands, alpha and beta, were used where the bands were continuously monitored and thus drowsiness is identified [29–31].

Aqsa Mehreen, Muhammad Haseeb, Muhammad Majid, Muhammad Obaid Ullah and Syed Muhammad Anwar [32] employed features such as signals and analyzing blinks to increase the accuracy of the result of the model. An electroencephalogram and an accelerometer, as well as gyroscope signals, were used to detect drivers' drowsiness. Finally in this review, Aleksey Minbaleev, Artem Starkov, Kseniia Nikolskaia and Vladislav Bessonov [33] used deep learning; this system detects drowsiness by analyzing environment variables. A convolutional neural network (CNN) model is used for the image classification of opened and closed eyes. This classification helps in determining the loss of driver's concentration.

17.3 EXISTING SYSTEMS

Existing systems have used methods such as the electroencephalogram (EEG), electrocardiogram (ECG), respiratory signal analysis, heart rate variability (HRV), mobile video processing, and PERCLOS Estimation. Some of these systems contain devices which have to be worn by the person, which can create problems when the driver is in the car. Sometimes an error might occur due to miswiring between the devices, which this might make the processor unable to perform properly, meaning that it might fail to alert the driver [34–36]. These kinds of system might be unsuitable for the detection of drowsiness. One of these techniques, the electroencephalogram (EEG), is a test which monitors brain activity by considering the electrical signal of the brain. In this instance, electrodes are placed on the scalp of a person. The ionic current present in neurons of the brain results in a voltage fluctuation, which is measured by the EEG [37–40].

17.4 SYSTEM ARCHITECTURE

An attempt is made to develop a system which monitors the driver, mainly focusing on the movement of the eyes. Not only an alarming sound but also some other features, such communication with the server side, the detection of alcohol content and the perception of road traffic incidents can also be included. The aim of this research is to design and develop a system which will only alert the driver and it is the responsibility of the driver to return to his normal driving condition and apply break if necessary. This research has focused on developing a system based on data science and IoT as domains and using algorithms, namely the Haar Cascade algorithm and the EAR algorithm [41–49].

The proposed system consists of the following modules:

1. Arduino
2. LCD Screen
3. Buzzer
4. Vibration Sensor
5. LED
6. Camera
7. System Running the Algorithm

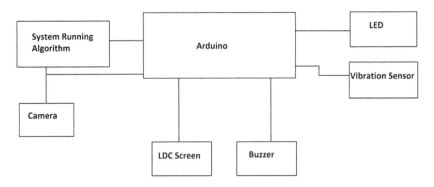

FIGURE 17.1 System architecture.

The system can be understood by considering it to be divided into two separate parts: hardware and software. The software part of the system consists of an algorithm which runs and monitors the driver constantly. This algorithm detects the face and eye coordinates or landmarks and triggers a return value when the eyes of the driver close for a certain number of seconds. The hardware part consists of multiple modules connected to an Arduino Uno chip, which is, in turn, linked to the system that runs the algorithm. The camera unit is connected to both the software system and the Arduino chipset.

17.5 HARDWARE REQUIREMENTS

17.5.1 LCD SCREEN

This is a type of flat panel display that primarily operates using liquid crystals. The liquid crystal display (LCD) screen is available in different formats, and the proposed system uses a 16X2 LCD screen where the screen can print 16 characters for one line and two such lines are present. A 16 X 2 LCD screen contains 16 pins, each of which are used for different purposes. The main advantage of an LCD screen over an LED one is the relatively low cost of the former. In addition, LCD has the ability to display more characters than LED. Two connected glasses make up the LCD panel, and it also contains a backlight. The liquid crystal molecules that make up the glasses are so constructed that will be affected by an electric current. They have a 90-degree distortion (e.g., light enters from one side, leaving a polarized glass at 90 degrees on the other side). The light originating from one side of the screen won't pass through a polarizing glass if there is no electricity transmitted into the molecule; otherwise, it will be rotated 90 degrees within the molecule and then pass through the second polarizing glass.

The LCD module is used to display the status of the driver, identifying whether the driver is sleeping or awake. This module is connected to the Arduino chipset via the pins mentioned (Table 17.1) and shown in the below sample figure of an LCD module (Figure 17.2).

Below table describes are details of the pins of the LCD module and their usage:

TABLE 17.1
LCD Pins

Pin	Input/Output	Description
vss	Nil	Ground (gnd)
vcc	Nil	+5 V power supply
vee	Nil	Power supply for controlling contrast
rs	Input	rs = 0 for command and rs = 1 for data register
rw	Input	rw = 1 for read and rw = 0 for write
e	Input/Output	Enable
db0…db7	Input/Output	8-bit data bus

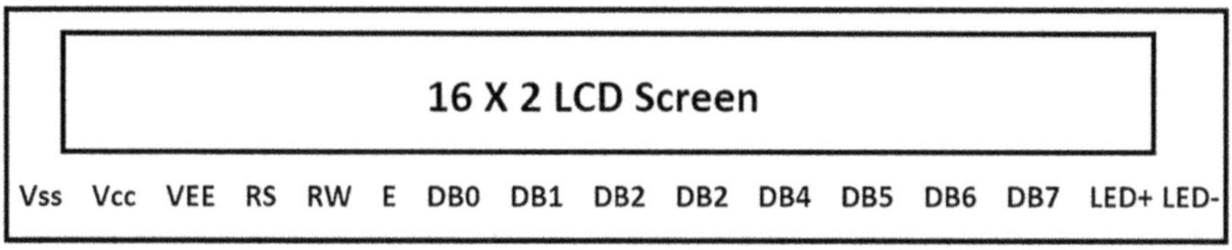

16 X 2 LCD Screen

Vss Vcc VEE RS RW E DB0 DB1 DB2 DB2 DB4 DB5 DB6 DB7 LED+ LED-

FIGURE 17.2   16 × 2 LCD screen.

17.5.2   LED

An electrical component that produces light when an electric current gets passed through, this it as a result of electrons reattaching with holes. Additionally, it is a light source built on semiconductors. It is a specific form of diode with properties similar to those of a p-n junction diode. This implies that an LED allows current to flow in one direction – forward – while blocking it in the opposite direction. Furthermore, we construct light-emitting diodes by employing a thin layer of semiconductor material that has been severely doped.

The LED module contains two pins, one negative and other one positive. The positive pin is connected to pin 9 and the negative pin to the ground pin of Arduino.

For the purposes of experimental setup, a small LED is used but for the actual implementation of the system in a vehicle, a larger light could be used, which turns on and flashes light on the driver's face when the driver closes their eyes for some seconds or the driver falls asleep.

17.5.3   Vibration Sensor

The name piezoelectric sensor is also used to refer to the vibration sensor. These flexible sensors are used to measure a variety of operations. This sensor converts changes in acceleration, pressure, temperature, force, or strain into an electrical charge by using the piezoelectric effects. By instantly determining capacitance and quality, this sensor is also utilized to determine airborne smells. There are three main categories of vibration sensors: velocity, acceleration and displacement. Displacement sensors track changes in the gap between the spinning component and the fixed housing of a machine (frame). Displacement sensors work by measuring displacement by inserting a probe into a hole which has been drilled down and tapped in the machine's frame, directly on top of a spinning shaft. On the other hand, velocity and acceleration sensors gauge the motion or acceleration of the object to which they are fastened, which is frequently a part of the machine frame that is visible from the outside. The vibration sensor contains three pins, namely D0, Vcc and Ground (GND). The Arduino chip is connected to vibration sensor via the following pin configuration:

D0 is a I/O signal pin to signal pin 13 of Arduino.
Vcc of sensor to 5 V pin of Arduino, Vcc is also known as the 5 V pin.
GND or ground pins of both Arduino and Vibration sensor are connected to each other.

17.5.4 Buzzer

A buzzer or beeper is a sound-producing signaling tool. It could be electromechanical, piezoelectric, or mechanical in nature. The mount holes on this piezo buzzer are 30mm apart and have a diameter of 23 mm. It comes with a 100 mm lead and is rated for between 3 and 20 volts. At 30 cm, it generates a 3k Hz tone at an 85 dB level. The basic working premise is that any time an electric potential is applied across a material which is piezoelectric, pressure variation is generated. The buzzer contains crystals placed between conductors: one conductor on top and the other on the bottom. Due to an inherent property, these crystals pull the opposing conductor when a potential difference is applied across them. Continual pulling and pushing causes a sharp soundwave to be produced. The buzzer contains two wires, namely a red one (which stands for positive) and a blue one (which represents the ground).

The buzzer is connected to Arduino chipset via the following configuration: Positive is connected to 8 pin and ground is connected to the ground pin of Arduino.

17.5.5 Arduino Uno

Arduino is a tool for controlling electronic items, including input devices such as temperature, light, touch, IR and humidity sensors, and output devices such as DC and stepper motors, LCD displays and LED lights etc. Arduino can be used to read input signals as well as control output signals. There are different types of Arduino boards, and Arduino Uno is the most popular. All Arduino boards share one common feature, which is the microcontroller at mega 328. One of the reasons why Arduino has become popular is that the use of microcontroller was made easier by its creators. While in general the documentation of microcontrollers contains a lot of technical jargon, Arduino is easier to understand, and anyone can try using it. The board is designed to be easy to use as, for example, we don't need any specialized cable such as pod or a blaster cable to connect Arduino to our computer. All we need is a simple USB cable, which acts as power supply to Arduino. This is generally not preferred in situations where we need large streams of input, such as big computations or video recordings.

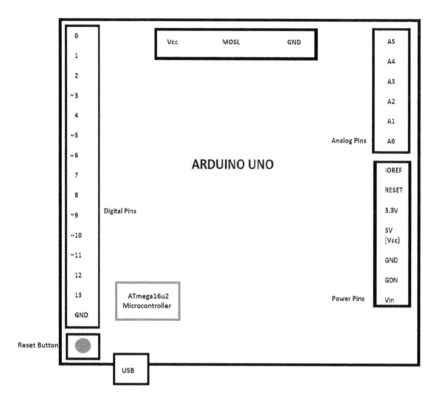

FIGURE 17.3 Arduino Uno.

This microcontroller contains the following types of pins to which multiple hardware devices are connected:

Digital Pins – 1 to 13 for I/O
Analog Pins – A0, A1, A2, A3, A4, A5
Power Pins – IOREF, RESET, 3.3 V, 5 V (V_{cc}), 2 GND or ground pins, Vin.
ICSP pins – V_{cc}, GND or ground, MOSI

17.6 SOFTWARE APPLICATIONS AND PROGRAMMING

Below are the software requirements for the proposed system:

17.6.1 IDE FOR ARDUINO

IDE stands for integrated development environment and this is used to write code and import our code into Arduino boards. This IDE can be installed and used in different operating systems such as Windows, Mac as well as Linux. Languages C and C++ programming languages are supported in this IDE. In the Arduino IDE, writing a program or piece of code is frequently referred to as "sketching." The Genuino unit, as well as the Arduino board, must be connected with the

IDE in order to upload the sketch that was developed in the IDE. The extension of the sketch file is ".ino." When you press the Upload button, a compiling and executing of our on-screen code takes place. Our new program replaces the old one in the connected board. We have to make sure that we already chose the board as well as the ports before submitting the drawing. We need a USB connectivity to connect our Arduino board to our computer. Once the previously mentioned processes have been finished, choose Upload option in the toolbar menu. More recent Arduino Uno chips have a feature that automatically resets them before an upload. On the earlier boards, there is a Reset button that needs to be pressed. As soon as the uploading is finished, the Tx (transmission) as well as Rx (receiving) LEDs will start to blink. If the uploading fails, the message will show up in the error window. We may upload our application using the bootloader without any additional hardware. This brief piece of software that is loaded into the board's microcontroller is referred to as a bootloader. The LED will sparkle as a result of PIN 13.

17.6.2 PYTHON PROGRAMMING LANGUAGE

Python, which was created by Guido van Rossum, is an interpreted, high-level and object-oriented programming language [16]. Python has replaced Java as the most popular entry-level language and allows learners to focus on completely understanding programming concepts instead of minute details because of its simplicity and easily accessible syntax. Python is renowned for its dynamic typing, built-in large data structures, and dynamic binding. To join together already existing components, Python is widely used as a scripting language. Python is also used for system programming, software development, math, and server-side web development. Python's simple syntax and emphasis on readability make it easier to learn, thereby minimizing the cost of program maintenance. The ability to create modular programs and reuse code is further simplified by Python's support for modules and packages. As an open forum language, Python is always being improved by multiple independent programmers. Python's features and advantages include compatibility with a wide range of operating systems. It has a straightforward structure similar to that of English, allowing programmers to use less lines and comparing these with the lines they would use with other languages. It allows the use of an interpreter system that enables instant code execution, speeding up prototyping able to be handled in a functional, procedural, or object-oriented manner.

17.6.3 PYSERIAL LIBRARY

The proposed system uses a Python library known as PySerial. PySerial makes serial communication easier. When the PySerial package is loaded, a computer running Python can interface with external hardware. PySerial is a useful tool for problem solvers since it facilitates data exchange between external devices like voltmeters, oscilloscopes, strain gauges, flow meters, actuators, lights etc. and computers. PySerial offers a user interface for the serial communication technology. One of the earliest computer communication protocols is serial communication. The Universal

Serial Bus (USB) specification, which is used by computers and other pieces of hardware such as the mouse, keyboards, and webcams, is older than the serial communication protocol. The basic serial communication interface is expanded and improved by USB.

17.6.4   OPENCV LIBRARY

A machine learning and computer vision software library is available for free under the name OpenCV. OpenCV's official name is Open-Source Computer Vision. It was introduced to give a standardized framework for applications that are made to work on computer vision and also to quickly integrate consumer goods with machine perception. The code is easily used and modifiable by businesses thanks to OpenCV, a BSD-licensed tool. This library, which is based on enhanced C++/C, incorporates Python and Java through an interface. Optimized algorithms above 2500 in number, containing a wide range of conventional and modern machine learning and computer vision techniques, are available in the library. Complex tasks such as the recognition of faces and objects, the classification of human actions from videos, camera movement tracking, object movement tracking, extracting models from 3D objects, and many others can be made simple by using OpenCV. In order to write C/C++ programs that require a lot of processing and to provide wrappers that can be utilized as modules, we use C/C++ to make Python better. Python is simpler to program than C/C++, so the code is quicker because the original C/C++ program was used to create it (C++ code which is actually executing in the background). Open CV's original C++ implementation contains a wrapper for Python called Open CV-Python.

17.6.5   HAAR CASCADE ALGORITHM

One of the few face-identification-capable object detection techniques is the Haar-Cascade classifier. This is used to detect facial landmarks, which are the coordinates of the parts present on the face. It is the act of locating prominent facial features, such as the eyes, nose, eyebrows, jawline, and mouth, on a face. Instead of relying on the individual pixel values of the image, the algorithm is based on the number of pixels inside the rectangle feature. The Haar-cascade technique provides rapid calculation. For the purpose of object detection, this method uses four steps: the Haar feature; cascade classified; a Boost learning; and an integral image. The Paul Viola and Michael Jones-proposed concept of features serves as the foundation for this approach. In the Haar feature selection stage, facial features such as nose, eyes, eyebrows, etc. are selected as edge features, line features and four rectangle features. These features are then divided into black and white parts, where black parts represent darker features of our face and white parts represent the brighter ones. In the second stage, i.e., creating integral images, multiple images are developed which contain black and white marks that represent the location of the features, the exact coordinates of the facial features are not yet identified at this stage. In AdaBoost learning, with the help of a decision term, the correctly and wrongly classified parts of the image are split and this takes place in multiple iterations. Finally, the strong classifier will come out as the result of this stage. In the final cascading classifier stage, all the previous stages will come together and the properly trained classifier is ready to go. The Haar Cascade classifier is pre-trained with both positive images (images that we want as output) as well as negative images. The Haar Cascade algorithm comes under OpenCV python library.

17.6.6 EAR – Eye Aspect Ratio Algorithm

Once the driver's face is detected, drowsiness is calculated according to the rate of eye blinking, i.e., based on the length between the upper and lower eye lids [50]. This method uses scalar value to detect the eye blink. For instance, if the driver's eyes are blinking more frequently and they are closing their eyes for longer than usual (measured in seconds), then this is a sign of drowsiness. In order to determine the frequency of eye blinking, it is therefore required to precisely detect the form of the eyes [45]. With the help of landmarks present in the facial image, the eye-opening state is estimated using the eye aspect ratio. The eye landmarks are identified for each video frame in between the computed height and the width of the eye. After finding the facial landmarks of the driver, the Eye Aspect Ratio algorithm detects the eye blink by considering the coordinates of the eyes. Drowsiness depends upon the time in which the eyes are closed. The EAR value describes whether or not the eyes are closed. If the value of EAR is zero, then it means that the eye is closed. Since complete eye closure signifies more than drowsiness, a threshold value is introduced. If EAR is less than this threshold value, then drowsiness will be detected.

17.6.7 NumPy Library

This is a Python library used for working with arrays. This library also contains functions to work with linear algebra and matrices as well. NumPy provides an array object which is much faster to work with large data as compared to Python lists. NumPy arrays are stored at one continuous place in memory unlike lists; hence processes can access and manipulate them very efficiently. This library is also optimized to work with latest CPU architectures. NumPy is generally written in Python; however, the majority of the parts that require fast computation are written in C++ or C. It is an open source library.

17.7 SYSTEM IMPLEMENTATION

The proposed system contains Arduino integrated into the vehicle's hardware. If the driver shows signs of being sleepy, a buzzer will sound an alarm and a camera will keep watch in front of the car. Alcohol is detected by the gas sensor, and accidents are discovered by the shaking sensor. The sensors and camera are connected to the Arduino Chip, and the IoT module sends a notification message so that the server is constantly updated on the condition of the driver. The Haar Cascade Algorithm is used to recognize the driver's face in order for the system to function. For object detection, the Haar Cascade technique is employed, and OpenCV is used to train the classifier. This program detects faces and eyes; if the eyes are closed, it is assumed

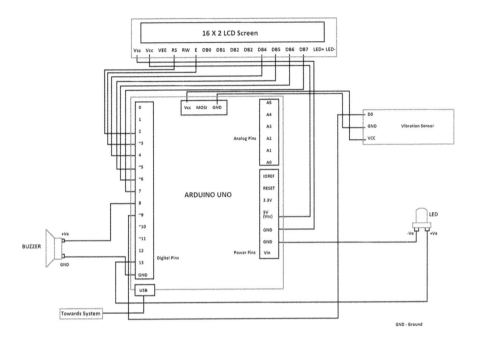

FIGURE 17.4   Experimental setup.

that the driver is sleepy and drowsy. The count begins when the driver's closed eye is discovered. A buzzer linked to the Arduino's USB ports emits a buzzing sound to alert the driver if the count exceeds the limit. If the driver does not awaken from sleep following the buzzer, the driver's image is taken and sent, from which the image processing is carried out. Normal images are converted into digital ones in a method known as Image Processing. In order to find out whether or not the driver is in a state of drowsiness, useful information is obtained by applying some operations on the digital images. Drowsiness is detected by the captured driver's image. The image, as well as the location of the driver, are sent by the Wi-Fi module. The vibration sensor measures the force that is being imparted on the vehicle in the case of accident. The motor of the car, which is running continuously, will be stopped, if the drowsiness or alcohol is sensed or in the event of an accident.

17.8   RESULT AND DISCUSSION

In this work, the driver's drowsiness is detected using the Eye Aspect Ratio Algorithm, which is implemented at the backend. If the eye aspect ratio value drops, then the system alerts the drivers so that they can get to their normal driving state. Other features, such as location, the detection that alcohol has been consumed, and the detection of accidents by considering the amount of force that has impacted on the vehicle, are implemented to make sure that every measure is taken for the safety of the driver.

17.9 CONCLUSION AND FUTURE SCOPE

There is a need for an alert to reduce the chances of getting into an accident. We proposed a system that will help drivers to return to their state of awakening. This system was developed, taking data science and IoT as domains. The methodology of this study is divided into two main phases: facial landmark detection and drowsiness detection. From facial landmark detection, we found the facial landmarks i.e., the coordinates of the face of the driver and drowsiness is detected based upon the value of the EAR. Furthermore, we included a vibration sensor which can detect whether or not an accident has occurred. This system is expected to support the drivers to come to their normal state of driving.

REFERENCES

1. Majumder, S., Guragain, B., Wang, C., & Wilson, N. (2019). On-board Drowsiness Detection using EEG: Current Status and Future Prospects. In *2019 IEEE International Conference on Electro Information Technology (EIT)*. doi:10.1109/eit.2019.8833866.
2. Nikolskaia, K., Bessonov, V., Starkov, A., & Minbaleev, A. (2019). Prototype of Driver Fatigue Detection System Using Convolutional Neural Network. In *2019 International Conference "Quality Management, Transport and Information Security, Information Technologies" (IT & QM & IS)*. doi:10.1109/itqmis.2019.8928341.
3. Mehreen, A., Anwar, S.M., Haseeb, M., Majid, M., & Ullah, M.O. (2019). A hybrid scheme for drowsiness detection using wearable sensors. *IEEE Sensors Journal*, 1–1. doi:10.1109/jsen.2019.2904222.
4. Dhanalakshmi, R., Anand, J., Sivaraman, A. K., & Rani, S. (2022). IoT-based water quality monitoring system using cloud for agriculture use. In *Cloud and fog computing platforms for internet of things* (pp. 183–196). Chapman and Hall/CRC.
5. Hong, Tianyi, & Qin, Huabiao. (2007). Drivers' Drowsiness Detection in Embedded System. In *2007 IEEE International Conference on Vehicular Electronics and Safety*. doi:10.1109/icves.2007.4456381.
6. Ritu, P., & Bhambri, P. (2023, February 17). Software effort estimation with machine learning – A Systematic literature review. In Susheela Hooda, Vandana Mohindru Sood, Yashwant Singh, Sandeep Dalal, Manu Sood (Eds.), *Agile Software Development: Trends, Challenges and Applications* (pp. 291–308). John Wiley & Sons, Inc.
7. Sangwan, Y. S., Lal, S., Bhambri, P., Kumar, A., & Dhanoa, I. S. (2021). Advancements in social data security and encryption: A review. *NVEO-Natural Volatiles & Essential Oils Journal|NVEO*, 8(4), 15353–15362.
8. Katyal, Y., Alur, S., & Dwivedi, S. (2014). Safe Driving by Detecting Lane Discipline and Driver Drowsiness. In *2014 IEEE International Conference on Advanced Communications, Control and Computing Technologies*. doi:10.1109/icaccct.2014.7019248.
9. Anilkumar, C. V., Ahmed, M., Sahana, R., Thejashwini, R., & Anisha, P. S. (2016). Design of Drowsiness, Heart Beat Detection System and Alertness Indicator for Driver Safety. In *2016 IEEE International Conference on Recent Trends in Electronics, Information & Communication Technology (RTEICT)*. doi:10.1109/rteict.2016.7807966.
10. Bhambri, P., Singh, M., Jain, A., Dhanoa, I. S., Sinha, V. K., & Lal, S. (2021). Classification of gene expression data with the aid of optimized feature selection. *Turkish Journal of Physiotherapy and Rehabilitation*, 32, 3.

11. Jafari Yazdi, M. Z., & Soryani, M. (2019). Driver Drowsiness Detection by Yawn Identification Based on Depth Information and Active Contour Model. In *2019 2nd International Conference on Intelligent Computing, Instrumentation and Control Technologies (ICICICT)*. doi:10.1109/icicict46008.2019.899.

12. Girish, I., Kumar, A., Kumar, A., & Anuradha, M. (2020). Driver Fatigue Detection. In *2020 IEEE 17th India Council International Conference (INDICON)*. doi:10.1109/indicon49873.2020.934.

13. Bhambri, P., Singh, S., Sangwan, S., Devi, J., & Jain, S. (2023). Plants recognition using leaf image pattern analysis. *Journal of Survey in Fisheries Sciences*, 10(2S), 3863–3871.

14. Babaeian, M., and Mozumdar, M. (2019). Driver Drowsiness Detection Algorithms Using Electrocardiogram Data Analysis. In *2019 IEEE 9th Annual Computing and Communication Workshop and Conference (CCWC)*. doi:10.1109/ccwc.2019.8666467.

15. Budak, U., Bajaj, V., Akbulut, Y., Atilla, O., and Sengur, A. (2019). An effective hybrid model for EEG-based drowsiness detection. *IEEE Sensors Journal, 1–1*. doi: 10.1109/jsen.2019.2917850.

16. Arya, V., Rani, S., & Choudhary, N. (2022). Enhanced Bio-Inspired Trust and Reputation Model for Wireless Sensor Networks. In *Proceedings of Second Doctoral Symposium on Computational Intelligence: DoSCI 2021* (pp. 569–579). Springer Singapore.

17. Bhambri, P., Singh, M., Dhanoa, I. S., & Kumar, M. (2022). Deployment of ROBOT for HVAC duct and disaster management. *Oriental Journal of Computer Science and Technology*, 15, 1–8.

18. Rachna, Bhambri, P., & Chhabra, Y. (2022). Deployment of distributed clustering approach in WSNs and IoTs. In Pankaj Bhambri, Sita Rani, Gaurav Gupta, Alex Khang (Eds.), *Cloud and Fog Computing Platforms for Internet of Things* (pp. 85–98). Chapman and Hall/CRC.

19. Rajevenceltha, J., Gaidhane, V. H., & Anjana, V. (2019). A Novel Approach for Drowsiness Detection Using Local Binary Patterns and Histogram of Gradients. In *2019 International Conference on Electrical and Computing Technologies and Applications (ICECTA)*. doi:10.1109/icecta48151.2019.8959669.

20. Tanveer, M. A., Khan, M. J., Qureshi, M. J., Naseer, N., and Hong, K.-S. (2019). Enhanced drowsiness detection using deep learning: An fNIRS study. *IEEE Access, 1–1*. doi:10.1109/access.2019.2942838.

21. Tipprasert, W., Charoenpong, T., Chianrabutra, C., & Sukjamsri, C. (2019). A Method of Driver's Eyes Closure and Yawning Detection for Drowsiness Analysis by Infrared Camera. In *2019 First International Symposium on Instrumentation, Control, Artificial Intelligence, and Robotics (ICA-SYMP)*. doi:10.1109/ica-symp.2019.8646001.

22. Ritu, & Bhambri, P. (2022). A CAD System for Software Effort Estimation. In *Paper presented at the International Conference on Technological Advancements in Computational Sciences*, 140–146. IEEE. doi:10.1109/ICTACS56270.2022.9988123.

23. Singh, M., Bhambri, P., Lal, S., Singh, Y., Kaur, M., & Singh, J. (2021). Design of the effective technique to improve memory and time constraints for sequence alignment. *International Journal of Applied Engineering Research (Netherlands)*, 6(02), 127–142.

24. Babu, G. C. N., Gupta, S., Bhambri, P., Leo, L. M., Rao, B. H., & Kumar, S. (2021). A semantic health observation system development based on the IoT sensors. *Turkish Journal of Physiotherapy and Rehabilitation*, 32(3), 1721–1729.

25. Bhambri, P., Singh, M., Jain, A., Dhanoa, I. S., Sinha, V. K., & Lal, S. (2021). Classification of the GENE expression data with the aid of optimized feature selection. *Turkish Journal of Physiotherapy and Rehabilitation*, 32(3), 1158–1167.

26. Singh, M., Bhambri, P., Dhanoa, I. S., Jain, A., & Kaur, K. (2021). Data mining model for predicting diabetes. *Annals of the Romanian Society for Cell Biology*, 25(4), 6702–6712.

27. You, F., Li, X., Gong, Y., Wang, H., & Li, H. (2019). A real-time driving drowsiness detection algorithm with individual differences consideration. *IEEE Access*, 1–1. doi:10.1109/access.2019.2958667.

28. Zhang, C., Wu, X., Zheng, X., & Yu, S. (2019). Driver drowsiness detection using multi-channel second order blind identifications. *IEEE Access*, 1–1. doi:10.1109/access.2019.2891971.

29. Rachna, Chhabra, Y., & Bhambri, P. (2021). Various approaches and algorithms for monitoring energy efficiency of wireless sensor networks. In *Lecture Notes in Civil Engineering* (Vol. 113, pp. 761–770). Springer, Singapore.

30. Bakshi, P., Bhambri, P., & Thapar, V. (2021). A review paper on wireless sensor network techniques in Internet of Things (IoT). *Wesleyan Journal of Research*, 14(7), 147–160.

31. Rana, R., Chhabra, Y., & Bhambri, P. (2021). Design and development of distributed clustering approach in wireless sensor network. *Webology*, 18(1), 696–712.

32. Guede-Fernandez, F., Fernandez-Chimeno, M., Ramos-Castro, J., & Garcia-Gonzalez, M. A. (2019). Driver drowsiness detection based on respiratory signal analysis. *IEEE Access*, 1–1. doi:10.1109/access.2019.2924481.

33. Lashkov, I., Kashevnik, A., Shilov, N., Parfenov, V., & Shabaev, A. (2019).Driver Dangerous State Detection Based on Open CV & Dlib Libraries Using Mobile Video Processing. In *2019 IEEE International Conference on Computational Science and Engineering (CSE) and IEEE International Conference on Embedded and Ubiquitous Computing (EUC)*. doi:10.1109/cse/euc.2019.00024.

34. Rana, R., Chhabra, Y., & Bhambri, P. (2021). Comparison and evaluation of various QoS parameters in WSNs with the implementation of enhanced low energy adaptive efficient distributed clustering approach. *Webology*, 18(1), 677–695.

35. Singh, Y. S., Lal, S., Bhambri, P., Kumar, A., & Dhanoa, I. S. (2021). Advancements in social data security and encryption: A review. *Natural Volatiles & Essential Oils*, 8(4), 15353–15362.

36. Bhambri, P. (2021). Electronic evidence. In Kamal Gulati, Narinder Kumar Bhasin (Eds.), *Textbook of Cyber Heal* (pp. 86–120). AGAR Saliha Publication. ISBN: 978-81-948141-7-7.

37. Bakshi, P., Bhambri, P., & Thapar, V. (2021). A Review Paper on Wireless Sensor Network Techniques in Internet of Things (IoT). In *Proceedings of the International Conference on Contemporary Issues in Engineering & Technology*.

38. Bhambri, P. (2020). Green compliance. In S. Agarwal (Ed.), *Introduction to Green Computing* (pp. 95–125). AGAR Saliha Publication. ISBN: 978-81-948141-5-3.

39. Bhambri, P., Kaur, H., Gupta, A., & Singh, J. (2020). Human activity recognition system. *Oriental Journal of Computer Science and Technology*, 13(2–3), 91–96.

40. Singh, G., Singh, M., & Bhambri, P. (2020). Artificial Intelligence Based Flying Car. In *Proceedings of the International Congress on Sustainable Development through Engineering Innovations*, pp. 216–227. ISBN 978-93-89947-14-4.

41. Rigane, O., Abbes, K., Abdelmoula, C., & Masmoudi, M. (2017). A Fuzzy Based Method for Driver Drowsiness Detection. In *2017 IEEE/ACS 14th International Conference on Computer Systems and Applications (AICCSA)*. doi:10.1109/aiccsa.2017.131

42. Wathiq, O., & Ambudkar, B. D. (2017). Optimized Driver Safety Through Driver Fatigue Detection Methods. In *2017 International Conference on Trends in Electronics and Informatics (ICEI)*. doi:10.1109/icoei.2017.8300787.

43. Artanto, D., Sulistyanto, M. P., Pranowo, I. D., & Pramesta, E. E. (2017). Drowsiness Detection System Based on Eye-Closure Using a Low-Cost EMG and ESP8266. In *2017 2nd International Conferences on Information Technology, Information Systems and Electrical Engineering (ICITISEE)*. doi:10.1109/icitisee.2017.8285502.

44. Gupta, I., Garg, N., Aggarwal, A., Nepalia, N., & Verma, B. (2018). Real-Time Driver's Drowsiness Monitoring Based on Dynamically Varying Threshold. In *2018 Eleventh International Conference on Contemporary Computing (IC3)*. doi:10.1109/ic3.2018.8530651.

45. Rani, S., Kataria, A., Kumar, S., & Tiwari, P. (2023). Federated learning for secure IoMT-applications in smart healthcare systems: A comprehensive review. *Knowledge-Based Systems*, 5(7), 110658.

46. Vasudevan, S. K., Kowshik, G., & Anudeep, J. (2019). Driver Feedback System with White Line Fever Detection. In *2019 International Conference on Vision Towards Emerging Trends in Communication and Networking (ViTECoN)*. doi:10.1109/vitecon.2019.8899665.

47. Oliveira, L., Cardoso, J. S., Lourenco, A., & Ahlstrom, C. (2018). Driver Drowsiness Detection: A Comparison Between Intrusive and Non-Intrusive Signal Acquisition Methods. In *2018 7th European Workshop on Visual Information Processing (EUVIP)*. doi:10.1109/euvip.2018.8611704.

48. Pratama, B. G., Ardiyanto, I., & Adji, T. B. (2017). A Review on Driver Drowsiness Based on Image, Bio-Signal, and Driver Behavior. In *2017 3rd International Conference on Science and Technology-Computer (ICST)*. doi:10.1109/icstc.2017.8011855.

49. Sathya, R. & Reddy, T & Reddy, S & Raghavendra, K. (2020). An IoT based driver drowsiness detection system and deterrent system for safety and driving. *International Journal of Future Generation Communication and Networking*, 13(3), 413–421.

50. Rani, S., Bhambri, P., & Gupta, O. P. (2022). Green smart farming techniques and sustainable agriculture: Research roadmap towards organic farming for imperishable agricultural products. In *Handbook of Sustainable Development through Green Engineering and Technology* (pp. 49–67). CRC Press.

18 Force/Position Control of Constrained Reconfigurable Manipulators Using Hybrid Backstepping Neural Networks Based Control Approach

Manju Rani

Gurugram University, Gurugram, India

Naveen Kumar

National Institute of Technology, Kurukshetra, India

18.1 INTRODUCTION

Reconfigurable manipulators are made up of interchangeable modules when compared with conventional robots, which have a fixed mechanism structure (Gierlak & Szuster, 2017). These manipulators have important qualities such as portability, ease of maintenance, large workspaces, affordability, and customization (Holcomb & Morari, 1991). Due to its standard joints, connection modules, and potential applications in areas like space exploration, high-risk operations, smart manufacturing, battlefields, etc., the control of reconfigurable manipulators has drawn a lot of interest from the control community (Li et al., 2019). Most current research on reconfigurable manipulators is carried out by robotic systems that are not constrained by their environment (Zhao and Li 2014; Ahmad et al. 2013). The manipulator really interacts with the environment in a variety of applications. There are many forms of control available to these manipulators that are based on centralized control (Ren et al. 2017; Li et al. 2008). But complexity results from robustness (Zhu et al., 2019). Additionally, the decentralized control structure offers not only the flexibility needed for various configurations but also a shorter computation time, which is ideal for real-time applications of reconfigurable manipulators

DOI: 10.1201/9781003383505-18

(Zhu & Li, 2010a; Wang et al., 2015). The decentralized control method for robot manipulators has been the subject of several studies (Zhou et al. 2017; Dong et al. 2017a; Du and Zhu 2018; Dong et al. 2017c, 2018, 2017b). A unique control strategy for reconfigurable systems was chosen by taking into account external disturbances and unidentified Nodal Analysis Framework (NAF) (Zhou et al., 2017). A new decentralized control strategy was explored for joint trajectory tracking control of the reconfigurable robot in the face of time-varying limitations (Dong et al., 2017a). An integral stacked sliding surface successfully reduced the chattering impact of the intended controller. The issue of trajectory tracking was resolved via a decentralized control strategy using data-based modeling (Du and Zhu 2018).

The aforementioned methods rely heavily on robust adaptive control algorithms that are model-based and try to convey an exact understanding of uncertain systems (Bali et al., 2023). Practically speaking, the biggest difficulty with the current methods is how to compute the regression matrix and collect precise data for the dynamic model of uncertain systems (Ritu and Bhambri, 2023). It becomes more challenging to govern the system using traditional model-dependent control techniques when the dynamics are complex (Sangwan et al., 2021). Furthermore, the limits on external disturbances and uncertainties should be established, notably in the case of the SMC's control regulations (Bhambri et al., 2021; Heck et al., 2016). Notably, the systems' performance may suffer due to the control laws' heavy dependence on the dynamic model, and all of these methods become ineffective when intelligent approaches have proven to be a more effective method for approximating the unknown smooth nonlinear functions, overcoming the limitations of model-dependent controllers (Liu et al., 2014; Liu et al., 2019; Li et al., 2016b; Li et al., 2016a). The adjustable features of neural network-based control technologies, such as nonlinear mapping, parallel distributed structure, and self-learning capability, which are successfully used to manage the more complex systems, are their main advantage on a broad scale (Bhambri, et al., 2023; Slotine & Li, 1991; Park & Sandberg, 1991). The combination of robust adaptive, sliding mode control, centralized and decentralized control schemes with neural network technology has also resulted in a number of outstanding control schemes that have been reported in the literature (Liu et al., 2014; Zhang et al., 2015; Sofi et al., 2016; Zhu and Li, 2010a; Zhu and Li, 2009; Ghajar et al. 2018; Cao et al., 2018; Naderi and Azab 2021; Dajer et al. 2022).

A back-propagation neural network was used in this study to train the more thorough and explicit data-based model. Decentralized neural network control rules for the reconfigurable manipulators were proposed by utilizing the Lyapunov stability analysis and backstepping techniques. Neural networks were used in this research as the most accurate approximation of the unknown dynamics. After that, a fuzzy logic-based controller was used to approximate the unknown dynamics of the reconfigurable manipulator by expressing the dynamics into a group of comparable structures. For limited manipulators, a reliable control strategy based on the neural network was developed (Ghajar et al., 2018). A new force/position control strategy was described by fusing terminal sliding mode with neural network technology, where the boundedness of force tracking and finite time convergence of position tracking were guaranteed by an adaptive control law (Cao et al., 2018).

This chapter suggests a high-precision guaranteed neural network-based hybrid force/position controller for the force and position control problem of constrained reconfigurable manipulators, even though the aforementioned significant control methods have been reported with significant control performance, both theoretically and practically (Bhambri et al., 2022). In light of this idea, the purpose of this effort is to offer a high-accuracy guaranteed NN-based hybrid backstepping method that combines the compensation of model-dependent and model-independent control strategies (Rachna et al., 2022). To the best of our knowledge, there hasn't been any research that bridges the gap between model-free and model-based control techniques for limited reconfigurable manipulators documented in the literature (Kumar et al., 2022).

In this research, we explore the hybrid force/position control strategy for reconfigurable manipulators in the face of environmental restrictions, which is motivated by the aforementioned talks. The following are the main contributions:

(i) By combining a model-free method with the partial system dynamics information that is already available, this work suggests a new control scheme for limited reconfigurable manipulators. The unknown dynamic component of the system is estimated via a radial basis function neural network (Rani et al., 2023).

(ii) An adaptive compensator controller added to the section of the controller mitigates the impacts of the neural network's reconstruction mistake as well as the effects of friction terms and external disturbances (Ritu and Bhambri, 2022).

(iii) The stability of the closed-loop system is examined using the Lyapunov theorem and Barbalat's lemma, and it is demonstrated that the position and force tracking errors are finite and that the tracking errors of the joints in all directions converge to zero asymptotically (Singh et al., 2021).

18.2 DYNAMICAL MODEL DESCRIPTION

$$M(\Theta)\ddot{\Theta}+V(\Theta,\dot{\Theta})\dot{\Theta}+G(\Theta)+F(\dot{\Theta})+D_d = U + \tau \qquad (18.1)$$

$$\tau = F = J_\varphi^T(\Theta)\eta \qquad (18.2)$$

The n-dimensional constraint equation is taken as:

$$\varphi(\Theta) = 0 \qquad (18.3)$$

where $M(\Theta) \in R^{(p \times p)}$ denotes the inertia matrix, $V\left(\Theta, \dot{\Theta}\right) \in R^{(p \times p)}$ is the centripetal-coriolis matrix, $G(\Theta) \in R^{(p \times 1)}$ is the gravity effects, $F\left(\dot{\Theta}\right) \in R^{(p \times 1)}$ represents the friction effects and $\tau \in R^{(p \times 1)}$ stands for the torque input vector. $D_d \in R^{(p \times 1)}$ represent the bounded unknown disturbances. The term $F = J_{\varphi}^{T}\left(\Theta\right)\eta$ "contact force" refers to the force created when the manipulator's end-effector makes contact with an external constraint. The jacobian matrix is $J_{\varphi}^{T}\left(\Theta\right) \in R^{(p \times n)}$ and $\eta \in R^{(p \times 1)}$ is the generalized force multiplier. The system has only $p - n$ one degree of freedom left after applying n constraints to the manipulator moving freely, so $p - n$ linearly independent positions will be used to express the system with constrained motion so that the joint position coordinate vector is separated as follows:

$$\Theta = \begin{bmatrix} \Theta_1 \\ \Theta_2 \end{bmatrix}; \Theta_1 \in R^{(p-n)}, \Theta_2 \in R^n \tag{18.4}$$

We formulate the constraint equation as follows by applying the implicit function theorem:

$$\Theta_2 = \phi\left(\Theta_1\right) \tag{18.5}$$

Eq. (18.4) can be rewritten as follows in view of (18.5):

$$\Theta = \begin{bmatrix} \Theta_1 \\ \phi\left(\Theta_1\right) \end{bmatrix} \tag{18.6}$$

Using (18.6), the joint position vector is differentiable with respect to time and yields:

$$\dot{\Theta} = Z\left(\Theta_1\right)\dot{\Theta}_1 \tag{18.7}$$

Here $Z\left(\Theta_1\right) = \begin{bmatrix} I_{p-n} \\ \partial\phi\left(\Theta_1\right)/\partial\Theta_1 \end{bmatrix}$ is an invertible matrix.

Equation (18.7) may be introduced as by obtaining the position joint vector's second derivative.

$$\ddot{\Theta} = \dot{Z}\left(\Theta_1\right)\dot{\Theta}_1 + Z\left(\Theta_1\right)\ddot{\Theta}_1 \tag{18.8}$$

Also the following relation is satisfied:

$$Z^{T}\left(\Theta_1\right)J_{\phi}^{T} = 0 \tag{18.9}$$

The dynamic model (18.1) is introduced by using (18.7) and (18.8) as follows:

$$M(\Theta_1)Z(\Theta_1)\ddot{\Theta}_1 + M(\Theta_1)\dot{Z}(\Theta_1)\dot{\Theta}_1 + V(\Theta_1,\dot{\Theta}_1)\dot{\Theta}_1$$
$$+G(\Theta_1)+F(\dot{\Theta}_1)+D_d = U + \tau \qquad (18.10)$$

After simplification, the equation above becomes:

$$M_1(\Theta_1)\ddot{\Theta}_1 + V_1(\Theta_1,\dot{\Theta}_1)\dot{\Theta}_1 + G(\Theta_1)+F(\dot{\Theta}_1)+D_d = U + J_\phi^T(\Theta_1)\eta \quad (18.11)$$

Here

$$M(\Theta_1)Z(\Theta_1) = M_1(\Theta_1); \; M(\Theta_1)\dot{Z}(\Theta_1)+V(\Theta_1,\dot{\Theta}_1)Z(\Theta_1) = V_1(\Theta_1,\dot{\Theta}_1)$$

When we multiply (18.11) by $Z^T(\Theta_1)$ both its sides and in view of (18.9), we get:

$$\bar{M}(\Theta_1)\ddot{\Theta}_1 + \bar{V}(\Theta_1,\dot{\Theta}_1)\dot{\Theta}_1 + \bar{F}(\dot{\Theta}_1)+\bar{G}(\Theta_1)+\bar{D}_d = Z^T(\Theta_1)U \qquad (18.12)$$

Where

$$\bar{M}(\Theta_1) = Z^T(\Theta_1)M_1(\Theta_1); \; \bar{V}(\Theta_1,\dot{\Theta}_1) = Z^T(\Theta_1)V(\Theta_1,\dot{\Theta}_1); \bar{G}(\Theta_1) = Z^T(\Theta_1)G(\Theta_1);$$
$$\bar{F}(\Theta_1) = Z^T(\Theta_1)F(\Theta_1); \bar{D}_d(\Theta_1) = Z^T(\Theta_1)D_d(\Theta_1)$$

At the same time, we suppose that the constrained manipulator system will be subject to the following attributes and assumptions for further study.

Assumption 1

The kinematic constraint is supposed to be a rigid, frictionless surface, and it states that the end-effector must follow a predetermined desired position without losing contact with it.

Assumption 2

It is assumed that any singularities should be kept at a distance from the reconfigurable manipulator so that the Jacobian matrix can continue to exist as a full rank matrix.

Assumption 3

The desirable terms, such as the desired joint position, wanted velocity, and intended acceleration, are all bounded, ensuring the closed-loop system's asymptotic stability.

Assumption 4

The intended constraint force and its derivative are all known, according to this presumption.

Assumption 5

Friction terms and external disturbances are bounded.

Property 1

The Inertia matrix is a symmetric, positive definite matrix.

Property 2

The skew-symmetric connection is satisfied by the inertia and centripetal-coriolis matrices.

18.3 PROBLEM IDENTIFICATION

The purpose of the current study is to build a workable controller specifically with the partial dynamic information of the manipulator so that reconfigurable manipulator can track the desired trajectory while retaining the force trajectory on the contact surface. More specifically, the design control law's primary goal is to ensure that the system is stable even when there are uncertainties (structured and unstructured). In light of this, we present

$$\tilde{\Theta} = \Theta - \Theta_d \tag{18.13}$$

$$\overline{\Theta}_1 = \Theta_1 - \Theta_{1d} \tag{18.14}$$

$$\tilde{\eta} = \eta - \eta_d \tag{18.15}$$

may reach zero levels.

18.4 DESIGN OF CONTROLLER

The filtered tracking error and a few additional helpful notations are presented prior to the creation of the control law as follows:

$$r = \dot{\tilde{\Theta}}_1 + \lambda \tilde{\Theta}_1; \ \Theta_n = \dot{\Theta}_{d_1} - \lambda \tilde{\Theta}_1 \tag{18.16}$$

Here $\lambda \in R^{(p-n)}$ is a matrix that is positive and definite.

The following steps can be used to determine the derivative of the filtered tracking error:

$$\dot{r} = \ddot{\tilde{\Theta}}_1 + \lambda \dot{\tilde{\Theta}}_1 = \ddot{\Theta}_1 - \ddot{\Theta}_{1r} \tag{18.17}$$

Consequently, as a result of (18.16) and (18.17), dynamic Eq. (18.12) produces:

$$\begin{aligned} \bar{M}(\Theta_1)\dot{r} + \bar{V}(\Theta_1, \dot{\Theta}_1)r \\ = Z^T(\Theta_1)U - \bar{M}(\Theta_1)\ddot{\Theta}_n \\ - \bar{V}(\Theta_1, \dot{\Theta}_1)\dot{\Theta}_n - \bar{G}(\Theta_1) \\ - \bar{F}(\dot{\Theta}_1) - \bar{D}_d \end{aligned} \tag{18.18}$$

The previous sentence can be organized to take the form:

$$\bar{M}(\Theta_1)\dot{r} + \bar{V}(\Theta_1, \dot{\Theta}_1)r = Z^T(\Theta_1)U - \kappa(\bar{z}) - \bar{F}(\dot{\Theta}_1) - \bar{D}_d \tag{18.19}$$

Where

$$\kappa(\bar{z}) = \bar{M}(\Theta_1)\ddot{\Theta}_n + \bar{V}(\Theta_1, \dot{\Theta}_1)\dot{\Theta}_n + \bar{G}(\Theta_1) \tag{18.20}$$

Constrained reconfigurable manipulators often presume that the dynamic knowledge of the control system is either totally known or completely unknown in light of the work documented in the literature. High nonlinearity and coupling terms make it impossible to fully ascertain all of the dynamic information about the dynamic system. Because of this, and with the addressing issue in mind, we will separate the non-linear dynamic element into the known dynamic part and the unknown dynamic part, respectively.

$$\hat{\bar{M}}(\Theta_1)\ddot{\Theta}_n + \hat{\bar{V}}(\Theta_1, \dot{\Theta}_1)\dot{\Theta}_n + \hat{\bar{G}}(\Theta_1) = \hat{\kappa}(\bar{z}) \tag{18.21}$$

$$\tilde{\bar{M}}(\Theta_1)\ddot{\Theta}_n + \tilde{\bar{V}}(\Theta_1, \dot{\Theta}_1)\dot{\Theta}_n + \tilde{\bar{G}}(\Theta_1) = \tilde{\kappa}(\bar{z}) \tag{18.22}$$

The nonlinear dynamic component of is given as in light of (18.21) and (18.22), respectively.

$$\kappa(\bar{z}) = \hat{\kappa}(\bar{z}) + \tilde{\kappa}(\bar{z}) \tag{18.23}$$

For the purpose of compensating the manipulator's unknown dynamic component, we shall use the radial basis function neural network (RBFNN) (Wang et al., 2015).

18.4.1 Radial Basis Function Neural Network

The radial basis function neural network has been demonstrated to be a universal approximate of the nonlinear functions and is frequently used to approximate unknown continuous functions due to its simplicity and amazing properties like a simple framework, faster training process, and convergence. Its structure was taken from the function approximation theory and is comparable to a feed forward neural network. The source node makes up the input layer of an RBF neural network, and each neuron in the hidden layer uses a radial basis function of the Gaussian function type to calculate its output. The output layer then frames the weighted sum of the hidden neuron outputs in linear form, and finally the network is appropriately supplied with a response.

The following introduces the structure of the Gaussian-type RBF neural network function:

$$\Upsilon_j(y) = \exp\left(\frac{-\|y - t_i\|^2}{2a_j^2}\right) \quad j = 1, 2, \ldots l \tag{18.24}$$

Where l is the number of hidden layers. The neural net j has the centre vector $t_i = [y_{j1}, y_{j2}, \ldots, y_{jl}]$, a_j^2, the variance of the jth radial basis function and Υ_j denotes the Gaussian activation function for neural net j.

In light of the RBF neural network's aforementioned structure, we therefore estimate the unknown dynamical portion as

$$\kappa(\bar{z}) = \Omega^T \Psi(\bar{z}) + \varepsilon(\bar{z}) \tag{18.25}$$

where $\Psi(.) : R^{4m} \to R^T$ the smooth basis functions are and the neural network weight matrix is $\Omega \in R^{(T \times m)}$. The number of nodes is T and the neural reconstruction error is $\varepsilon(.) : R^{4m} \to R^m$.

For large T, $\|\varepsilon(\bar{z})\| \leq \varepsilon_T$.

By incorporating (18.23) and (18.25) into (18.19), one can get:

$$\bar{M}\dot{r} = Z^T U - \kappa(\bar{z}) - \Omega^T \Psi(\bar{z}) - \varepsilon(\bar{z}) - \bar{F}(\dot{\Theta}_1) - \bar{D}_d - \bar{V}(\Theta_1, \dot{\Theta}_1)r \tag{18.26}$$

For the construction of the force/position ideal controller, we choose the input in accordance with the restricted dynamical model (18.26).

$$U = \bar{U} + \bar{\bar{U}} \tag{18.27}$$

Where $\bar{\bar{U}}$ is described as

$$\bar{\bar{U}} = -J_\phi^T \left(\Theta\right)\left(\Lambda_d - v_{\bar{\Lambda}} \bar{\Lambda}\right) \tag{18.28}$$

In light of (18.27) and (18.28), (18.26) can be further rearranged to have the following form:

$$\bar{M}\left(\Theta_1\right)\dot{r} = Z^T\left(\Theta_1\right)\bar{U} - \kappa\left(\bar{z}\right) - \Omega^T \Psi\left(\bar{z}\right) - \varepsilon\left(\bar{z}\right) - \bar{F}\left(\dot{\Theta}_1\right) - \bar{D}_d - \bar{V}\left(\Theta_1, \dot{\Theta}_1\right)r \tag{18.29}$$

The following control law is then taken into consideration:

$$Z^T\left(\Theta_1\right)\bar{U} = \bar{\kappa}\left(\bar{z}\right) - \rho_r r + \bar{\Omega}^T \Psi\left(\bar{z}\right) + \tilde{\Theta} + \Delta \tag{18.30}$$

The above control law adds an additional adaptive compensator Δ to the controller component, which is built as follows, to counteract the impacts of the neural network's estimating inaccuracy as well as the effects of friction terms and external disturbances.

Using the Properties (1) and (2) as well as the error bound on neural network reconstruction error, we have

$$\left\| \bar{F}\left(\dot{\Theta}\right) + D_d + \varepsilon\left(\bar{z}\right) \right\| \leq a_1 + a_2 \left\| \dot{\Theta} \right\| + a_3 + \varepsilon_T \tag{18.31}$$

The above calculation leads to:

$$\varpi = \left[1 \; \left\|\dot{q}\right\| \; 1 \; 1\right]\left[a_1 \; a_2 \; a_3 \; \varepsilon_T\right]^T = N^T \Phi \tag{18.32}$$

Taking into account (18.31)–(18.32), the following introduces an adaptive stabilizing compensator:

$$\Delta = \frac{-\hat{\varpi}^2 r}{\hat{\varpi}\left\|r\right\| + \delta} \tag{18.33}$$

The error dynamics are finally produced by combining (18.30) and (18.33) and applying to (18.26) as

$$\bar{M}\dot{r} = -\rho_r r - \tilde{\Omega}^T \Psi\left(\bar{z}\right) - \varepsilon\left(\bar{z}\right) - \bar{F}\left(\dot{\Theta}_1\right) - \bar{D}_d - \bar{V}\left(\Theta_1, \dot{\Theta}_1\right)r + \Delta - \tilde{\Theta}$$

18.5   STABILITY ANALYSIS

$$\dot{\hat{\Omega}} = -\Gamma_\Omega \Psi\left(\bar{z}\right) r^T \tag{18.34}$$

$$\dot{\hat{\Phi}} = \Gamma_\Phi N \|r\| \tag{18.35}$$

where $\Gamma_\Omega \in R^{c_1 \times c_2}$ and $\Gamma_\Phi \in R^{l_1 \times l_2}$ are the positive definite matrices.

$$H = \frac{1}{2} r^T \bar{M} r + \frac{1}{2} tr\left(\tilde{\Omega}^T \Gamma_\Omega^{-1} \tilde{\Omega}\right) + \frac{1}{2} tr\left(\tilde{\Phi}^T \Gamma_\Phi^{-1} \tilde{\Phi}\right) + \frac{\delta}{\gamma}$$

The differentiation of Lyapunov function with respect to time gives

$$\dot{H} = r^T \bar{M} \dot{r} + \frac{1}{2} r^T \dot{\bar{M}} r + tr\left(\tilde{\Omega}^T \Gamma_\Omega^{-1} \dot{\tilde{\Omega}}\right) + tr\left(\tilde{W}_1^T \Gamma_{W_1}^{-1} \dot{\tilde{W}}_1\right) + tr\left(\tilde{\Phi}^T \Gamma_\Phi^{-1} \dot{\tilde{\Phi}}\right) + \frac{\dot{\delta}}{\gamma}$$

By making use of adaptive laws, Properties 1–2, and adaptive bound part, finally, we get:

$$\ddot{H} \leq -2 r^T \rho_r r \tag{18.36}$$

From Equation (18.36), we have $\ddot{H} \leq 0$. With the time t, $\dot{H}$ goes to zero by Barbalat's Lemma and this implies that and states of the system is bounded as well as all error terms also goes to zero as $t \to \infty$. Overall, the dynamic system is asymptotically stable.

18.6   SIMULATION STUDY

In a comparable manner, this section shows the effectiveness of the suggested control method and its benefit over the adaptive position/force hybrid neural network-based control scheme as provided in Liu et al. (2014). The dynamical model's specifics as well as configuration details can be found in Kumar and Rani (2021). The computer simulation findings are based on two distinct configurations of 2-DOF restricted reconfigurable manipulators, and their analytic charts are displayed in Figure 18.1.

Configuration I: According to configuration I, it is assumed that the reconfigurable manipulator has been given the task of polishing, and the environmental constraint equation is assumed to be as follows:

The simulation results are run with various configurations to look at the variations in position errors and velocity errors in order to demonstrate the likely advantages, precision, and robustness of the suggested control technique. We have used simulation results from two different control strategies, including the suggested hybrid

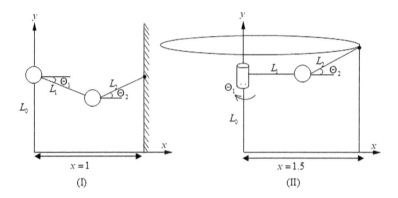

FIGURE 18.1 Analytic graphs (a) Configuration I (b) Configuration II.

control strategy and the current adaptive neural network control scheme described in Liu et al. (2014) for the comparison purposes.

First, Figures 18.2, 18.3 show the simulation results of the position tracking errors of the joint 1 and 2 for configuration I using both the suggested control approach and the method in Liu et al. (2014).

The simulation results for velocity tracking error for configuration I using the method in Liu et al. (2014) and the suggested control method are given in Figures 18.4 and 18.5, respectively. The following findings can be seen from Figures 18.2–18.5: Compared to the method in Liu et al. (2014), the suggested method successfully drives the manipulator to follow the required trajectory profile and the tracking errors fast converge to zero values. The approach in Liu et al., (2014) clearly has a

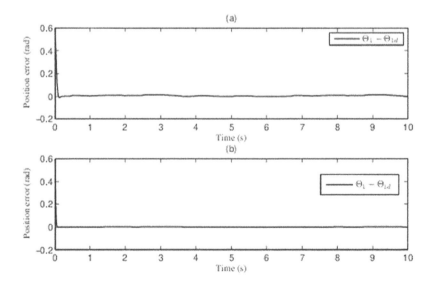

FIGURE 18.2 Errors in tracking Joint 1 position for Configuration I with (a) controller (Liu et al., 2014); (b) recommended controller.

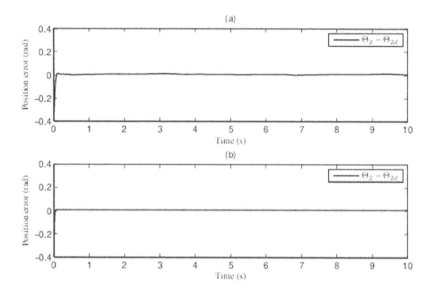

FIGURE 18.3   Errors in tracking Joint 2 position for Configuration I with (a) controller (Liu et al., 2014); (b). recommended controller.

longer convergent time for tracking velocity and location. The suggested control approach effectively makes use of the available dynamic partial information, has a faster convergence rate, and is less impacted by uncertainties.

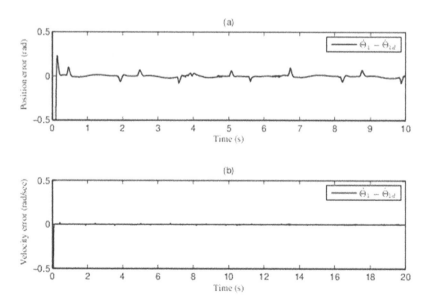

FIGURE 18.4   Errors in Joint 1 velocity tracking for Configuration I with (a) controller (Liu et al., 2014); (b) recommended controller.

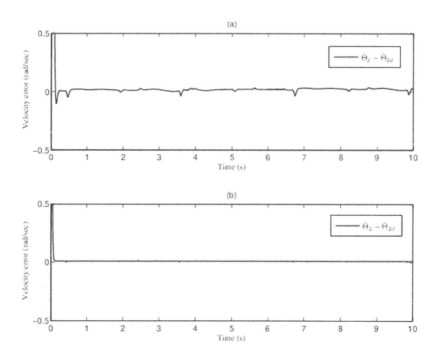

FIGURE 18.5 Errors in Joint 2 velocity tracking for Configuration I with (a) controller (Liu et al., 2014); (b) recommended controller.

Figures 18.6–18.7 show, respectively, the evolution of the constraint force tracking error for Configuration I using the method in Liu et al. (2014) and the suggested control method. It is evident that the suggested control strategy almost achieves the intended force tracking profile and keeps the real force almost entirely within the chosen one region. Following that, the effectiveness of the suggested control mechanism is evaluated by assuming that the manipulator will follow a circular path, namely Configuration II. Contrary to Configuration II, where the relationship between the constraint and the independent joint is constant, Configuration I's relationship between them is an explicit function. The attainable workspace of the manipulator serves as the basis for the constraint equation in this instance. The Joint 1's position and velocity tracking error profiles for Configuration II are shown in Figures 18.9 and 18.10, respectively, using the method in Liu et al. (2014) and the suggested control method.

From Figures 18.8–18.9, it is clear that the suggested technique has a faster rate of convergence and a shorter convergence time for tracking errors than the method in Liu et al. (2014) demonstrating its advantage in terms of high tracking accuracy. Next, Figures 18.10 and 18.11 show the development of the constraint force tracking error curves for Configuration II using the method in Liu et al. (2014) and the proposed control method, respectively. The comparison between the suggested control method and the method in Liu et al. (2014) shows that force tracking errors are extremely minor under the proposed control system.

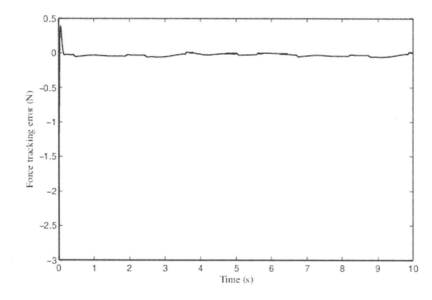

FIGURE 18.6   Error in constraint force tracking for (Liu et al., 2014) controller in configuration I.

Finally, it is evident from the simulation results for both configuration situations that the suggested control strategy has improved the controller's performance and provided great robustness against the system's inherent uncertainties.

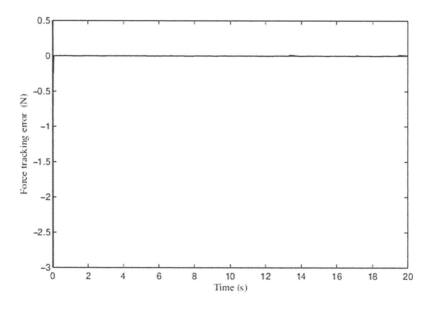

FIGURE 18.7   Force tracking error due to constraints for Configuration I under the suggested control strategy.

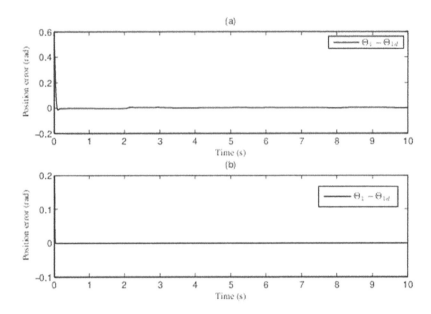

FIGURE 18.8   Errors in tracking Joint 1 position for Configuration II with (a) controller (Liu et al., 2014); (b) recommended controller.

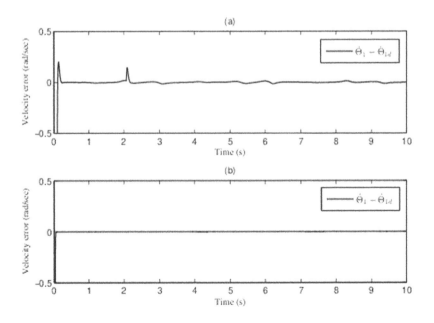

FIGURE 18.9   Errors in Joint 1 velocity tracking for Configuration II with (a) controller (Liu et al., 2014); (b) recommended controller.

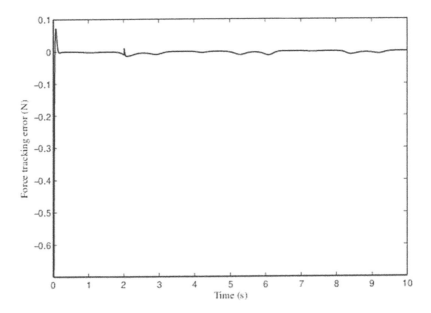

FIGURE 18.10 Error in constraint force tracking for (Liu et al., 2014) controller in Configuration II.

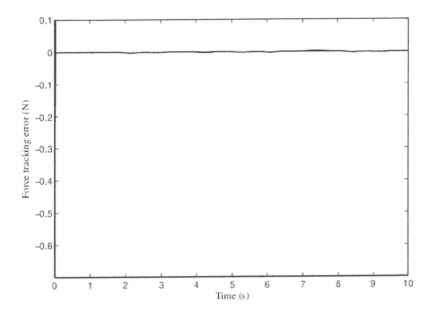

FIGURE 18.11 Tracking error due to constraints for Configuration II using the suggested control strategy.

18.7 CONCLUSION

The issue of force/position control for limited reconfigurable manipulators has been addressed in this work. By combining the advantages of the model-dependent controller with the RBF neural network-based controller, the authors have advanced a brand-new control strategy for limited reconfigurable manipulators. The application of a neural network-based controller has increased the inefficiency of the model-based control method i.e. radial basis method With the addition of an adaptive compensator to the controller, the neural network compensates for system uncertainties and handles the impacts of friction terms, external disturbances, network reconstruction error, and more. The Lyapunov approach makes advantage of online learning of neural network weights to ensure system stability and error convergence. The simultaneous force and the joint tracking have progressed extremely slowly as a result of the suggested approach. As a result, we see that, while maintaining the boundedness of the restricted force tracking and the asymptotic convergence of the joint tracking errors, both of these tracks also converge to the appropriate values when various constraints are applied to various configurations.

REFERENCES

Ahmad, S., Zhang, H., & Liu, G. (2013). Distributed fault detection for modular and reconfigurable robots with joint torque sensing: A prediction error based approach. *Mechatronics*, 23(6), 607–616.

Bali, V., Bali, S., Gaur, D., Rani, S., & Kumar, R. (2023). Commercial-off-the shelf vendor selection: A multi-criteria decision-making approach using intuitionistic fuzzy sets and TOPSIS. *Operational Research in Engineering Sciences: Theory and Applications*, 12(4), 100–113.

Bhambri, P., Singh, M., Dhanoa, I. S., & Kumar, M. (2022). Deployment of ROBOT for HVAC duct and disaster management. *Oriental Journal of Computer Science and Technology*, 15, 1–8.

Bhambri, P., Singh, M., Jain, A., Dhanoa, I. S., Sinha, V. K., & Lal, S. (2021). Classification of gene expression data with the aid of optimized feature selection. *Turkish Journal of Physiotherapy and Rehabilitation*, 32, 3.

Bhambri, P., Singh, S., Sangwan, S., Devi, J., & Jain, S. (2023). Plants recognition using leaf image pattern analysis. *Journal of Survey in Fisheries Sciences*, 10(2S), 3863–3871.

Cao, C., Wang, F., Cao, Q., Sun, H., Xu, W., & Cui, M. (2018). Neural network–based terminal sliding mode applied to position/force adaptive control for constrained robotic manipulators. *Advances in Mechanical Engineering*, 10(6), https://doi.org/10.1177/1687814018781288

Dajer, M., Ma, Z., Piazzi, L., Prasad, N., Qi, X. F., Sheen, B., & Yue, G. (2022). Reconfigurable intelligent surface: Design the channel–A new opportunity for future wireless networks. *Digital Communications and Networks*, 8(2), 87–104.

Dong, B., Li, Y., & Liu, K. (2017a). Decentralized control for harmonic drive–based modular and reconfigurable robots with uncertain environment contact. *Advances in Mechanical Engineering*, 9(4), 43–56.

Dong, B., Li, Y., Liu, K., & Li, Y. (2017b, July). Decentralized adaptive super-twisting control for modular and reconfigurable robots with uncertain environment contact. In *2017 36th Chinese Control Conference (CCC)* (pp. 6644–6651). IEEE.

Dong, B., Liu, K., & Li, Y. (2017c). Decentralized control of harmonic drive based modular robot manipulator using only position measurements: Theory and experimental verification. *Journal of Intelligent & Robotic Systems*, 88, 3–18.

Dong, B., Zhou, F., Liu, K., & Li, Y. (2018). Torque sensorless decentralized neuro-optimal control for modular and reconfigurable robots with uncertain environments. *Neurocomputing, 282*, 60–73.

Du, Y., & Zhu, Q. (2018). Decentralized adaptive force/position control of reconfigurable manipulator based on soft sensors. *Proceedings of the Institution of Mechanical Engineers, Part I: Journal of Systems and Control Engineering, 232*(9), 1260–1271.

Ghajar, M. H., Keshmiri, M., & Bahrami, J. (2018). Neural-network-based robust hybrid force/position controller for a constrained robot manipulator with uncertainties. *Transactions of the Institute of Measurement and Control, 40*(5), 1625–1636.

Gierlak, P., & Szuster, M. (2017). Adaptive position/force control for robot manipulator in contact with a flexible environment. *Robotics and Autonomous Systems, 95*, 80–101.

Heck, D., Saccon, A., Van de Wouw, N., & Nijmeijer, H. (2016). Guaranteeing stable tracking of hybrid position–force trajectories for a robot manipulator interacting with a stiff environment. *Automatica, 63*, 235–247.

Holcomb, T., & Morari, M. (1991, June). Local training for radial basis function networks: towards solving the hidden unit problem. In *1991 American Control Conference* (pp. 2331–2336). IEEE.

Kumar, N., & Rani, M. (2021). Neural network-based hybrid force/position control of constrained reconfigurable manipulators. *Neurocomputing, 420*, 1–14.

Kumar, P., Banerjee, K., Singhal, N., Kumar, A., Rani, S., Kumar, R., & Lavinia, C. A. (2022). Verifiable, secure mobile agent migration in healthcare systems using a polynomial-based threshold secret sharing scheme with a blowfish algorithm. *Sensors, 22*(22), 8620.

Li, Y., Ding, G., Zhao, B., Dong, B., & Liu, G. (2016b, July). Decentralized adaptive neural network sliding mode control for reconfigurable manipulators with data-based modeling. In *2016 International Joint Conference on Neural Networks (IJCNN)* (pp. 595–602). IEEE.

Li, Y., Lu, Z., Zhou, F., Dong, B., Liu, K., & Li, Y. (2019). Decentralized trajectory tracking control for modular and reconfigurable robots with torque sensor: Adaptive terminal sliding control-based approach. *Journal of Dynamic Systems, Measurement, and Control, 141*(6).

Li, Y. C., Ding, G. B., & Zhao, B. (2016a). Decentralized adaptive neural network sliding mode position/force control of constrained reconfigurable manipulators. *Journal of Central South University, 23*(11), 2917–2925.

Li, Z., Ge, S. S., Adams, M., & Wijesoma, W. S. (2008). Robust adaptive control of uncertain force/motion constrained nonholonomic mobile manipulators. *Automatica, 44*(3), 776–784.

Liu, C., Liu, X., Wang, H., Zhou, Y., & Lu, S. (2019). Observer-based adaptive fuzzy funnel control for strict-feedback nonlinear systems with unknown control coefficients. *Neurocomputing, 358*, 467–478.

Liu, Y., Zhao, B., & Li, Y. (2014, December). Adaptive neural network position/force hybrid control for constrained reconfigurable manipulators. In *2014 IEEE 17th International Conference on Computational Science and Engineering* (pp. 38–43). IEEE.

Naderi, B., & Azab, A. (2021). Production scheduling for reconfigurable assembly systems: Mathematical modeling and algorithms. *Computers & Industrial Engineering, 162*, 107741.

Park, J., & Sandberg, I. W. (1991). Universal approximation using radial-basis-function networks. *Neural Computation, 3*(2), 246–257.

Rachna, Bhambri, P., & Chhabra, Y. (2022). Deployment of distributed clustering approach in WSNs and IoTs. In Pankaj Bhambri, Sita Rani, Gaurav Gupta, Alex Khang (Eds.), *Cloud and Fog Computing Platforms for Internet of Things* (pp. 85–98). Chapman and Hall/CRC.

Rani, S., Bhambri, P., & Kataria, A. (2023). Integration of IoT, Big data, and cloud computing technologies. Big Data, Cloud Computing and IoT: Tools and Applications.

Ren, Y., Chen, Z., Liu, Y., Gu, Y., Jin, M., & Liu, H. (2017). Adaptive hybrid position/force control of dual-arm cooperative manipulators with uncertain dynamics and closed-chain kinematics. *Journal of the Franklin Institute, 354*(17), 7767–7793.

Ritu, & Bhambri, P. (2022). A CAD system for software effort estimation. *Paper presented at the International Conference on Technological Advancements in Computational Sciences* (pp. 140–146). IEEE. https://doi.org/10.1109/ICTACS56270.2022.9988123

Ritu, P., & Bhambri, P. (2023, February 17). Software effort estimation with machine learning – A systematic literature review. In Susheela Hooda, Vandana Mohindru Sood, Yashwant Singh, Sandeep Dalal, Manu Sood (Eds.), *Agile software development: Trends, challenges and applications* (pp. 291–308). John Wiley & Sons, Inc.

Sangwan, Y. S., Lal, S., Bhambri, P., Kumar, A., & Dhanoa, I. S. (2021). Advancements in social data security and encryption: A review. *NVEO-Natural Volatiles & Essential Oils Journal|NVEO*, 8(4), 15353–15362.

Singh, M., Bhambri, P., Lal, S., Singh, Y., Kaur, M., & Singh, J. (2021). Design of the effective technique to improve memory and time constraints for sequence alignment. *International Journal of Applied Engineering Research (Netherlands)*, 6(02), 127–142.

Slotine, J. J. E., & Li, W. (1991). *Applied nonlinear control* (Vol. 199, No. 1, p. 705). Englewood Cliffs, NJ: Prentice Hall.

Sofi, A., Ding, Y., Weng, F., Jiang, X., & Tang, M. (2016). Vibration-attenuation controller design for uncertain mechanical systems with input time delay. *Shock and Vibration*, 2016, 9686358. https://doi.org/10.1155/2016/9686358

Wang, G., Dong, B., Wu, S., & Li, Y. (2015, October). Sliding mode position/force control for constrained reconfigurable manipulator based on adaptive neural network. In *2015 International Conference on Control, Automation and Information Sciences (ICCAIS)* (pp. 96–101). IEEE.

Zhang, G., Zhuang, Z., & Guo, X. (2015). Bloch surface plasmon enhanced blue emission from InGaN/GaN light-emitting diode structures with Al-coated GaN nanorods. *Nanotechnology*, 26(12), 125201. https://doi.org/10.1088/0957-4484/26/12/125201

Zhao, B., & Li, Y. (2014). Local joint information based active fault tolerant control for reconfigurable manipulator. *Nonlinear Dynamics*, 77, 859–876.

Zhou, F., Li, Y., & Liu, G. (2017). Robust decentralized force/position fault-tolerant control for constrained reconfigurable manipulators without torque sensing. *Nonlinear Dynamics*, 89, 955–969.

Zhu, L., & Li, Y. (2010a). Decentralized adaptive neural network control for reconfigurable manipulators. In *2010 Chinese Control and Decision Conference* (pp. 1760–1765). https://doi.org/10.1109/CCDC.2010.5498523

Zhu, M., & Li, Y. (2009). Decentralized adaptive fuzzy sliding mode control for reconfigurable modular manipulators. *International Journal of Robust and Nonlinear Control*. Advance online publication. https://doi.org/10.1002/rnc.1444

Zhu, Q., Zhang, W., Zhang, J., & Sun, B. (2019). U-neural network-enhanced control of nonlinear dynamic systems. *Neurocomputing*, 352, 12–21.

Index

Pages in *italics* refer to figures and pages in **bold** refer to tables.

Milton Keynes UK
Ingram Content Group UK Ltd.
UKHW051658141024
449570UK00005B/57